DATE DUE

DEMCO 128-5046

SOMETHING ABOUT THE AUTHOR®

Something about
the Author *was named
an "**Outstanding
Reference Source**,"
the highest honor given
by the American
Library Association
Reference and User
Services Association.*

ISSN 0276-816X

SOMETHING ABOUT THE AUTHOR®

**Facts and Pictures about Authors
and Illustrators of Books for Young People**

**EDITED BY
ALAN HEDBLAD**

VOLUME 107

GALE GROUP

*Detroit
San Francisco
London
Boston
Woodbridge, CT*

STAFF

Editor: Alan Hedblad
Associate Editor: Melissa Hill
...phy Features Coordinator: Motoko Fujishiro Huthwaite

...ing Editors: Sheryl Ciccarelli, Sara L. Constantakis, Catherine Goldstein, Maria Job, Arlene M. Johnson
Editorial Assistant: Erin E. White

Editorial Technical Specialist: Karen Uchic

Managing Editor: Joyce Nakamura
Publisher: Hal May

Research Manager: Victoria B. Cariappa
Project Coordinator: Cheryl L. Warnock
Research Associates: Patricia Tsune Ballard, Corrine A. Boland, Tamara C. Nott,
Wendy K. Festerling, Tracie A. Richardson
Research Assistants: Phyllis J. Blackman, Patricia L. Love

Permissions Manager: Maria L. Franklin
Permissions Associates: Sarah Chesney, Edna Hedblad, Michele Lonoconus

Production Director: Mary Beth Trimper
Production Assistant: Deborah Milliken

Graphic Artist: Gary Leach
Image Database Supervisor: Randy Bassett
Imaging Specialists: Robert Duncan, Michael Logusz
Imaging Coordinator: Pamela A. Reed

Library of Congress Catalog Card Number 72-27107

ISBN 0-7876-3216-3
ISSN 0276-816X

Printed in the United States of America

10 9 8 7 6 5 4 3 2 1

Contents

Authors in Forthcoming Volumes vii
Introduction ix
Acknowledgments xi
Illustrations Index 221
Author Index 245

Authors in Forthcoming Volumes

Below are some of the authors and illustrators that will be featured in upcoming volumes of *SATA*. These include new entries on the swiftly rising stars of the field, as well as completely revised and updated entries (indicated with *) on some of the most notable and best-loved creators of books for children.

Michael Coleman: The English author of dozens of books in a variety of genres, including detective fiction, sports stories, nonfiction, and picture books, Coleman received the 1997 Carnegie Medal for the novel *Weirdo's War.*

*Tomie dePaola: The author and/or illustrator of more than two hundred books as well as a professional artist, designer, and art teacher, dePaola is one of the most prolific and popular contemporary creators of books for children in the early and middle grades. His most recent efforts include installments in the popular "Strega Nona" and "Bill and Pete" picture-book series, as well as a new edition of 1973's *Nana Upstairs and Nana Downstairs,* republished with full-color illustrations.

Ted Dewan: Dewan cast a robot in the title role of his self-illustrated adaptation of *The Sorcerer's Apprentice,* which was released to coincide with the two-hundredth anniversary of the tale's original publication in Germany.

Francisco Jimenez: Jimenez is an award-winning educator and author of numerous scholarly publications on Spanish language and literature. His works for children, *The Circuit* and *La Mariposa,* reflect his experiences growing up in a family of Mexican migrant workers.

*Diana Wynne Jones: The recipient of three Carnegie commendations as well as other prestigious awards, Jones continues to turn out her unique brand of fantasy fiction, as in her recent novel, *Dark Lord of Derkholm.*

*Peg Kehret: Blending exciting action, likable characters, and hi-lo language, Kehret writes books that lead her readers on to more difficult fiction and nonfiction. The prolific novelist has produced more than a dozen new works in the last five years, including *The Richest Kids in Town, Earthquake Terror,* and *Small Steps,* a memoir of her childhood battle with polio.

*Holly Keller: Known for her lovable animal protagonists, including Geraldine, Horace, and Henry, Keller is praised for the minimalist, flat, cartoon style of her illustrations and the wit and wisdom of her texts. Her latest efforts include the picture book *Brave Horace* and the children's chapter book *I Am Angela.*

Jon Krakauer: In his best-selling *Into Thin Air: A Personal Account of the Mount Everest Disaster,* Krakauer documents the 1996 expedition up the famous mountain that claimed the lives of eight of his fellow climbers.

*Gordon Parks: A published poet, filmmaker, novelist, composer, and photojournalist, Parks has recounted the events of his life in several autobiographical works, including *To Smile in Autumn* and *Voices in the Mirror.*

Kerri Strug: Strug's autobiography, *Landing on My Feet: A Diary of Dreams,* recounts the gymnast's career from her entrance into the sport at the age of four through her dramatic performance at the 1996 Olympic games.

Cynthia Zarin: Zarin's poetry offers a purity of language and a slightly offbeat perspective on mundane, typically overlooked topics. Her picture books for children, including *Rose and Sebastian* and *What Do You See When You Shut Your Eyes?,* encourage her preschool audience to look at things a from fresh perspective.

Introduction

Something about the Author (*SATA*) is an ongoing reference series that examines the lives and works of authors and illustrators of books for children. *SATA* includes not only well-known writers and artists but also less prominent individuals whose works are just coming to be recognized. This series is often the only readily available information source on emerging authors and illustrators. You'll find *SATA* informative and entertaining, whether you are a student, a librarian, an English teacher, a parent, or simply an adult who enjoys children's literature.

What's Inside SATA

SATA provides detailed information about authors and illustrators who span the full time range of children's literature, from early figures like John Newbery and L. Frank Baum to contemporary figures like Judy Blume and Richard Peck. Authors in the series represent primarily English-speaking countries, particularly the United States, Canada, and the United Kingdom. Also included, however, are authors from around the world whose works are available in English translation. The writings represented in *SATA* include those created intentionally for children and young adults as well as those written for a general audience and known to interest younger readers. These writings cover the entire spectrum of children's literature, including picture books, humor, folk and fairy tales, animal stories, mystery and adventure, science fiction and fantasy, historical fiction, poetry and nonsense verse, drama, biography, and nonfiction.

Obituaries are also included in *SATA* and are intended not only as death notices but also as concise overviews of people's lives and work. Additionally, each edition features newly revised and updated entries for a selection of *SATA* listees who remain of interest to today's readers and who have been active enough to require extensive revisions of their earlier biographies.

New Autobiography Feature

Beginning with Volume 103, *Something about the Author* will feature three or more specially commissioned autobiographical essays in each volume. These unique essays, averaging about ten thousand words in length and illustrated with an abundance of personal photos, present an entertaining and informative first-person perspective on the lives and careers of prominent authors and illustrators profiled in *SATA*.

Two Convenient Indexes

In response to suggestions from librarians, *SATA* indexes no longer appear in every volume but are included in alternate (odd-numbered) volumes of the series, beginning with Volume 57.

SATA continues to include two indexes that cumulate with each alternate volume: the Illustrations Index, arranged by the name of the illustrator, gives the number of the volume and page where the illustrator's work appears in the current volume as well as all preceding volumes in the series; the Author Index gives the number of the volume in which a person's biographical sketch, autobiographical essay, or obituary appears in the current volume as well as all preceding volumes in the series.

These indexes also include references to authors and illustrators who appear in Gale's *Yesterday's Authors of Books for Children, Children's Literature Review,* and *Something about the Author Autobiography Series.*

Easy-to-Use Entry Format

Whether you're already familiar with the *SATA* series or just getting acquainted, you will want to be aware of the kind of information that an entry provides. In every *SATA* entry the editors attempt to give as complete a picture of the person's life and work as possible. A typical entry in *SATA* includes the following clearly labeled information sections:

- *PERSONAL:* date and place of birth and death, parents' names and occupations, name of spouse, date of marriage, names of children, educational institutions attended, degrees received, religious and political affiliations, hobbies and other interests.

- *ADDRESSES:* complete home, office, electronic mail, and agent addresses, whenever available.

- *CAREER:* name of employer, position, and dates for each career post; art exhibitions; military service; memberships and offices held in professional and civic organizations.

- *AWARDS, HONORS:* literary and professional awards received.

- *WRITINGS:* title-by-title chronological bibliography of books written and/or illustrated, listed by genre when known; lists of other notable publications, such as plays, screenplays, and periodical contributions.

- *ADAPTATIONS:* a list of films, television programs, plays, CD-ROMs, recordings, and other media presentations that have been adapted from the author's work.

- *WORK IN PROGRESS:* description of projects in progress.

- *SIDELIGHTS:* a biographical portrait of the author or illustrator's development, either directly from the biographee—and often written specifically for the *SATA* entry—or gathered from diaries, letters, interviews, or other published sources.

- *FOR MORE INFORMATION SEE:* references for further reading.

- *EXTENSIVE ILLUSTRATIONS:* photographs, movie stills, book illustrations, and other interesting visual materials supplement the text.

How a SATA Entry Is Compiled

A *SATA* entry progresses through a series of steps. If the biographee is living, the *SATA* editors try to secure information directly from him or her through a questionnaire. From the information that the biographee supplies, the editors prepare an entry, filling in any essential missing details with research and/or telephone interviews. If possible, the author or illustrator is sent a copy of the entry to check for accuracy and completeness.

If the biographee is deceased or cannot be reached by questionnaire, the *SATA* editors examine a wide variety of published sources to gather information for an entry. Biographical and bibliographic sources are consulted, as are book reviews, feature articles, published interviews, and material sometimes obtained from the biographee's family, publishers, agent, or other associates.

Entries that have not been verified by the biographees or their representatives are marked with an asterisk (*).

Contact the Editor

We encourage our readers to examine the entire *SATA* series. Please write and tell us if we can make *SATA* even more helpful to you. Give your comments and suggestions to the editor:

BY MAIL: Editor, *Something about the Author,* The Gale Group, 27500 Drake Rd., Farmington Hills, MI 48331-3535.

BY TELEPHONE: (800) 877-GALE

BY FAX: (248) 699-8054

Acknowledgments

Grateful acknowledgment is made to the following publishers, authors, and artists whose works appear in this volume.

AARDEMA, VERNA. From an illustration in *Who's in Rabbit's House?* by Verna Aardema. Dial Books for Young Readers, 1977. Pictures copyright (c) 1977 by Leo and Diane Dillon. Reproduced by permission of Dial Books for Young Readers, a division of Penguin Putnam Inc. In the UK by Sheldon Fogelman, Esq.

ALBERT, SUSAN. Albert, Susan Wittig, photograph. From a jacket of *Witches' Bane* by Susan Wittig Albert. Berkley Publishing Group, 1993. Copyright (c) 1993 by Susan Wittig Albert. Reproduced by permission.

ASQUITH, CYNTHIA. Asquith, Cynthia, photograph.

BAILEY, LINDA. Cupples, Pat, illustrator. From a cover of *How Come the Best Clues Are Always in the Garbage?* by Linda Bailey. Albert Whitman and Company, 1996. Cover illustration copyright (c) 1994 by Pat Cupples. Reproduced by permission of Kids Can Press Ltd., Toronto, Canada.

BEST, CARI. Best, Cari, photograph. Reproduced by permission. / Daly, Niki, illustrator. From an illustration in *Red Light, Green Light, Mama and Me* by Cari Best. Orchard Books, 1995. Illustrations copyright (c) 1995 by Niki Daly. Reproduced by permission of the publisher, Orchard Books, New York. / Gottlieb, Dale, illustrator. From an illustration in *Taxi! Taxi!* by Cari Best. Orchard Books, 1994. Illustrations copyright (c) 1994 by Dale Gottlieb. Reproduced by permission of the publisher, Orchard Books, New York.

BISHOP, NIC. Bishop, Nic, photograph. Reproduced by permission. / From a cover of *The Secrets of Animal Flight* by Nic Bishop. Houghton Mifflin Company, 1997. Jacket photographs copyright (c) 1997 by Nic Bishop. Reproduced by permission of Houghton Mifflin Company.

BORNSTEIN, RUTH LERCHER. Bornstein, Ruth Lercher (about 2 years old), photograph. Reproduced by permission. / Bornstein, Ruth Lercher (age 11), with brother Bruce (age 8), formal photograph. Reproduced by permission. / Bornstein, Ruth Lercher, (casually posing with children), photograph. Reproduced by permission. / Bornstein, Ruth Lercher (in pasture with goats), 1950, photograph. Reproduced by permission. / Bornstein, Ruth Lercher (painting), 1948, photograph. Reproduced by permission. / Bornstein, Ruth Lercher, photograph by Marti Friedlander. Reproduced by permission. / Bornstein, Ruth Lercher (standing amongst corn stalks), about 1971, photograph. Reproduced by permission. / Bornstein, Ruth Lercher with grandson Jacob (in her studio), 1984, photograph. Reproduced by permission. / Bornstein, Ruth Lercher (with her children seated behind), photograph. Reproduced by permission. / Illustration from *Little Gorilla* by Ruth Lercher Bornstein. Clarion, 1976. Reproduced by permission. / Lercher, Adolf and Bertha, formal photograph. Reproduced by permission.

BOSMAN, PAUL. Bosman, Paul, photograph. Reproduced by permission.

BOYNTON, SANDRA. From a cover of *Blue Hat, Green Hat* by Sandra Boynton. Little Simon Books, 1995. Copyright (c) 1984, 1995 by Sandra Boynton. Reproduced by permission of Little Simon Books, an imprint of Simon & Schuster Macmillan. / From an illustration in *A is for Angry: An Animal and Adjective Alphabet* by Sandra Boynton. Copyright (c) 1983, 1987 by Sandra Boynton. Used by permission of Workman Publishing Co., New York. All rights reserved.

BRIGHTON, CATHERINE. From a cover of *My Napolean* by Catherine Brighton. The Millbrook Press, 1997. Text and illustration copyright (c) 1997 by Catherine Brighton. Reproduced by permission.

BUFFIE, MARGARET. Buffie, Margaret, photograph by Bob Carmichael. Reproduced by permission. / Bogdan, Florentina, illustrator. From a cover of *Angels Turn Their Backs* by Margaret Buffie. Kids Can Press, 1998. Jacket/cover painting copyright (c) 1998 by Florentina Bodgan. Used by permission of Kids Can Press Ltd., Toronto.

CLARKE, KENNETH. Clarke, Kenneth, 1996, photograph. Archive Photos, Inc. Reproduced by permission.

something about the author

AARDEMA, Verna 1911-

Personal

Surname is pronounced "*ar*-da-ma"; born June 6, 1911, in New Era, MI; daughter of Alfred Eric (in business) and Dora (maiden name, VanderVen) Norberg; married Albert Aardema, May 29, 1936 (died, 1974); married Joel Vugteveen, 1975 (now deceased); children: (first marriage) Austin, Paula. *Education:* Michigan State College of Agriculture and Applied Science (now Michigan State University), B.A., 1934. *Politics:* Republican. *Religion:* Protestant.

Addresses

Home—23 Shady West Nursing Home, Rm. 333, 2310 North Airport Road, Fort Myers, FL 33907.

Career

Grade school teacher in Pentwater, MI, 1934-35, in Muskegon, MI, 1935-36 and 1945-46, and at Lincoln School, Mona Shores, 1951-73; *Muskegon Chronicle,* Muskegon, staff correspondent, 1951-72; writer. Sunday school teacher for twelve years. Frequent guest at book fairs held throughout the United States. *Member:* National Education Association, Juvenile Writers' Workshop (publicity chair, 1955-65), Michigan Education Association, Mona Shores Education Association (corresponding secretary, 1965-70).

Awards, Honors

Children's Book Showcase Award, 1974, for *Behind the Back of the Mountain: Black Folk Tales from Southern Africa; Why Mosquitoes Buzz in People's Ears* was named a *New York Times* Notable Book, 1975; Randolph Caldecott Medal, American Library Association, 1976, and Art Books for Children citation, 1977, both for *Why Mosquitoes Buzz in People's Ears;* Lewis Carroll Shelf Award, 1978, for *Who's in Rabbit's House?;* Children's Reading Round Table Award, 1981; Parents' Choice Award for Children's Books, literature category, 1984, for *Oh, Kojo! How Could You!,* 1985, for *Bimwili and the Zimwi,* 1989, for *Rabbit Makes a Monkey of Lion,* and 1991, for *Pedro and the Padre; What's So Funny, Ketu?, Bimwili and the Zimwi,* and *Princess Gorilla and a New Kind of Water* were named among the New York Public Library's 100 Best Books of the Year for 1982, 1987, and 1988, respectively; *Redbook* Ten Best Books of 1991 and Junior Library Guild selection, 1992, both for *Borreguita and the Coyote.*

Writings

RETELLINGS; AFRICAN AND MEXICAN FOLKTALES

Tales from the Story Hat, illustrated by Elton Fax, Coward, 1960.
Otwe, illustrated by Elton Fax, Coward, 1960.
The Na of Wa, illustrated by Elton Fax, Coward, 1960.
The Sky-God Stories, illustrated by Elton Fax, Coward, 1960.

More Tales from the Story Hat, illustrated by Elton Fax, Coward, 1966.

Tales for the Third Ear: From Equatorial Africa, illustrated by Ib Ohlsson, Dutton, 1969.

Behind the Back of the Mountain: Black Folk Tales from Southern Africa, illustrated by Leo Dillon and Diane Dillon, Dial, 1973.

Why Mosquitoes Buzz in People's Ears: A West African Tale, illustrated by Leo Dillon and Diane Dillon, Dial, 1975.

Who's in Rabbit's House?: A Masai Tale, illustrated by Leo Dillon and Diane Dillon, Dial, 1977.

Ji-Nongo-Nongo Means Riddles, illustrated by Jerry Pinkney, Four Winds, 1978.

The Riddle of the Drum: A Tale from Tizapan, Mexico, illustrated by Tony Chen, Four Winds, 1979.

Half-a-Ball-of-Kenki: An Ashanti Tale, illustrated by Diane Stanley Zuromskis, Warne, 1979.

Bringing the Rain to Kapiti Plain, illustrated by Beatriz Vidal, Dial, 1981.

What's So Funny, Ketu?, illustrated by Marc Brown, Dial, 1982.

The Vingananee and the Tree Toad: A Liberian Tale, illustrated by Ellen Weiss, Warne, 1983.

Oh, Kojo! How Could You!: An Ashanti Tale, illustrated by Marc Brown, Dial, 1984.

Bimwili and the Zimwi: A Tale from Zanzibar, illustrated by Susan Meddaugh, Dial, 1985.

Princess Gorilla and a New Kind of Water: A Mpongwe Tale, illustrated by Victoria Chess, Dial, 1988.

Rabbit Makes a Monkey of Lion: A Swahili Tale, illustrated by Jerry Pinkney, Dial, 1989.

Pedro and the Padre, illustrated by Friso Henstra, Dial, 1991.

Traveling to Tondo: A Tale of the Nkundo of Zaire, illustrated by Will Hillenbrand, Knopf, 1991.

Borreguita and the Coyote, illustrated by Petra Mathers, Knopf, 1991.

Anansi Finds a Fool, illustrated by Bryna Waldman, Dial, 1992.

Sebgugugu the Glutton: A Bantu Tale from Rwanda, illustrated by Nancy L. Clouse, W. B. Eerdmans and Africa World Press, 1993.

Misoso: Once Upon a Time Tales from Africa, illustrated by Reynold Ruffins, Knopf, 1994.

Jackal's Flying Lesson: A Khoikhoi Tale, illustrated by Dale Gottlieb, Knopf, 1995.

How the Ostrich Got Its Long Neck: A Tale from the Akamba of Kenya, illustrated by Marcia Brown, Scholastic, 1995.

The Lonely Lioness and the Ostrich Chicks: A Masai Tale, illustrated by Yumi Heo, Knopf, 1996.

Anansi Does the Impossible!: An Ashanti Tale, illustrated by Lisa Desimini, Atheneum, 1997.

This for That: A Tonga Tale, illustrated by Victoria Chess, Dial, 1997.

Koi and the Kola Nuts: A Tale from Liberia, illustrated by Joel Cepeda, Simon and Schuster, 1999.

OTHER

A Bookworm Who Hatched (photographs by Dede Smith), Owen Publishers, 1992.

Works represented in several reading textbooks published in the United States and England. Also author of *Write a Folktale.*

Translations of Aardema's books have been published in Japan, France, South Africa, Taiwan, and the Netherlands.

Adaptations

Bringing the Rain to Kapiti Plain was adapted for television by Reading Rainbow, and *Why Mosquitoes Buzz in People's Ears* was adapted as an animated film by Weston Woods. Many of Aardema's stories have been released on audio cassette.

Sidelights

Children's book writer Verna Aardema is well known for her retellings of African stories and tall tales, among them such award-winning efforts as *Why Mosquitoes Buzz in People's Ears, Who's in Rabbit's House?, Rabbit Makes a Monkey of Lion,* and *Princess Gorilla and a New Kind of Water.* Additionally, two of her tales from Mexico, *Pedro and the Padre* and *Borreguita and the Coyote* have also won awards and critical acclaim. Aardema has retold tales from all directions of the compass in Africa, including tales from the Masai, the Ashanti, the Mpongwe, the Nkundo of Zaire, the Tonga, and the Swahili. Her stories deal with puzzles, tricksters, and heroes, and are all adapted from original tales held in the African and Mexican oral tradition. Known for her clear use of language as well as linguistic devices such as ideophones and repetitive sounds, Aardema has enjoyed a career spanning some four decades since the publication of her first title in 1960, *Tales from the Story Hat.* Beginning her writing career late in life, Aardema has sought retirement several times, only to be talked out of it by her agent or editors. She acknowledged in an essay in *Something about the Author Autobiography Series* (*SAAS*), "I don't know if I'll ever retire. Maybe I will just go out of print."

Born in 1911, the third of nine children, Aardema grew up in the small Michigan town of New Era. Reading was an early passion for Aardema, and until the sixth grade she was considered something of a family malingerer because of the time she spent with books. Then a teacher gave her an A for a poem she had written, and suddenly at home her fortunes and reputation changed. Her mother finally recognized her for something positive, comparing her to her own grandfather, a writer. "That is the first time I can recall being noticed for any good reason," Aardema wrote in *SAAS.* Thereafter, she was largely excused from chores, and allowed to retire to a private place in the swamp behind the family home, there to dream of stories she might write. "It really was in the dark secret room of that swamp that I made up my first stories," Aardema recalled in *SAAS.* "I would sit on one of three logs which formed the boundaries of that room, dig my heels into the spongy black earth, and think and think until I'd think my sisters must be finished with the dishes."

Behind the curtain the actors prepare the set and the props, rehearse their lines, and don their masks.

Verna Aardema retells a Masai tale in which a rabbit enlists the aid of his animal friends to remove a monster who has taken up residence in his home. (*From* Who's in Rabbit's House?, *illustrated by Leo and Diane Dillon.*)

Deciding to become a writer, Aardema promptly formed a writer's group which met under the maple tree in front of the house. Attending high school in nearby Shelby, she put her writing skills to use penning a column on school news for the local newspaper, the *Oceana Herald.* After high school, Aardema determined to go on to college, attending Michigan State College in East Lansing where she helped put herself through school by working in the Publications Department of the college. On this job she came into daily contact with journalists from the AP and UPI covering college news, and during her undergraduate years she took every writing class the

college offered. The noted humor writer, Peter DeVries, was one her favorite instructors, and he encouraged her fledgling efforts. During her senior year she won three different writing awards, and upon graduation was offered jobs at several different newspapers in Michigan. However, with the low pay offered to female newspaper writers, Aardema opted instead for teaching school.

After two years of teaching, Aardema married and over the years became a fulltime homemaker and the mother of two children. Nearing forty, she began writing for newspapers again, working for the *Muskegon Chronicle,* and she also resumed teaching, in kindergarten and the primary grades. But during all this time, she had never given up her dreams of becoming a professional writer. Finally Aardema's young daughter Paula goaded her into storytelling when, as a little girl, she refused to eat without a story accompanying the food. Once Aardema had exhausted the usual store of European tales, she began making up her own stories based on the books about Africa which she had been reading for many years. One of these stories, "An Egg for Chop," was good enough to sell, she thought, and in fact she did just that. This early effort appeared in the January, 1959, edition of *Instructor* magazine, and Aardema's career as a professional writer was officially launched.

Aardema continued to wear several hats throughout the 1960s—mother and wife, teacher, journalist, and writer of children's books. When an editor at Coward-McCann suggested she enlarge "An Egg for Chop" into a juvenile novel, Aardema proposed instead that she write a series of stories based on African folktales, something that at that time had not been done for young readers. Soon she had enough tales to fill a book. *Tales from the Story Hat* was published in 1960 and stayed in print for two decades. Employing animals in each of nine stories to portray different character traits, Aardema retold African legends about the origins of things, of tricksters and tricked, and about the wise and the foolish. These stories "possess humor and shrewd observation," noted a writer for *Kirkus Reviews,* who called them "charmingly told" as well as "refreshingly uncluttered."

Aardema had found a successful use for her passionate interest in things African, and with her next several books she presented further African legends and tales, but in simplified vocabulary, influenced by the early works of Dr. Seuss. Additionally, in titles such as *Behind the Back of the Mountain,* Aardema not only "maintained the atmosphere of the stories' origins in her spirited, entertaining retelling," as Denise M. Wilms noted in *Booklist,* but she also "admirably indicates the sources of the stories (English-language volumes published from 1868 to 1938)," according to *Horn Book*'s Virginia Haviland. Aardema collected folktales and stories from translations of Zulu, Bantu, Tshindao, Thonga, Bushman, and Hottentot for these collections.

With Aardema's eighth book, she finally hit on the format of picture book rather than story collections, and picture books have continued to be her main production, with over two dozen such efforts to her credit. That eighth book, *Why Mosquitoes Buzz in People's Ears,* was adapted from one of a batch of stories submitted to Dial Press as yet another folktale collection, and was illustrated by Leo and Diane Dillon. This West African tale ultimately won a Caldecott Medal for illustration, as well as a *New York Times* Notable Book Award. A pourquoi (or "why") tale, *Why Mosquitoes Buzz in People's Ears,* follows a chain of events from the initial teasing of an iguana by a cheeky mosquito to the failure of the sun to wake up—and all the mosquito's fault. With this story Aardema first adapted her use of ideophones, or onomatopoeic devices for her animal

characters. The snake in this story moves to the sound of "wasawusu, wasawusu," for example, and this actual ideophone comes from African folklore.

Critical response to *Why Mosquitoes Buzz in People's Ears* was very positive. "A 'why' story from Africa is retold with verve in a picture book that should delight young listeners and adult readers," observed Zena Sutherland in *Bulletin of the Center for Children's Books.* Writing in the *New York Times Book Review,* Carol Stevens Kner commented that this "charming narrative of cause and effect is an African legend retold, one of the nicest of many such adaptations of African folklore."

Aardema's first husband died in 1974, and shortly before publication of *Why Mosquitoes Buzz in People's Ears,* she remarried. After that book won the Caldecott Medal, Aardema's editor encouraged her to find a really excellent story for a follow-up; this she culled from an earlier collection of hers, *Tales for the Third Ear,* which was going out of print with rights reverting to the author. Aardema adopted the story entitled "The Long One" from that collection for the picture book, *Who's in Rabbit's House?* In this work, Aardema retells a Masai tale about a poor little rabbit who must deal with the scary presence of the Long One who has taken over his house. A story with a comic twist at the end, *Who's in Rabbit's House?* was awarded the Lewis Carroll Shelf Award for 1978. Eileen A. Archer observed in a *Book Window* review that the "language used in the text is attractive with wonderful rhythms," while *Books for Your Children* contributor Ann Pilling called the picture book "a marvelous read aloud."

Aardema's first book to move from an African setting was *The Riddle of the Drum,* which is a tale from Tizapan in which the king of that region promises that his daughter will not marry any ordinary prince. Suitors must guess what the king's magic drum is made of or die in the attempt to win the young girl's hand. *Publishers Weekly* called this book a "fast, exciting version of a favorite Mexican legend." Aardema returned to Mexican legend with later titles as well, including *Pedro and the Padre* and *Borreguita and the Coyote.* In the former title, the young boy Pedro is not only lazy but also a liar of quite astounding ability. Sent out into the world to earn his living, he is at first sheltered by a padre, but is soon sent packing again because of his wily ways, off to adventures in the big world. After learning that he must mend his ways, Pedro finally returns to the padre. *Publishers Weekly* commented that "young readers will find the hero of this story so engaging and entertaining that they won't even realize he is teaching them an important lesson." A trickster tale from Ayutla is at the heart of Aardema's *Borreguita and the Coyote,* in which "a gullible coyote is pitted against a fetchingly fluffy lamb," according to a *Publishers Weekly* commentator. Betsy Hearne concluded in *Bulletin of the Center for Children's Books:* "Here's a picture book that will hold young listeners' attention with traditional suspense while opening their eyes to new shapes and surprising contrasts."

Though Aardema has retold Mexican folktales, by far the majority of her writing has been on African themes, an interesting intellectual passion for a girl who grew up in Michigan and has never been closer to the shores of Africa than Florida, where she and her second husband retired in 1984. Rather, where her husband retired; Aardema has kept up her same ambitious publishing schedule, producing such acclaimed books as *Bringing the Rain to Kapiti Plain, Bimwili and the Zimwi, Princess Gorilla and a New Kind of Water, Rabbit Makes a Monkey of Lion, Anansi Finds a Fool, Misoso,* and *This for That.* Many of these tales have been culled from Aardema's early story collections, now out of print.

Aardema retells a folktale from Zanzibar, now part of Tanzania, in *Bimwili and the Zimwi,* employing her fetching ideophones to describe waves and the movement of a crab. *Booklist* reviewer Carolyn Phelan called the work a "tightly written, slightly scary story with a heroine who uses her wits and courage to overcome a powerful enemy," and dubbed it "a favorite for reading aloud." King Gorilla discovers a barrel of vinegar and determines that whoever can drink it shall marry his daughter in *Princess Gorilla and a New Kind of Water.* A writer for *Kirkus Reviews* concluded that this book is "embellished with engaging animal noises and dialogue that varies entertainingly," and that the "funny-wise story should make good telling." "Aardema has created a high-spirited, infectiously funny story," commented a reviewer for *Publishers Weekly,* "and the language of the tale is jaunty, playful and sure—perfect for reading aloud." The sly Jackal of *Jackal's Flying Lesson* gets his comeuppance in a story "retold with energy and rhythm and lots of animal action," according to *Booklist*'s Hazel Rochman, while an explanation for why the ostrich looks like it does is supplied in the Kenyan tale, *How the Ostrich Got Its Long Neck.* Reviewing the latter story in *Booklist,* Rochman called it "a laugh-out-loud picture book."

Aardema continues to write of trickster rabbits and bunnies, of amorous cats and lonely lions, making gentle lessons and morals along the way. With her 1994 *Misoso,* she returned to the collected-tales format with which she began her writing career. *Kirkus Reviews* called *Misoso* a "treasure." In a fitting summation to Aardema's entire career, this same reviewer observed that "If there were any doubts about Aardema's ... preeminence as a teller of African tales, this collection puts them to rest."

Works Cited

Aardema, Verna, essay in *Something about the Author Autobiography Series,* Volume 8, Gale, 1989, pp. 1-16.

Archer, Eileen A., review of *Who's in Rabbit's House, Book Window,* summer, 1981, p. 18.

Review of *Borreguita and the Coyote, Publishers Weekly,* June 7, 1991, p. 65.

Haviland, Virginia, review of *Behind the Back of the Mountain, Horn Book,* December, 1973, p. 587.

Hearne, Betsy, review of *Borreguita and the Coyote, Bulletin of the Center for Children's Books,* December, 1991, p. 83.

Kner, Carol Stevens, review of *Why Mosquitoes Buzz in People's Ears, New York Times Book Review,* November 9, 1975, p. 48.

Review of *Misoso, Kirkus Reviews,* October 15, 1994, p. 1403.

Review of *Pedro and the Padre, Publishers Weekly,* December 7, 1990, p. 81.

Phelan, Carolyn, review of *Bimwili and the Zimwi, Booklist,* December 1, 1985, p. 564.

Pilling, Ann, review of *Who's in Rabbit's House, Books for Your Children,* spring, 1981, p. 15.

Review of *Princess Gorilla and a New Kind of Water, Kirkus Reviews,* February 1, 1988, p. 197.

Review of *Princess Gorilla and a New Kind of Water, Publishers Weekly,* February 26, 1988, p. 196.

Review of *The Riddle of the Drum, Publishers Weekly,* March 5, 1979, p. 105.

Rochman, Hazel, review of *How the Ostrich Got Its Long Neck, Booklist,* June 1, 1995, p. 1773.

Rochman, Hazel, review of *Jackal's Flying Lesson, Booklist,* July, 1995, p. 1880.

Sutherland, Zena, review of *Why Mosquitoes Buzz in People's Ears, Bulletin of the Center for Children's Books,* November, 1975, p. 37.

Review of *Tales from the Story Hat, Kirkus Reviews,* April 1, 1960, p. 288.

Wilms, Denise M., review of *Behind the Back of the Mountain, Booklist,* December 1, 1973, p. 384.

For More Information See

BOOKS

Children's Literature Review, Volume 17, Gale, 1989.

PERIODICALS

Booklist, March 15, 1987, p. 1142; March 8, 1989, p. 1131; January 15, 1991, pp. 1060-61; September 15, 1991, p. 153; September 1, 1992, p. 62; April 1, 1993, p. 1425; December 15, 1994, p. 750; March 15, 1997, p. 1244; December 1, 1997, p. 638.

Bulletin of the Center for Children's Books, June, 1989, p. 241; July, 1995, p. 374; February, 1997, p. 198; March, 1997, p. 238; January, 1998, p. 152.

Five Owls, June 1991, p. 99.

Horn Book, September-October, 1991, pp. 605-06; March-April, 1995, p. 202; January-February, 1997, pp. 71-72.

Kirkus Reviews, February 15, 1989, p. 287; July 15, 1992, p. 917; September 1, 1996, p. 1318.

New York Times Book Review, September 24, 1989, p. 26; April 9, 1995, p. 25; October 8, 1995, p. 31.

School Librarian, May, 1993, p. 53; August, 1995, p. 107.

School Library Journal, March, 1991, p. 181; August, 1991, p. 158; September, 1992, p. 214; June, 1993, p. 93; June, 1995, p. 98; December, 1996, p. 110; September, 1997, pp. 198-99.

Wilson Library Bulletin, June, 1992, pp. 118-20; February, 1995, p. 97.*

—Sketch by J. Sydney Jones

ALBERT, Susan Wittig 1940-
(Robin Paige, a joint pseudonym)

Personal

Born January 2, 1940, in Maywood, IL; daughter of John H. and Lucille (Franklin) Webber; married (divorced); married William J. Albert (a writer), 1986; children (first marriage): Robert, Robin, Michael. *Education:* University of Illinois, B.A., 1967; University of California-Berkeley, Ph.D., 1972. *Hobbies and other interests:* Gardening.

Addresses

Office—Drawer M, Bertram, TX 78605. *Agent*—Deborah Schneider, Gelfman Schneider Literary Agents, 250 West 57 St., New York, NY 10107. *Electronic mail*—(Agent) dcschneider@msn.com.

Career

University of San Francisco, San Francisco, CA, instructor, 1969-71; University of Texas, Austin, assistant professor, 1972-77, associate professor, 1977-79, associate dean of graduate school, 1977-79; Sophie Newcomb College, New Orleans, LA, dean, 1979-81; Southwest Texas State University, San Marcos, professor of English, 1981-87, graduate dean, 1981-82, vice president for academic affairs, 1982-86; full-time writer, 1987—. Editor, *China's Garden* newsletter, 1994-97; president, Story Circle Network, Inc., 1997—; editor,

Susan Wittig Albert

Story Circle Journal, 1997—. *Member:* Sisters in Crime, Mystery Writers of America, Garden Writers of America, International Herb Association, Herb Society of America, Story Circle Network.

Awards, Honors

Danforth graduate fellowship, 1967-72; nominee, Agatha and Anthony Awards, Best First Mystery, 1992, for *Thyme of Death.*

Writings

"CHINA BAYLES" MYSTERY NOVELS

Thyme of Death, Scribner, 1992.
Witches' Bane, Scribner, 1993.
Hangman's Root, Scribner, 1994.
Rosemary Remembered, Berkley, 1995.
Rueful Death, Berkley, 1996.
Love Lies Bleeding, Berkley, 1997.
Chile Death, Berkley, 1998.
Lavender and Lies, Berkley, 1999.
Death of a Mistletoe Man, Berkley, 2000.

*"KATE and CHARLES" MYSTERY NOVELS; WITH WILLIAM
J. ALBERT UNDER JOINT PSEUDONYM ROBIN PAIGE*

Death at Bishop's Keep, Berkley, 1994.
Death at Gallow's Green, Berkley, 1995.
Death at Daisy's Folly, Berkley, 1997.
Death at Devil's Bridge, Berkley, 1998.
Death at Rottingdean, Berkley, 1999.
Death at Whitechapel, Berkley, 2000.

NONFICTION

(Translator with Valentina Zavarin, and editor) Boris Uspensky, *The Poetics of Composition: The Structure of the Artistic Text and Typology of a Compositional Form,* University of California Press, 1973, reprinted 1983.
Steps to Structure: An Introduction to Composition and Rhetoric (textbook), Winthrop Publishing, 1975.
(Editor) *Structuralism: An Interdisciplinary Study,* Pickwick Press, 1976.
Stylistic and Narrative Structures in the Middle English Verse Romances, University of Texas Press, 1977.
(With Franklin Holcomb and Anne Dunn) *The Participating Reader* (textbook), Hall, 1979.
Work of Her Own: How Women Create Success and Fulfillment off the Traditional Career Track, Putnam, 1992, published as *Work of Her Own: A Woman's Guide to Success off the Career Track,* foreword by Diane Fassell, Putnam, 1994.
Writing from Life: Telling Your Soul's Story, Putnam, 1997.

OTHER

Also author/co-author of more than sixty children's books, including several mysteries in the "Nancy Drew" and "Hardy Boys" series; (editor) *Soundings* (journal), vol. 58, no. 2, summer, 1975.

Work in Progress

Bloodroot, publication expected in 2001; research into the evolution of women's memoirs.

Sidelights

The protagonist of Susan Wittig Albert's "China Bayles" mystery series is a former attorney who leaves the career fast track to open an herb shop in the west Texas hill town of Pecan Springs. In many ways the concept is autobiographical: Albert, a university professor and administrator, was herself on the fast track in the 1970s and 1980s. She held several positions at colleges and universities in Texas and Louisiana before leaving her vice presidency at Southwest Texas State University. Since her departure, she has written full-time. Starting with *Thyme of Death* in 1992, she began writing the "China Bayles" mysteries. Then, in the mid-1990s, she and her husband, Bill, began working on a series of Victorian mysteries under the joint pseudonym of Robin Paige. While most of her works are written for adults, young adults enjoy them as well.

In the first book of the "China Bayles" series, readers are introduced to China and her best friend, Ruby. Forty-two years old when the series begins, China has left the legal profession to open an herb shop called Thyme and Seasons. In the store next to hers is the flamboyant Ruby, who sells crystals and other New Age paraphernalia. As *Thyme of Death* begins, another friend of China's, Jo Gilbert, dies from an overdose of sleeping pills and vodka. China knows that her late friend was battling breast cancer, but she is not willing to accept the explanation that Jo simply committed suicide. Soon China and Ruby uncover a whole rash of suspects, most notably Roz Kotner, the host of a children's television program. But she is not the only likely suspect: there is also the local developer who tried to put an airport in Pecan Springs, a plan opposed by Jo and the activist group she organized to lobby against it.

Thyme of Death was nominated for both the Agatha and Anthony awards as Best First Mystery of 1992. A *Publishers Weekly* reviewer called the resolution of the plot "slightly disappointing," however, and concluded by suggesting that readers might have "mixed feelings about the story's conclusion." A *Kirkus Reviews* critic gave *Thyme of Death* an unenthusiastic review as well, calling it "heavy-handed in its attempts to be both hip and cozy." But John Benson observed in an *Armchair Detective* review that "China is an interesting character who has the potential to grow in later installments." Benson concluded by saying that the projected China Bayles series "holds considerable promise." Similarly, *Booklist* reviewer Stuart Miller wrote, "This murder-in-a-small town story keeps your interest."

Witches' Bane, the next book in the "China Bayles" series, begins at Halloween. Ruby has provoked a local preacher by offering a class in reading tarot cards, a form of fortune-telling considered satanic by many Christians. The preacher, the Reverend Billy Lee Har-buck of the Everlasting Faith Bible Church, is not the only one opposed to Ruby's classes, since there have been several recent murders in Pecan Springs attributed to satanism. Other bizarre crimes follow: animals are found dead, ritually slaughtered as though for sacrifice, and Ruby discovers that the ritual knife from her shop has been stolen. To further complicate speculation about the source of the crimes, a cross has been burned on the lawn of a Jewish woman, an apparent act of the Ku Klux Klan. Ruby suspects that the reverend is behind all this; but China digs deeper.

A number of reviewers observed that Albert was starting to hit her stride with *Witches' Bane.* Gail Pool of *Wilson Library Bulletin* called it "a stronger entry than the first," and particularly praised Albert's portrayal of a visit from China's mother, which is "vexing to the narrator" but "proves entertaining for us." A *Kirkus Reviews* critic was less effusive in his commentary, criticizing the "dysfunctional family psychobabble" of China's relationship with her recovering-alcoholic mother. As for the mystery, "even mystery novices will spot the villain early on." Nonetheless, the reviewer called the second book "an improvement over China's debut." Likewise a *Booklist* critic pronounced it "on the whole, an entertaining and engaging story," while a reviewer in *Publishers Weekly* wrote that "Albert's lively mystery captures the flavor of a modern small town being reshaped by big-city refugees." Echoing a similar sentiment, a *Library Journal* critic assessed *Witches' Bane* as "even better than *Thyme of Death.*"

Continuing the herbal theme of her titles, Albert's next book was called *Hangman's Root.* This time the mystery revolves around the murder of a biology professor who has earned plenty of enemies both with his acerbic nature and with his experiments involving animals. Police suspect Dottie Riddle, a friend of China's who loves animals, but China is not convinced and determines to find the real culprit. With earlier books in the series, some critics had declared the digressions concerning facts about herbs to be a bit excessive, but this time a *Publishers Weekly* reviewer offered an opposite opinion: "Despite a slow start and little herbal lore, the plot unfolds briskly and with sly humor." Gail Pool of the *Wilson Library Bulletin* commented that "Albert writes with fine observation and humor about small-town life, academic life, and the personal life of China Bayles." A reviewer in *Kirkus Reviews,* who had offered negative appraisals of the first two books, praised this one. Albert, the reviewer stated, had "written herself through" the problems of the earlier novels and the present volume offered "more serious plotting and a more generous distribution of suspicion."

Whereas in earlier books China's female friends such as Ruby had been the strongest presence besides the protagonist herself, *Rosemary Remembered* was the first of several to place greater emphasis on China's boyfriend, Mike McQuaid. The Rosemary of the title is Rosemary Robbins, McQuaid's accountant, who bears a striking resemblance to China. When Rosemary winds up murdered, it appears that someone is out to get China.

Teaming up with McQuaid, the herb shop proprietress searches for Rosemary's killer. "Herb lore and China's game approach to everyday problems, as well as extraordinary ones," wrote a *Publishers Weekly* contributor, "make this Rosemary memorable, indeed." Emily Melton of *Booklist* concluded that "readers will enjoy Albert's wonderfully original characters and her amusing descriptions of life in a small Texas town as much as the intriguing plot"; and a critic in *Kirkus Reviews* called *Rosemary,* "Albert's strongest book yet."

With *Rueful Death,* China becomes closer to McQuaid and his son—so close, in fact, that she needs a break. She goes away to a remote monastery for a retreat, but of course she can't get away from murder and intrigue. The sisters are in turmoil over a plan to turn the quiet monastery into a glitzy conference center, and China has to sort through two deaths, a parcel of poison-pen letters, and a spate of arson. *Rueful Death,* in the words of a *Publishers Weekly* reviewer, is "an intelligent addition" to the series, "a page-turner [with] soul to spare." A *Library Journal* critic called the book "more quality diversion," and Stuart Miller of *Booklist* appraised it as a "well-plotted mystery with strong characters." The book appeared for several weeks on the *USA Today* bestseller list.

Love Lies Bleeding marks a departure from the previous five novels. Returning from the monastery, China is determined to marry McQuaid—but when she gets back to Pecan Springs, she discovers that he has found someone else. Her personal situation is further complicated when, after being urged by Ruby to look into the murder of a former Texas Ranger, she discovers that McQuaid has a connection to the killing. In the end, China must join forces with McQuaid's new girlfriend to solve the case and save the man they both love. A reviewer in *Publishers Weekly* complained about the change in China's character, observing that she had "turn[ed] unexpectedly wimpish" after being dumped by McQuaid. However, in a *Booklist* review, Melton deemed it "warm, witty, New Agey, and fun—the best yet in an appealing series that just keeps getting better."

Albert is also the author, with her husband Bill, of several Victorian mystery novels published under the joint pseudonym Robin Paige. The novels feature sleuths Kate Ardleigh, an Irish-American author of penny-dreadful books, and Sir Charles Sheridan, an amateur scientist with an interest in forensic technology. As the series begins, Kate travels to England, inheriting some money and an estate, and eventually marries Charles as they become involved in different mysteries. Along the way the pair encounters such historical figures as Rudyard Kipling, Jennie Churchill, the Prince of Wales, Beatrix Potter, as well as Henry Rolls and Charles Royce.

In addition to writing mystery novels for older readers, Albert has written and co-written fiction for children. Among her sixty-plus works for this audience are several mysteries in the "Nancy Drew" and "Hardy Boys" series. About her writing career, Albert commented: "I've thought of myself as a writer ever since I could hold a pencil and make letters, but my first paid publication didn't come until I was nineteen and began a short-lived career—three or four years—as a juvenile fiction writer. After that, I went on to college and graduate school and learned how to write literary criticism in an appropriately academic style. When enough was enough, I went back to children's fiction and then turned to women's mystery fiction.

"I enjoy the multiple challenges of writing books in a series: developing characters over time and trying circumstances, creating multi-leveled plots that link several books, and keeping the themes and ideas fresh. This often means defying critics' and readers' expectations and helping them to see new possibilities for growth in a familiar genre, with familiar characters and settings. I also find great pleasure in working with my co-author/husband, Bill Albert, who has a strong plot sense and a fine understanding of the dynamics of character development. It is always a fascinating challenge to work together to craft a coherent narrative out of two different stories—his and mine. (This is something like two architects designing a house, drawing the plans, building it, and then living in it together.) I am interested, as well, in women's stories and memoirs and look forward to doing more work with that subject in a few years—perhaps my own memoir, perhaps a critical study of the development of women's memoirs. The world is full of things to write about. I'll never run out of projects."

Works Cited

Benson, John, review of *Thyme of Death, Armchair Detective,* spring, 1993, p. 109.

Review of *Hangman's Root, Kirkus Reviews,* August 1, 1994, p. 1023.

Review of *Hangman's Root, Publishers Weekly,* September 12, 1994, p. 85.

Review of *Love Lies Bleeding, Publishers Weekly,* October 13, 1997, p. 59.

Melton, Emily, review of *Rosemary Remembered, Booklist,* November 1, 1995, p. 456.

Melton, Emily, review of *Love Lies Bleeding, Booklist,* November 1, 1997, p. 456.

Miller, Stuart, review of *Thyme of Death, Booklist,* November 15, 1992, pp. 581, 585.

Miller, Stuart, review of *Rueful Death, Booklist,* October 1, 1996, p. 324.

Pool, Gail, review of *Witches' Bane, Wilson Library Bulletin,* October, 1993, p. 98.

Pool, Gail, review of *Hangman's Root, Wilson Library Bulletin,* January, 1995, p. 95.

Review of *Rosemary Remembered, Kirkus Reviews,* September 15, 1995, p. 1308.

Review of *Rosemary Remembered, Publishers Weekly,* September 4, 1995, p. 52.

Review of *Rueful Death, Library Journal,* October 1, 1996, p. 131.

Review of *Rueful Death, Publishers Weekly,* September 16, 1996, p. 73.

Review of *Thyme of Death, Kirkus Reviews,* September 1, 1992, p. 1089.

Review of *Thyme of Death, Publishers Weekly,* September 7, 1992, p. 81.

Review of *Witches' Bane, Booklist,* October 1, 1993, p. 256.

Review of *Witches' Bane, Kirkus Reviews,* August 15, 1993, p. 1028.

Review of *Witches' Bane, Library Journal,* October 1, 1993, p. 130.

Review of *Witches' Bane, Publishers Weekly,* October 4, 1993, p. 67.

For More Information See

PERIODICALS

Alfred Hitchcock Mystery Magazine, February, 1995; April, 1995.

Armchair Detective, spring, 1994, p. 233; spring, 1995, p. 210; winter, 1997, p. 97.

Belles Lettres, winter, 1993, p. 53.

Booklist, November 15, 1992, pp. 581, 585.

Bookwatch, January, 1993, p. 4; September, 1996, p. 1.

Horticulture, August, 1993, p. 72; June, 1994, p. 76; February, 1995, p. 72.

Kirkus Reviews, September 1, 1996, p. 1270; September 15, 1997, p. 1420.

Library Journal, October 1, 1992, p. 122; October 15, 1992, p. 78; October 10, 1993; October 1, 1995, p. 124; September 15, 1996, p. 131; November 15, 1996, p. 69.

Los Angeles Times, November 15, 1995.

Los Angeles Times Book Review, December 10, 1995, p. 15.

Publishers Weekly, August 3, 1992, p. 55; September 9, 1996, p. 66; December 2, 1996, p. 52.

*   *   *

ARTHUR, Robert
See FEDER, Robert Arthur

*   *   *

ASQUITH, Cynthia Mary Evelyn (Charteris) 1887-1960

Personal

Born September 27, 1887, in Wiltshire, England; died March 31, 1960, in Oxford, England; married Herbert Asquith (a poet), 1910.

Career

Author, biographer, editor, contributor to magazines and newspapers. Secretary to J. M. Barrie, 1918-37.

Writings

The Child at Home, Scribner, 1923.

Martin's Adventure, Scribner, 1927.

The Duchess of York: An Intimate and Authentic Life Story, Hutchinson (London), 1928.

God Save the King, Chapman and Hall (London), 1935.

The Spring House, M. Joseph (London), 1936.

Not Long for This World (anthology), Telegraph Press (New York City), 1936.

The Family Life of Queen Elizabeth, Hutchinson, 1937, E. P. Dutton (New York City), 1937.

The Queen: An Entirely New and Complete Biography, Written with the Approval of Her Majesty, Hutchinson, 1937.

The King's Daughters, Hutchinson, 1937, E. P. Dutton, 1938.

One Sparkling Wave, M. Joseph, 1943.

This Mortal Coil (ghost stories), Arkham House (Sauk City, WI), 1947.

I Wish I Were You (juvenile), Children's Books (London), 1949.

Haply I May Remember, J. Barrie (London), 1950, Scribner, 1950.

What Dreams May Come, J. Barrie, 1951.

Remember and Be Glad (autobiography), J. Barrie, 1952.

Portrait of Barrie, J. Barrie, 1954, Dutton (New York City), 1955.

Married to Tolstoy, Icon Books (London), 1960, Houghton Mifflin, 1961.

Diaries, 1915-18, edited by E. M. Horsley, with a foreword by L. P. Hartley, Hutchinson, 1968, Knopf (New York City), 1969.

Cynthia Mary Evelyn Asquith

Thomas Hardy at Max Gate, Toucan P. (St. Peter Port), 1969.

EDITOR

The Treasure Ship: A Book of Prose and Verse, Scribner, 1926.
The Ghost Book (anthology), Scribner, 1927.
Sails of Gold, Scribner, 1927.
The Treasure Cave: A Book of New Prose and Verse, Scribner, 1928.
The Funny Bone: New Humorous Stories, Scribner, 1928.
The Black Cap: New Stories of Murder and Mystery (anthology), Scribner, 1928.
Shudders (anthology), Scribner, 1929.
The Children's Cargo, Eyre and Spottiswoode (London), 1930.
When Churchyards Yawn: Fifteen New Ghost Stories, Hutchinson, 1931.
The Silver Ship (stories, poems, and pictures), Putnam (London and New York City), 1932.
My Grimmest Nightmare (short stories), G. Allen and Unwin (London), 1935.
The Princess Elizabeth Gift Book: In Aid of the Princess Elizabeth of York Hospital for Children, Hodder and Stoughton (London), 1935.
The Children's Ship, J. Barrie, 1950.
The Second Ghost Book (anthology), J. Barrie, 1952, published as *A Book of Modern Ghosts,* Scribner, 1953.
The Third Ghost Book (anthology), J. Barrie, 1956.

Sidelights

Cynthia Asquith was married to poet Herbert Asquith, son of the British prime minister during the last years of World War I. In 1918, Asquith's husband returned from the war too ill to work, and Asquith took a position as secretary to J. M. Barrie, the creator of *Peter Pan,* organizing his social and personal affairs until his death in 1937. Asquith's wide circle of friends included many literary figures, including L. P. Hartley, Hugh Walpole, D. H. Lawrence, Algernon Blackwood, and Arthur Machen. She collected from them many mystery and ghost stories and compiled anthologies of their work. Asquith also wrote ghost stories, children's books, biographies, and novels.

For More Information See

BOOKS

Fane, Julian, *Best Friends: Memories of Rachel and David Cecil, Cynthia Asquith, L. P. Hartley, and Some Others,* Sinclair Stevenson and St. George's Press (London), 1990.
Reginald, R., *Science Fiction and Fantasy Literature,* Volume 1, Gale (Detroit), 1979.
Sullivan, Jack, editor, *The Penguin Encyclopedia of Horror and the Supernatural,* Viking (New York City), 1986.

PERIODICALS

Booklist, June 1, 1969, p. 1105.
Choice, September, 1969, p. 892.
Library Journal, March 15, 1969, p. 1140.
New York Times Book Review, February 23, 1969, p. 7.
Publishers Weekly, January 6, 1969, p. 49.
Times Literary Supplement, May 9, 1968, p. 474; October 2, 1987, p. 1064.*

B

BAILEY, Linda 1948-

Personal

Born in 1948.

Addresses

Home—Winnipeg, Manitoba, Canada.

Career

Writer.

Awards, Honors

Arthur Ellis Award nominee for best juvenile, 1997, for *What's a Daring Detective Like Me Doing in the Doghouse?*

Writings

FOR CHILDREN; "STEVIE DIAMOND" MYSTERY SERIES

How Come the Best Clues Are Always in the Garbage?, illustrated by Pat Cupples, Kids Can Press (Toronto, Ontario), 1992.
How Can I Be a Detective If I Have to Baby-sit?, illustrated by Pat Cupples, Kids Can Press, 1993.
Who's Got Gertie? And How Can We Get Her Back?, illustrated by Pat Cupples, Kids Can Press, 1994.
How Can a Frozen Detective Stay Hot on the Trail?, illustrated by Pat Cupples, Kids Can Press, 1996, Albert Whitman (Morton Grove, IL), 1996.
What's a Daring Detective Like Me Doing in the Doghouse?, illustrated by Pat Cupples, Kids Can Press, 1997, Albert Whitman, 1997.

OTHER FICTION FOR CHILDREN

Petula, Who Wouldn't Take a Bath, illustrated by Jackie Snider, HarperCollins (Canada), 1996.
Gordon Loggins and the Three Bears, illustrated by Tracy Walker, Kids Can Press, 1997.

Sidelights

Canadian author Linda Bailey is the creator of the Stevie Diamond Mystery series for middle graders. In *How Come the Best Clues Are Always in the Garbage?* eleven-year-old Stevie and her friend Jesse Kulniki set out to find out who stole the funds of Garbage Busters, an environmental group that is protesting a fast-food restaurant's excessive use of packaging. Reviews of the book were mixed. In *Horn Book Guide*, Carolyn Shute described the main characters as "appealing" and "down-to-earth" but lacking in sophistication, while David Bennett in *Books for Keeps* called the novel "heady stuff." Joseph J. Rodio, writing in *Catholic Library World*, commented on the book's "humorous insights" into the adult world and the well-developed friendship of Stevie and Jesse, while a *Times Educational Supplement* reviewer described the way in which Stevie solved the mystery as "triumphant panache." Joanne Findon, writing in *Quill & Quire*, compared the brisk tempo of *How Come the Best Clues are Always in the Garbage* to the Encyclopedia Brown or Great Brain series, yet she also found the ecological message too obvious and faulted Stevie's "forced" voice. Conversely, Gisela Sherman, writing in *Canadian Children's Literature*, praised the quick-paced plot, "great dialogue, comic timing, odd clues and hilarious situations," adding that the environmental message "fits in naturally."

In *How Can I Be a Detective If I Have to Baby-sit?* Stevie and Jesse spend a week in a British Columbian reforestation camp, where Stevie's father is working. Although the girls think they will be able to enjoy the great outdoors, they were invited so that they could baby-sit five-year-old Alexander, the camp cook's son. When Stevie and Jesse discover that Alexander's family is in some kind of trouble, their vacation becomes a sleuthing job. Calling the novel "a cut above most detective series for the age group," *School Library Journal* contributor Linda Wicher described the plot as "nimble," but found that the secondary characters lacked depth and character development. Chris Sherman of *Booklist* found the story "entertaining," its heroine

A STEVIE DIAMOND MYSTERY

How Come the Best Clues Are Always in the Garbage?

LINDA BAILEY

In the first title in Linda Bailey's mystery series, sixth-grader Stephanie adopts the alias Detective Stevie Diamond and solves the case of who stole money from the Garbage Busters, an environmental group for which her mother works. (Cover illustration by Pat Cupples.)

"engaging," and predicted that its fast pace would appeal to young readers.

With *Who's Got Gertie? And How Can We Get Her Back?* and *How Can a Frozen Detective Stay Hot on the Trail?* one critic noted that Bailey seemed to hit her stride. *Who's Got Gertie?*, which centers on Stevie and Jesse's efforts to find a missing neighbor, a retired actress, was praised by Sarah Ellis of *Quill & Quire,* who called the book a successful example of "middle-grade-mayhem." Praising its quick pace and "buoyant" humor, Ellis concluded: "*Gertie* is colourful, lively, ephemeral, attention-getting, extravagant, and a crowd pleaser."

In *Frozen Detective* the sleuthing duo are on the trail of missing carnivorous plants in chilly Winnipeg, and one of the suspects is Stevie's uncle. Tanya Auger, writing in *Horn Book Guide,* called the story "refreshingly off-beat," and Janet McNaughton, reviewing for *Quill & Quire,* praised Bailey's characterization, plotting, and use of local color. "This is a likeable pair," wrote

McNaughton, adding, "The mystery works well, too." A fifth Stevie Diamond mystery, *What's a Daring Detective Like Me Doing in the Doghouse?,* was published in 1997. In this installment, Stevie is working at a day care center for dogs while the "Vancouver Prankster" maraudes, going so far as to steal the prime minister's underwear. A stray dog seems to hold a connection to the joker, so Stevie and Jesse begin to investigate.

Bailey is also the author of two other books for children, *Petula, Who Wouldn't Take a Bath* and *Gordon Loggins and the Three Bears.* The latter is a send-up of the classic Goldilocks story in which young Gordon slips through a door in the school library bookshelf and ends up starring in the story-hour tale. There are a few twists, however—Gordon doesn't much care for porridge and he isn't hefty enough to break Baby Bear's chair. But according to Deborah Stevenson of the *Bulletin of the Center for Children's Books,* "the reinvention and the living-the-book fantasy are amiable and inviting." Anne Louise Mahoney of *Quill & Quire* asserted: "This hilarious story will be a big hit with kids who know the classic tale."

Works Cited

Auger, Tanya, review of *How Can a Frozen Detective Stay Hot on the Trail?, Horn Book Guide,* spring, 1997, p. 62.

Bennett, David, review of *How Come the Best Clues Are Always in the Garbage?, Books for Keeps,* September, 1996, p. 13.

Ellis, Sarah, review of *Who's Got Gertie?, Quill & Quire,* December, 1994, p. 31.

Findon, Joanne, review of *How Come the Best Clues Are Always in the Garbage?, Quill & Quire,* September, 1996, p. 74.

Review of *How Come the Best Clues Are Always in the Garbage?, Times Educational Supplement,* July 5, 1996, p. R8.

Mahoney, Anne Louise, review of *Gordon Loggins and the Three Bears, Quill & Quire,* July, 1997, p. 51.

McNaughton, Janet, review of *How Can a Frozen Detective Stay Hot on the Trail?, Quill & Quire,* September, 1996, p. 74.

Rodio, Joseph J., review of *How Come the Best Clues Are Always in the Garbage?, Catholic Library World,* December, 1996, p. 55.

Sherman, Chris, review of *How Can I Be a Detective If I Have to Baby-sit?, Booklist,* March 15, 1996, p. 1264.

Sherman, Gisela, review of *How Come All the Best Clues Are Always in the Garbage?, Canadian Children's Literature,* winter, 1994, p. 66.

Shute, Carolyn, review of *How Come the Best Clues Are Always in the Garbage?, Horn Book Guide,* fall, 1996, p. 289.

Stevenson, Deborah, review of *Gordon Loggins and the Three Bears, Bulletin of the Center for Children's Books,* December, 1997, p. 117.

Wicher, Linda, review of *How Can I Be a Detective If I Have to Baby-sit?, School Library Journal,* July, 1996, p. 82.

For More Information See

PERIODICALS

Canadian Book Review Annual, 1994, p. 545.
Children's Book Review Service, spring, 1996, p. 141.
Canadian Materials, March, 1994, p. 44.
Emergency Librarian, September, 1994, p. 56.
Quill & Quire, August, 1992, p. 26.
School Library Journal, May, 1996, p. 110.

* * *

BEALE, Fleur

Personal

Married (husband deceased); children: daughters. *Hobbies and other interests:* Reading.

Addresses

Home—Hamilton, New Zealand. *Office*—Melville High School, 6 Collins Road, Hamilton 2011, New Zealand.

Career

Teacher, writer. Teaches English at Melville High School in Hamilton, New Zealand.

Awards, Honors

Senior fiction honour book, New Zealand *Post* Children's Book Awards, 1999, for *I Am Not Esther.*

Writings

Great Pumpkin Battle, Shortland, 1988.
Slide the Corner, Scholastic, 1993.
Against the Tide, HarperCollins (Auckland, NZ), 1993.
Over the Edge, Scholastic, 1994.
Driving a Bargain, HarperCollins, 1994.
Fifteen and Screaming, HarperCollins, 1995.
The Fortune Teller, HarperCollins, 1995.
Rockman, HarperCollins, 1996.
I Am Not Esther, Hyland House (South Melbourne, Aus.), 1998.
Further Back Than Zero, Scholastic, 1998.

Stories broadcast on the children's radio program *Grandpa's Place.*

Sidelights

A writer of young adult novels set in her native New Zealand, Fleur Beale is credited with producing realistic, fast-paced stories that have wide appeal for teens, particularly reluctant male readers. From her post as a teacher of English at the secondary school level, Beale is able to tap into issues that most affect young people of the 1990s, according to *Magpies* interviewer Julie Harper. "Without doubt Beale is well-versed in what will appeal to teenagers, she has the ability to identify that which is significant in their lives," Harper contended. Although Beale's novels often address serious matters, many reviewers have applauded her ability to explore important themes without overshadowing her exciting plots filled with tension and action.

Beale's works often center on pivotal issues in the lives of young people, including first experiences with sexuality, drug and alcohol use, and the escalating problems of despair and teen suicide. She is often praised for her sensitive handling of these matters, as she manages to avoid didacticism while pointing out sensible alternatives to dangerous or self-destructive behavior. For example, in *I Am Not Esther,* young Kirby is abandoned by her mother to the care of relatives who practice a brand of strict fundamentalist Christianity. *Reading Time* reviewer John McKenzie praised Beale's complex treatment of the sensitive issues raised in this novel, noting that she portrays both "the kindness and certainty in submerging one's self into a strong community" and "the ugliness of religious conformity and power ... in all its self-righteous intolerance." In the end, Kirby grows in maturity as she learns to stand up for herself and her younger relatives against the rigid authoritarianism of adults who neglect the emotional needs of their children while endeavoring to care for their spiritual needs. "Although the setting is recognisably New Zealand this novel will have relevance where ever there are attempts to control the minds and emotions of children," concluded *Magpies New Zealand* reviewer Joan Brockett.

Teenage suicide is explored in *Rockman,* which features an emotionally isolated and vulnerable adolescent who has been physically abused by his father. As in Beale's other novels for young adults, "the real life dilemmas of modern families, especially as they relate to fathering and machoism as male identity," are central themes, according to McKenzie. In her well-received novel *Further Back Than Zero,* Beale portrays a teenager, Ash, whose ability to cope with an abusive, alcoholic stepfather is threatened by his attraction to his stepbrother Sam's freewheeling lifestyle, which includes a growing dependence on alcohol. Although a subplot concerns a girl who contracts AIDS while under the influence of alcohol, McKenzie asserted: "We are not talking about a moral treatise here: it is an exciting story—in fact highly recommended by this interviewer!"

Of *Further Back Than Zero,* Fleur commented: "I wrote the book because I have listened to so many kids talk about getting wasted and how they woke up the next day in jail or couldn't remember anything that had happened the night before.

"I wanted to write about alcohol and teenagers and tell a story about what can happen. I guess I just wanted to make kids think. Alcohol can be such a lethal substance and while most kids are lucky and don't get their lives messed up, there are those that wreck their futures with one bottle of spirits."

Works Cited

Brockett, Joan, review of *I Am Not Esther, Magpies New Zealand,* May, 1998, p. 8.

Harper, Julie, "Know the Author: Fleur Beale," *Magpies New Zealand,* September, 1998, pp. 4-6.

McKenzie, John, "Fleur Beale: A Writer for 1990s Teenagers," *Reading Time,* February, 1999, pp. 39-40.

For More Information See

PERIODICALS

Magpies New Zealand, March, 1997, p. 8.*

*   *   *

BEST, Cari 1951-

Personal

Born May 30, 1951, in New York, NY; daughter of Morris (a jeweler) and Anne (a secretary; maiden name, Boltan) Best; married Morton Schindel (a filmmaker and educator), March 16, 1988; children: Alexandra, Peter, David. *Education:* City University of New York (CUNY), Queens College, B.A., 1972; Drexel University, M.L.S., 1975. *Hobbies and other interests:* "Butterfly and bird watching, gardening, biking, dog walking and dog talking. The best things in life are free!"

Addresses

Home—389 Newtown Turnpike, Weston, CT 06883.

Career

International Reading Association, Newark, DE, librarian, 1975-76; Weston Woods Studios, Westport, CT, editorial director, 1986—. *Member:* American Library Association.

Awards, Honors

Ezra Jack Keats New Writer's Award, New York Public Library, 1995, for *Taxi! Taxi!*

Writings

Taxi! Taxi!, illustrated by Dale Gottlieb, Little, Brown, 1994, Orchard, 1997.

Red Light, Green Light, Mama and Me, illustrated by Niki Daly, Orchard, 1995.

Getting Used to Harry, illustrated by Diane Palmisciano, Orchard, 1996.

Top Banana, illustrated by Erika Oller, Orchard, 1997.

Last Licks: A Spaldeen Story, illustrated by Diane Palmisciano, DK, 1999.

Montezuma's Revenge, illustrated by Diane Palmisciano, Orchard, 1999.

Three Cheers for Catherine the Great!, illustrated by Giselle Potter, DK, 1999.

Cari Best

Sidelights

Cari Best told *SATA:* "Many times in my books, I will use my power as a storyteller to make something positive from something gray and grim. If certain events did not play out happily in my life, those very same events might now play out happily in my stories. *Taxi! Taxi!,* for example, is the story of a young girl who gets to spend a glorious day in the country with her beloved father. He returns her love unconditionally and promises more sweet times together—even though he must deliver her back to her mother at the end of the day. The universality of the ache and emptiness created by the reality of one parent living elsewhere most probably will be felt deep in the hearts of children everywhere. I still feel it."

Taxi! Taxi! is, in fact, a book that creates a positive situation from a difficult reality. Every Sunday Tina stands on her street counting the red cars she sees and visiting with neighbors as she looks expectantly for her father's taxi. On Sundays, Papi, a taxi driver, picks Tina up in his cab and takes her on outings to special surprise places. Papi does not live with Tina, so the outings are an especially important part of their relationship. Wistful wishes are woven through the story, as when Tina says to Papi: "This is the best Sunday ever. I wish you lived with me and Mama. Then I could see you every day." Papi too shares his wistfulness, when he tells Tina that he talks to his plants about her whenever he is lonely. Despite the less-than-perfect situation, Tina decides that she is lucky to have two families—"Papi and me, and Mama and me." Deeming the book's tone to be "generally upbeat," Ellen Fader praised *Taxi! Taxi!* in *Horn Book,* citing its "positive look at one day in the life of a girl" with two families. *School Library Journal* contributor John Peters called *Taxi! Taxi!* "a story with plenty of subtext and a premise that will strike a chord with many readers."

Sharing with *SATA* some thoughts about her next book, Best related: *"Red Light, Green Light, Mama and Me* was borne out of the feelings of love and warmth and security that overwhelmed me each time I stood next to my mother whenever we went somewhere together. In my heart I always knew that come heat or high water, monster or madman, nothing and no one in the whole world (certainly not in New York City) would ever harm me as long as my mother was there. What soon followed in my mind was her image—looking so beautiful and so important, as she left me each day to go to work, while I, a helpless young child was left behind to cry over her picture. But never again! In my story, Lizzie, an enchantingly bold and charming little girl (much more like my daughter than like myself), gets to spend an entire day with her mother at work—not behind a heavy gray metal desk like my mother's—but at the dynamic Downtown Children's Library, where Mama is part of an energetic team, a real 'work family' that makes new and exciting things happen every hour!"

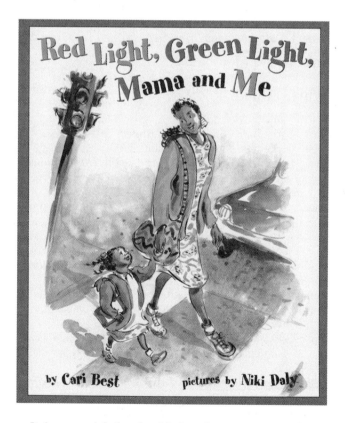

It is a special day for Lizzie, who accompanies her mother to her job; the two ride the subway, buy muffins, and before long, Lizzie finds herself working alongside Mama and her co-workers in the public library. (Cover illustration by Niki Daly.)

In *Bulletin of the Center for Children's Books,* critic Susan Dove Lempke lauded *Red Light, Green Light, Mama and Me* for its celebration of "the everyday details of grownup life that seem so appealing to a small child." Similarly, a *Publishers Weekly* reviewer praised Best for "wisely realiz[ing] that an average workday needs no embellishment to enthrall a child." The same commentator credited Best's story with providing an introduction to the working world that "just might [make young readers] feel better about saying good-bye in the mornings to come." Lempke, noting the book's tenor of encouraging independence in young readers, wrote that *Red Light, Green Light, Mama and Me* "presents the world of work as something wonderful to grow into." *School Library Journal* contributor Virginia Opocensky pronounced the work "a warm wonderful story," adding: "Don't miss this gem."

While *Red Light, Green Light, Mama and Me* was inspired by an emotion, Best's next project was inspired by one of her five senses. *"Getting Used to Harry* started with a smell," Best explained to *SATA.* "For me it was the loathsome, lingering, stale smell of cigar associated with a loathsome, lingering, stale person who was very much a part of my childhood. The hard part for me was to find the good in this character and, at the same time, provide children in a similar situation with a way to cope—again, to create something positive out of something seemingly hopeless. When Cynthia's mother marries Harry, her home becomes his home, and there is absolutely nothing she can do to change that. There must be an awful lot of Cynthias out there who are having to get used to an awful lot of Harrys. The fact that Cynthia is a child and Harry is an adult is secondary. After all, who would disagree that we would all be a lot better off with a little less bickering.

"Interestingly enough, the smell of the real Harry's cigar carried me through the writing of the book—although an actual cigar never appears in the story. I never *did* get used to the smell, and, therefore, could not convincingly persuade Cynthia to get used to it either."

Though she couldn't convince Cynthia to adapt to the smell of cigars, Best *did* persuade her to adjust to the equally pungent personality of Harry. Several reviewers, including *Booklist* critic Susan Dove Lempke, remarked on Best's "upbeat tone" and "gentle humor." A writer for *Publishers Weekly* especially liked the way Harry and Cynthia bonded over a nighttime walk, "bringing Best's funny, heartwarming tale to a reassuring close." Calling Cynthia's narration "a nice combination of sulky and snappy," Elizabeth Bush commended the book's upbeat humor in *Bulletin of the Center for Children's Books,* writing that the "reassurance to new stepkids [is] delivered with a goofy sweetness that makes the lesson go down easy."

"Being in touch with what I felt as a child," Best told *SATA,* "has never been difficult; the challenge has been to convert those feelings, however ill and negative, into something that would help a child deal with similar situations in his or her life today."

When they pass a man selling balloons, Papi buys one. "For my best girl," he says, presenting it to Tina. "*Para mi chica la más preciosa.*" Tina squeezes Papi's big hand. "I love you so-o-o much," she says. "This is the *best* Sunday ever. I wish you lived with me and Mama. Then I could see you every day."

Tina, a little girl with two families, spends this particular Sunday with her father, who takes her on many adventures in his taxi, including a drive in the country, a picnic lunch, and a visit to a farm. (From Taxi! Taxi!, *illustrated by Dale Gottlieb.*)

In *Top Banana,* Best helps children deal with sibling rivalry. Benny the parrot, true to his title role, is top banana; he is Flora Dora's one and only pampered pet. In return for Flora Dora's devotion, he "fanned [Flora] when she was faint. He helped fertilize her ferns. He fluted the edges of her fruit pies." Basically, Benny revels in his own unique beauty and his idyllic life until the day that Flora brings Scarlett O'Hara, a stunner of an exotic orchid, into their previously perfect home. When Flora tells Scarlett and Benny that they are both "the sweetest, most beautiful creatures on earth," Benny begins dreaming up ways to hurt Scarlett. The dreams fade away, however, as Scarlett falls ill, and Benny sets about nursing his nemesis back to health by converting Flora Dora's bathroom into her ideal environment—a rainforest. "Best writes good-humoredly," wrote a *Publishers Weekly* critic, "with judicious doses of alliteration." A *Kirkus Reviews* critic praised *Top Banana* for its "offbeat funny take on sibling rivalry."

Best's strong sense of self has contributed to her writing success. She noted in *SATA:* "Something children always find amusing is that, despite the fact that I grew up wearing other kids' clothes, most notably a neighbor's—Ellen Katz's name-tagged underwear, blouses, shorts, and dresses—I had a strong sense of who I was

and what I could and couldn't do. I knew that I liked hot dogs and not hamburgers. I knew that I liked the color red and not the color green. I knew that I liked stories about families, and I hated stories about monsters. I knew that if I wanted to, I could make myself run fast in a race, spell all the words correctly on a spelling test, and not eat that one last bite of liver that I knew would make me burst. I wasn't very interested in science, and I didn't care very much about what I wore. But I did hate wearing galoshes in the rain, and I hated being sent to bed when it was still light outside.

"Understanding who I am helps me in my writing. Sometimes after I've toiled over something for months, I'll read it over and come to the conclusion that I can do better still, or I'll admit that this is the absolute best that I can do—even though the writing might leave much to be desired.

"Something I try never to do when I'm writing is to write about anything I don't care much about. If it doesn't matter to me, then why will it matter to children? I always hope that readers will care as much as I do— even if the story is about *my* grandmother and not theirs, and how much I loved her knees and her cheeks and the sound of the Russian language. I try to awaken in each of them a passion for my passion—whether it's for playing ball, a dog named Pansy, a puny parrot, a walk in the city, or a ride in a taxi. And, of course, when the child then feels like indulging the passion in himself or herself, I am rewarded. There goes a child who, one day I hope, will grow up to be a caring adult."

Works Cited

Best, Cari, *Taxi! Taxi!,* Little, Brown, 1994.

Best, Cari, *Top Banana,* Orchard, 1997.

Bush, Elizabeth, review of *Getting Used to Harry, Bulletin of the Center for Children's Books,* October, 1996, p. 49.

Fader, Ellen, review of *Taxi! Taxi!, Horn Book,* May-June, 1994, p. 306.

Review of *Getting Used to Harry, Publishers Weekly,* September 2, 1996, p. 130.

Lempke, Susan Dove, review of *Getting Used to Harry, Booklist,* November 1, 1996, p. 506.

Lempke, Susan Dove, review of *Red Light, Green Light, Mama and Me, Bulletin of the Center for Children's Books,* September, 1995, p. 6.

Opocensky, Virginia, review of *Red Light, Green Light, Mama and Me, School Library Journal,* October, 1995, p. 96.

Peters, John, review of *Taxi! Taxi!, School Library Journal,* June, 1994, p. 96.

Review of *Red Light, Green Light, Mama and Me, Publishers Weekly,* July 31, 1995, p. 80.

Review of *Top Banana, Kirkus Reviews,* February 15, 1997, p. 296.

Review of *Top Banana, Publishers Weekly,* March 10, 1997, p. 66.

For More Information See

PERIODICALS

Booklist, September 1, 1995, p. 82.
Bulletin of the Center for Children's Books, May, 1999, p. 308.
New York Times Book Review, September 25, 1994, p. 32.
Publishers Weekly, March 7, 1994, p. 69.
School Library Journal, April, 1997, p. 90; May, 1999, p. 85.

*   *   *

BISHOP, Nic 1955-

Personal

Born August 26, 1955; father is a biology teacher and science writer, mother has worked as a scientist. *Education:* University of Nottingham, B.Sc. (with honors), 1976; University of Canterbury, Ph.D. (plant science), 1989.

Addresses

Home—Newton, MA.

Career

Massey University, Palmerston North, New Zealand, research fellow, 1977-80; University of Canterbury, Canterbury, New Zealand, tutor and researcher, 1980-86; writer and photographer, 1988—. Appeared in television documentaries, including an episode of the series *Beyond 2000,* broadcast by the Discovery Channel, 1994; guest on radio programs in New Zealand.

Awards, Honors

Wattie Book Award (now Montana Book Award), and selected among ten best books of 1992 by both *Metro* and *North and South* magazines, all 1993, all for *Natural History of New Zealand;* Montana Book Award, 1995, for *From the Mountains to the Sea;* New Zealand's National Library Award, best children's nonfiction book of 1996, and New Zealand *Post* Children's Book Award, 1997, both for *The Garden;* New Zealand's National Library Award, one of five best children's nonfiction books of 1996, for *The Field;* Reading Magic Award from *Parenting* Magazine, 1997, Best Books, *School Library Journal,* 1997, Blue Ribbon Book, *Bulletin of the Center for Children's Books,* 1998, and John

Nic Bishop

Burroughs Nature Books for Young Readers Award, 1998, all for *The Secrets of Animal Flight.*

Writings

AUTHOR AND PHOTOGRAPHER

Untouched Horizons: Photographs from the South Island Wilderness (for adults), Hodder & Stoughton (Auckland, New Zealand), 1989.

Natural History of New Zealand (for adults), illustrations by Chris Gaskin, Hodder & Stoughton, 1992.

From the Mountains to the Sea: The Secret Life of New Zealand's Rivers and Wetlands (for adults), Reed Books (Auckland), 1994.

Leap Frog, Scott, Foresman (Glenview, IL), 1994.

New Zealand Wild: The Greenest Place on Earth (for adults), Reed Books, 1995.

Ready, Steady, Jump, Scott, Foresman, 1995.

The Secrets of Animal Flight, Houghton (Boston, MA), 1997.

Strange Plants, Richard C. Owen, 1997.

The Green Snake, Wright Group (San Diego, CA), 1998.

The Katydids, Richard C. Owen, 1998.

Gecko Flies, Wright Group, 1998.

Mudskipper, Wright Group, 1998.

Canoe Diary, Scott, Foresman, 1998.

Caught in a Flash, Scott, Foresman, 1998.

PHOTOGRAPHER

(Contributor) Mark Pickering, *The Hills,* Reed Books, 1988.

Pat Quinn, *The Bumble Bee,* Scott, Foresman, 1993.

The Praying Mantis, Scott, Foresman, 1993.

Owen Neville Bishop, *Wildflowers of New Zealand* (for adults), Hodder & Stoughton, 1994.

Owen Neville Bishop and Audrey Bishop, *New Zealand Wild Flowers Handbook* (for adults), Hodder & Stoughton, 1994.

Joy Cowley, *Pukeko Morning,* Scott, Foresman, 1994.

Jane Buxton, *Snap, Splash,* Scott, Foresman, 1994.

Diane Noonan, *I Spy a Fly,* Lands End (New Zealand), 1994.

Diane Noonan, *On the Move,* Lands End, 1994.

(Contributor) Mark Pickering, *Wild Walks,* Shoal Bay Press (New Zealand), 1995.

Diane Noonan, *The Rocky Shore,* Heinemann (New Zealand), 1996.

Diane Noonan, *The Garden,* Heinemann, 1996.

Diane Noonan, *The Pond,* Heinemann, 1996.

Diane Noonan, *Lake Critter Journal,* Scott, Foresman, 1996.

Joy Cowley, *Sky to the Sea,* Scott, Foresman, 1996.

Diane Noonan, *The Field,* Heinemann, 1996.

Joy Cowley, *Swans,* Heinemann, 1997.

Jill Eggleton, *Spider Legs,* Wright Group, 1997.

Sy Montgomery, *The Snake Scientist,* Houghton, 1999.

Joy Cowley, *The Red-Eyed Tree Frog,* Scholastic Press, 1999.

Photographs have appeared in calendars and magazines, including *Ranger Rick, Animals, Natural History, Pacific Way, International Photographer,* and *New Zealand Geographic.*

Work in Progress

Natural history books for children on topics "from prehistoric life to forest critters."

Sidelights

Nic Bishop told *SATA:* "I have always been fascinated by nature. When I was young, my parents lived in Bangladesh, Sudan (in Africa), New Guinea, and Indonesia, where my father worked for UNESCO. My interest in photography began at age nine, when I borrowed my older sister's camera to record my time in the Sudan. Since then, I have not looked back. My teenage years in New Guinea were an especially wonderful experience. I was educated at home there for several years in the highlands and, without others of my age and race for company, I often spent my weekends hiking to local villages. I always took my camera to record the adventures.

"It was also in New Guinea that I was first exposed to the extraordinary diversity of life. The richness of species was amazing—especially insects—and they made fascinating subjects for home-school biology studies. My father was a biology teacher, so there was always lots of encouragement for me to learn about natural history. It really wasn't surprising that I continued to study in the field of biology when I went to the university. I studied botany at a university in England, and then I moved to New Zealand, where I completed a doctorate in plant physiology.

"I maintained a strong interest in photography, natural history, and hiking, and I decided to find my future as a natural history author and photographer. With my background as a scientist, it was the smaller and more everyday animals that I found the most fascinating for photography. Our view of nature is very biased toward the big and seemingly spectacular animals, but biologically the small critters are the most important. On close and thoughtful inspection, they are also usually the most beautiful and intriguing.

"My interest in writing has followed my interest in photography. In many ways, I feel they are similar endeavors. Both are thoughtful processes that force one to articulate—on film or paper—what it is about the subject that one finds interesting or challenging. Having involved myself with the process of learning and inquiring photographically, it is natural for me to want to put words on paper, too.

"In photographing small animals I have aimed to depict my subjects on their terms, taking the viewer into their small world. My special camera techniques include high-speed photography of insects and birds in flight. It took a while to build the equipment I needed, and I had electronics help from my father. In the end we made a complex system of special flash guns and a shutter, with laser beams to trip the camera just as the subject flies into view. The equipment is not always reliable, and given that animal subjects have their moods, too, it can

Enhanced by the author's photographs, Bishop's book makes accessible to middle graders the more technical aspects of animal flight, including such topics as wing structure, soaring, gliding, and landing, as well as some issues that continue to puzzle scientists. (Cover photographs by Nic Bishop.)

take a long time to get good results. It often takes a hundred shots just to get one that looks great.

"The thrill of high-speed photography is getting a picture of something that cannot be observed by eye. The results are also instructive, showing the wing motions that animals use to stay airborne, and this helped me explain the mechanisms of flight for my book *The Secrets of Animal Flight.*"

Critics agree that Bishop hit the mark with *The Secrets of Animal Flight.* In this book, the author explores all aspects of flight in the animal kingdom. With clear prose and full-color, stop-action photography he explains the mechanics of the flight of birds, bats, and insects. Of special interest are a series of photos isolating the individual motion stages of flight in a chickadee, wasp, and butterfly. "The many colorful photographs expand the text with precision and beauty," stated Carolyn Phelan in *Booklist.* Bishop even touches on fascinating aspects of flight that scientists don't fully understand, like why Monarch butterflies migrate to the same area in Mexico year after year, or why some birds can fly 2,000 miles nonstop, but the unanswered questions "won't

keep this title from flying off the shelf," noted Susan S. Verner in *Bulletin of the Center for Children's Books.* "This is the best type of science book—it really communicates the excitement of unlocking nature's secrets and leads readers on to discoveries of their own," enthused Ruth S. Vose in *School Library Journal.*

"When I began as a natural history author and photographer," Bishop continued to *SATA,* "my books were aimed at the adult audience, but I soon realized that many of my favorite photographs were appealing to children. Most of my books seemed to feature bugs, frogs, and reptiles. With their open and inquisitive minds, children find these subjects fascinating, just as I did when I was young. So now I work solely in the children's field. Nature is endlessly wonderful, and if I can use my photographs to help encourage a child's natural curiosity about the living world, then I feel I have achieved something really worthwhile."

Works Cited

Phelan, Carolyn, review of *The Secrets of Animal Flight,* *Booklist,* March 15, 1997, p. 1236.

Verner, Susan S., review of *The Secrets of Animal Flight*, *Bulletin of the Center for Children's Books*, June, 1997, pp. 350-51.

Vose, Ruth S., review of *The Secrets of Animal Flight*, *School Library Journal*, April, 1997, p. 120.

For More Information See

PERIODICALS

Horn Book, May-June, 1997, p. 337.
Kirkus Reviews, February 1, 1997, p. 219.

Autobiography Feature

Ruth Lercher Bornstein

1927-

If I were to close my eyes and draw a picture of my life, I'd make a small figure of a woman on the horizon looking up at an enormous, cloud-filled sky. The sun would be low, the clouds dark with light around the edges. If I were to draw a picture of what sustains me, I'd show the same scene, only close-up, and the woman would be holding a child in her arms. If I were to draw what I need, I'd repeat the scene, the woman with the child, but also moving back to view the big, open space.

I had been thinking about telling some of my story to my children and grandchildren and, after avoiding it for many years, I recently began reading my teenage diaries. The memories are piling up. So here goes, sifting through the layers, trying to organize my life into an essay.

I'm first-generation American, born and growing up at a time when being American was the first priority, especially for greenhorn immigrants like my parents. I never heard them speak Yiddish.

My mother, Baila Friedman, was born in 1903 near Grudno in Russia and was one of two girls in a family of eight living children. Though Jews had to pay taxes, their children were not allowed to attend public school. A schoolteacher was hired to come to their home after school. The Cossacks were feared and, during the first World War, the area was overrun by Polish and German soldiers. Only the Germans left the family some of the potatoes in the fields.

Only once did I hear my mother utter a language other than English, only once did I hear her sing. One night, when I was around thirteen and she was at the kitchen sink and didn't know I was listening, she sang *"Oichee chornia,"* the Russian song "Dark Eyes." I wished she would sing more.

After the war my mother followed two older married brothers to Milwaukee, Wisconsin. Entering the United States at Ellis Island, her name was changed to Bertha.

Born in 1896, my dad grew up near Pshmenshel in Austria. Under duress he was drafted into the German army in World War I and, though he also was from a large and religious family, he often said that the war was so horrible he became an atheist in the foxhole. After the war he followed two married sisters to Milwaukee. His name, Abraham, became Adolph. You can tell my dad's innocent nature from his autobiography which he painstakingly wrote out in lined notebooks and gave to my brother and me and to each one of his six grandchildren. He wrote how proud he was that he had lived to see Halley's comet twice, and how amazing to live throughout the twentieth century, from horse-drawn carriages to men landing on the moon. I edited his journal, made typewritten copies for the relatives, and gave it to him for his ninetieth birthday. My dad wanted to be "known."

My mother pooh-poohed going over the past. "Why think about what is over and done with?" But before she died I interviewed her and have twenty audio tapes that I hope to transcribe into text.

My parents never wanted to set foot in Europe again. Whenever we criticized the U.S.A., the conversation would always end with, "Yes, but you don't know what it's like to live without freedom." When he finally bought his own home, my dad installed a tall flagpole and every Fourth of July he proudly displayed the American flag. He also cast the only vote in 1948, in New London, Wisconsin, for the Progressive Party candidate, idealistic Henry Wallace.

My parents met in Milwaukee in a Labor Zionist class to learn English. He was unambitious, content with his job as a skilled glove cutter. She was smart, fiercely independent, and proud. Despite her independence, it seems she was a woman of her times. She was twenty-two years old. It was time to get married.

Many years later, when I was a grandmother myself, I asked her why she had married my dad. She replied, "Because he was good to his sisters." She also told me that when I was little, I would beg them to stop fighting. My parents were married for sixty-two years.

Ruth Lercher Bornstein

I must have been very young. I thought I was connected by a thread to a tiny, invisible person, who looked just like me. I was sure that she was always with me, that she never left me. When I walked down the street she was right behind me. When I wore a red dress, she wore a red dress too. I'm not sure when she disappeared and I knew I was alone in the world, not connected by a thread to anyone. I must have been three or four.

We lived in a poor immigrant neighborhood, upstairs in back of a building with a clothesline strung to the one in front. My brother, Bruce, was born three years after me, and I've been told that I called him *"my baby."* I was very well dressed; my mother made all my clothes. I don't know where she found the scraps, but when I was a year old I wore a coat with fur collar and cuffs and a hat to match.

When I was three, my favorite song was "Summertime" from the musical opera *Porgy and Bess,* and I sang it constantly. It must have been quite a feat, because my mother took me downtown on the streetcar to audition for a radio talent show. Standing in front of a roomful of people, I froze. No sound came out of me. My mother took me home.

Of kindergarten I have a memory of boys running away from my kisses. In second grade I wrote a poem about a valentine coming alive that was mimeographed in the school paper. And my ambition at age six, and I quote from an essay I wrote in college at age seventeen, was "to become the world's greatest artist. The world's greatest masterpiece, painted by me naturally, would be a huge rainbow colored version of a sunset with soft dark trees outlining a rippling lake. I happily dreamed of my forthcoming fame."

Not only that. In age I was in between Princess Elizabeth of England and Shirley Temple of Hollywood, so naturally I had curls and was enrolled in tap dancing and acrobatic lessons. I was not brave. It took me a long time to

master a back bend, much less a forward flip. I can still do a shuffle-ball-change.

When I was eight or nine, my dad's back was badly injured and he could no longer work in the glove factory. My mother's brothers, Sam and Jake, agreed to hire him to work as a salesman in their men's clothing stores. It was 1936, the time of the depression, and my dad was glad to get the work. My mother was less happy. She knew that her brothers were doing us a "favor." She hated being beholden.

We moved to West Allis, a suburb of Milwaukee, to be closer to the stores. The new neighborhood was considered a step up. We still lived in an upstairs flat but there was a green lawn in front. The neighborhood kids were different, unfriendly. My mother intervened with another mother and soon after I was allowed to join in on the wild night games of kick-the-can. In school I made friends. And got a crush on Dickie Chesley.

One evening I walked some distance to Dick's house; it was already dark when I knocked on the front door. The door opened and I asked his mother if Dickie could come out and play. She looked down at me with an expression of horror. "It's past Dickie's bedtime," she said. "He's in bed asleep."

I got my first pet, a small green chameleon, from the Wisconsin State Fair. He (I called it "he") came with a safety pin on the end of a tiny gold chain so I could wear him on my blouse. He changed color slightly—green and brown shades—depending on what I wore. I can still feel his cool, soft, silky skin. I watched his long tongue lap up the sugar water I fed him, constantly petted him, and thought my pet loved me too. One day, to give him a tiny taste of freedom, I let him loose in the grass. In a flash, he was gone. I was heartbroken and searched for him for days.

I loved robin redbreasts. When a pair of robins began a nest on our narrow windowsill, Bruce and I were frantic. What if the nest fell off? Our gentle dad built a platform, the robins continued nest building, and just inches away we could watch the baby robins hatch and begin to grow. I remember the sharp, black points of their new sticking-out feathers. When they were ready and flew off, we cheered. After all we had helped raise them.

Later that summer I found a robin on the grass. I picked him up and cradled him in my hands, and I could hear his heart beating, loud, like a clock. Suddenly the clock stopped, the robin's eyes covered over with white, and he turned stiff and cold. Oh, how I cried. I made the neighborhood kids come to the funeral, complete with a grave, a cross, flowers, and sad songs.

My few books were hand-me-downs from Aunt Rose. I shed many tears over *Heidi* and gazed over and over at the book's glossy, colored illustrations. I admired the well-drawn, realistic pictures in *Illustrated Bible Stories* and the "folk-art" drawings in *Folk Tales Children Love.* I still have these books.

I also loved my hand-me-down clothes from cousin Ginka. My mother may not have been so happy. She wasn't happy staying home either, housebound with us. I never suffered from being a poor relative, but when I was nine years old and was called to the phone downstairs in our landlady's apartment, I was afraid to talk into it. And when we got a ride out to the countryside, my little brother

"My parents, Bertha and Adolph Lercher, in 1926. My mother is pregnant with me."

pointed out the car window and said, "Look! a real human being cow!"

I was drawing a lot, often copying the illustrations of pretty women in magazines. Again, quoting my college freshman essay, "By the age of ten I realized that my ambition of becoming the world's greatest artist might not be possible or practical. I certainly had no fears for my future anyway. Commercial art and being a career woman had attracted my attention by then."

But the important thing was having friends. All of us ten-year-old girls wanted to change our names. I wanted Bonnie but couldn't have it. Another girl had chosen it first. When I was almost eleven, I was told that we would move again. I said, "I won't go!"

With the help of my uncles, my parents had found a vacated dry-goods store in a town of four thousand people some hours north of Milwaukee. It was cold and rainy on the day we arrived, but I immediately fell in love with the muddy streets and the "country" one block away. And on the first day of school, when they asked me my name, I said, "Bonnie."

New London was bigger than the other hamlets around, so it was where the surrounding farmers did their shopping on Friday night. Together with the few Jewish families in the area, my parents formed the Jewish Welfare Club. They met in each other's homes, and with poker and other card games they raised money for Jewish causes. In 1938 and 1939 when they heard of the happenings in Germany, help was even more urgent. But I knew nothing about it.

My mother's parents and other siblings had emigrated from Russia to Palestine in the early 1930s. I never heard about my father's family, never learned what happened to them in the Holocaust. Till the day he died, my father never talked about his brothers and sisters in Europe. At some point I learned that close relatives on my mother's side perished.

I always thought my parents were silent because they wanted to protect us. But much later when I asked my mother why she chose not to share her fear and sorrow, she said, "You didn't want to hear it."

Later, whenever my dad visited me in the various places I lived, he always looked for "Lercher" in the phone books. He never found any relatives. I wish that I had kept my maiden name; I use it now for my books on the slight chance that someone will contact me.

My dad was a heavy smoker and my brother and I enjoyed the bric-a-brac furniture "bought" with Raleigh cigarette coupons. Some of our dishes came from give-aways at the movies. My father was invited to join the Lions Club as well as the Rotary and Oddfellows clubs, and my mother joined the ladies' auxiliaries.

My new name stuck. Even with my parents. My brother and I each skipped half a grade because of the difference in school systems. Not yet twelve, I was in junior high, the top floor of Lincoln Elementary School. I was asked to join two competing girls' clubs and Donnie and Leslie, two boys in class, sent me a note. They both wanted me to be their girl friend and said I had to choose between them. I wrote back, democratically saying I liked them equally. I lost them both.

I remember uncontrollable giggling spells and lots of note passing. I still drew lots of pictures.

In Girl Scouts we won badges and sang lots of songs. Once, at a Girl and Boy Scout Jamboree in the area, I saw dozens of chickens running around with their heads cut off. One of the badges, I found out, was learning how to slaughter chickens. We didn't have to pass that badge in our troop.

At our "Scout" cottage at the Waupaca Chain O'Lakes, I had to swallow a live minnow. I couldn't even swallow a pill. But our twenty-one-year-old assistant leader said I couldn't belong to the special "club within the club" unless I did. I wanted to belong! So I kept on gagging. The minnow was dry and dead by the time I got it down.

Uncle Shimon, newly arrived from Palestine, gave me my first bike and, at age eleven, I learned to ride. Riding into the countryside, often to the Little Wolf River, I lay in the long grass and drew and daydreamed. Daydreaming was probably what I did best.

And I got one of my wishes. Uncle Jake came to town with a puppy. My mother was upset with Uncle Jake and said to me, "No! I know you won't take care of it." I begged. She gave in. She was right. I often forgot to clean up after Mitzi, even to feed her. All I wanted was to hug her tight and have her love me back. Mitzi began to ran away whenever she saw me coming. While I was at school she was hit by a car, probably because I didn't tie her up. A neighbor boy was asked to tell me; my parents were afraid to tell me themselves. I sobbed for a long time.

I was thirteen when World War II started. I was impressed when my mother was visited by the F.B.I. and instructed to keep her eyes and ears open. People of German ancestry lived in the area and there were suspicions of Nazi sympathizers, even collaborators.

My mother was the driver in the family, my father the passenger. She even drove to Milwaukee and Chicago on buying trips for the store. She was the driver in every sense. In the store she tried to pretend that my dad was the boss. The conflict was saved for later, at home.

With our parents working into the night, Bruce and I usually made do with heated-up Campbell's Chicken Noodle Soup and fried Spam for supper. I was jealous of the other kids who sat down for supper with their families and actually talked together. I was jealous of their Christmas too. I sneaked my brother out with me late one Christmas eve, and we dragged a fir tree branch home. I stuffed two stockings with apples and oranges for a "surprise" on Christmas morning. From then on my parents let us have Christmas trees and gave us presents too.

Bruce took after Mom; he was the smart one. He became class valedictorian and later had a long career as a mathematics professor at Binghampton State University in New York.

Ruth about two years old.

I was the flighty "artistic" one. I was unsure of my ability, but the label "class artist," like the name Bonnie, stuck. All through junior high and high school, I was asked to make signs for every event, every school department, and to draw for the school newspaper. I didn't know how to say no.

Did I want to be in the band? I said yes and was given the only instrument left, a clarinet. I loved being part of the whole and hearing all the instruments come together to create beautiful music. In high school we traveled on a bus to football and basketball games, singing "Oh the deacon went down to the cellar to pray," and "Sipping cider through a straw," at the top of our lungs. When the guys started up "My Bonnie lies over the ocean, won't you bring back my Bonnie to me," I blushed and got a nice, warm feeling inside.

I cry at parades. I can sob when a high school band comes by. I cried even then when I was marching, wearing a way-too-big red and white uniform and trilling on my clarinet. I've tried to figure out why I cry. I think it's the humanness of it; human beings showing themselves, being connected. Being "known."

I couldn't stop giggling and was often kicked out of English class and study hall. But in my diary, there was also, "I'm beginning to think my happy days take turns with my not so happy days." and "I try to think but I get more mixed up about myself, life and everything under the sun," I loved Biology and dropped out of Typing (if I only knew then). My mother was a skilled seamstress but I could barely sew an apron, in the required Home Economics.

Seeing the movie *The Moon and Sixpence* made me write, "I long to be able to paint or even to appreciate real art." I also wrote, "Oh, when will this awful war be over? How can people kill each other? Please make everyone understand all the world is one brotherhood," and "Just thinking—why do I keep a diary? It's silly to write stuff down—maybe it's because I don't confide in my parents and you *have* to tell someone." But I did tell. I needed to talk, to touch. I confided in Norma and Esther who also felt alone and couldn't talk to their parents.

I took on a big job. Writing to servicemen in the navy, the army, the marines, even the coast guard. Some were boys I knew who had quit school to join up. Some were guys I didn't know. In any case it was my duty. They all needed long letters from home.

My friends and I joked that we lived in a hick town and that every other store in New London was a bar. No foreign language was offered in high school and no art. But I loved being in the country, loved ice skating to school and on the wavy-iced Wolf River, stopping to get warm at the various bars along the shore. Some of us drank too early and smoked.

On May 7, I wrote, "Mom started off on how spoiled I am and what a fool I make of myself over men. I told her that if I was spoiled it's always the parents' fault—and it is!!" There were loud lectures from my mother. "You're Jewish, different from the others; people are talking about you, you have to behave better than the others!" But I didn't know why I was different. I just wanted to be one of the gang.

Often there was a heavy silence at home. A few times my mother stayed in bed, two days at a time, and we tiptoed around the house. I didn't know why she was so

"My brother, Bruce, and me. I'm eleven; he's eight."

depressed, and I was afraid to ask. I thought that, somehow, it was my fault. And at least once I heard that it was.

My mother became an officer in the Business and Professional Women's Club in town. She made most of the crucial decisions in the store, did all the bookkeeping and the clothes alterations, went on buying trips, put up the best dill pickles and red raspberry jam.... Now I wonder how she did it all. On the other hand, how did I find the time to see forty movies in 1943 what with my heavy social life, my extra-curricular activities like band, oratory, debate, doing all those signs for school activities and cartoons for the school annuals, helping out in the store some Friday nights, being in school plays (I was murdered on stage in one play and had to give a blood curdling scream—I was good at that—fall down, be dragged across the stage, and stuffed into a closet), besides faithfully keeping up the spirits of our fighting men with letter after letter *and* writing in my diary every single night?

Next to Bonnie Lercher in the 1944 High School Annual it says, "Wherever she goes, whatever she's done, she has a bright smile for everyone." I did. But at the same time I was writing, "What is the meaning of life?" and, "I'm so mixed up!"

My parents must have breathed huge sighs of relief when I attended Layton Art School in Milwaukee for part of two summers. I wanted to be an artist. Most of my friends were going to be nurses. I wrote, "Gee, I hope I won't waste myself sitting in art school. I could be a nurse cadet and do something for my country!"

I lived at Aunt Rose's in West Allis and felt brave taking the streetcar downtown. On my first day in art school I saw my first nude model. I turned beet red; there were boys my age in the class. I soon got over it and tried hard to concentrate on the work. I never did understand perspective. On July 21, 1994, I wrote, "An artist should know how to draw everything. They have to observe everything too—which I don't," and "Oh, I wish I had something to say!"

Cousin Ginka, a modern dancer, introduced me to dance, and I loved taking the classes. Cousin Trudi gave me *The Lonely Ones* by William Steig. The "human condition" drawings had captions like, "My true love will come someday," "I can't express it," "Forgive me, I'm only human," and "People are no damn good."

I sang "Sometimes I Feel Like a Motherless Child" a lot after I saw Paul Robeson in a concert. On my first trip to Chicago, I was stunned by the Van Goghs and Picassos in the Chicago Art Institute, and I received my first art books, Van Gogh and Picasso, from Ginka and Trudi. I bought myself a book of illustrated fairy tales and thought it might be fun to illustrate a fairy tale one day. And that summer I wrote in my diary, "Oh, to find my own true love and get married and have lots of kids—and paint!"

I hadn't given much thought to which college to attend, so by default and because it was less expensive I went off to the University of Wisconsin in Madison. I was seventeen, a little scared, but glad to get away from home. Looking back, I was much too young, and the school was too big. Hundreds of us took notes in the history and economics lecture halls. I almost flunked the first and dropped out of the second. And I was too scattered to ever find a real mentor. I wanted to be part of the swirling social life in the Student Union, even learned to like the 3.2 beer served in the Rathskeller.

Sometimes I lashed out at anti-semitic remarks I overheard, sometimes I didn't. I never knew how I was going to react. Not having a secure base, I turned the remarks inward and wondered if there was something wrong with *me*. Was being Jewish something less than human? Now I have compassion for the needy adolescent I was, but I'm still ashamed to say that though I swore I wanted to be "independent," it was a blow when my friend told me, "I'm sorry, Bonnie, you're nice and we like you, but you can't join our sorority because you're Jewish."

One night in the Rathskeller around that time, I met a very bitter African-American soldier. He told me that even the graveyards in the army were segregated into black and white.

I discovered poetry. The book we used in the freshman English class was *Modern American and British Poetry,* edited by Louis Untermeyer. Over and over I read William Butler Yeats' "I will arise now and go to Innisfree ..." and "I shall have some peace there, for peace comes dropping slow." And in another Yeats poem, "Adeh Wishes for the Cloths of Heaven," I loved the lines, "tread softly because you tread on my dreams." A. E. Houseman appealed to me too. "When I Was One and Twenty" is full of "endless rue" and "oh, 'tis true, 'tis true."

We wrote essays. On one paper the professor noted that I had "unusual promise, a pleasing humanity." The comment pleases me now, but then I didn't give it a thought . . . . I was going to be a painter.

I began to spend long hours in the printmaking studio, etching and lithographing lonely lost souls. One etching shows a nude girl with a big weight on her head. Al Sessler, the printmaking teacher, was worried about us "little girl" art students. How would we be able to earn a living, that is, if we didn't get married right away? The answer. Major in Art Education. So along with studio art classes, I practice-taught art and enjoyed it, especially in the outlying rural schools.

There was a condescending term, "woman artist." I knew I wasn't a dilettante, but could I, a female, be a real artist? And then I fell in love.

Ed was already an army veteran, going to school on the GI bill and serious about his art studies. We were in a painting class together, we talked about everything but,

mainly, I just wanted to be held. For long hours. Ed wanted more. At last he said he couldn't take it and went back to an old girl friend. We were still in the same art class. I suffered terribly.

One rainy night, as I stood reading *Crime and Punishment* in a Madison bookstore, a Norwegian exchange student approached me. Dostoevsky was his favorite writer too! Bjorn was some years older, had been in the Norwegian underground during the war, was a poet, a ski-jumper, and an exotic character with his long blond hair, long fur coat, and leather pouch filled with hardtack and blood sausage, which he'd gnaw whenever he was hungry.

I hoped Ed would see us and be jealous. He did and he wasn't. But Bjorn and I had many soulful times together. And he thought *I* was exotic; before he returned to Norway, he told me that he had never met a Jewish girl before. Years later I got a letter from Bjorn. He wondered why I hadn't come to Norway as I'd planned. It was a turn not taken.

The summer I was twenty, I landed a job as the arts and crafts teacher at an unusual children's arts camp in

At home during the college years, 1948.

As a goatherd in Israel, 1950.

Maine. Up until then, except for Chicago, I had never left Wisconsin. Traveling by train, I stopped and visited in New York City, walked Manhattan from one end to the other, and vowed I'd come back after I graduated.

At Camp Bearnstow the best day of the week for me was my day off. With watercolors and a sketchbook, a cantaloupe to eat and a knife to cut it, I took a canoe out on Parker Pond (a very big lake) and paddled to an island to observe, and write and draw all day. One poem inspired by the quiet and the dragonflies ends like this:

Suddenly I can hear insects speak, trees whisper,
waves singing of old and ceaseless caresses.
And in that instant I am that form,
a winged creature not quite human.
For the first time I live
and this my dream
is more real than my earth bound body.

I spent the summer after graduation in New London, painting scenes around town and making friends with Bert Sampson, the town hobo who lived in a boxcar on the old railroad tracks by the local brewery. He'd direct me to an outside faucet and, while he rocked in his rocking chair, I'd siphon beer for him. I admired Bert's old weatherbeaten face and asked him to pose for me. He handed me a quarter. "For painting my picture," he said. "And for the paints you're using." Bert became the model for Walt in my present, on-going novel.

I exhibited my summer's work in the redbrick, Andrew Carnegie Library in town, and later my folks displayed the watercolor of Bert in Lercher's store window. I heard that Bert often came by and stood admiring his portrait. The picture now hangs in the New London Museum, the bottom floor of the library.

New York! New York! Through cousin Trudi I interviewed for a job as art teacher at Lenox Hill Settlement House just after the big, mature man-teacher quit. It seems he couldn't handle the teenage-and-older gangster types who "interrupted" his night classes. The settlement house

director thought she'd try something daring.... I was hired. It didn't work. After beer bottles were thrown out of the second story window and the police came, the night classes were cancelled.

Settled with a room and board, every morning I was able to attend Julian Levi's painting class at the Art Students League. At noon I walked back through Central Park to the settlement house and conducted art classes for elementary age children. Saturday morning, I taught crafts to old people who came primarily for the soup and sandwiches I prepared for them. They good-naturedly tolerated the crafts.

Never without my sketchbook, on my days off I drew people in the subways and buses, hung out in Central Park and sketched King Kong, the poor gorilla behind bars in the Central Park Zoo. And I fell in love again. With Don, who lived in Greenwich Village.

Back in Wisconsin, my mother, who seemed to know everything, asked me to accompany her to Israel. Her father and her younger sister had recently died there and her mother was now in her eighties. It had been twenty-nine years since my mother had seen her. It was April, 1949. Israel had become a state in May, 1948. I didn't even know the difference between Yiddish and Hebrew. My romance had cooled for the moment. I accepted her offer.

I planned to stay in Israel for two weeks, then go to Paris and look up some artist friends from college. But as soon as the plane landed at Lod Airport I was hooked. The airfield was covered with wildflowers. I had never smelled orange blossoms, or jasmine, had never seen a fig tree. I fell in love with the physical country first.

My young Israeli cousins crowded around me, touching my clothes, my hair. I couldn't understand a word they said and began to cry. They immediately began teaching me Hebrew and, soon after, they took me to visit a neighbor, Dov Noy, the editor of a children's newspaper in Tel Aviv. Dov took me to Cafe Caseet and introduced me to the young painters and writers who congregated there.

These were attractive, good-natured people only a bit older than me, who just months before had been in the underground, had spirited people away from Europe, who had risked their lives over and over. I thought the name Bonnie was too frivolous for Israel and told them my real name, Ruth. They all welcomed me. I was swept away.

My instant new boyfriend, Dahn, took me with him on the back of a truck with the Chizbatron, the troop of army entertainers who were journeying for the first time into the Negev desert. While they sang and joked for the troops, I sat in the hot desert and painted watercolors of the multi-colored mountains. I held up on the extremely rugged trip, then was sick for a week in my grandmother's house when we got back.

After six weeks, my mother left for home. I stayed. I visited Yemenite people, just flown in on what they called "The wings of an eagle." Housed in temporary tent cities, these refugees from another world crowded around me, touching me and smiling as I sketched them and handed them the drawings. Later, in a hospital, I visited some of them again. They had arrived wearing all their silver finery, but they were poor and many were sick with typhoid fever or malaria.

In Tel Aviv, I took modern dance classes with the eminent teacher, Gertrude Kraus, helped paint theater sets

"With my children: (from left) Noa, Jonah, Adam, and Jesse."

designed by the artist, Moshe Mokady, and did a few illustrations for *Davar Le-Yeladim,* the children's newspaper. I visited newly formed kibbutzim founded by people younger than me, where they rode wild Arab steeds and took turns sleeping in the limited number of cots.

Wandering the country with my sketchbook, I walked among Roman ruins and into Arab villages along the Mediterranean and into a Druse village on Mount Carmel.

I spent the summer months in Tzfat (Safed), the ancient village and art colony in the Galilee mountains. My room was furnished with candles and a mattress loaned to me by the army stationed on the hill. I also had a balcony and a view. I washed myself and my one dress (I had given most of my clothes to my admiring cousins) in the shower at a writer's house. I walked the hills, painted in the wadis, and spent a memorable day by a stream in Meron, feeling like part of the landscape. And when I slept on my roof and stared up at the night sky, the stars were so big, so bright and so close, I felt that I was being pulled up into them, and I held on tight to the roof.

One day I acted as a tour guide for a couple of bus loads of American tourists, leading them down the narrow, winding lanes to the tiny, blue-painted medieval synagogue that Chagall had painted not long before. Though I was only a tourist myself, I was given food stamps. I felt guilty; people had so little. I gave the food stamps away and ate scrambled eggs at the cafe and ripe figs off the trees. And I got sick.

I had had the three anti-typhoid shots in New York but that's what it turned out to be. Typhoid fever. I was rushed by ambulance to a hospital for infectious diseases and spent a month in bed in a ward with women patients, all from Middle Eastern countries.

I hallucinated whole movies of stories and was force-fed soft-boiled eggs. When my friends were at last allowed to visit me, the doctor told them that I giggled because I was weak. I was also too weak to walk so was sent to a rest and recuperation hostel in Tzfat for a month where I began to eat and walk ... and get the giggles.

Back in Tel Aviv, my long hair fell out, in clumps. Somehow I wasn't worried, but my Israeli friends were and spirited me away to Kibbutz Bet Alfa where they had a machine that was supposed to make hair grow back. I sat under it for an hour a day and my hair did grow back ... like steel wool. I wanted to work so at 4:30 A.M. I was out in the fields harvesting carrots and cauliflower.

It was spring and baby goats were being born. After work I hung out in the goat shed (shades of Heidi?) and was thrilled when I was given the job of baby-goat goatherd. With a staff and a special trilling call, I tried to get the young ones to follow me through the kibbutz and out to the fields. Visiting Bet Alfa twenty years later, the kibbutzniks were still laughing about the many times I tried to chase one kid out of the roses while all the others ran every which way. It got better. Those were happy days, alone in the fields with my sketchbook, and being a mother to my family of goat-kids. Whenever a shadow passed overhead ... a hawk or an eagle ... all the kids would rush over and crowd around me for protection.

Most of my kibbutz friends were married and settled. Some already had children. I still had bouts of weakness and after four months the goats were almost grown. I was restless. Vowing I'd be back in a year, I traveled steerage class on a ship across the Mediterranean to Marseilles.

Paris in 1950 was an exciting place to be, the mecca for art students from all over the world, most of them on some kind of GI Bill. Besides the spectacular museums and parks, there were the ateliers run by famous French artists and the active cafe life along Boulevard Montparnasse. But I was filled up with the intense experiences I had had in Israel. I needed to let it spill out, needed to be quiet and paint.

I found my friends from college and in Cafe Select I met Harry Bornstein, a fellow painter and former refugee from Vienna who had become an American citizen in the U.S. Army. He was dashing, charming, witty, and he lived in Meudon, a twenty-minute train ride from Paris.

Through Harry I rented a spacious room in Meudon with a French family. Every morning the family could be seen in the garden, hunting for the snails they'd have for lunch. When they invited me to eat with them. I said, "Merci, no!"

I borrowed an easel, cooked leek soup on a Bunsen burner, but mostly lived on long loaves of French bread and Camembert cheese. Harry was painting nearby in his own rented room but we did make time to explore Paris. We climbed to the top of Notre Dame Cathedral to be eye level with the gargoyles, and biked to the village of Chartres to spend hours in and around the inspiring Chartres Cathedral.

In the garden, about 1971.

After I had been in France four months, Harry unexpectedly had to return by plane to New York. I used his ticket on the Dutch troop ship, Vollendam, and returned to the U.S.A. on a two-week trip over the Atlantic.

Back in Wisconsin I didn't know what to do with myself. I was twenty-three. I went to Milwaukee, got iron shots for my anemia, and, during the Christmas season, worked in Uncle Jake's store.

Harry was at Cranbrook Academy of Art in Michigan, accepted for a Master's of Fine Arts. I joined him there and we were married by a Justice of the Peace. At Cranbrook, wanting to do something different, I learned to throw pots on a kick wheel and soon realized that ceramics could be as compelling a life work as painting. My pots usually came out of the kiln earth toned and burnished, as if they were dug up from a time long ago, and I liked it that way. Then the semester was over. Harry had his M.F.A. And I was very pregnant.

Neither of us had been West. We headed for California by car. As we drove off the Golden Gate Bridge and into Marin County, Harry said, "Looks like Italy." So we settled in Sausalito, and our daughter Noa was born. Pushing the baby buggy, I could walk by the bay or into the redwoods in Muir Woods. My art work was mostly sketching my baby. After a year, Harry's parents needed him and we drove to New York.

We lived in Greenwich Village for a summer, then moved uptown, across the street from Inwood Park on the Hudson River. Even then people were afraid to walk into the park, which was a real woods, only better; the tulip and copper beech trees were allowed to grow to their full magnificence. I took Noa there every day and when she was fourteen months old I made an 8-millimeter movie of her titled *Babe in the Woods.*

Harry worked for his father in a sweat shop. And then, when his parents moved to Los Angeles and needed him, we followed. I was pregnant again.

Jonah was born. We moved into an unfinished tract house in the San Fernando Valley and the first thing I did was plant a fig tree and an olive tree to remind me of Israel and a deciduous Liquid Amber tree whose leaves, I hoped, would turn red and gold in the autumn, like Wisconsin and the East coast.

The tract was a good place to raise children with its winding streets and little traffic. The garage became the studio and then Adam was born. I enjoyed juggling kids and art and mostly painted at night. Art materials were always on the table and I did lots of drawings of my children while they drew pictures of their own.

When I was pregnant with Jesse I knew I wouldn't be able to paint for awhile. I also knew I had to have an outlet. I loved folk music so I took up the guitar and learned song after song. For the children, there was "Hush Little Baby," "All the Pretty Little Horses," and "Down in the Valley." For the hootenanies at the Valley Center of Arts, there was "I Never Will Marry"and "Wally Wally." It felt good singing all those sad Scottish dirges and Irish ballads about lost love.

But I was safe. Married. And busy. A mother. With children to love and to love me. At home we danced and drummed and played with clay. We went to the park, camped out at the beach and sang in the car.

I discovered picture books and every two weeks we all went to the library. *Goodnight Moon, Babar, Green Eggs and Ham,* and the *Little Bear* books were some of our favorites. As time passed the bedtime stories were *Pinocchio, Charlotte's Web,* and *Stuart Little.* From *The Borrowers* the term "Human Bean" became part of my vocabulary. I continued to enjoy the children's books with them on into junior high.

While my children played, I painted in my studio-garage. I made sure they'd stay near the pecan tree in the front yard by supplying the whole neighborhood with popcorn and kool-aid. I made three rather surrealistic films of my children and their friends one year titled, *Spring, Summer,* and *Celebration.*

We had dogs and puppies, cats and kittens. Our glossy, be-jeweled cookies looked as if they had been dug up from some fabulous tomb. To watch the sunset there was a ladder to the roof.

I wanted them to have a secure base, and when the time came, Noa had a Bat Mitzvah, the boys, Bar Mitzvahs.

With each new period of painting I looked through all my past work, needing to find the thread (I called it the "core") to make sure it was "me." And sometimes as I worked on a canvas, I searched so hard that I painted everything out.

I was inspired by the trees in the park, by the sun and shadow at the front door, by my children. When we put a pool in the backyard, I moved my studio to the back of the house so I could keep an eye on them. And through every period, along with books on the Gothic painters, Picasso, Paul Klee, Bonnard, Matisse, the Fauves and the German Expressionists, *Goodnight Moon* remained on the coffee table.

Harry and I had helped found the Valley Center of Arts, and we attended weekly painting-critique sessions. My art went through an abstract period and, at the same time, I did my best work in the weekly life-drawing workshops. I exhibited in many juried shows in California, won a few prizes, and had two one-person exhibits at the Center.

I was glad when the abstract and figurative work came together and I developed a body of work that I knew was even more "true." At that point I wanted a larger audience, wanted to gain validation from the art world. I suppose I wanted to be "known."

There were two reviews in the *Los Angeles Times* in 1963. The first reviewer said that the "souls" in my paintings "shine through," that my work was "poetically expressed." The second reviewer commented that my paintings were "peculiarly personal," that they suggested "illusion" more than "reality," and that there was a "crudeness" in my dealing with form that was "both primitive and highly sophisticated."

I was devastated by the second review. Now I wonder why. The review was not bad. And it was accurate. But, somehow, I felt that I was being rejected and I cried.

I got over it. Drawn to the "old country," the world of my ancestors I'd never experienced, I created another body of work, still bittersweet but more open, sometimes with two figures instead of one "lonely one."

We moved to Pacific Palisades, a beautiful area in the Santa Monica Mountains. Harry was now an architect and a builder and, with his remodeling, made us a spacious home. I had a studio in the garage and a ladder to the roof to watch the sunsets over the sea. And I could hike up our hill and wait for the glow in the sky that meant the full moon was about to rise over the city.

Inspired by the beauty around me, my work grew lighter, more fanciful. I started to do strange, funny little drawings, one after the other: rabbits peeking out of holes in the ground, little green elephants talking to flowers, flowers flying away.... Sometimes, I made notes around the edges. I didn't know what was happening, but I was having fun and, as usual in my work, I let it happen. In 1971 I grew my first vegetable garden. My youngest child was going on twelve years old.

As I began to dig and prepare the soil, it seemed to grow more and more rocks, and I discovered that the backyard had once been a rock garden. I kept on digging, turning over the soil, putting in manure. For mulch I bought bales of straw. I wanted the yard to smell like a farm. It did.

I planted and the garden grew. Like a wild, green jungle. Later I wrote, "It was like a celebration going on, everything growing, putting out flowers, whispering among themselves, holding onto each other." Crops I didn't plant came up, like the surprise corn stalks that produced real ears of corn. I spent more time in the garden, holding hands with the cucumber vines, than I did in my studio. I even wondered if maybe a little green elephant was hiding under the leaves.

The watermelon vines kept flowering and spreading but they never produced a full-grown watermelon. They made me think of us "human beans" and I wrote later about "the 'hoots,' the parades, of people getting up and revealing themselves, persevering, maybe not producing much but still trying to grow." In November the vines began to die. But even as they were sinking and fading into the ground, they were still putting out flowers ... trying to grow.

I felt that I had witnessed the whole cycle of life in one summer. And that I had had a hand in it. I had even helped grow the huge red and green, horned tomato worm that made me scream when I reached into the vines to pick a tomato.

Then, one day, while sitting on my second-story deck, I reached up and found words. It was as if they had always been there and, now that I was ready, I could pull them down. Words like *seed* and *green* and *grow* felt as real to me as paint. My first poem that autumn was titled "I Love My Garden."

I couldn't stop writing, kept a notebook under my pillow, barely slept. I knew that what was coming out of me was from the same source as my painting, that it must be part of the thread I was always searching for.

My ideas centered around themes I thought were important: to be aware of the drama of the day unfolding, and that we're all part of the natural world around us.

The little green elephant became a character in a sketchbook. The rabbit came out of the ground and wandered the woods the way I liked to wander. The flower flying away became the germ of a fairy story. I filled up sketchbook after sketchbook with words and pictures, began to "use" my wishes, fantasies, feelings in a way that I couldn't do with paint alone.

I'd always loved gorillas. When they were little my boys had reminded me of robust, little gorillas. But I had never wanted to do a *portrait* of a gorilla!

"With my grandson Jacob, age seven, in my studio," 1984.

From **Little Gorilla,** *1976.*

I was always making lists: the children's schedules, food shopping, errands. I wrote this list too.

Daily List

Let's see ... the Big Things
Making the nest.
Rearing the young.
Looking at the sky.
Feeling the mystery.

The Little Things
Digging in the ground.
Shopping for light bulbs and candles.
Looking for robins.
Feeling the mystery.

I had ten sketchbooks I thought said something, and I wanted to share them. I didn't know how to send them to a publisher so I took them into a children's book store. A salesgirl said she knew of a local publisher and told me to leave the sketchbooks with her. Two weeks later I got a call.

Out of the ten dummies, one was accepted for publication. When I met with Marjorie Thayer, the editor of Golden Gate Books, I asked her what was wrong with the other nine! *Indian Bunny* was a complete story, she explained, with a beginning, a middle, and an end. Hmm.... Also I had never heard of color separation. To help me, a printer from Ward Ritchie Press was sent to my home. I didn't like working in black and gray overlays on a light table, only imagining the colors and how they would mix, but as a painter, I wasn't afraid of the process. So I was stuck. I would have to do color separation for eleven more books. And after I illustrated *Son Of Thunder,* a Lapland folktale retold by Ethel Kharasch McHale, I said to myself, "I guess I *am* an illustrator."

There are only one hundred and thirty-three words in *Little Gorilla,* including all the "and's." But it took me two years to get clear on what it was that I really wanted to say. (Love goes on!) When I got an illustration award for the book, my daughter made a surprise (to the audience) appearance at the awards dinner, hidden under a very realistic gorilla costume. On the podium, I introduced her as one of my children.

In one notebook, I wrote, "There is so much to say, to find out, to learn. I think of the vine quietly growing in its own place and yet how it keeps spreading out as far as it can go. I don't know if I am up to the challenge of making beautiful and satisfying picture books. But I am going to try."

The hero of *Indian Bunny* is like a real little boy (and me) exploring his surroundings, alone but feeling safe even in the night. The tiny green elephant in *The Dream of the Little Elephant* takes risks to find where he belongs, what *I* secretly dreamed of doing. In both books the sub-plot is the whole day passing.

One day, walking in the Santa Barbara Botanical Gardens, I saw a bud on a bush and I said to myself, "I wonder what could be in there?" Naturally, I had seen hundreds of buds. This time I was ready to see something more (was it my long ago, invisible child?). The idea grew through many stages and years and, together with my "flower flying away," it became *The Seedling Child.*

As night descends and the book comes to an end, the seedling child flies away with the birds. But the girl still hears the song.

Once upon a time
when the world was new,
when the sun was new,
when the moon was new,
inside a flower
a seedling child grew
and stayed in my heart a long, long time.

I was surprised when I was asked to speak at a Psychological Convention. The psychiatrist who invited me told me that the "message" of *The Seedling Child* was what he was trying to say in his practice.

And of course I had to write about goats. In *Of Course a Goat* the boy climbs a mountain to search for a baby goat, then carries her "down the dark mountain," and is welcomed home by his mother, " ... and you'll be waiting" under a rising, full moon.

The Dancing Man evolved over a period of seven years and is the story of a creative life from beginning to end ... and beyond. I chose dance as the medium because I love to dance myself, have folk danced for many years, and because I believe in the power of dance to bring people together.

First published in 1978, I was asked to re-illustrate the book for its twentieth anniversary. Quoting the 1998 edition's jacket copy, "An orphan boy is given the gift of a pair of silver shoes and with them, the ability to dance joy and courage into the lives who need it most. Over the years and down many paths, Joseph dances through the land and into the hearts of the people, bringing them an awareness of the world around them. And when his bones grow old with

"With my children behind me: (from left) Adam, Jonah, Noa, and Jesse."

time, he passes on his gift and thus continues the circle of the celebration of life."

The illustrations for the book are set in Eastern Europe and have a shtetl flavor. I'm gratified that *The Dancing Man* is told and performed by many storytellers and dance groups. In April 1999, it was performed by the University of Utah's Children's Dance Theatre for its fiftieth anniversary.

I didn't want it to happen but our marriage came to an end. I had an illustration contract to fill, set up a studio in my present condominium in Santa Monica and fulfilled the contract. But I was deeply depressed. With the help of a psychologist, I finally was able to see that I had done the right thing, both for my husband and myself. Harry married the year after we divorced and thanked me for taking the step. Sadly he died in 1994. The day before he died he called me from Ashland, Oregon, and said, "Keep working."

I found a companion too. Ralph is a hiker, fisherman, tennis player, and he balances my checkbook. He's a supportive anchor, gives me the space I need, and consents to wearing outlandish get-ups at Halloween folk dance parties. And who else would put on white tights and a billowing, silver Hershey Kiss costume and go with me (also a Hershey Kiss) to my mother's retirement home at lunchtime and pass out Hershey's Kisses? My mother got a huge kick out of it. Most of the other people went on eating. I don't think they believed their eyes.

My dad died in 1988, my mother in 1992. Whatever I feel that I lacked growing up, I know that my parents were generous, upstanding, and courageous human beings. And, of course, like all of us, they did the best they could with what they had.

The work went on. More challenges illustrating books written by other authors. My own book, *A Beautiful Seashell,* contains a story within a story as well as a gift from a great-grandmother, an immigrant from the old country, to her great-granddaughter.

I was offered a job, teaching at U.C.L.A. Extension. I accepted, knowing it would be good for me to have to prepare lesson plans and consult, in other words, to pull myself together. I titled my class Creating the Picture Book.

The focus of my class was for the students (of all ages) to find their own "voices." As well as delineating the picture book process, my handouts were often exhortations to "Do what makes your heart sing," a quote, I was told, by Ladybird Johnson, and poems such as "Landscape with Yellow Birds" by the Japanese poet, Shuntaro Tanikawa.

I made signs:

"What are you trying to say?"

"The more you become yourself, the more style you have."

"Play, juggle, brainstorm, take chances, don't get locked in too soon."

"Work for the child you were."

"Persevere; have faith. They are not rejecting *You!*"

"Go for it! What do you have to lose?"

I continued the class off and on for seven years. Finally I had to stop. I've always felt more like a student than a teacher—and a very slow learner. The days pass so quickly; I needed time to find my own way.

Through Nan Hackett Jo, a fiber artist, I got hooked on free-wheeling basket making; combining natural fibers with shells, yarns ... whatever. (I named one basket "Letting It All Hang Out.") From baskets came handmade paper, paper weaving and laminating, and for three years my studio was the base for evolving art work, including xeroxing photos from the old country and using them in the big paper "quilts," collages and sewn assemblages. It was a passionate, happy-to-wake-up-in-the-morning period.

For two years I participated in Sharon Kagan's Creative Journal Workshop. To guided imagery we drew with our eyes closed and with our sub-dominant hands. I worked fast, not thinking, just following my "gut" feeling, as my pencil moved across sheet after sheet of paper. Then, when I felt sated and opened my eyes, I saw which images I wanted to develop in color. This "process" oriented, non-self-judgmental way of working has given me the courage to dig deep past the "adult mind." Often there are breakthroughs, surprises. I need to play a lot.

I've shown this kind of work in three one-person exhibits. They have titles like *Seed Talk, Serene Goat, Blue Ribbon Baby,* and *Truckin' Along.* But there's also a lot of dark in some of my "playful" paintings. They have titles like *Memorial, Goodbye,* and *Forgive.*

Ever a self-doubting writer, I took a poetry workshop with poet Jack Grapes and learned again that we are bottomless, that there is much more inside of us than we know.

For my manuscript, *The Gift of the Wind,* I received inspiring rejection letters from Charlotte Zolotow, the editor-in-chief at Harper and Row. "... if only you could dig a little deeper you could give us...."

I tried! But finally I had to settle for less than the "Universe" I had been aiming for. After many, many revisions, *The Gift of the Wind* became *Rabbit's Good News.* The book is dedicated "For all the new ones." The wind in the world has become "a soft green sound," and on the last page it reveals that, "Spring is here!"

Creating the illustrations for *Rabbit's Good News,* I finally got the courage to be "loose," painterly. I thought of Matisse. The artist was asked, "How do you know when you're finished with a painting?" Matisse answered, "When it says what I want it to say."

I didn't worry about details with *Rabbit.* In fact, many details were lost in the sweep of the pastel. It didn't matter. The art said what I wanted it to say. I also made use of a quote of Bonnard's, "You can never use too much yellow."

For every illustration project, I pour over my own art work and my favorite art books. For *Rabbit* and *The Seedling Child,* I looked at Bonnard. For *A Beautiful Seashell,* I studied Milton Avery. For *The Dancing Man,* Edvard Munch and the German Expressionists. Finally the moment has to come. I get down to work and think only of how best to enhance the text.

Poetry had always come naturally to me but I felt I wanted to learn more about it. In 1991, I took Myra Cohn Livingston's Writing Poetry for Children class at U.C.L.A. Extension, and after two sessions I was accepted into her Master Class. We worked with the many forms of poetry, agreed, disagreed, delved into, brought forth. The class encouraged me to write to my left hand drawings, and the twelve poems gleaned from the process became my "statement" about the many aspects of making art.

My book, *That's How It Is When We Draw,* begins with,

A small seed in the muddle,
A sprout coming up for air,
A blooming....

and is dedicated to ... "every growing and surprising thing."

It was hard to choose, but here are three poems from the book. But sometimes ...

There are bad times,
And I go away under the table,
And scribble everyone away.
Until the paper rips to pieces,
Until I punch it and scrunch it,
Until it's a tighter ball than anyone,
Until I throw everyone
Away.
And then
Another time ...
A rainbow!

And here is a bird above me,
Here is the ground below.
The ground feels good
As if it knows me,
As if the bird knows me,
And the sky.
As if they're all saying to me,
"You're here in the world,
And we know it."

Newspaper,
Wrapping paper,
Brown paper bags.
Cereal box insides,
Envelope back sides,
Junk mail other sides,
I collect it all.
Because ...
An important thing about drawing
Is ...
Having lots of stuff to draw on!

"Success is going from failure to failure without losing enthusiasm," Winston Churchill once said. Many of my books have gone out of print. Naturally, it's disappointing. But, as my friend Clyde Bulla philosophically says, "Out of print books may still be found in libraries."

Many of my ideas have been rejected by editors. Often I learn from the rejections, let the project sit, work on it again, persevere. At any rate, in the book world, my skin has grown thick. I know they're not rejecting *me.*

And after all, I didn't stop painting just because most of my paintings didn't sell. It's the same with writing. Focusing in on an idea, walking with it, waking up with it.... Writing or painting, I'm happiest when I'm working.

One of my story-poems tells of an imaginary day in the life of a pond. Another attempts to express what I feel was the magical and "organic" way that I began to write. It's also an attempt to inspire "human beans" of all ages to dig deep and "let it out," which I was saying in a different way in *That's How It Is When We Draw.*

Even if my stories and poems aren't accepted, I hope one day to complete the art for them—the way I did at the beginning—not for publication, but for myself, for the joy and satisfaction of "doing it."

In 1987, on a trip to New Zealand, I visited my friend Beryl. Beryl was dying of cancer. I was so moved by her courage, even her humor, that on the flight home I began to write about her. I thought about it, worked on it, wanted to do something with it. I knew the piece wasn't a picture book; I didn't know what it was. Slowly I began to realize that I had begun a process that would take a long time. I didn't know anything about writing a novel. I re-read Anne Tyler's *The Accidental Tourist,* re-read *Tuck Everlasting* by Natalie Babbitt, *The Great Gilly Hopkins* by Katherine Paterson, and *Good-bye, Chicken Little* and *The Midnight Fox* by Betsy Byars. And I wrote. Volumes. In long hand. I moved to 19-by-24-inch newsprint pads. Trying to keep some kind of order became impossible. I bought a computer.

The only aspect left of the original Beryl is a bit of her sweet nature and the butterflies she "grew." There have been a few bites from editors but mainly the rejections I've received have helped me to delve deeper and I don't begrudge the years this project is taking me.

The book is not autobiographical but in this story I can be both eleven-year-old girl, Charley, and her "crazy" old mentor, Beryl. I've given myself a second chance to grow up, given myself that mentor. Through Beryl's love, Charley can validate herself and have compassion for her mother "who is trying to grow in hard rocky soil." And through sad times and hard, at the end, Charley can say, "at least for this minute the space inside of me is big enough, and wide enough, to hold it all."

When I wake before dawn and think about the terrible events in the world, or slip back into sadness about my own past or fear of what will be, Joseph Campbell's words, "Joyful participation in the sorrows of the world," help bring me back to the only thing I can do, that is to live in the "Now." I take a deep breath, look at what I've scribbled during the night, get out of bed, and begin the day. The first important thing to do is to walk down the hill to the beach and look out over the far horizon of ocean and into the wide sky. On the way I'll encounter trees, birds, dogs, cats, people——aware that all of us are living at the same time in the world, and under the same sky.

Here in my light-filled, all-purpose, living, dining, writing-by-hand room, I can be a recluse, do my stretches, and think and read. Some of my present reading is poetry by William Stafford and Mary Oliver and philosophy by the Vietnamese Buddhist monk, Thich Nhat Hanh. I can make myself a big batch of popcorn and watch the light change and grow dark.

Here I'm surrounded by a zoo full of stuffed toy animals, whirligigs, and folk art toys. Noa's sculptures are on a shelf along with stones, shells, and driftwood I've collected from everywhere. A bulletin board is full of family and friend's notes and successes. On a wall is the glove stretcher my dad used in the factory and art work by my children, grandchildren, other people's children, and Harry and me. Upstairs, I have a ladder to the roof. One of my left-hand paintings is titled *Containing All.*

In January I found a little brown-needled but still sweet-smelling fir tree in the trash, carried it home, and decorated it with my cut-out, recycled, cardboard people. One grinning, devilish angel is saying, "What's the alternative? Happy New Year!"

I'm lucky that on most days I can retreat, and lucky at other times that I can reach out. Lucky I've had the time to slowly develop—and still keep on "beginning." I was lucky to be able to stay home when my children were growing up, lucky that they have grown to be resourceful and creative adults. Noa is a visual artist living in New York, Jonah is a poet, editor, and director of the Ashland Writing Conference, Adam is a yoga instructor in Australia, and Jesse is an architect here in Santa Monica. All are happily married. I have six very special grandchildren.

I'm lucky that I've had other people's art and poetry in my life. I'm lucky that children's books found me.

Sometimes, when I'm drawing or writing in the car, Ralph will say, "Can't you ever stop?" When I told this to my friend, Lea, she said, "Yes, one day you will stop." Meanwhile . . . .

The need to fill up and spill out never lets go. But I've always felt lucky, always knew that art "saves" me. Following my thread with painting and writing has helped me be "known"—to myself.

To you, the reader: We are all connected here in this world. At the same time we each have our own personal, unique life. I wish you all the best in yours.

Writings

FOR CHILDREN; AUTHOR AND ILLUSTRATOR

Indian Bunny, Children's Press/Scholastic, 1973.
Little Gorilla, Seabury Press, 1976.
The Dream of the Little Elephant, Seabury Press, 1977.
Annabelle, Harper/Crowell, 1978.
The Dancing Man, Seabury Press, 1978, New 20th Anniversary edition, Clarion, 1998.
Jim, Seabury Press, 1978.
I'll Draw a Meadow, Harper, 1979.
Of Course a Goat, Harper, 1980.
The Seedling Child, Harcourt, 1987.
A Beautiful Seashell, Harper, 1990.
Rabbit's Good News, Clarion, 1995.
That's How It Is When We Draw (poetry collection), Clarion, 1997.

ILLUSTRATOR

Ethel K. McHale, reteller, *Son of Thunder: An Old Lapp Tale,* Children's Press, 1974.
Crescent Dragonwagon, *Your Owl Friend,* Harper, 1977.
Charlotte Zolotow, *Flocks of Birds,* Crowell, 1981.
Patricia MacLachlan, *Mama One, Mama Two,* Harper, 1982.
Charlotte Zolotow, *Summer Is . . . ,* Harper, 1983.
Lyn Hoopes, *Mommy, Daddy, Me,* Harper, 1988.

Adaptations

The Dancing Man has been performed by the Spence School of Dance in Riverton, Utah, the Children's Dance Theater of the University of Utah, and the Children's Theater of Madison, Wisconsin.

BOSMAN, Paul 1929-

Personal

Born August 2, 1929, in South Africa; immigrated to the United States, 1982, naturalized citizen; son of Ferdinand Hugo (a director of agriculture) and Edith Cecilia (a pianist; maiden name, Townshend) Bosman; married Elaine Roos (a homemaker), July 7, 1957; children: Christopher, Simon, Kate. *Education:* Attended Johannesburg School of Art, 1948-50, and Central School of Art, London, England, 1952.

Addresses

Home and office—Wildlife Investment, Inc., 55 Rock Top Rd., Sedona, AZ 86351. *Electronic mail*—Bosman@sedona.net.

Career

Coleman, Prentis & Varley Advertising, London, England, layout artist, 1955; Bomac Ltd., Montreal, Quebec, designer, 1956; Afamal Advertising, Durban, South Africa, layout artist, 1957-59; Lindsay Smithers Advertising, Durban, layout artist, 1959-61; Lindsay Smithers Advertising, Johannesburg, South Africa, group head, 1961-63, head of design group, 1963-66, art director, 1966-67, creative director, 1967-68, member of board of directors, 1968; operator of a luxury photographic safari lodge in Zimbabwe, beginning in 1969; artist and illustrator. Work has been exhibited in South Africa, the United States, Canada, and West Germany and is represented in private collections; designer of postage stamps. Endangered Wildlife Trust, fellow; Rhino and Elephant Foundation, former adviser. Participant in a South African wildlife painting safari as part of a cultural exchange, arranged by *Wildlife Art Magazine,* 1992; Academic at St. Andrews College, Grahamstown. *Member:* Society of Animal Artists.

Awards, Honors

Four awards of excellence, Society of Animal Artists; Elliott Liskin Award for painting; Italian Gold Stamp Award, for a stamp design.

Illustrator

Anthony Hall-Martin, *Elephants of Africa,* C. Struik (Cape Town, South Africa), 1986, Safari Press (Long Beach, CA), 1989.

David E. Brown, *Arizona Game Birds,* University of Arizona Press (Tucson, AZ), 1989.

Anthony Hall-Martin, *The Magnificent Seven and the Other Great Tuskers of the Kruger National Park,* Human & Rousseau (Cape Town), 1994.

Anthony Hall-Martin, *Cats of Africa,* Fernwood Press (South Africa), 1997, Smithsonian Institution Press (Washington, DC), 1998.

Contributor of artwork to periodicals, including *American Artist, Defenders of Wildlife, Gray's Sporting Journal, Game Country, International Wildlife, Reader's Digest, Safari, Sporting Classics, South African Wildlife, Wildlife Art Magazine, Southwest Art,* and *Shooting Sportsman.*

Sidelights

Paul Bosman told *SATA:* "I was born in South Africa and have always had opportunities to travel and see exciting things. When I was a teenager, my family moved from South Africa to Bechuanaland Protectorate (now Botswana) where my father was the director of agriculture. Our home was a long way from civilization. We had no grocery stores, so we had to stock up on supplies once a month 'in town.' The roads were so bad that we had a light aircraft to make the trip to Northern Rhodesia (now Zambia).

"At that time, there were no schools where we lived, and my brother and I were sent to boarding school. I still remember my two-day train trip to school in southeastern Africa. Coming home for vacation was the highlight of the year. Panda Matenga, where we were stationed, was the most exciting place in the world! We were surrounded by bush and forests and had the opportunity to get to know the wildlife that abounded. Once, we even had lions drinking from our swimming pool!

Paul Bosman

"I started sketching people and places and eventually decided to pursue art as a profession. Three years at the Johannesburg Art School and another year at the Central School of Art in London prepared me for a career in advertising, first in England, then in Canada, and finally back in South Africa. I enjoyed my work and eventually became the creative director and a member of the board of a large advertising agency. I decided, however, to retire by the time I reached forty years of age.

"In 1969 we moved to Zimbabwe, where my wife and I built and operated a photographic safari lodge. That was the ultimate life for me. We were surrounded by all kinds of wildlife. Buffalo came at night to eat the banana trees. Elephants pulled at the branches over our house, and lions roared frequently. Our two sons were six and nine years old and enjoyed fishing in the river near our house, collecting wild honey, or walking together in search of something exciting. I began painting the wildlife and had my first solo exhibition in Johannesburg in 1973. It was successful beyond my expectations, and I seemed to have profession number three!

"When the war broke out in southeastern Zimbabwe, we returned to South Africa. It was then that I met Dr. Anthony Hall-Martin, a biologist in the Kruger National Park. We decided to work together and publish a series of art prints of the largest elephants in the park, known as the Magnificent Seven. These prints were so successful that we attempted a book on the elephants of Africa.

"In preparation for the ambitious project, we visited fourteen countries over the length and breadth of Africa. It was exciting and, at times, dangerous. We traveled in many types of transportation—small aircraft, helicopters, canoes—some in much need of repair! On land, we walked great distances through the rain forests of West Africa. We saw rare animals such as so-called pygmy elephants, Jentink's duiker, and a golden cat. We waded through swamps where leeches attached themselves to our bodies and had to be hastily removed. We negotiated the raffia palms of Azagny in a canoe, and climbed the mountains of Kahuzi Biega to see the gorillas.

"On these trips, we collected enough interesting information to collaborate on another book, *Cats of Africa*. I have been to many wonderful places and continue to enjoy my travels. Who knows what exciting destinations the future holds?"

For More Information See

PERIODICALS

American Artist, September, 1988, p. 32.
Art in America, June, 1994, p. 96.
Field and Stream, West edition, September, 1990, p. 151.
New York Times, October 7, 1990, p. 40.
Science Books & Films, August-September, 1998, p. 176.

BOYNTON, Sandra (Keith) 1953-

Personal

Born April 3, 1953, in Orange, NJ; daughter of Robert Whitney (an English teacher) and Jeanne Carolyn (Ragsdale) Boynton; married James Patrick McEwan (a writer), October 28, 1978. *Education:* Yale University, B.A., 1974; graduate study at the University of California- Berkeley Drama School, 1974-75, and Yale University School of Drama, 1976- 77. *Religion:* Quaker.

Addresses

Office—c/o Workman Publishing, 708 Broadway, New York, NY 10003-9555.

Career

Author, illustrator, cartoonist. Recycled Paper Products, Inc., Chicago, IL, designer of greeting cards, 1974—. *Member:* Authors Guild.

Awards, Honors

Irma Simonton Black Award, Bank Street College of Education, 1985, for *Chloe and Maude;* Children's Choice Award, Children's Book Council and the International Reading Association, for *Hester in the Wild.*

Writings

FOR CHILDREN; SELF-ILLUSTRATED

Hippos Go Berserk, Little, Brown, 1977, revised and redrawn, Simon & Schuster, 1996.
Hester in the Wild, Harper, 1979.
If at First ..., Little, Brown, 1980.
But Not the Hippopotamus, Simon & Schuster, 1982, revised, 1995.
The Going to Bed Book, Simon & Schuster, 1982, revised, Little Simon, 1995.
Opposites, Simon & Schuster, 1982, revised, 1995.
Moo, Baa, La La La, Simon & Schuster, 1982, revised, 1995.
A Is for Angry: An Animal and Adjective Alphabet, Workman, 1983.
A to Z, Simon & Schuster, 1984, revised, 1995.
Blue Hat, Green Hat, Simon & Schuster, 1984, revised, 1995.
Doggies, Simon & Schuster, 1984, revised, 1995.
Horns to Toes and in Between, Simon & Schuster, 1984, revised, 1995.
Chloe and Maude, Little, Brown, 1985.
Good Night, Good Night, Random House, 1985.
Hey! What's That?, Random House, 1985.
Oh My, Oh My, Oh Dinosaurs!, Workman, 1993.
Birthday Monsters!, Workman, 1993.
One, Two, Three!, Workman, 1993.
Barnyard Dance!, Workman, 1993.
Rhinoceros Tap and 14 Other Seriously Silly Songs, (children's songbook and tape), Workman, 1996.

Snoozers: 7 Short Short Bedtime Stories for Lively Little Kids, Simon & Schuster, 1997.
Dinosaur's Binkit, Simon & Schuster, 1998.
Boynton's Greatest Hits: Volume One, Simon & Schuster, 1998.
Bob, Simon & Schuster, 1999.

OTHER SELF-ILLUSTRATED BOOKS

Gopher Baroque and Other Beastly Conceits (cartoons), Dutton, 1979.
The Compleat Turkey, Little, Brown, 1980.
Chocolate: The Consuming Passion, Workman, 1982.
Don't Let the Turkeys Get You Down, Workman, 1986.
Christmastime, Workman, 1987.
Grunt: Pigorian Chant from Snouto Domoinko de Silo (book and CD recording), Workman, 1996.

ILLUSTRATOR

Jamie McEwan, *The Story of Grump and Pout,* Crown, 1988.
Jamie McEwan, *The Heart of Cool,* Simon & Schuster, in press.

Sidelights

Sandra Boynton's whimsical animals seem like old friends. In award-winning titles for children such as *Hester in the Wild* and *Chloe and Maude,* this author-illustrator has created a cast of creatures which are immediately familiar. A trip to any drugstore or market which sells greeting cards will explain such familiarity: Boynton has created a line of cards that has been tickling funny bones since the 1970s. Her creative cards have sent mainstream manufacturers scrambling back to the drawing boards in the most literal fashion. Boynton's most famous card is the legendary "Hippo Birdie Two Ewes" (1975, Recycled Paper Greetings).

Whether working on adult cartoon and picture books or children's books, Boynton imbues in her art the same sense of silliness and tongue-in-cheek humor that she brought so successfully to greeting cards. "My animals are not people," Boynton commented to Victoria Irwin in an interview for *Christian Science Monitor.* "But they are not really animals, either. They are philosophers."

Born in Orange, New Jersey, in 1953, Boynton grew up in Philadelphia, Pennsylvania. She attended the German-town Friends School there and then went on to Yale University, where she earned her undergraduate degree. While at Yale, Boynton took a course in illustrating children's books from Maurice Sendak, who told her that her illustrations looked like they belonged on greeting cards. ("He didn't mean it as a compliment," Boynton told *SATA.*) While attending drama school as a post-graduate, Boynton began creating greeting cards, ultimately selling 10,000 of them, which she had independently printed, to craft shops on the East Coast. This mini-success encouraged her to seek out greeting card companies directly, and she soon made contact with a start-up company called Recycled Paper Products.

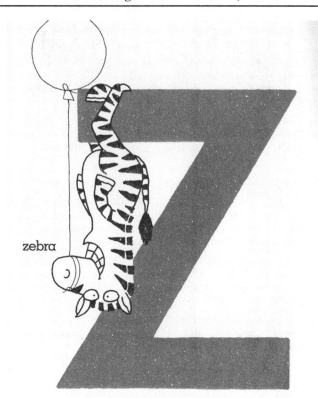

zebra

is for ZANY

Letters of the alphabet are introduced to young children by Sandra Boynton's exuberant and alliteratively described animals. (From A Is for Angry, *written and illustrated by Boynton.)*

The rest is industry history: Boynton's off-the-wall humor charmed purchasers and receivers alike, and brought men into the market for the first time as major purchasers of such cards. Soon her furry friends were appearing on calendars, posters, stationery, and T-shirts.

Boynton's first book for children, *Hippos Go Berserk,* is a visually vibrant counting book in which Boynton explored her talents with rhyme. A contributor to *Wilson Library Bulletin* dubbed this "a small, unpretentious book, but a special one in terms of overall unity, not to mention its warmth and whimsicality.... The total effect is light, airy, and tender." Another picture book, *If at First ...,* hinges on the old adage, "If at first you don't succeed, try, try again." Serving as an example of this adage is a little mouse who tries desperately to push a rather large purple elephant up a hill. The mouse tries leading the disinterested elephant, tempting it with a peanut, screaming at it, and other methods of coaxing. Finally, when the pachyderm falls asleep, the clever rodent startles it awake with a trumpet blast that sends the elephant scurrying up the hill. Like the mythological Sisyphus, the brown mouse's work is not yet done: eight more purple beasts wait at the bottom of the hill. In a review for *Booklist,* Denise M. Wilms approved of Boynton's subject matter, promising that children "will chuckle at the absurdity of elephant versus mouse." Also noted by Wilms were "the expressions Boynton manages to get into her characters with the fewest possible lines." Gemma DeVinney concluded in *School Library Journal* that the "practically perfect pace of the cartoonlike illustrations make this a universally appealing chuckle."

With her second effort, *Hester in the Wild,* Boynton set the tone for her future picture book productions. Zena Sutherland of *Bulletin of the Center for Children's Books* summarized the story's plot: "A bouncy little blunt-snouted pig, Hester, runs into a series of problems when she goes on a canoe trip." The trip turns into an adventure as the canoe begins to leak and then the tent takes up the same soggy refrain. The last straw, an invasion of gophers who turn Hester's tent into a crowded train station, sends Hester paddling away from her zany adventure. "The illustrations are cartoon-like but uncluttered, clean in line and softly pastel," observed Sutherland. *Booklist* reviewer Denise M. Wilms "admire[d] this solitary pig's pluck as she meets with one bit of bad luck after another." Wilms lauded the "comical illustrations in bright, spring colors" as well as the story's "ingenuous telling."

In *A Is for Angry,* Boynton takes on the alphabet—with a twist: She pairs an adjective with each letter rather than a noun, avoiding the traditional *A-is-for-apple* configuration. A reviewer for *Bulletin of the Center for Children's Books* marveled that the book "should not work, but it does—con brio!" Large clear letters are provided, and humorous, cartoon animal characters act out the meaning of the adjectives. Readers will meet an array of emoting animals, including an angry anteater, a bashful

In her self-illustrated **Blue Hat, Green Hat,** *Boynton employs her unique brand of humor and whimsy to present basic colors and familiar articles of clothing to very young children.*

bear, and an ill iguana. A *Publishers Weekly* contributor reviewing *A Is for Angry* called Boynton "the Duchess of Daft" and noted that the author had created a book "that grownups won't mind a bit going over and over again as their little ones will certainly demand."

One of Boynton's most popular publications for young readers is the chapter book, *Chloe and Maude,* featuring watercolor cats as the title characters. A *Kirkus Reviews* critic called the escapades of this feline duo "endearing and familiar." The kitties romp through three short tales that highlight some delightfully juvenile antics. In the first story, Chloe's talent with a drawing pen upsets Maude, who stomps away in a jealous snit, overturning a paint pot in the process. Chloe admires the resulting accidental picture and encourages Maude to take up abstract art. Maude adopts a stuck-up alter ego named Sophia in the second story, and it takes good friend Chloe to return Maude to her former self. An overnight at Maude's house provides plenty of adventure for the final tale of the two companions. Noises in halls and cracks in walls threaten to scare away Chloe and Maude's fun, but the creative cats use their imaginations to invent much safer surroundings. *Booklist's* Denise M. Wilms called these stories "amusing," while a writer for *Kirkus Reviews* found them "enjoyable ... with happy conclusions, and very lively illustrations." Janet French, writing in *School Library Journal,* concluded that Boynton's illustrations "have made the leap from card to book with considerable success."

Three of Boynton's books—*The Going to Bed Book,* its expanded picture book version, *Good Night, Good Night,* and *Snoozers: 7 Short Short Bedtime Stories for Lively Little Kids*—all address the toddler-troubling issue of bedtime. One of *Snoozers'* seven rhymes, "Silly Lullaby," looks at bedtime for a host of wacky characters, from chickens in the bathtub to sneakers in the freezer. Lauding *Snoozers* in the *Bulletin of the Center for Children's Books,* Pat Mathews wrote, "Textual humor, enhanced by droll illustrations ... will turn the bedtime ritual into a giggle fest."

Boynton covers the concepts of counting, opposites, music, and social skills with a series of board books called "Boynton on Board." One of these books, *Barnyard Dance!,* boasts farm animals dancing a rollicking reel. Reviewing *Barnyard Dance!,* a *Publishers Weekly* contributor hailed the entire "Boynton on Board" series as a "fresh and buoyant" source of "good clean fun." In addition to Boynton's many self-illustrated books, the author-artist has also provided illustrations for her husband's children's book, *The Story of Grump and Pout.* A *Publishers Weekly* contributor described this joint effort as "a deliciously silly story," with "hairy, ornery protagonists." The protagonists, another husband and wife team, are grouchy Grump and her husband, Pout. Slightly less cranky than Grump, Pout obtains an extremely comfortable pair of shoes and actually shares his good fortune with his wife. The couple dances with happiness at Pout's generosity and Grump's new shoes. With more praise for *The Story of Grump and Pout,* a *Publishers Weekly* critic wrote, "McEwan's text and

Boynton's cartoony illustrations are packed with droll expressions and witty details."

It is Boynton's droll humor combined with witty cartoons that readers have come to expect from the author-illustrator, making her as popular with adults as she is with the younger set.

Works Cited

Review of *A Is for Angry, Publishers Weekly,* January 20, 1984, p. 88.

Review of *A Is for Angry, Bulletin of the Center for Children's Books,* March, 1984, p. 122.

Review of *Barnyard Dance!, Publishers Weekly,* January 31, 1994, p. 88.

Review of *Chloe and Maude, Kirkus Reviews,* December 15, 1985, p. 1396.

DeVinney, Gemma, review of *If at First ...,* *School Library Journal,* April, 1980, p. 90.

French, Janet, review of *Chloe and Maude, School Library Journal,* March, 1986, p. 144.

Review of *Hippos Go Berserk, Wilson Library Bulletin,* January, 1980, p. 325.

Irwin, Victoria, "Sandra Boynton Takes the Cake with 'Hippo Birdy, Two Ewes ...,'" *Christian Science Monitor,* December 30, 1980.

Mathews, Pat, review of *Snoozers, Bulletin of the Center for Children's Books,* March, 1998, p. 237.

Review of *The Story of Grump and Pout, Publishers Weekly,* March 11, 1988, p. 101.

Sutherland, Zena, review of *Hester in the Wild, Bulletin of the Center for Children's Books,* October, 1979, p. 22.

Wilms, Denise M., review of *Hester in the Wild, Booklist,* June 1, 1979, p. 1488.

Wilms, Denise M., review of *If at First ...,* *Booklist,* March 1, 1980, p. 938.

Wilms, Denise M., review of *Chloe and Maude, Booklist,* March 1, 1986, p. 1014.

For More Information See

PERIODICALS

Kirkus Reviews, September 15, 1996, p. 1410.
New York Times Book Review, March 13, 1994, p. 20.
Publishers Weekly, November 4, 1996, p. 78.

*   *   *

BRIGHTON, Catherine 1943-

Personal

Born May 20, 1943, in London, England; daughter of Stuart (an artist) and Vera (a writer; maiden name, White) Boyle; married Andrew Brighton (an art critic), July 16, 1966; children: Shane, Henry. *Education:* St. Martin's School of Art, Diploma in Art and Design, 1966; Royal College of Art, M.A., 1969.

Career

Worked as a freelance illustrator during the 1970s; writer and illustrator of children's books.

Awards, Honors

Children's Book of the Year selection, Child Study Association of America, 1986, for *My Hands, My World;* Premio-Grafico Prize, 1987, for *The Fantastic Book of Board Games.*

Writings

AUTHOR AND ILLUSTRATOR

Cathy's Story, Evans (London), 1980.
Maria, Faber (London), 1984, published in the U.S. as *My Hands, My World,* Macmillan, 1984.
The Picture, Faber, 1985.
Five Secrets in a Box, Methuen (London), 1987, Dutton, 1987.
Hope's Gift, Faber, 1988, Doubleday, 1988.
Nijinsky, Methuen, 1989, published in the U.S. as *Nijinsky: Scenes from the Childhood of the Great Dancer,* Doubleday, 1989.
Mozart, Lincoln (London), 1990, published in the U.S. as *Mozart: Scenes from the Childhood of the Great Composer,* Doubleday, 1990.
Dearest Grandmama, Faber, 1991, Doubleday, 1991.
The Brontes: Scenes from the Childhood of Charlotte, Branwell, Emily and Anne, Lincoln, 1994, Chronicle Books (San Francisco, CA), 1994.
Rosalee and the Great Fire of London, Jonathan Cape (London), 1994.
My Napoleon, Lincoln, 1997, Millbrook Press (Brookfield, CT), 1997.

OTHER

(Illustrator) J. J. Strong, *Emily's a Guzzleguts,* Evans, 1979.
(Illustrator) Sian Victory, *Two Little Nurses,* Methuen, 1983, Faber, (Boston), 1983.
(Illustrator) J. J. Strong, *I Was Only Trying to Help,* Evans, 1984.
(Editor and illustrator) Walter de la Mare, *The Voice: A Sequence of Poems,* Faber (London), 1986, Delacorte, 1986.
(Illustrator with Fulvio Testa, Ralph Steadman, Tony Ross and Quentin Blake) *The Fantastic Book of Board Games,* St. Martin's (New York), 1988.

Contributor to *Modern Painters.*

Sidelights

Children's author and illustrator Catherine Brighton is the creator of sumptuous picture books that portray, in rich and precise detail, the lives of both famous and obscure children. Many of her titles focus on historical events or the accomplishments of famous figures, and her settings—Renaissance Italy, the Vienna of Mozart's time—offer a delicious opportunity for a devotee of the visual riches of the past. Brighton has occasionally been criticized for the sense of detachment her works evince,

Catherine Brighton based her self-illustrated story about a young girl's friendship with Napoleon Bonaparte on actual excerpts from Betsy Balcombe's 1855 journal.

partly because of certain visual conceits she uses in her illustrations, such as frames and windows. In other cases, she has been faulted for not including enough background information for young readers, or for delving into topics and themes that are somber or even psychologically dire. "The subjects that Catherine chooses are atypical of what might be expected in a picture book: isolation, loneliness, vulnerability," explained Maggi Waite in the British journal *School Librarian.* However, Waite observed that "Catherine is 'always on the child's side,' recognising the validity of childhood fears and traumas. In the happiest of childhoods there are times of anxiety, fear and loneliness. Catherine's understanding will strike a chord in a world where images of total happiness and perfection assail us from every form of media."

Brighton was born Catherine Boyle in 1943 in London. "As a thoughtful and rather solitary child within a large family, she lost herself in books and in an inner life,"

related Waite in her *School Librarian* article. Though there were many books in the Boyles's home, relatives in America also sent them children's titles, as Brighton recalled in a *Publishers Weekly* interview with Kimberly Olson Fakih. "That sense of being different is at the core of my books," Brighton explained. "I pored over the tiniest details of everyday life in those books, looking for the differences."

After earning degrees from the prestigious St. Martin's School of Art and the Royal College of Art, Brighton worked as a freelance illustrator for several years before illustrating J. J. Strong's *Emily's a Guzzleguts* in 1979. The next year, she published *Cathy's Story,* the first of several books for which she created both text and illustrations. Cathy is a young girl who likes to pass the quiet afternoons before her mother returns from work by delivering the mail in her building. In this way she meets an elderly neighbor, Mrs. Slinger, who enjoys Cathy's visits; Cathy, in turn, enjoys the stories Mrs. Slinger tells about each of her framed photographs of family and friends. When Mrs. Slinger passes away, Cathy must come to terms with her first experience of loss, but finds that her friend has left her a meaningful parting gift. In a *Growing Point* review, Margery Fisher asserted that the story "is conceived in large, well-composed pictures in which the child's environment, her relationships and her mood are forcefully and elegantly expressed."

Brighton's next book, *Maria,* published in the United States as *My Hands, My World,* is a collection of vignettes from a day in the life of a blind girl named Maria. Maria shows readers how she uses her other senses to learn about her environment, as she feels the window glass to tell the weather and smells her father's work overalls. Maria also has a make-believe friend— Bumpers, a girl from the Elizabethan era—to keep her company. Fisher praised Brighton's "eloquent, richly coloured pictures" in a *Growing Point* review. Brighton continued the Elizabethan theme in *The Picture,* in which a little girl, confined to her bed with a fever, is transported to another era through a piece of art on the wall. Brighton relates much of the protagonist's sense of wonder through her illustrations, which are framed in her characteristic style: either employing an actual frame designed onto the page, or endeavoring to capture a scene as viewed through a window.

Another of Brighton's works with historical overtones is *Five Secrets in a Box.* The book's protagonist is Virginia Galileo, the daughter of the famous scientist. Little Virginia wanders around her fifteenth-century Florentine home while her astronomer father sleeps during the day. The house, shown in Brighton's detailed illustrations, is elegant and full of beautiful objects, but the ones that Virginia loves best rest inside a box in her father's observatory. To Virginia they have magical, but also troublesome, properties. In the end, her preoccupied and politically persecuted father sends her to a convent, a place where the real-life Virginia died 22 years later. Brighton illustrated her scenes in hues of pink, brown, and turquoise, mimicking the Tuscan light and marbly decorative elements of the period. Margery Fisher, reviewing the book for *Growing Point,* found that Brighton had "succeeded brilliantly" in her task, while a *Publishers Weekly* critic termed *Five Secrets in a Box* a "captivating and imaginative work."

Brighton again presents an unusual setting with unique visual characteristics in *Hope's Gift,* her portrayal of life in a traveling theater troupe in sixteenth-century Europe. The story's focus is Hope, considered the least intellectually blessed among three Van Missen actor-siblings. Hope possesses a magical power, which she discovers when she holds a parakeet in her hand and heals its broken wing. Her sister Mercy goads her into doing the same for a paralyzed girl. Though disturbed by her newfound power, Hope finally accepts her gift, and the parakeet as payment. A reviewer for *Junior Bookshelf* called *Hope's Gift* "a clever and original story" and praised Brighton's artistry. Margery Fisher, writing in *Growing Point,* termed the work "a remarkable marriage of words and illustrations."

As in *Five Secrets in a Box,* the protagonist of Brighton's *Dearest Grandmama* is the daughter of a scientist. The story is related through Maudie-Ann's letters to her grandmother while the girl is on board a ship with her naturalist father. Brighton's profusion of drawings detail the unusual plants, animals, and even bone specimens that Maudie-Ann's father is busy collecting. Maudie-Ann, however, is preoccupied with her new friend, a young boy who does not speak, nor cast a shadow. He also carries a letter saying that he is a passenger on a ship called the *Marie Celeste* in the year 1872, forty years into the future. An explanatory endnote from Brighton reveals a real-life mystery behind the story. Though some reviewers found the plot a bit complex for its age group, most lavished praise upon Brighton for her efforts. A *Junior Bookshelf* contributor lauded Brighton's illustrations, asserting that they demonstrated "her extravagantly brilliant technique and her feeling for atmosphere." Karen K. Radtke, writing for *School Library Journal,* called *Dearest Grandmama* a work "designed to capture readers' imagination and take them on a mysterious journey."

In 1989 Brighton changed direction somewhat and produced two works that take a more biographical approach to the lives of famous personages from history, focusing in particular on their childhoods. The author conducted extensive research into the subject of *Nijinsky,* as she had for *Five Secrets in a Box.* For her look at the doomed Russian ballet dancer, Brighton visited Nijinsky's hometown, Leningrad. The inspiration for the book, explained Maggi Waite in her *School Librarian* profile on Brighton, came when Brighton saw a vintage photograph of a Russian ballet master standing in the snow, holding a child. Brighton noted in *Publishers Weekly* that after she saw the photograph, she recalled and tracked down a biography she had once read on the dancer's tragic life that was written by his wife. It was just as she had remembered. "And there was this amazing, powerful childhood," Brighton said. "It was all there for the taking. Even the tragedy was built in at an early age." The 1989 publication of *Nijinsky* coincided with the one-hundredth anniversary of the subject's birth. As Brighton recounts through words and images, Nijinsky grew up in Tsarist Russia after being abandoned by his father, who was also a dancer. Yet his own promise was evident soon after, when his mother took him to audition at the Imperial School of Ballet. Brighton's endnote explains that Nijinsky's fame and fortune did not save him from a tragic end. The book was well received. "Atmospheric illustrations—both rich and sombre . . . convey the feel of old Russia," noted Jennifer Taylor in *School Librarian.* "Handsome and clearly a labor of love," wrote *Booklist* reviewer Denise Wilms. In *Mozart,* Brighton tells the composer's life story through the eyes of his sister, Nannerl, who recounts the excitement of various occasions in the life of the eighteenth-century musical prodigy, including performing before emperors and kings and traveling all the way to England. The work is told in diary form, and its creamy pink, blue, and gold-toned illustrations, done in the style of the era, are framed in similarly appropriate baroque swirls.

Brighton's next book, *Rosalee and the Great Fire of London,* presents a little girl and her adventures at the time of the 1663 fire that destroyed much of London. Rosalee possesses an ancestral book of mystic recipes that the Cunning Man, an evil alchemist, would like to steal; he pursues her and her pet pig, Roger Bacon, as the flames engulf the city. The pig is named after a 13th-century thinker whose ideas about science were far ahead of his time, and foreshadowed the Enlightenment. "This remarkable book offers a feast, in terms of literary appreciation and visual spectacle," asserted Mandy Cheetham in *Magpies,* who went on to term the book "a treasure that should not be missed." Julia Marriage, writing in *School Librarian,* declared *Rosalee and the Great Fire of London* "a book to rival the best of the year."

The Brontes: Scenes from the Childhood of Charlotte, Branwell, Emily and Anne helps to underscore a revival of interest in the lives and works of the nineteenth-century literary family. Told through the voice of Charlotte—author of *Jane Eyre*—it follows the rural English lives of a very imaginative family. The girls release geese in the house of their parson father, make up elaborate fantasies, and eventually begin setting their ideas to paper. "The life of the young Brontes is recorded as if by the eye of a camera," noted *School Librarian* contributor Waite, "with [Brighton's] now familiar sense of detachment. Life at Haworth is depicted with great attention to detail, interspersed with visual references to the children's imaginary world."

In *My Napoleon,* Brighton once again creates a fictional situation from an actual event. The French emperor was exiled to the island of St. Helena, and years later the daughter of his prison-keeper wrote in her journal about her friendship with the diminutive but formidable dictator. *My Napoleon* presents in words and pictures the story of Betsy Balcombe and her unusual older friend. At first, Betsy admits to being intimidated by Napoleon's impending visit, until she discovers he is not that much greater in height than herself. It pleases him that she can speak French—Betsy is English—and at one point he allows her to have so much candy that she becomes ill all over his imported rug. *School Library Journal* contributor Amelia Kalin maintained that Brighton's illustrations were "truly descriptive," and laid out in a format that "contributes to the sense that readers are unfolding a rediscovered time and place."

Brighton has occasionally been criticized for giving readers a limited view of a time and place, for not including more explanatory detail. But Brighton views her style in a different light—she seeks to give just a brief glimpse into a past event. "When you're walking down a dark street, and someone has the curtains open, you have a glimpse of their lives," she told Kimberly Olson Fakih in *Publishers Weekly.* "Someone else's life is going on and you get that and then move on."

Works Cited

Cheetham, Mandy, review of *Rosalee and the Great Fire of London, Magpies,* May, 1995, p. 31.

Review of *Dearest Grandmama, Junior Bookshelf,* August, 1991, p. 143.

Fakih, Kimberly Olson, interview with Brighton in *Publishers Weekly,* July 28, 1989, pp. 132-34.

Fisher, Margery, review of *Cathy's Story, Growing Point,* November, 1980, p. 3793.

Fisher, Margery, review of *Five Secrets in a Box, Growing Point,* November, 1987, p. 4892.

Fisher, Margery, review of *Hope's Gift, Growing Point,* September, 1988, pp. 5044-45.

Fisher, Margery, review of *Maria, Growing Point,* January, 1985, p. 4375.

Review of *Five Secrets in a Box, Publishers Weekly,* July 10, 1987, p. 67.

Review of *Hope's Gift, Junior Bookshelf,* August, 1988, pp. 179-80.

Kalin, Amelia, review of *My Napoleon, School Library Journal,* June, 1997, p. 79.

Marriage, Julia, review of *Rosalee and the Great Fire of London, School Librarian,* February, 1995, p. 21.

Radtke, Karen K., review of *Dearest Grandmama, School Library Journal,* November, 1991, p. 90.

Taylor, Jennifer, review of *Nijinsky, School Librarian,* November, 1989, p. 142.

Waite, Maggi, "Children Waiting in the Wings," *School Librarian,* November, 1993, pp. 136-37.

Wilms, Denise, review of *Nijinsky: Scenes from the Childhood of the Great Dancer, Booklist,* November 15, 1989, p. 660.

For More Information See

PERIODICALS

Booklist, November 1, 1988, p. 479.

Bulletin of the Center for Children's Books, December, 1990, p. 79; November, 1991, p. 57; July-August, 1994, p. 351; May, 1997, pp. 314-15.

Growing Point, March, 1986, p. 4584.

Junior Bookshelf, February, 1981, pp. 10-11; February, 1985, pp. 10-11; April, 1986, p. 59; August, 1989, pp. 157-58; October, 1990, pp. 217-18.

Kirkus Reviews, September 15, 1989, p. 1400; March 15, 1997, p. 459.

Publishers Weekly, August 9, 1991, p. 57; February 28, 1994, p. 88.*

*   *   *

BUFFIE, Margaret 1945-

Personal

Born March 29, 1945, in Winnipeg, Manitoba, Canada; daughter of Ernest William John (a lithographer) and Evelyn Elizabeth (Leach) Buffie; married James Macfarlane (an artist), August 9, 1968; children: Christine Anne. *Education:* University of Manitoba, received degree, 1967, certificate in education, 1976.

Addresses

Home—1020 Grosvenor Ave., Winnipeg, Manitoba, Canada R3M 0N6.

Career

Hudson's Bay Co., Winnipeg, Manitoba, illustrator, 1968-70; Winnipeg Art Gallery, Winnipeg, painting instructor, 1974-75; River East School Division, Winnipeg, high school art teacher, 1976-77; freelance illustrator and painter, 1977-84; writer, 1984—. University of Winnipeg, writing instructor, 1992-97. *Member:* Canadian Authors Association, Canadian Society of Children's Authors, Illustrators, and Performers, International Board on Books for Young People (IBBY).

Awards, Honors

Young Adult Canadian Book Award, 1987-88; Canadian Library Association Young Adult Book Award, 1989, for *Who Is Frances Rain?;* Ontario Arts Council grants, 1987 and 1989, Canada Council Grant, 1995; McNally Robinson Book for Young People Award, 1996. Vicky Metcalf Award, 1996, for body of work. Works placed on Notable Canadian Young Adult Fiction Lists, Canadian Children's Book Centre Our Choice Lists, Canadian Library Association Notable Canadian Fiction Lists, and American Library Association and New York Public Library Best Books for Young Adults Lists.

Writings

Who Is Frances Rain?, Kids Can Press (Toronto), 1987, published in the U.S. as *The Haunting of Frances Rain,* Scholastic, 1989.
The Guardian Circle, Kids Can Press, 1989, published as *The Warnings,* Scholastic, 1991.
My Mother's Ghost, Kids Can Press, 1992, published in the U.S. as *Someone Else's Ghost,* Scholastic, 1995.
The Dark Garden, Kids Can Press, 1995.
Angels Turn Their Backs, Kids Can Press, 1998.

Sidelights

Margaret Buffie told *SATA:* "I was born, raised, and continue to live in Winnipeg, Manitoba, a city full of the history of the Canadian fur trade and, later, the gateway to the settlement of western Canada. I love the Manitoba prairies to the south and the lakes and tundra to the north. East of Winnipeg, just over the border of Ontario, is a small lake called Long Pine. In 1919, my grandfather built a log cabin there as a summer home for his family. My mother and father built another log house on their own property across the bay in 1943. My sisters and I have, in turn, built cottages all around this log cabin and on any given summer day you will find someone sunning on the docks or picking blueberries on the pine-covered, rocky hills that surround Long Pine. That wonderful place has wound its spell around three generations of my family and is now onto its fourth.

Margaret Buffie

"As a very young child, I loved the long summers spent at my grandpa's log cabin. But I had a secret I kept from everyone else. You see, I knew that the big, swaybacked log cabin breathed quietly—watching and waiting and listening. Oh, its beds were comfortable and the smell of varnished logs and wood smoke hung in the air, but I knew that for the cabin, there was another world beyond my family's—a world that went on when we weren't there, or perhaps even while we slept—a world that belonged to the shadowy places in the deep woods surrounding us.

"Even the inside of the cabin made of spruce logs seemed to belong to that other world. High above were the rafters spun with cobwebs, and down below were the hidden entrances for nocturnal mice to slide through and raid the kitchen. I never could find their private doors into the night.

"It was those secret places that I wanted to capture in *Who Is Frances Rain?* [published in the United States as *The Haunting of Frances Rain*]. When Lizzie McGill digs through an old cabin site and discovers a pair of spectacles, she puts them on and finds herself looking at the flickering shadows of a time past—a time that the cabin remembers and shares with her in order that she can help a restless spirit find peace on the other side."

The highly regarded *Who is Frances Rain?* blends elements of a mystery, ghost story, and time-travel fantasy with Buffie's sensitive depiction of a fractured modern family. In the novel, fifteen-year-old Lizzie, anxious to get away from her moody mother, new stepfather, and quarreling siblings, decides to explore the deserted Rain Island, considered by her grandmother to be unsafe and off-limits. There Lizzie discovers a pair of magic glasses through which she peers more than half a century into the past, viewing two female figures who lived on the island in the 1920s. What she learns from them helps her to appreciate her own family history and to work at resolving her personal problems. A reviewer in *Children's Book News* called *Who Is Frances Rain?* "a thoroughly absorbing young adult novel filled with characters who are bound to intrigue teenagers. It's full of the resonance of Canadian summer, the mystique of forest and water, and is sure to linger in the reader's mind long after the last page is turned."

"My second novel, *The Guardian Circle* [published in the United States as *The Warnings*]," Buffie continued to *SATA*, "takes place in an old house in Winnipeg. The central character, fifteen-year-old Rachel MacCaw, abandoned by her parents, arrives at 135 Cambric Street one drizzly fall day. She describes the place as a crumbling pile of bricks the color of raw beef liver, set

Buffie's young-adult novel is a poignant first-person narrative about a girl who develops a fear of leaving her house after her parents' marriage ends and she and her mother move to a new town. (Cover illustration by Florentina Bogdan.)

in a yard of tangled yellowing weeds and wild hedges. Leafless vines like licorice whips crawl all over the outside, and Rachel decides that they are probably the only things holding the building together. When Rachel enters 135 Cambric, she is acted upon by the magic within it. How she deals with the old people in the house and how she deals with the ghostly magic make up the story in *The Warnings*.

"I knew when I sat down with my notebooks and pencils to begin a first draft that I would have to draw on what poet Archibald MacLeish called 'the brain's ghostly house'—to walk through its darkened rooms, perhaps hear a door slam behind me or the creak of a secret stair tread. Slowly, I began to create a world that Rachel and other characters such as Luther Dubbles and Gladys Snodgrass and Dunstan Gregor could live in. A world that was made up of bright sunshine one minute and darkened hallways the next. A world of reality, but a world, also, where magic could happen at the flick of a cat's shadow." *Canadian Children's Literature* contributor Margery Stewart called Rachel a "believable" character and noted that "despite the spooky nature of the subject, Buffie's book sparkles, stitched together as it is with deft touches of humour, catching the reader with unexpected jolts and dollops of surprise and delight." In a *Voice of Youth Advocates* review, Catherine M. Dwyer highly recommended *The Warnings*, asserting: "Buffie has written a wonderful supernatural mystery."

Buffie's *My Mother's Ghost* (published in the United States as *Someone Else's Ghost*) takes place in Willow Creek, Alberta. Following the tragic death of her younger brother, Scotty, sixteen-year-old Jessica Locke moves from Winnipeg to a dude ranch with her parents. Jessica's father is going about his life as if nothing had happened; Jessica is working very hard on the ranch, trying to put her life back in order, and her mother, who has become very withdrawn and depressed, begins to think that she sees Scotty's ghost. Jessica finds the journal of Ian Shaw, a little boy who died on the ranch long ago, and suspects the ghost that her mother sees is actually the ghost of Ian. The story of the Locke family is juxtaposed with the story of Ian Shaw and his family. The two stories intersect as both families are faced with collapse as the result of the death of a family member. In the end, the Shaw family is able to rest in peace, while Jessica's family is able to move on. *My Mother's Ghost* received a favorable assessment from several commentators. *Voice of Youth Advocates* contributor Sister Mary Veronica described the book as "a real sit-on-the-end-of-your-seat page turner." Julia Rhodes noted in *Quill and Quire:* "It's refreshing to read YA fiction that respects the intelligence and maturity of its readers. [Buffie] proves once again that the realities of modern life need not come at the expense of an engrossing narrative."

Buffie followed *My Mother's Ghost* with another story of the supernatural, *The Dark Garden*. In a book that *Kirkus Reviews* called "a first-rate blend of a ghost story and problem novel," sixteen-year-old Thea is recovering from injuries sustained in a biking accident. After returning home from the hospital, she must cope not only with her amnesia but with her dysfunctional family that seems to be falling apart. Joanne Stanbridge of *Canadian Children's Literature* stated that "adolescents will sympathize with [Thea's] moody defiance right up to the last page." Thea also experiences encounters with the supernatural world in the novel, especially the ghost of Susannah who helps her uncover the secret behind a century-old tragedy. Stanbridge claimed that *The Dark Garden* is a challenging story that "requires an agile reader to keep up with the twists and turns of the plot." She added: "Buffie has once again written a book teenagers will love."

Buffie serves up more mystery and magic in *Angels Turn Their Backs,* another tale of a teen girl encountering the paranormal. In this work, fifteen-year-old Addy has recently moved from Toronto to Winnipeg with her mother, and because of a severe panic attack, convinces her mother to let her home-school. While home all day in the apartment house, Addy finds a talking parrot and several exquisite pieces of needlework that belonged to the former owner of the building, agoraphobic needle-point artist Lotta Engel. With clues hidden in the angel designs in the needlepoint and help from the parrot, Addy begins to unravel the mystery of Lotta. Teresa Toten commented in *Quill and Quire* that "the story is peopled with likeably flawed major and minor characters," and concluded that "the chills are warmer than a horror story in this tale, which is first and foremost a good story." *Voice of Youth Advocates* contributor Ann Bouricius offered similar commendation in another favorable assessment of *Angels Turn Their Backs,* concluding: "Populated with nicely developed secondary characters who also change and grow, Buffie's book should appeal to thoughtful readers who want stories driven by character rather than plot." A critic in the Brantford, Ontario, *Expositor* asserted that "*Angels* is a fine addition to Buffie's collection of award-winning work."

In summing up Buffie's work, *Quill and Quire* contributor Peter Carver commented: "The ghostly world of Buffie's novels is not necessarily threatening but rather a manifestation of the strong personalities of those who have gone before—hardly surprising in a writer who has such a strong sense of where she comes from."

Works Cited

Review of *Angels Turn Their Backs,* the Brantford, Ontario, *Expositor,* August 1, 1998.

Bouricius, Ann, review of *Angels Turn Their Backs, Voice of Youth Advocates,* April, 1999, p. 35.

Carver, Peter, "Margaret Buffie's Spirit Circle," *Quill and Quire,* November, 1989, p. 13.

Review of *The Dark Garden, Kirkus Reviews,* July 15, 1997, p. 1107.

Dwyer, Catherine M., review of *The Warnings, Voice of Youth Advocates,* June, 1991, p. 93.

Rhodes, Julia, review of *My Mother's Ghost, Quill and Quire,* August 15, 1992, p. 25.

Sister Veronica, Mary, review of *Someone Else's Ghost, Voice of Youth Advocates,* April, 1995, p. 19.

Stanbridge, Joanne, review of *The Dark Garden, Canadian Children's Literature,* summer, 1996, pp. 84-85.

Stewart, Margery, "Our Ghostly Co-habitants: The Seen and the Unseen," *Canadian Children's Literature,* spring, 1996, pp. 63-64.

Toten, Teresa, review of *Angels Turn Their Backs, Quill and Quire,* September, 1998, p. 65.

Review of *Who Is Frances Rain?, Children's Book News,* September, 1987, p. 13.

For More Information See

PERIODICALS

Booklist, October 15, 1997, p. 397.

Canadian Children's Literature, Number 81, 1996, pp. 63-65.

Horn Book, September, 1997, p. 568.

Kirkus Reviews, September 1, 1998, p. 1282.

Quill and Quire, December, 1995, p. 37.

C

CARSON, J(ohn) Franklin 1920-1981

OBITUARY NOTICE—See index for *SATA* sketch: Born August 2, 1920, in Indianapolis, IN; died October 23, 1981. High school teacher, principal, and education professor. J. Franklin Carson received his B.S. degree in 1948 from Butler University, and his M.S. (1954) and Ph.D. (1972) degrees from Indiana University. He served with the U.S. Coast Guard Reserve for three years before he began his career as a biologist for the Grassyfork Fisheries in Martinsville, Indiana, in 1948, and as a naturalist for the Indianapolis Children's Museum in 1949. He was a high school teacher of English and biology in Martinsville, Indiana, from 1950 to 1956. He left teaching briefly to serve as magazine editor, educational coordinator, and field representative for the Indiana Lumber and Builders' Supply Association. Carson returned to public education as a high school principal in Indiana, from 1957 to 1961, and in Taiwan for Taipei American Schools, from 1961 to 1964. In 1966 he joined the faculty at Central Michigan University as an associate professor of secondary education, a position he held for the rest of his career. His first book, *Floorburns,* was published in 1957. Carson wrote eight books altogether, all for young people. Two of his works were Junior Library Guild Selections: *The Boys Who Vanished* (1959) and *The Coach Nobody Liked* (1960). He was a member of the National Association of Secondary School Principals and Phi Delta Kappa, and served as president of the North Judson, Indiana, Chamber of Commerce in 1961. Carson twice participated in UNESCO-Chinese Ministry of Education projects.

—Robert Reginald and Mary A. Burgess

CHAMBERS, Robert W(illiam) 1865-1933

Personal

Born May 26, 1865, in Brooklyn, NY; died December 16, 1933; son of William (a lawyer) and Caroline (Boughton) Chambers; married Elsa Vaughn Moller, July 12, 1898; children: one son. *Education:* Attended Art Students' League, New York; attended Ecole des Beaux Arts and Academie Julien, both Paris, France, c. 1886-93.

Career

Writer. Illustrator for *Life, Truth,* and *Vogue* magazines, New York City, c. 1893. *Member:* National Institute of Arts and Letters.

Writings

FICTION; FOR CHILDREN

Outdoorland, Harper, 1902.
Orchard-land, Harper, 1903.
River-land, Harper, 1904.
Forest-land, Appleton (New York City), 1905; published as *Hide and Seek in Forest Land,* Appleton, 1909.
Mountain-land, Appleton, 1906.
The Younger Set, Appleton, 1907.
Garden-land, Appleton, 1907.
The Green Mouse, Appleton, 1910.
Blue-bird Weather, Appleton, 1912.
Japonette, Appleton, 1912.
The Hidden Children, Appleton, 1914.
Quick Action, Appleton, 1914.
Anne's Bridge, Appleton, 1914.
Police!!!, Appleton, 1915.
Who Goes There, Appleton, 1915.
The Laughing Girl, Appleton, 1918.
The Happy Parrot, Appleton, 1929.

NOVELS

In the Quarter, Neely (New York City), 1894.

The Red Republic: A Romance of the Commune, Putnam, 1895.

The King and a Few Dukes, Putnam, 1896.

Lorraine, Harper, 1897.

Ashes of Empire, Stokes (New York City), 1898.

The Cambric Mask, Stokes, 1899.

The Conspirators, Harper, 1899.

Outsiders: An Outline, Stokes, 1899.

Cardigan, Harper, 1901.

The Shining Band, Ward, Lock (London), 1901.

The Maid-at-Arms, Harper, 1902.

The Maids of Paradise, Harper, 1902.

In Search of the Unknown, Harper, 1904.

Iole, Appleton, 1905.

The Reckoning, Appleton, 1905.

The Fighting Chance, Appleton, 1906.

The Tracer of Lost Persons, Appleton, 1906.

The Firing Line, Appleton, 1908.

The Danger Mark, Appleton, 1909.

Special Messenger, Appleton, 1909.

Ailsa Page, Appleton, 1910.

The Common Law, Appleton, 1911.

The Streets of Ascalon: Episodes in the Unfinished Career of Richard Quarren Esq., Appleton, 1912.

The Business of Life, Appleton, 1913.

The Gay Rebellion, Appleton, 1913.

Between Friends, Appleton, 1914.

Athalie, Appleton, 1915.

The Girl Philippa, Appleton, 1916.

Barbarians, Appleton, 1917.

The Dark Star, Appleton, 1917.

The Restless Sex, Appleton, 1918.

In Secret, Doran, 1919.

The Moonlit Way, Appleton, 1919.

The Crimson Tide, Appleton, 1919.

The Slayer of Souls, Doran, 1920.

The Little Red Foot, Doran, 1921.

The Flaming Jewel, Doran, 1922.

Eris, Doran, 1923.

The Talkers, Doran, 1923.

America; or, The Sacrifice: A Romance of the American Revolution, Grossett & Dunlap, 1924.

The Mystery Lady, Grossett & Dunlap, 1925.

Marie Halket, Unwin (London), 1926, Appleton, 1937.

The Men They Hanged, Appleton, 1926.

The Drums of Aulone, Appleton, 1927.

Beating Wings, Cassell (London), 1928; Appleton, 1930.

The Rogue's Moon, Appleton, 1928.

The Sun Hawk, Appleton, 1929.

The Rake and the Hussy, Appleton, 1930.

The Painted Minx, Appleton, 1930.

Gitana, Appleton, 1931.

War Paint and Rouge, Appleton, 1931.

Whistling Cat, Appleton, 1932.

Whatever Love Is, Appleton, 1933.

Secret-Service Operator, Appleton, 1934; published as *Spy Number 13*, Philip Allan (London), 1935.

The Young Man's Girl, Appleton, 1934.

The Gold Chase, Appleton, 1935.

Love and the Lieutenant, Appleton, 1935.

The Girl in Golden Rags, Appleton, 1936.

The Fifth Horseman, Appleton, 1937.

Smoke of Battle, Appleton, 1938.

SHORT FICTION

The King in Yellow, Neely, 1895.

The Maker of Moons, Putnam, 1896.

The Mystery of Choice, Appleton, 1897.

The Haunts of Men, Stokes, 1899.

A Young Man in a Hurry and Other Short Stories, Harper, 1904.

The Tree of Heaven, Appleton, 1907.

Some Ladies in Haste, Appleton, 1908.

The Better Man, Appleton, 1916.

The Mask and Other Stories, Whitman (Racine, WI), 1929.

OTHER

With the Band (poetry), Stone and Kimball (New York City), 1896.

Iole (musical comedy), produced in New York City, 1913.

Also author of *The Witch of Ellangowan* (play), produced at Daly's Theatre.

Sidelights

Considered one of the most important authors of supernatural-horror fiction since Edgar Allan Poe, Robert W. Chambers is best remembered for his bizarre, imaginative tales of the supernatural, especially those included in his 1895 book, *The King in Yellow*, a collection comprising prose poems, sketches of Parisian life, and the five tales of the supernatural for which it is renowned. A prolific writer of best-selling romance novels, Chambers was accused of commercialism by many critics. While his once-popular novels are largely unread today, Chambers's supernatural stories are considered classics of the genre.

Chambers was born in Brooklyn, New York, the son of a distinguished lawyer. Deciding to pursue a career as an artist, Chambers attended art school in New York and in 1886 traveled to Paris to study at the Ecole des Beaux Arts and later at the Academie Julien. On returning to New York in 1893, he worked as an illustrator for the magazines *Life*, *Truth*, and *Vogue*, and published his first book, *In the Quarter*. With the success of his second work, *The King in Yellow*, Chambers abandoned art for a literary career, a decision which proved extremely lucrative. Few of the society novels and historical romances that he subsequently produced are considered more than potboilers which catered to the market for love and adventure stories. Chambers's works—including *The Restless Sex*, *The Rake and the Hussy*, and *Love and the Lieutenant*—ensured his status as one of the most popular writers of his time. He died in 1933.

For More Information See

BOOKS

Cooper, Frederic Taber, *Some American Story Tellers*, 1911, reprinted by Books for Libraries Press, 1968.

Daniels, Les, *Dying of Fright: Masterpieces of the Macabre*, Scribner, 1976.

Kilmer, Joyce, *Literature in the Making by Some of Its Makers*, 1917, reprinted by Kennikat Press, 1968.

Lovecraft, H. P., "Supernatural Horror in Literature," *Dagon and Other Macabre Tales,* edited by August Derleth, Arkham House, 1965.

Punter, David, *The Literature of Terror: A History of Gothic Fictions from 1765 to the Present Day,* Longman, 1980.*

*   *   *

CLARKE, Kenneth 1957-

Personal

Born March 22, 1957, in Wichita, KS; son of Carolyn Gunnels Clarke. *Education:* El Centro Junior College, A.A.S., 1981; East Texas State University, B.S., 1986. *Politics:* Republican. *Religion:* Protestant. *Hobbies and other interests:* Collecting vintage radio tapes.

Addresses

Home—3130 Royal Gable Dr., Dallas, TX 75229-3787. *Electronic mail*—KClarke3@juno.com.

Career

Sprint Corp., Dallas, TX, customer service associate, 1987—. *Member:* Mystery Writers of America, National Writers Association, Society of Children's Book Writers and Illustrators.

Kenneth Clarke

Writings

The Case of the Magnolia Murders (mystery novel), 1stBooks Library (Bloomington, IN), 1998.

Sidelights

Kenneth Clarke once commented: "I've always liked mystery books. I guess it's because of the challenge involved with finding the killer and bringing him or her to justice.

"Every good mystery author should attempt to expand the perimeters of the genre, instead of depending upon pre-existing plots. New, innovative plots are vital and, if given a chance, can provide satisfaction to all concerned."

*   *   *

CRAY, Roberta
See EMERSON, Ru

*   *   *

CUMMINGS, Pat (Marie) 1950-

Personal

Born November 9, 1950, in Chicago, IL; daughter of Arthur Bernard (a management consultant) and Christine M. (a librarian; maiden name, Taylor) Cummings; married Chuku Lee (a real estate appraiser and entrepreneur), 1975. *Education:* Attended Spelman College, 1970-71, and Atlanta School of Art, 1971-72; Pratt Institute, B.F.A., 1974. *Religion:* "Raised Catholic but practice no religion in an organized way now." *Hobbies and other interests:* Travel and foreign languages (especially French and Italian), swimming.

Addresses

Home and office—28 Tiffany Pl., Brooklyn, NY 11231.

Career

Freelance author and illustrator, 1974—. *Exhibitions:* Society of Illustrators group show, 1990, 1991; Museum of Fine Arts, Grand Rapids, MI, Bush Gallery, MA, and Ohio Cultural Arts Center, Athens, OH, all 1991; National Museum of Women in the Arts group show, and Newark Museum, Newark, NJ, both 1992; Discovery Center, Binghamton, NY, Cinque Gallery, New York, NY, and Peale Museum, Baltimore, MD, all 1993; Memorial Art Gallery, Rochester, NY, 1994; California Afro-American Museum, Los Angles, CA, 1996. *Member:* Society of Children's Book Writers and Illustrators, Graphic Artists Guild, Children's Book Illustrators Group, Authors Guild, Writers Guild of America (eastern chapter).

Pat Cummings

Awards, Honors

Notable Children's Trade Book in the Field of Social Studies, National Council for the Social Studies-Children's Book Council, 1982, for *Just Us Women;* Coretta Scott King Honorable Mention, American Library Association (ALA), 1983, for *Just Us Women,* and 1987, for *C.L.O.U.D.S.;* Coretta Scott King Award, ALA, 1984, for *My Mama Needs Me;* Black Women in Publishing Illustration Award, 1988; nonfiction award, *Boston Globe/Horn Book,* and Editor's Choice, *Booklist,* both 1992, and Children's Choice Award, 1996, all for *Talking with Artists;* Best Books, *School Library Journal,* 1998, for *Talking with Adventurers.*

Writings

AUTHOR AND ILLUSTRATOR; FOR CHILDREN

Jimmy Lee Did It, Lothrop, 1985.
C.L.O.U.D.S., Lothrop, 1986.
Clean Your Room, Harvey Moon!, Bradbury, 1991.
Petey Moroni's Camp Runamok Diary, Bradbury, 1992.
Carousel, Bradbury, 1994.
Dear Mabel!, Celebration Press, 1996.
My Aunt Came Back, HarperCollins, 1998.

ILLUSTRATOR; FOR CHILDREN

Eloise Greenfield, *Good News* (formerly titled *Bubbles*), Coward, McCann, 1977.
Trudie MacDougall, *Beyond Dreamtime: The Life and Lore of the Aboriginal Australian,* Coward, McCann, 1978.

Cynthia Jameson, *The Secret of the Royal Mounds: Henry Layard and the First Cities of Assyria,* Coward, McCann, 1980.
Jeannette Franklin Caines, *Just Us Women,* Harper, 1982.
Mildred Pitts Walter, *My Mama Needs Me,* Lothrop, 1983.
Cathy Warren, *Fred's First Day,* Lothrop, 1984.
Jeannette Franklin Caines, *Chilly Stomach,* Harper, 1986.
Cathy Warren, *Springtime Bears* (also known as *Playing with Mama*), Lothrop, 1986.
Jeannette Franklin Caines, *I Need a Lunch Box,* Harper, 1988.
Mary Stolz, *Storm in the Night,* Harper, 1988.
Barrett, Joyce Durham, *Willie's Not the Hugging Kind,* Harper, 1989.
Mildred Pitts Walter, *Two and Too Much,* Bradbury, 1990.
Mary Stolz, *Go Fish,* HarperCollins, 1991.
Nikki Grimes, *"C" is for City,* Lothrop, 1994.
Angela Shelf Medearis, *Barry and Bennie,* Celebration Press, 1996.
Margaret Read MacDonald, reteller, *Pickin' Peas,* Harper-Collins, 1998.

OTHER; EDITOR AND COMPILER

Talking with Artists, Volume 1, Bradbury, 1992, Volume 2, Simon & Schuster, 1995, Volume 3, Clarion, 1999.
(With Linda Cummings) *Talking with Adventurers: Conversations with Christina M. Allen, Robert Ballard, Michael L. Blakey, Ann Bowles, David Doubilet, Jane Goodall, Dereck & Beverly Joubert, Michael Novacek, Johan Reinhard, Rick C. West and Juris Zarins,* National Geographic Society, 1998.

Willie's Not the Hugging Kind was translated into Spanish.

Work in Progress

Angel Baby, for Lothrop; *Lulu's Birthday,* text by Elizabeth Fitzgerald Howard, for Greenwillow; *The Blue Lake* and *Purrrrr,* both for HarperCollins; *Talking with Adventurers,* Volume 2, for National Geographic Society.

Sidelights

Pat Cummings is a children's author and illustrator whose works feature people of various races taking positive, constructive approaches to everyday problems. Her interest in diversity developed after spending her childhood living in Germany, Japan, and such U.S. states as Illinois, New York, Virginia, Kansas, and Massachusetts; her father's career with the U.S. Army involved moving to a new base every few years. Being immersed in different cultures as a child sensitized Cummings to the importance of including people of all races in her work. "I've chosen at times not to illustrate stories that contained what seemed to be negative stereotypes," Cummings affirmed in an essay for *Something about the Author Autobiography Series* (SAAS). "When the vast majority of books published for children still reflects a primarily white, middle-class reality, I've always felt it was essential to show the spectrum of skin tones that truly make up the planet. I want any child to

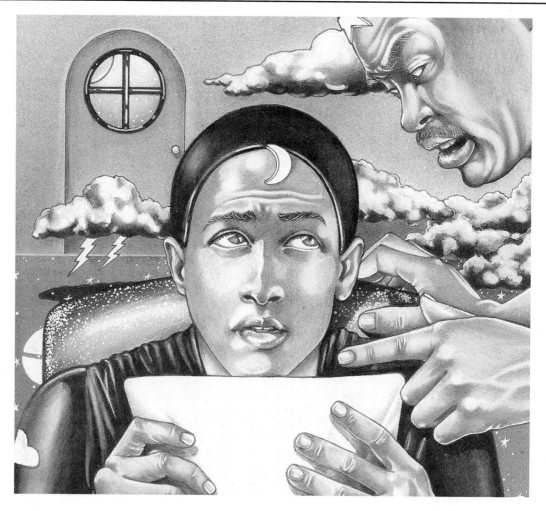

Chuku, cloud designer for Creative Lights, Opticals, and Unusual Designs in the Sky, finds himself in trouble after spelling out "Hello Down There" over New York City. (From C.L.O.U.D.S., *written and illustrated by Cummings.*)

be able to pick up one of my books and find something of value in it, even if only a laugh. The stories have truly universal themes: a jittery first day of school, the arrival of a new baby, attacking a messy room."

Born in 1950 in Chicago, Illinois, Cummings was the second of four children. Her brother and sisters were her closest friends while she was growing up, mainly because moving so often made it difficult to develop lasting friendships. She had already moved to Virginia and back to Chicago by the age of five, when she first left American soil to live in Germany. In her essay for *SAAS,* she recalled the impact of living in a foreign country: "I remember exotic little details from Germany: the strange-smelling gnome-like dolls from the Black Forest, seeing my first gingerbread house one Christmas, and climbing castles that stood along the Rhine River. My mother read fairy tales to us from a book that I believe was called *Tales of the Rhine....* What I realized later, when I began illustrating children's books, was that the thin line between fantasy and reality began for me when I climbed those castle steps that seemed fashioned right out of the fairy tales my mother had read to us."

One memorable event happened in Germany that proved to have a lasting effect on Cummings's life and career. While out one day with Linda, her older sister, Cummings decided to hop on board a school bus full of other girls—uninvited—after Linda had left her alone for a moment. The bus traveled deep into Germany's Black Forest and stopped at a ballet school. Cummings got out with the rest of the girls, pretending to belong, and spent an enchanting afternoon practicing ballet. When she finally returned home, she discovered that her distraught mother had alerted the German and army police. She was grounded for a long time after that incident. "As it turned out, I found myself with quite a bit of time on my hands to practice drawing," she recollected in *SAAS.* "I was not allowed out alone for thousands of years after that, and stuck in my room, I began drawing ballerinas. They all had pinpoint waists and enormous skirts.... As I perfected my ballerinas, I found that my classmates would pay me for them. I got a nickel for a basic ballerina, a dime for the more elaborate ones. If they had glitter, or were special requests (hearts on Valentine's Day or monsters for Halloween, for example), I might even get some M & Ms or Twinkies as payment. Candy was as good as money in those days. So, at a very early age, I realized that artwork could be thoroughly enjoy-able and good business as well."

Cummings went on creating ballerinas and other works of art throughout her school years. She never spent two years in a row at the same school, except for her junior and senior years of high school. Though many of her school experiences were positive—she used her artistic talents to help out with school projects and meet new friends—one incident at a Virginia elementary school taught her some of the harsh realities of life. "At recess I ran to the playground and hopped on a merry-go-round," she wrote in *SAAS*. "One of the nuns hastily came and led me away from the slides and see-saws, jungle gyms and sandbox I had my sights on next. She took me over to a dirt lot where there was a lone basketball hoop. My sister Linda was there. The nun told me that this was 'my' playground but that seemed ridiculous. There was nothing there. I remember that Linda was crying, having probably just found out the same on our first day. I always expected Linda to explain things, to know everything before I did, but she couldn't tell me what we had done to get kicked out of the 'real' playground. We were black and we couldn't play with the white kids we sat next to in the classroom. That wasn't clear to me then, even looking around at the other black children that had been steered to the dirt lot. It took me several years and more of such encounters to make any connection . . . . That non-inclusion puzzled me, troubled me, and finally, as I was growing up, led me to an awareness of America's deeply rooted racism." This experience laid the foundation for Cummings's profes-sional goal of creating works that appeal to people of all races.

After graduating from high school in 1968, Cummings decided to attend Pratt Institute in New York City. She majored in fashion because illustration was not offered as a major at that time. Though she dropped out of Pratt, worked for a year, and traveled to Georgia to attend Spelman College and the Atlanta School of Art, Cummings eventually returned to Pratt to earn her bachelor of fine arts in 1974. During her last year of school she began working as a freelance commercial artist. She landed her first job after a man in a car saw her hauling her portfolio down the street after school. He informed her that a job awaited her if she would get in the car. "I sized up the situation, took a chance and went with him. That was exactly the sort of thing my parents had worried about when I went to New York. But I had developed, I thought, a fairly reliable intuition by that time and it proved to be an excellent move," Cummings related in *SAAS*. The job was drawing posters for the Billie Holiday children's theater, and before long Cummings had clients from other theaters as well.

Cummings's break into book illustration came after some of her artwork was featured in a publication distributed by the Council on Interracial Books for Children. Without any experience with books, Cum-mings was offered the chance to draw the pictures for Eloise Greenfield's *Good News*. Cummings quickly informed her editor that she knew exactly what to do,

but in fact she knew nothing about book illustration. Once the job was hers, Cummings drew upon her network of friends to set up a meeting with illustrator Tom Feelings, who gave her a crash course on every-thing she would be expected to know and do. To this day Cummings feels a professional debt to Feelings that she tries to repay by helping other beginning artists. After her lessons with Feelings, she still had trouble starting. "I stared at the blank paper before me," she remarked in *SAAS*. "I was convinced that this book should rival *Alice in Wonderland* and that the art should make Johnny Carson's staff call to book me. I wanted the cover of *Time* magazine. I was dizzy with panic. I finally took a pad of paper into the bedroom . . . . I drew all afternoon. Not artwork that would bump [*Alice in Wonderland* illustrator John] Tenniel out of place, but drawings that began to give shape to the story at hand . . . . I look at it today and see the hundreds of mistakes I made and remember the agony and the ecstasy it produced. When I saw the book on a shelf in Bloomingdale's it was almost like being on Carson."

Since that first book, Cummings has gone on to illustrate more than a dozen works for others, and has written some of her own, including *Jimmy Lee Did It*, *C.L.O.U.D.S.*, and *Clean Your Room, Harvey Moon!* All three have strong ties to Cummings's family. The inspiration for *Jimmy Lee Did It* came from Cummings's brother Artie, who during childhood had his own "Jimmy Lee," an imaginary friend conveniently blamed when trouble occurred. Cummings got the idea for *C.L.O.U.D.S.* after sitting on the porch in Virginia with her mother and applauding a stunning sunset. The

Galloping verse and colorful illustrations combine to highlight the bond between a little girl and her beloved aunt, a traveler who brings her niece delightful gifts from exotic destinations. (From My Aunt Came Back, *written and illustrated by Cummings.)*

story's main character, Chuku—the name of Cummings's husband—is a cloud designer for Creative Lights, Opticals, and Unusual Designs in the Sky who finds himself in trouble after spelling out "Hello Down There" over New York City. A critic for *Kirkus Reviews* declared that "Cummings's brilliantly hued pictures delight the eye," while a *Publishers Weekly* reviewer called Cummings's artwork "fantastic and futuristic."

A tale of the unusual things a boy keeps in his room, *Clean Your Room, Harvey Moon!* is also based on her brother and was produced while Cummings stayed with her younger sister Barbara in Jamaica. Young Harvey's Saturday-afternoon cartoons are interrupted by his mother's demands that he clean his room—immediately. Eager to get back to the TV, Harvey begins "cleaning" by stuffing everything under his rug and bedspread, but his unusual housekeeping methods fail to impress his mother. Deborah Abbott, writing for *Booklist,* asserted that the text of this story "comes alive in the perky color drawings, filled with details that youngsters will savor." A *Publishers Weekly* critic noted, "Cummings's art is a boisterous clutter of color, providing just the right mood for her bouncy, rhyming text."

Cummings also created the text and illustrations for *Carousel,* the story of Alex, a young African-American girl whose father is not able to make it home from a business trip in time for her birthday party. Stomping off to bed in an angry huff, Alex breaks a zebra off the miniature carousel her father has left her as a present. That night, the other carousel animals come alive in Alex's dreams and carry her on a magical ride through the night sky. Her father is there when she wakes up, and all is well. A *Kirkus Reviews* commentator maintained that "Cummings's depiction of the disappointed child . . . is refreshingly true to life, while the nuances of her emotions are also warmheartedly portrayed." A reviewer for *Publishers Weekly* also praised Cummings's "affecting, vividly hued art, which depicts the realistic and the fanciful scenes with equal vibrancy," while *Booklist*'s Deborah Abbott asserted, "Cummings's vibrant double-page-spread illustrations depict the moods accurately and sensitively."

Cummings interviewed thirteen fellow children's illustrators for her highly acclaimed *Talking with Artists.* The collection profiles such noted artists as Jerry Pinkney, Leo and Diane Dillon, Victoria Chess, and Lane Smith. Each entry includes a recent photo of the illustrator, a full-color reproduction of a sampling of their work, and their answers to eight questions commonly asked by children. In a review for *The Five Owls,* Karen Nelson Holye declared, "among the many biographies and autobiographies about authors and illustrators of children's books, Cummings's compilation proves the most accessible." *Horn Book* critic Mary M. Burns called *Talking with Artists* "an innovative approach to informational books . . . an inspired concept, executed with class!" The work was expanded to two more editions; volume 2 looks at Floyd Cooper, Keven Henkes, and Vera B. Williams, and volume 3 includes Lisa Desmini, Peter Sis, and Paul O. Zelinsky. Stephanie Zvirin called

volume 2 "a special treat for budding artists and wonderful for teachers" in a *Booklist* review, while *School Library Journal* contributor Carol Schene declared of the same volume: "Full of insight and inspiration, this is an entertaining resource that young people, teachers, and librarians will enjoy. Cummings has another hit on her hands."

In addition to illustrating her own texts, Cummings has provided drawings for the works of other writers. Her collaborations with Jeannette Franklin Caines include *Chilly Stomach* and *I Need a Lunch Box.* The first book explores the difficult and sensitive issue of child molestation. Young Sandy is uncomfortable when her Uncle Jim hugs her and kisses her on the lips, but Jim's behavior is not overt enough to attract the attention of Sandy's parents. Sandy confides her fears to her friend Jill, who urges her to tell her parents. *School Library Journal* contributor Karen K. Radtke noted that "Cummings's impressionistic chalk pictures provide a comfortable background for an uncomfortable subject." Zena Sutherland of *Bulletin of the Center for Children's Books* asserted, "intensely bright colors and a dramatic use of space make each page a vivid tableau." In *I Need a Lunch Box,* a little boy wants a lunch box just like his older sister, who is starting first grade. Cummings's illustrations depict the boy's dreams, in which he has a lunch box of a different color and shape for each day of the week. "Cummings has depicted sturdy, healthy-looking children who almost push out of the pages' bounds," declared a *Kirkus Reviews* critic. *Booklist*'s Denise M. Wilms maintained, "Cummings's pictures are exuberant paintings that don't stint on strident displays of strong color."

Cummings's illustrations also grace the pages of Mary Stolz's *Storm in the Night* and *"C" is for City* by Nikki Grimes. *Storm in the Night* is a tender portrayal of the relationship between a young African-American boy and his grandfather, who are left alone together one night when the lights go out during a thunderstorm. Grandfather tells the boy of his own childhood when he was scared of thunderstorms too, but summoned up the courage to rescue his dog, who was caught in a storm. Cummings's illustrations for this work "effectively evoke the stormy night world," according to a critic for *Kirkus Reviews.* *Horn Book* reviewer Ethel L. Heins asserted, "every illustration is imbued with the boy's sensory awareness during a night of wonder and discovery." In *"C" is for City,* each letter of the alphabet represents different New York City experiences. Each of Cummings's illustrations "is a hearty slice of urban life," according to *Booklist* critic Julie Yates Walton. Sally R. Dow noted in *School Library Journal* that "many of the arresting images reflect the ethnic, religious, and economic diversity" of life in a big city.

Whether working on her own books or illustrating for others, Cummings maintains her philosophy that children's books ought to encourage optimistic, constructive approaches to life: "There is a responsibility attached to making books for young readers," she stated in *SAAS.* "A lot of stories focus on the children's emotions and scratching up those feelings is pointless unless there is a positive resolution by the book's end. I feel the best stories allow a child to discover a solution or approach to their own situation. My parents' positive outlook on life gave me and my brother and sisters the tools we needed to construct any future we envisioned. I hope to pass that feeling of capability on through the characters I write about or draw."

Works Cited

Abbott, Deborah, review of *Carousel, Booklist,* July, 1994, p. 1953.

Abbott, review of *Clean Your Room, Harvey Moon!, Booklist,* February 15, 1991, p. 1201.

Burns, Mary M., review of *Talking with Artists, Horn Book,* July-August, 1992, pp. 465-66.

Review of *Carousel, Kirkus Reviews,* April 1, 1994, p. 478.

Review of *Carousel, Publishers Weekly,* March 21, 1994, p. 72.

Review of *Clean Your Room, Harvey Moon!, Publishers Weekly,* February 8, 1991, p. 56.

Review of *C.L.O.U.D.S., Kirkus Reviews,* January 15, 1986, p. 130.

Review of *C.L.O.U.D.S., Publishers Weekly,* June 27, 1986, p. 86.

Cummings, Pat, essay in *Something about the Author Autobiography Series,* Volume 13, Gale, 1992, pp. 71-88.

Dow, Sally R., review of *"C" is for City, School Library Journal,* November, 1995, p. 71.

Heins, Ethel L., review of *Storm in the Night, Horn Book,* July-August, 1988, p. 486.

Hoyle, Karen Nelson, review of *Talking with Artists, The Five Owls,* May-June, 1992, pp. 62-63.

Review of *I Need a Lunch Box, Kirkus Reviews,* July 15, 1988, p. 1057.

Radtke, Karen K., review of *Chilly Stomach, School Library Journal,* August, 1986, p. 79.

Schene, Carol, review of *Talking with Artists, Vol. 2, School Library Journal,* October, 1995, p. 145.

Review of *Storm in the Night, Kirkus Reviews,* January 15, 1988, p. 129.

Sutherland, Zena, review of *Chilly Stomach, Bulletin of the Center for Children's Books,* July-August, 1986, p. 203.

Walton, Julie Yates, review of *"C" is for City, Booklist,* October 1, 1995, p. 322.

Wilms, Denise M., review of *I Need a Lunch Box, Booklist,* September 15, 1988, p. 156.

Zvirin, Stephanie, review of *Talking with Artists, Vol. 2, Booklist,* September 15, 1995, pp. 157-58.

For More Information See

BOOKS

Behind the Covers, Vol. II, Libraries Unlimited, 1989.

Children's Literature Review, Volume 48, Gale, 1998, pp. 31-57.

PERIODICALS

Booklist, February 15, 1991, p. 1201; May 15, 1991, p. 1800; May 1, 1992, p. 1598; July, 1998, p. 1887.

Bulletin of the Center for Children's Books, May, 1990, p. 229; April, 1992, p. 202; October, 1992, p. 41; October, 1995, p. 50.

Horn Book, July-August, 1991, pp. 454-55; November-December, 1995, pp. 755-56; November, 1998, p. 753.

Kirkus Reviews, February 1, 1991, pp. 181-82; July 15, 1992, p. 919; September 1, 1995, p. 1279; February 1, 1998, p. 194.

Language Arts, January, 1993, pp. 52-59.

Publishers Weekly, February 23, 1990, pp. 216-17; June 8, 1998, p. 59.

School Library Journal, April, 1990, p. 100; April, 1991, p. 94; May, 1991, p. 84; December, 1992, pp. 78, 80; August, 1994, pp. 127-28; October, 1995, p. 145; April, 1999, p. 145.

*   *   *

CUNNINGHAM, E. V.
See FAST, Howard

*   *   *

CURTIS, Gavin 1965-

Personal

Born July 8, 1965, in New York, NY. *Education:* School of Visual Arts, New York City, B.F.A.; Hunter College of the City University of New York, M.S., 1999.

Addresses

Agent—Marilyn Marlow, Curtis Brown, Ltd., 10 Astor Pl., New York, NY 10003.

Career

Elementary schoolteacher in New York state.

Writings

(Self-illustrated) *Grandma's Baseball,* Crown, 1990.

The Bat Boy and His Violin, illustrated by E. B. Lewis, Simon & Schuster, 1998.

Contributor of stories and drawings to Marvel Comics.

Sidelights

Gavin Curtis told *SATA:* "Growing up in a public-housing project in New York City, I had to look for my literary and artistic role models wherever I could find them. I was inspired by creative individuals who possessed numerous facets to their talents—like Gordon Parks, who was not only a photographer, but also an author, filmmaker, and composer. In *The Bat Boy and His Violin,* I based Reginald's passion for his music on my own passion for writing and illustrating. It was frustrating when, as a child, I had to convince family members and friends that spending hours in the corner of our living room writing and drawing superhero stories

Gavin Curtis

was not a colossal waste of time. Everyone liked my efforts but, never having met an actual author from the projects, they just did not see the practicality of it. Then, at the age of twenty-two, I started writing and drawing stories for Marvel Comics.

"In that same year, I wrote and illustrated my first picture book, *Grandma's Baseball.* Usually I illustrate my own stories so, with *The Bat Boy and His Violin,* it was exciting to see how another illustrator interpreted what I wrote. It was also a chance to prove to myself that I was not just selling stories on the basis of my art—an anxiety harbored by many author-illustrators.

"I received a Bachelor of Fine Arts degree from the School of Visual Arts, where I studied illustration, animation, and film. At Hunter College, I received a Master of Science degree in education. I teach kindergarten and would like to teach older grades, possibly moving on to administrative service in the public school system.

"Though I am not a particularly good player, I like to dabble on the keyboard. Like Reginald in *The Bat Boy and His Violin,* I enjoy classical music. One year, I even took my class of four-year-olds to the Lincoln Center for a concert of Tchaikovsky's music. Many patrons and the conductor expressed apprehension that the young children would be disruptive, but my well-behaved students made them eat their words. The children even applauded politely when the members of the orchestra tuned their instruments."

Set in 1948, *The Bat Boy and His Violin* features a young violin player named Reginald whose father insists that he is wasting his time with the instrument. Reginald's father, who is the manager of the worst team in the Negro Leagues, makes Reginald trade his bow for a bat and become the team's bat boy. Having little interest in baseball, the aspiring musician brings his instrument to the game and entertains the players in the dugout. Surprisingly, the team begins to win, convincing Reginald's father that his son's talent should be encouraged and appreciated. In a starred *School Library Journal* review, Judith Constantinides applauded not only the "interesting" portrayal of life in the Negro Leagues, but also the "wonderfully delineated father-son relationship." According to a *Publishers Weekly* contributor, "this imposing book will score high marks with youngsters whether their tastes run to sports or to Mozart." *Booklist* critic GraceAnne A. DeCandido praised the large amount of material about the Negro Leagues as well as the "quiet message about bridging the gap between what a parent wants and what a child needs."

Curtis continued, "If there is a lesson that readers and future artists can learn from Reginald's tale, I guess it is to follow your dreams, even when loved ones are not as encouraging as you would like them to be. Eventually they will 'come around.' I like to imagine that Reginald (named after Reggie Jackson, my favorite baseball player of all time) did ultimately realize *his* dream to play in a famous orchestra."

Works Cited

Review of *The Bat Boy and His Violin, Publishers Weekly,* April 6, 1998, p. 77.

Constantinides, Judith, review of *The Bat Boy and His Violin, School Library Journal,* July, 1998, pp. 72-73.

DeCandido, GraceAnne A., review of *The Bat Boy and His Violin, Booklist,* June 1 & 15, 1998, p. 1765.

D

DiCIANNI, Ron 1952-

Personal

Born March 26, 1952, in Chicago, IL; son of John and Leona (Gentile) DiCianni; married Patricia Rybowicz (an executive assistant), August 25, 1973; children: Grant, Warren. *Education:* American Academy of Art, Chicago, AA. *Religion:* Pentecostal.

Addresses

Home—340 Thompson Blvd., Buffalo Grove, IL 60089. *Office*—Art2See, 310 E. Chicago St., Elgin, IL 60120. *E-mail*—art2see@aol.com and ron@art2see.com. *Agent*—Alive Communications, Colorado Springs, CO.

Ron DiCianni

Career

MasterPeace Collection, Arkansas, cofounder and partner, 1990-97; Art2See, Elgin, IL, chief executive officer, 1997—.

Awards, Honors

Four gold medallions for the "Tell Me" Series; painting award for "Simeon's Moment" and two Visitors' Choice awards, Sacred Arts Show, Billy Graham Center.

Writings

Beyond Words: A Treasury of Paintings and Devotional Writings, Tyndale (Wheaton, IL), 1998.

ILLUSTRATOR

Frank Peretti, *This Present Darkness,* Crossway, 1986.
Frank Peretti, *Piercing the Darkness,* Crossway, 1988.
Paul Hughes, *Shadow of Death,* Bridge-Logos (South Plainfield, NJ), 1993.
R. Kent Hughes, *The Gift: Seven Meditations on the Events Surrounding Jesus' Birth,* Crossway (Wheaton, IL), 1994.
R. K. Hughes, *The Saviour,* Crossway, 1995.
Calvin Miller, *My Son, My Saviour: The Awesome Wonder of Jesus' Birth,* Chariot Victor (Colorado Springs, CO), 1997.
Calvin Miller, *My Lord & My God,* Chariot Victor, 1998.

ILLUSTRATOR; "TELL ME" SERIES

Max Lucado, *Tell Me the Story,* Crossway, 1992.
Lucado, *Tell Me the Secrets: Treasures for Eternity,* Crossway, 1993.
Joni Eareckson Tada and Steve Jensen, *Tell Me the Promises: A Family Covenant for Eternity,* Crossway, 1996.
Tada and Jensen, *Tell Me the Truth: God's Eternal Truths for Families,* Crossway, 1997.
Michael Card, *Tell Me Why: Eternal Answers to Life's Timeless Questions,* Crossway, 1999.

Sidelights

Author and illustrator Ron DiCianni is a devout Christian who uses his talent to create for his audience visual translations of Bible events and themes. Through his own artwork and his encouragement of other Christian artists, DiCianni hopes to inspire a second Renaissance, in which the arts are used effectively by the Christian Church.

According to DiCianni's forward in *Beyond Words,* the artist became aware of his gifts and God's calling to use them while still a child. Throughout DiCianni's adolescence, Pat, "the woman who would later become my only date and my wife," reported DiCianni, "kept reminding me of the call for my life and demonstrated her belief in it by giving me my first set of paints and an easel." The young couple worked hard, Pat at an insurance company and Ron at a church as a janitor, to pay for DiCianni's tuition at the American Academy of Art in Chicago. For eighteen years, DiCianni devoted his talents to the secular community, because he found that "the Church had no apparent interest in using art for anything more than decoration." Consequently, DiCianni noted, "my career ... went in the secular direction and prospered beyond my wildest dreams." Chosen as the official illustrator for the Moscow Olympics in 1980, DiCianni was soon disappointed to discover that the United States would be boycotting that year's Olympic Games. Despite the setback, his work began gaining international attention. DiCianni decided, though, that it was time to return his attention to Christian spiritual art. After what the artist himself termed "a halfhearted attempt" to move towards more religious content, DiCianni had a humbling experience and began devoting himself entirely to Christian spiritual art. Through mentorship and artistry DiCianni aims to create the second Renaissance he has hoped for since his youth.

DiCianni takes cues from several admired artists, including Newell Convers (N. C.) Wyeth, who said, "you can only paint out of conviction." He also admires Norman Rockwell for his ability to make viewers notice the subject of his work rather than the techniques used to produce it. DiCianni believes that "painters and every other kind of artist have a choice when executing the finished piece. They can either cause you to focus on what they painted or how they painted it. They cannot do both with equal power." Like Wyeth and Rockwell, DiCianni has chosen to focus on his subject matter, about which he is most definitely passionate: "As a speaker aims to tell you the truth," DiCianni asserted, "I aim to show you the truth."

In *Tell Me the Secrets* DiCianni aims to elucidate truths about some very weighty subjects, such as peace, forgiveness, and death. In the story, a retired missionary makes friends with three children and acquaints them with a book that reveals life's spiritual secrets. A *Publishers Weekly* contributor maintained that *Tell Me the Secrets* "beautifully combines the efforts of [writer] Pastor Lucado and artist DiCianni," and the same commentator called the book a "lovely story for all ages."

In all his works, whether for child or adult audiences, Ron DiCianni aims for excellence: "I believe that if you have been gifted with artistic ability, you are responsible to develop it to the fullest."

Works Cited

DiCianni, Ron, *Beyond Words: A Treasury of Paintings and Devotional Writings,* Tyndale, 1998.

Review of *Tell Me the Secrets: Treasures for Eternity, Publishers Weekly,* November 8, 1993, p. 48.

*   *   *

DUBOSARSKY, Ursula 1961-

Personal

Born June 25, 1961, in Sydney, Australia; daughter of Peter (a writer) and Verna (a writer) Coleman; married Abel Dubosarsky, December 17, 1987; children: Maisie, Dover, Bruno. *Education:* Sydney University, B.A. (with honors), 1982, Diploma in Education, 1989.

Addresses

Office—c/o Penguin Books, Maroondah Highway, Ringwood, Victoria, Australia 3134. *E-mail*—dubosar @ar.com.au.

Career

Writer. Australian Public Service, Canberra, Australia, researcher, 1983-84; *Reader's Digest* magazine, Sydney Australia, freelance researcher, 1986—.

Awards, Honors

Notable Book, Children's Book Council of Australia (CBCA), for *High Hopes, Zizzy Zing, Bruno and the Crumhorn,* and *Black Sails White Sails;* shortlist, CBCA Young Readers Award, 1994, for *The Last Week in December;* New South Wales (NSW) commendation for Family Therapy Award, 1990, for *High Hopes;* NSW State Literary Award and Victorian Premier's Award for Children's Literature, both 1994, and shortlist, CBCA Award for Older Readers, 1995, all for *The White Guinea Pig;* NSW State Literary Awards Ethnic Affairs Commission Award, 1995, and shortlist, Royal Blind Society Talking Book Award, inclusion in United Nations White Raven library collection, and CBCA Honour Book, all 1996, all for *The First Book of Samuel.*

Writings

Maisie and the Pinny Gig, illustrated by Roberta Landers, Macmillan, 1989.

High Hopes, Penguin, 1990.

Zizzy Zing, HarperCollins, 1991, Penguin, 1998.

The Last Week in December, Puffin, 1993.

The White Guinea-Pig, Viking, 1994.
The First Book of Samuel, Viking, 1995.
Bruno and the Crumhorn, Viking, 1996.
Black Sails White Sails, Penguin, 1997.
The Strange Adventures of Isador Brown, illustrated by Paty Marshall-Stace, Puffin, 1998.
Honey and Bear, illustrated by Ron Brooks, Viking, 1998.
My Father Is Not a Comedian, Penguin, 1999.

Work in Progress

Special Days for Honey and Bear and *The Game of the Goose,* a junior fantasy novel.

Sidelights

Australian author Ursula Dubosarsky is noted for her young adult novels, commonly referred to as comedies with a dark streak. In award-winning books such as *Zizzy Zing, High Hopes, The White Guinea Pig, The First Book of Samuel,* and *Black Sails White Sails,* Dubosarsky has created a pageant of vivid characters and closely wrought incident. Reviewing *The Last Weekend in December,* Robyn Sheahan of *Magpies* called Dubosarsky "one of the very few truly original and talented voices speaking to children through literature in Australia today." Although her books sometimes contain Australian expressions that prove challenging to younger American readers, Dubosarsky's themes and subject matter have garnered a loyal readership and critical praise in the United States.

Born in Sydney, Australia, Dubosarsky was raised by parents who were both writers. As she told an *ACHUKA* interviewer, "I was pretty scatty as a child ... always losing things and forgetting things—and certainly a daydreamer." Graduating from Sydney University in 1982, she spent two years in Canberra as a researcher for the Australian Public Service. She began writing in the evenings to create her first novel, ultimately published nearly a decade later as *Zizzy Zing.* Meanwhile the author spent a year on a kibbutz where she met her Argentine-born husband. Returning to Sydney in 1986, Dubosarsky took work as a researcher for *Reader's Digest* and continued her writing in the little free time afforded her by a growing family.

Dubosarsky's first book, *Maisie and the Pinny Gig,* was published in 1989. A picture book, *Maisie and the Pinny Gig* tells the story of Maisie, her dreamtime friend, Pinny Gig, and Maisie's skeptical parents, who have never encountered a Pinny Gig. Dubosarsky's *High Hopes* was released the following year. Serendipitously, the manuscript had been pulled from publisher Penguin's slush pile by editor and writer Jane Godwin; the two have worked together ever since.

High Hopes is the story of twelve-year-old Julia, who is very protective of her father, George. Widowed, George is a native Spanish speaker and has trouble understanding the customers at his delicatessen. Julia's grandmother also has trouble with English, so Julia takes advantage of an offer of free language tutoring and finds a teacher to give English lessons. Unexpectedly, Julia sees Anabel, the teacher, kissing her father and decides she must save her naive father from this inappropriate woman. Julia's plot leads her to bake a "poisoned" cake—one with an entire bottle of vanilla in it. When George is enticed by the aroma of the poisonous dessert, Julia's plot fails, but she begins accepting her father's need for companionship and decides to tolerate the addition of a stepmother to the family.

Reviewing this debut novel, Andrea Davidson commented in *Voice of Youth Advocates:* "This is a funny, offbeat novel about growing up, remarriage, and family ups and downs." Davidson concluded that Dubosarsky's "very skillful writing" contributes to a "most entertaining read." *Horn Book*'s Ellen Fader deemed *High Hopes* "a breezy novel with realistic underpinnings that will please fans of contemporary fiction," while *Booklist*'s Mary Romano observed that Dubosarsky "deftly captures the immigrant experience and a child's fear of change." Contributor Adrian Jackson concluded his assessment of *High Hopes* in *Books for Keeps* with what could be a summation of Dubosarsky's style: "There's a lovely confidence in the story telling and a clever blending of the comic and serious."

A mysterious letter is at the heart of Dubosarsky's third published work, *Zizzy Zing.* The letter ultimately leads young Phyllis, who is spending the summer at a convent, back in time to 1938. Faced with a perplexing tragedy, Phyllis is launched into the most horrifying summer of her life. Commenting on the somewhat manic tone of *Zizzy Zing,* Dubosarsky told *ACHUKA,* "A friend of mine once said that she found *Zizzy Zing* notable for its tone of near hysteria, and she was worried about how I must have been feeling when I wrote it." Dubosarsky, though, attributes any such edginess in the book to the fact that she wrote it almost entirely at night, while working a full-time job during the day. Dubosarsky cut her teeth on this novel, written years before the publication of her first two books, and discovered that a planned plot was not her style. "I only really find out what's going to happen in my books as I'm writing," Dubosarsky told *ACHUKA.* "Really for me, the best analogy for writing is dreaming—it's all happening in your head, so of course at some level you're controlling it, or deciding what's happening, but on the whole it's not a conscious thing." As she began writing this first novel, Dubosarsky knew only that she wanted to create a murder mystery where the child was the detective; what she ended up with was perhaps a bit more of a ghost story than mystery.

The last week in December, usually filled with anticipation, supplies the trepidation-filled setting as well as the title of Dubosarsky's *The Last Week in December.* The book's eleven-year-old main character, Bella, is dreading the impending arrival of her English relatives because she has a guilty secret. When her relatives last visited three years earlier, Bella stole something from them, and Bella is sure they have come to confront her with her crime. The visit is full of surprises, however, for both Bella and for readers. Reviewer Robyn Sheahan commented in *Magpies* that "Bella is woundingly credible and engaging." Sheahan, in fact, had praise for all of the author's characterizations, writing, "Dubosarsky's command of her characters is born of observational skills honed to a razor sharp and sometimes disturbing edge." Further emphasizing an appreciation of *The Last Week in December,* Sheahan asserted that the work is "destined to fall into the canon of classic Australian works for children."

Dubosarsky views herself as a slow writer who is more concerned with character, language, and individual sentences than with the overall plot. In her *ACHUKA* interview, she revealed that though she thinks of herself "as a comic writer essentially," when writing first person novels, "the sadder bits just creep out."

Though written in the third person, some sadder bits still creep out of Dubosarsky's *The White Guinea Pig.* While Geraldine is reluctantly taking care of her friend's white guinea pig for six weeks, her domestic world seems to be falling apart. Her father is going bankrupt and selling their house; her older sister is torn between two boyfriends; and the neighbor, Ezra, on whom Geraldine has a crush, appears to be guarding an awful secret. Though the white guinea pig of the title is lost and ultimately killed, the novel is not tragic but uplifting. "A sad tale?" pondered a reviewer for the *Observer.* "Actually not. You'll be moved by the sudden, warm ending; with its lightness and wit, this is a comedy of some depth." *Booklist* contributor Chris Sherman felt that the "surreal quality" of the novel "sets it apart from the usual crop of middle-school problem novels about families," while Deborah Stevenson of the *Bulletin of the Center for Children's Books* noted that "Dubosarsky, a talented writer, weaves ... strands together into a story of humor and notable eccentricity." Stevenson concluded that "readers with particularly offbeat literary tastes will appreciate this Australian import."

Other critically acclaimed young adult novels by Dubosarsky include *The First Book of Samuel, Bruno and the Crumhorn,* and *Black Sails White Sails. The First Book of Samuel* is inspired by the Biblical story of Samuel, who disappears on his twelfth birthday, leaving family members trying to piece together his life using the scraps of information available to them. Reviewing *The First Book of Samuel* in *Magpies,* Jo Goodman observed that "Every word, every nuance is carefully judged." *Bruno and the Crumhorn* is about a boy taking lessons on a Renaissance musical instrument which has an embarrassing honking sound. Val Randall, writing in *Books for Keeps,* called *Bruno and the Crumhorn* "a whimsical story, peopled with eccentric characters," and went to note that the "narrative has a dry, whacky humour." Reviewing that same novel in *Magpies,* Anne Hanzl called it "a 'hoot' of a story full of sly humour, and interesting, quirky characters." Less humor is served up in *Black Sails White Sails,* a novel with Greek mythology at its center. Wendy Caveneti, writing in the on-line magazine *Between the Lines,* compared this work to "the desolation of Wim Wender's *Paris, Texas.*"

Dubosarsky gave *SATA* some exclusive firsthand insights into her experience in writing her next book, *Honey and Bear:* "I came to writing *Honey and Bear,* a book for early readers and listeners, after writing several novels for older children. Honey and Bear came to me in the middle of the night, if not exactly in a dream, at least in a near-dreamlike state! My third child, Bruno, was very active at night, and as a result, so was I. I was suffering a great deal from sleeplessness. One night lying there staring at the dark feeling rather desperate, the very first story of *Honey and Bear,* which is called 'Good Idea, Bad Idea,' came into my head, word for word, virtually as it appears on the page today. It was as though the characters of Honey the bird and Bear the bear and their life together dropped down from heaven, in just the right voice. In fact, all five of the little stories in Honey and Bear came to me that very night. Then, at last, feeling both very excited and content, I fell asleep.

"When I woke up, I remembered my nocturnal visitors, and I was both happy and nervous—altogether too nervous to rush to the word processor to write them down! What if they were no good? I walked around for several days keeping the stories a secret in my head, like someone who has witnessed something strange and is in two minds about telling anyone about it. Finally, about a week later, I sat down and typed the stories out. Wonderful to relate, I seemed to have remembered them all—every word.

"I had never had what you might call a creative experience quite like that—one that came like something given, and brought its creator so much pleasure in the process. Ron Brooks was eventually chosen to illustrate the stories, which he did with such beautiful warmth. For me, the book feels like a blessing; writing it was one of those experiences, which as I remember Rumer Godden saying in reference to *The Mousewife,* comes to a writer perhaps once in a life time. And I am so grateful for it."

Dubosarsky summarized, in her *ACHUKA* interview, some of the differences she's noticed between writing for children and writing for young adults: "Little children are, as we all know, very concerned with what you might call the Great Questions of Life—by the time they're eleven or twelve, the other age group I write for, the social dilemmas are more preoccupying, both for writer and reader." For both age groups, however, Dubosarsky maintains her humorous take on life, with her usual cast of quirky characters often teetering on the edge between the comic and the tragic.

Works Cited

Caveneti, Wendy, review of *Black Sails White Sails, Between the Lines,* www.thei.aust.com/btl/btlrvursula.html.

Davidson, Andrea, review of *High Hopes, Voice of Youth Advocates,* October, 1991, p. 226.

Fader, Ellen, review of *High Hopes, Horn Book,* September-October, 1991, p. 596.

Goodman, Jo, review of *The First Book of Samuel, Magpies,* May, 1995, p. 32.

Hanzl, Anne, review of *Bruno and the Crumhorn, Magpies,* May, 1996, p. 42.

Jackson, Adrian, review of *High Hopes, Books for Keeps,* May, 1991, pp. 14-15.

Marks, Mary Romano, review of *High Hopes, Booklist,* August, 1991, pp. 2146-47.

Randall, Val, review of *Bruno and the Crumhorn, Books for Keeps,* September, 1996, p. 16.

Sheahan, Robyn, review of *The Last Week in December, Magpies,* July, 1993, p. 34.

Sherman, Chris, review of *The White Guinea Pig, Booklist,* July, 1995, p. 1878.

Stevenson, Deborah, review of *The White Guinea Pig, Bulletin of the Center for Children's Books,* June, 1995, p. 107.

"Ursula Dubosarsky Interview," *ACHUKA,* www.achu ka.co.uk/udint.htm.

Review of *The White Guinea Pig, Observer,* November 20, 1994, p. 12.

For More Information See

PERIODICALS

Junior Bookshelf, December, 1994, p. 223.
School Librarian, February, 1994, p. 31.
School Library Journal, September, 1991, p. 252; July, 1995, p. 76.
Times Educational Supplement, November 7, 1997, p. 7.
Voice of Youth Advocates, August, 1995, p. 156.

—Sketch by J. Sydney Jones

*   *   *

DUNN, Anne M. 1940-

Personal

Born November 9, 1940, in Red Lake, MN; daughter of Guy Gabriel George (a laborer) and Maefred (an educator; maiden name, Vanoss; present surname, Arey) LaDuke; married Wallace Humphrey (divorced, 1976); married John Dunn (a custodian), April 9, 1982; children: Wallis, Steven, Thomas, Annette, Esther, Charles.

Addresses

Home—P.O. Box 721, Cass Lake, MN 56633.

Career

Indian Health Service, Eagle Butte, SD, worked as a licensed practical nurse; *Grand Forks Herald,* Grand Forks, ND, worked as a feature writer; Minnesota Clergy and Laity Concerned, worked as program coordinator; Cass Lake High School, Cass Lake, MN, worked as coordinator of Stipend Program; *Native American Press/Ojibwe News,* area correspondent. Battered Women Services of Hubbard County, past member of board of directors; Northern Minnesota Religious Freedom Council, founding member; Warriors in the Struggle, founding member; Peace Lantern Committee, past

Anne M. Dunn

member; member of women's peace delegation to Chiapas, Mexico, 1996; U.S. delegate to the Mothers of the Earth World Peace Summit, Vienna, Austria, 1997; member of Pastors for Peace caravan to raise funds for humanitarian aid to the people of Chiapas and Nicaragua, 1997.

Awards, Honors

Nomination for Minnesota Book Award, 1996, for *When Beaver Was Very Great: Stories to Live By;* Bridging the Gap Recognition Award, 1997.

Writings

When Beaver Was Very Great: Stories to Live By, illustrated by Sharon L. White, Midwest Traditions (Mount Horeb, WI), 1995.

Grandmother's Gift: Stories from the Anishinabe, Holy Cow! Press (Duluth, MN), 1997.

Author of plays, including *Our Relatives Are Coming* (three-act), *Cora the Battered* (one-act soliloquy), and *Crow's Disgrace* (four-act). Columnist for *News from Indian Country.* Contributor of poems and essays to periodicals. *Beaver Tail Times,* past editor and publisher; coeditor, *Solidarity,* and *We the People....*

Selections from *When Beaver Was Very Great* have been translated into lyrics by Carson Gardner and some were set to music, released as "The Whispering Tree" by Mikoche (Bismark, ND).

Sidelights

Anne M. Dunn told *SATA:* "I am an Anishinabe Ojibwe grandmother who has walked many paths. I am a long-time advocate of protecting our natural resources and improving the way we educate our children. I coordinated the Cass Lake High School Stipend Program, the components of which included a cross-age tutoring project, student interns, and a panel of student speakers who addressed the issues of preventing early pregnancy and teenage parenting. For five years I edited and published the *Beaver Tail Times,* a monthly newsletter promoting positive human values, and I served for three years on the Peace Lantern Committee, which endeavors to promote peace and racial justice.

"My play, *Our Relatives Are Coming,* focuses on reconciliation among all nations. *Cora the Battered* is a one-act soliloquy which addresses the issues of domestic violence. *Crow's Disgrace* is a four-act play based on a traditional Ojibwe myth. Along with my mother, Maefred Arey, and my daughter Annette Humphrey I also produced a cassette collection of Anishinabe 'grandmother stories.'"

E

ELDON, Kathy 1946-

Personal

Born June 26, 1946, in Cedar Rapids, IA; daughter of Russell and Louise Knapp; married Michael Eldon, September 14, 1969; children: Dan (deceased), Amy. *Education:* Wellesley College, B.A., 1968. *Avocational interests:* Constant travel, films, Blazers Safe Haven, Kenya, photojournalism, talented young people.

Addresses

Home—Los Angeles, CA. *Agent*—Jane Dustel, 1 Union Square West, New York, NY 10003.

Career

Freelance journalist, film producer, author, art teacher, broadcaster, lecturer, media consultant, mother. *Member:* Committee to Protect Journalists, Overseas Press Club of America.

Writings

(Compiler, with Jean Kane and Nancy Swanborg) *Nairobi, All You Need to Know, But Don't Know Who to Ask: A Guide for Visitors and Residents in Kenya,* American Women's Association (Nairobi), 1979.

(With Eamon Mullan) *Tastes of Kenya: Epicurean Cuisine,* illustrated by Moyra Owens, Kenway Publications (Nairobi), 1981.

Making Music in Kenya, Macmillan, 1981.

Kathy Eldon's Eating Out Guide to Kenya, Kenway Publications, 1983.

(Compiler) *Specialties of the House from Kenya's Finest Restaurants,* edited by Clare Taylor, Kenway Publications, 1985.

Safari Journal, Kenway Publications, 1985.

(Compiler) *More Specialties of the House,* Kenway Publications, 1987.

(Editor) Dan Eldon, *The Journey Is the Destination: The Journals of Dan Eldon,* Chronicle Books, 1997.

Kathy Eldon

(With Amy Eldon) *Angel Catcher: A Journal of Loss and Remembrance,* Chronicle Books, 1998.

(With Amy Eldon) *Soul Catcher: A Journal to Help You Become Who You Really Are,* Chronicle Books, 1999.

(Editor) *The Art of Life,* Chronicle Books, 2000.

Also author, with Mike Eldon, of *Kitchens and Cooking, The Story of Medicine,* and *Tom-Tom to Television,* all in the "Eyewitness" series from Wayland.

Work in Progress

With Amy Eldon, *Stay in Touch,* a communications kit for parents and children; an autobiography titled *Soul on Fire.*

Sidelights

Kathy Eldon is a freelance journalist, author, producer, and editor with an eclectic assortment of publications to her name. With Mike Eldon, she published several works in Wayland's "Eyewitness" series for young readers. Their *Kitchens and Cooking* was praised by Eric Korn in *New Statesman* for its "confident" tone. *Times Educational Supplement* critic Rosemary O'Day wrote positively of *The Story of Medicine* and *Tom-Tom to Television,* the latter title concerning the history of human communication from early developments in writing to the latest in satellite transmitting. O'Day praised the authors' comprehensive coverage of their topics and said that the books are also written with "clarity and simplicity," in a style that "will have a wide appeal." On her own, Eldon has published several works on cooking and restaurants in Kenya, where she and her family lived for several years.

In 1993, Eldon's twenty-two-year-old son was killed while working as a freelance photojournalist for Reuters news service in Somalia. Dan Eldon, who had led an extraordinarily accomplished short life, was stoned to death by a mob reacting to the bombing of Mogadishu by an American helicopter. At the time of his death, Dan, who was the youngest photojournalist Reuters had ever employed, had accumulated seventeen volumes of journals, many of them containing collages of the young man's personal photographs and drawings. Kathy Eldon determined to have a selection from the journals published. One result of that determination was *The Journey Is the Destination,* a work that Joan Levin in *Library Journal* called "a somewhat offbeat, scrapbook-type publication" composed of bits of artwork from the journals. Kathy Eldon selected the pages and prefaced them in what Levin called "a painful tribute to her son." A reviewer for the online media retailer Amazon.com praised the journals, stating that the work testifies to Dan Eldon's "sophisticated vision and the purity and naivete of youth on the brink of adulthood." *USA Today* critic Deirdre R. Schwiesow, noting that Dan's death "resulted directly from a belief that he could make a positive difference," stated that the book is "ultimately hopeful and inspiring, despite its dark ending."

The Journey Is the Destination is only the first of several works inspired by the death of Dan Eldon. Others include *Angel Catcher: A Journal of Loss and Remembrance,* written by Eldon with daughter Amy for people who have lost a loved one; a Turner Television documentary on photojournalists, *Dying to Tell the Story,* that interweaves Dan Eldon's story with the lives of other journalists who risk their lives to do their jobs; plans for a Columbia Pictures film based on Eldon's life story to be written by Jan Sardi, directed by Bronwen Hughs, and co-produced by Kathy Eldon; and many exhibitions of the art and photography of Dan and the three colleagues who died with him in Somalia.

Eldon once commented: "I am in awe of great writers, whose words inspire us to be more than we think we can ever be. I would like to have known Ralph Waldo Emerson, whose irrepressible spirit makes me want to fling my laptop into Walden Pond and simply celebrate the gift of being alive."

Works Cited

Review of *The Journey Is the Destination: The Journals of Dan Eldon,* Amazon.com, http://www.amazon.com (July 28, 1998).

Korn, Eric, "Chefs Proper," *New Statesman,* May 24, 1974, p. 742.

Levin, Joan, review of *The Journey Is the Destination: The Journals of Dan Eldon, Library Journal,* November 1, 1997, p. 72.

O'Day, Rosemary, "Way of Progress?", *Times Educational Supplement,* May 26, 1978.

Schweisow, Deirdre R., "An Extraordinary 'Journey'," *USA Today,* January 5, 1998, p. 5D.

For More Information See

PERIODICALS

Baltimore Sun, March 27, 1994.
Publishers Weekly, August 25, 1997, p. 25.

*   *   *

EMERSON, Ru 1944-
(Roberta Cray, a pseudonym)

Personal

Born December 15, 1944, in Monterey, CA; daughter of William Hanan (an electrical technician) and Marcella Maxine (a commercial artist; maiden name, Case) Emerson; companion of Doug Garrety (a carpenter and photographer), 1972—. *Education:* Attended University of Montana, 1963-66; Los Angeles County Bar Association, bachelor's equivalent, 1977. *Politics:* Liberal.

Addresses

Home—2600 Rueben-Boise Rd., Dallas, OR 97338. *Agent*—Richard Curtis, 171 East 74th St., New York, NY 10021.

Career

Writer. Worked as a legal secretary in Century City, CA, 1975-86. *Member:* Science Fiction Writers of America.

Writings

FANTASY NOVELS

The Princess of Flames, Ace, 1986.
Spell Bound, Ace, 1990.
Masques (novelization of _Beauty and the Beast_ television
script), Avon, 1990.
(As Roberta Cray) _The Sword and the Lion,_ DAW, 1993.
(With Mercedes Lackey) _The Bard's Tale: Fortress of
Frost and Fire,_ Baen, 1993.
(With A. C. Crispin) _Voices of Chaos_ (seventh volume of
"Starbridge" series), Ace, 1998.

"NEDAO" TRILOGY

To the Haunted Mountains, Ace, 1987.
In the Caves of Exile, Ace, 1988.
On the Seas of Destiny, Ace, 1989.

"NIGHT-THREADS" SERIES

The Calling of the Three, Ace, 1990.
The Two in Hiding, Ace, 1991.
One Land, One Duke, Ace, 1992.
The Craft of Light, Ace, 1993.
The Art of the Sword, Ace, 1994.
The Science of Power, Ace, 1995.

"XENA, WARRIOR PRINCESS" SERIES

The Empty Throne, Boulevard, 1996.
The Huntress and the Sphinx, Boulevard, 1997.
The Thief of Hermes, Boulevard, 1997.
Warrior Princess Hunter, Boulevard, 1998.
The Xena Scrolls, HarperCollins, 1998.
Go Quest, Young Man, Ace, 1999.

OTHER

Against the Giants, TSR, 1999.

Also author of short stories and novellas.

Work in Progress

More novels, including installments in the "Xena"
series.

Sidelights

Ru Emerson is noted for her sword-and-sorcery fantasy
novels, including her series based on the popular _Xena,
Warrior Princess_ television series. According to _St.
James Guide to Fantasy Writers_ essayist Pauline Morgan, Emerson's strengths are her character development
and her "ability to tell an action-packed story."

Emerson was born in California but moved to Butte,
Montana, when she was five. She remained in Montana
until her early teens, and still considers it "home." "One
of the greatest things about Butte was the fact that the
teachers I had really encouraged reading," she once told
SATA, "and so did the public library. I started reading
long before first grade, thanks to my parents, and found
it easy to keep it up with that kind of encouragement."

By the time Emerson was nine she had embarked on a
career as a writer, although she did not know it at the
time. "At that time I was reading the 'Nancy Drew' and
'Hardy Boys' mysteries and almost had gone through all
of the existing books, so I fiddled with my own plots for
these characters. Sometime around then, I also began
writing stories for the westerns I watched on television.
Even though I was writing stories, I never thought I
might one day write for a living: I hadn't found a class
of book that filled me with lots of my own ideas, though
I tried a little of almost everything I read."

After graduating from high school, Emerson received a
music scholarship to the University of Montana. In
between course work, she read "voraciously," recalling:
"Oddly enough, with all the reading I did, I never once
read science fiction or fantasy in high school or college."
In 1966 Emerson moved to Los Angeles, where she
finally discovered fantasy literature. Finding a copy of J.
R. R. Tolkien's classic _The Hobbit_ in a local bookstore,
she was hooked: "I was back in the bookstore the next
day to buy the entire 'Lord of the Rings' trilogy," she
told _SATA._ By the early 1970s she had discovered the
works of such science-fiction writers as Andre Norton,
Anne McCaffrey, Alan Dean Foster, Roger Zelazny, and
C. J. Cherryh. "Suddenly, there simply couldn't be
enough of this kind of no-boundaries writing for me,"
she recalled, "and suddenly, too, I found myself full of
ideas for my own books." In 1978 Emerson began
working on what would eventually be published as the
"Nedao" trilogy, although she would publish other
works first.

Finding a publisher proved to be difficult, and in the
summer of 1983, while in the process of relocating to
Oregon, Emerson decided to commit herself to six
months of steady writing. She reworked a fantasy novel
that she had completed, and submitted it to Ace. _The
Princess of Flames_ was published three years later, and
Ace acquired the rights to Emerson's "Nedao" trilogy as
well.

In _The Princess of Flames,_ Elfrid is forced into exile
with her father, King Alster, after her older brother
Sedry usurps the throne. Disguising herself as a boy,
Elfrid enjoys numerous adventures in her travels with
her father, encountering many forms of magic in their
quest to regain the King's throne. In her essay in _St.
James Guide to Fantasy Writers,_ Pauline Morgan
praised _The Princess of Flames_ as "an excellent debut
for a fresh, enthusiastic writer" and commented on
Emerson's "great sense of pace" and the parallels
between the novel's plot and that of William Shakespeare's _King Lear._

In the "Nedao" trilogy, Emerson introduces readers to
the fantastic kingdom of Nedao as seen through the eyes
of the story's narrator, a magical cat named Nisana.
Forced to flee from her castle home after an invasion of
warriors, Princess Ylia finds herself orphaned and alone,
save for Nisana. The three novels recount Ylia's travels,
both across the treacherous landscape bordering the
kingdom of Nedao, and into adulthood, as she learns to

take care of herself and to develop the magical skills inherited from her mother. Ylia becomes a super-heroine and the leader of her refugee clan; the final book of the series, *On the Seas of Destiny,* finds her defending her people against an attack by her evil cousin, Vess.

One of the characteristics of Emerson's fiction is the "coming of age" theme, which is embodied in several of her main characters. "I'm not certain I originally planned this," she commented, "though I am fascinated by people of whatever age who lack nerve or social skills, or inner strength, and what kinds of events would push them to becoming brave and strong." In Emerson's "Night-Threads" series, a boy named Chris must learn new skills necessary to adapt to his changing circumstances. Introduced in *The Calling of the Three,* Chris is the son of Jennifer, an attorney who, along with her laid-back sister Robyn, is drawn into another world where they attempt to help the spoiled Lialla and her handicapped brother Aletto. A conflict of personalities as well as of cultures ensues, mediated by Chris, and the three women work together to help Aletto gain the throne that should, by rights, be his. Praising the first three volumes of the "Night-Threads" series in *Booklist,* contributor Roland Green noted that Emerson's work "could be held up as a model of how to write readable fantasy adventure."

Later volumes of the series find Chris full grown and engaging in adult pursuits. In *The Art of the Sword* he is tricked into marriage with Ariadne by her conniving father in order to gain favor with the ruling family. Gradually learning to get along, the couple are soon bound together by a common thread: because they have not helped him in his machinations, Ariadne's father would like to see them both dead. Praising the novel as part of an "excellent series," *Voice of Youth Advocates* contributor Vicky Burkholder advised reading the series from the beginning, so that "the reader gets the background to make what happens in this book understandable."

Emerson has contributed to other series of novels in addition to creating her own. *The Bard's Tale: Fortress of Frost and Fire* was co-authored with veteran fantasy writer Mercedes Lackey; Lackey drafted the outline and Emerson fleshed it out into a full-length novel. With A. C. Crispin, Emerson created *Voices of Chaos,* a part of Crispin's "Starbridge" science-fiction series about a growing space-based league of nations and the efforts of an undesirable race to gain entrance. "Crispin and Emerson keep the writing ... as intelligent as ever," according to *Booklist* contributor Roland Green.

In an interview with Phil Howell for the Web site *Whoosh!,* an online journal devoted to *Xena, Warrior Princess,* Emerson described her experiences as a professional author: "To me, character is the driving force of all my writing. I will come up with a loose plot idea on my own and then sit down and figure out who the characters are, where they came from, and I might go down to what color underwear they wear and what they eat for breakfast before I start writing. With the Xena books I had a little more of an outline on each of them, but things will come in mid-book, half-way through, three-quarters of the way through in characterization that surprise the heck out of me. I just had no clue these people were going to be in there. So it's more character building, but I always do start out with a beginning, a middle, and an end, at least, and sometimes more than that in the way of structure .... I try to write at least three and a half chapters before I go back and do any cleaning up on the early stuff .... Generally by the time I get down to the last three or four chapters it doesn't need rewrite at all." Her advice to fledgling writers? "Write a lot and read everything you can. Then, write a lot more .... The winnowing out process is going to be hellish and harsh. If you've got two typos on the first page, if you've got three grammatical errors in the first chapter, ... you're going to get it kicked back and you'll never know why."

"Something I've always believed, particularly since my books have hit the stands, is that I have a responsibility to try and instill in others the kind of love of writing I grew up with," Emerson once confided to *SATA.* "Too many kids pick up on an attitude in school that reading is 'what I have to do' .... I think that [getting kids to turn off the TV and pick up a book] can only be done by writing exciting, immediate fiction, and possibly someday I'll feel I've really done a good job of that."

Works Cited

Burkholder, Vicky, review of *The Art of the Sword, Voice of Youth Advocates,* April, 1995, p. 33.

Emerson, Ru, interview with Phil Howell, *Whoosh!,* http://whoosh.org/issue5/emerson.html (January 26, 1999).

Green, Roland, review of *One Land, One Duke, Booklist,* February 1, 1992, p. 1014.

Green, Roland, review of *Voices of Chaos, Booklist,* March 1, 1998, p. 1098.

Morgan, Pauline, essay on Emerson in *St. James Guide to Fantasy Writers,* St. James Press, 1996, pp. 182-83.

For More Information See

PERIODICALS

Booklist, February 15, 1989, p. 976; September 15, 1990, p. 104; October 15, 1990, p. 421; April 15, 1991, p. 1627.

Kliatt, January, 1991, p. 20; July, 1993, p. 16.

Voice of Youth Advocates, June, 1986, p. 87; June, 1988, p. 95; October, 1990, p. 228; April, 1991, p. 42.

*   *   *

ERICSON, Walter
See FAST, Howard

F

Howard Fast

1914-

My father, Barney Fast, was a workingman all of his life. He was born in 1869 in the town of Fastov in the Ukraine and was brought to the United States in 1878, aged nine, by his older brother, Edward. Immigration shortened Fastov to Fast, gave it to him as a last name, and so it remained.

In 1897, working in a tin factory in Whitestone, Long Island, my father made friends with a young man named Daniel Miller. Miller's family had moved from Lithuania to London a generation before, and Daniel, one of a family of five sons and two daughters, had made his way to America alone. When the war with Spain began, Barney and Dan and a few other Jewish boys working at the tin factory organized a regiment to fight in Cuba and thereby revenge themselves for the expulsion of Jews from Spain in 1492. They persuaded enough non-Jews to join up to make a regiment of three hundred men, and one of the bookkeepers at the plant, a man in his middle sixties named Charlie Hensen, who claimed to have been a cavalry officer during the Civil War, offered to train the three hundred as a cavalry regiment. That was not as loony a proposition as it sounds, for the war in Cuba was disorganized, with all sorts of citizens getting into the act—as witness Theodore Roosevelt and his Rough Riders.

Hensen collected twenty-five percent of each man's pay, with which he proposed to buy uniforms, sabers, and horses. But after a few months, Hensen and the money disappeared, and Barney never did get to Cuba. He did, however, become bosom pals with Danny Miller, and Danny showed Barney a picture of his beautiful sister. My father fell in love with the picture, began to correspond with Ida Miller, saved his money, sent her a steamship ticket for passage to America, and in due time married her. In 1904 their first child, Rena, was born, and in 1906 they had a son named Arthur, a sensitive, beautiful boy that I know only from photographs. He died of diphtheria six

years later. My brother Jerome was born in March of 1913, and I came in November of the following year. My mother's last child, Julius, was born in 1919. My mother died of pernicious anemia in the spring of 1923, when I was eight-and-a-half years old.

We were always poor, but while my mother lived, we children never realized that we were poor. My father, at the age of fourteen, had been an ironworker in the open-shed furnaces on the East River below Fourteenth Street. There the wrought iron that festooned the city was hammered into shape at open forges. As a kid, Barney had run for beer for the big, heavy-muscled men who hammered out the iron at the blazing forges, and there was nothing else he wanted to do. But the iron sheds disappeared as fashions in building changed, and Barney went to work as a gripper man on one of the last cable cars in the city. From there to the tin factory and finally to being a cutter in a dress factory. He never earned more than forty dollars a week during my mother's lifetime, yet with this forty dollars my mother made do. She was a wise woman, and if a wretched tenement was less than her dream of America, she would not surrender. She scrubbed and sewed and knitted. She made all of the clothes for all of her children, cutting little suits out of velvet and fine wools and silks; she cooked and cleaned with a vengeance, and to me she seemed a sort of princess, with her stories of London and Kew and Kensington Gardens and the excitement and tumult of Petticoat Lane and Covent Garden. Memories of this beautiful lady, whose speech was so different from the speech of others around me, were wiped out in the moment of her death. I remember my father coming into the tiny bedroom where I slept with Jerome, waking us gently, and saying, "Momma died last night." Although I was very young, I must have known what death meant—my mother had been sick for over a year—for at that moment my mind had to choose between memory and madness, and forget-

Howard Fast, 1992

fulness and sanity. My mind chose forgetfulness so that I could remain sane. The process is not uncommon and is called infantile amnesia; it was not until years later that my memories of my mother began to return.

Because my memories of my mother were wiped out in a flash, the dark-haired woman who lay in the open coffin in our tiny living room—packed with family and curious neighbors—was strange to me. I wept dutifully. My mother's brother Gerry, a young physician and the only solvent member of the family, pressed a silver dollar into my hand, and it quieted my tears. I had never seen anything like it before.

All the dismal business of a death in poverty, of the tragedy of my poor father left with three small children and a nineteen-year-old girl who had been coddled and treasured by her mother to the point of becoming a spoiled child, shattered by her mother's death, does remain in my memory. For a few months after my mother's death, my sister tried to keep the family together, but more and more she saw herself trapped, doomed to spinsterhood by the responsibility of caring for three little boys. So acute was

her fear that she plunged into marriage, compounding the tragedy and leaving my bewildered father to take care of the three small children. Jerome and I hated the man she married. His only virtue in our eyes was that he was British, somehow distantly related to us by marriage, but he was insensitive and stupid.

I loved my sister—and did so to the day of her death—but my father was shattered by her departure. My maternal grandmother—I never saw my father's parents—took my brother Julius to live with her in Long Island. He was only four years old, and there was no way my father could take care of him. Indeed, there was no way my father could take care of Jerome and me.

My father was a dear and gentle man, a gentleman in every sense of the word, but his own mother had died when he was seven years old, and the death of his wife threw him into a deep depression. I know that several women loved him, but he never married again. If he had, possibly my life would have been different, but as it was, my brother and I were left from morning to night on our own, with no one to turn to, no one to care for or feed us—with a father who was depressed and disoriented and often did not come home until well past midnight, plunging Jerome and me into periods of terror that were to be repeated again and again.

The years that followed provided an experience in poverty and misery that was burned into my soul. In time, nothing much changed in the scheme of poverty; what did change was my ability to face and alter circumstances. I ceased to be wholly a victim. The place where we lived was a wretched slum apartment, made lovely by the wit and skill and determination of my mother; but after her death and the departure of my sister, the place simply disintegrated. Jerome and I, two small boys essentially on our own, had to be mother and father and brother to each other. Jerome cared for me; to the best of my ability, I cared for him. My father disappeared each morning at 8 A.M. and rarely did he return until after midnight; periodically, he was out of work. We made some efforts to keep the apartment clean, but that's not within the scope of small boys. The apartment became dirty; the cheap furniture began to come apart; trash accumulated. In his depression, my father seemed unaware of what was happening. We had holes in our clothes, our shoes were coming apart, and Pop made only an occasional effort to rectify things.

In actuality, we had no childhood; it slipped away. When I was ten and Jerome was eleven, we decided to take things in hand. My brother was like a rock, and without him I surely would have perished. We needed money, and Jerome had heard somewhere that you could make money delivering newspapers, in particular the *Bronx Home News,* which existed entirely on home delivery with a system worked out by a man named Keneally. I don't recall his first name, and there's no way I can find it, but I remember

The author in 1946.

him with great fondness. He had an office in Washington Heights, and one day after school, Jerry and I made our way there and presented ourselves to Mr. Keneally, a tall, lean, long-faced man.

I can imagine how we appeared to him, two ragged kids with long, shaggy hair, holes in our shoes, holes in our stockings. "We can do it!" Jerry pleaded, and Keneally said okay, he'd give us a chance, even though we were too young to do a proper route. But one of his boys had left, and maybe the two of us together could do one route. He was very kind. He was of the generation of Irish who had fought their way up from the starkest poverty, and he understood. We were given a book of some ninety customers who took daily papers, including Saturday and Sunday, and each week we had to collect twelve cents from each customer. We paid a straight price for our bundle, and it amounted to about two out of every twelve cents—a price we paid whether we were able to collect or not.

So my working life began, at age ten, and from then until I was twenty-two years old I had one job or another: for three years delivering the *Bronx Home News,* then working for a cigarmaker on Avenue B on the East Side, then a hatmaker on West Thirty-eighth Street, then making deliveries and cleaning at an uptown butcher shop, and then at the 115th Street branch of the New York Public Library. When I left the library, I worked for a year in a dress factory, first as a shipping clerk and then as a presser—at least a presser in training. Meanwhile, I finished grade school, went to high school, got a scholarship to the National Academy of Design, and worked there for a year. I gave it up when, at the age of seventeen, I sold my first short story.

The first toll poverty takes is human dignity, and no family in abject poverty lives like the Crachits in Charles Dickens's *A Christmas Carol.* He was faulted on that, and he wrote *The Chimes* to show the other side of the coin, but he left out the sense that every poverty-stricken family has of a world put together wrong. It was particularly evident in New York, where the poor lived cheek by jowl with the rich. The rich were always evident, the people I so catalogued then, those who lived on Riverside Drive and Fort Washington Avenue. They were middle-class people, but we had nothing, and to us they were wealthy in the only way we knew wealth. In those days of the 1920s, there was no safety net beneath the poor, no welfare, no churches handing out free dinners. Survival in poverty was your own affair. I have tried to explain this to people who expressed indignant wonder at the fact that I joined the Communist party. The absence of unemployment insurance is educational in a way that nothing else is.

One of the main reasons, perhaps, for our survival as a family unit was the place where we lived. The anti-Semitism that prevailed was maniacal; there is no other way to describe it. And this crazed Christian sickness forced Jerry and me at first, then Julius with us, into a closed, defensive unit. Aside from my uncle's family in the summer, no relative held out a hand to us. Some of them were well-to-do; all of them lived comfortably, but my father's pride forbade his asking for help, and none was offered. They were a lousy crew, and I'll say no more about them.

We didn't complain, Jerry and I, and in a sense the challenge of keeping the family alive was a game we

Howard and Bette Fast with their two children, Jonathan, five, and Rachel, nine, winter 1953-54.

played. We lived in two worlds, the wretched world of reality and the marvelous, endlessly exciting world of the books we read. In those days, bread, milk, and cheese were delivered very early in the morning to the doors of the prosperous. When we had no food, we'd be up at six in the morning to find bread and milk and cheese that would keep us alive. We did not consider it stealing; we never questioned our right to remain alive. Once, we appropriated—a better word—an entire stalk of bananas from a truck. Some we kept for ourselves, eating bananas until we could not face another. The rest we sold for a nickel a hand. When we were utterly penniless and my father was unemployed, we scoured the neighborhood for milk bottles, a nickel for each returned. We knew the back way into every house in the area; we knew the rooftops.

When I turned fourteen, in 1928, I reached an age of maturity, the difference from childhood being, to my mind, the difference between being a victim without recourse and a sort of adult with recourse. My brother and I had arrived at an age where we could change things. Filth was no longer a permanent part of our existence; it could be dealt with and done away with. We were working and Barney was working, making fifty dollars a week, the most he had ever earned per week in all his life. Julius was living with us now, aged nine years old, and both Jerry and I felt a sense of responsibility toward him. We informed Barney that we were going to move out of that miserable slum apartment, and when he put up a storm of protest—he was incapable of altering his living place—we said that we'd move without him. Jerry and I were both working for the

New York Public Library at that point, paid thirty cents an hour, a sum that was reduced to twenty-five cents an hour after the great stock market crash; and with extra time on Wednesday and Saturday, I took home nine dollars a week and Jerry eleven. Twenty dollars was not to be sneezed at—indeed, in our world it was a princely sum—and it bought us food and clothes. With Barney's fifty dollars added to our twenty, there was an income of seventy dollars a week, unimaginable riches. It did not last very long, but long enough to get us out of 159th Street and up to Inwood at the northern tip of Manhattan.

I began to think. From the time when the street became my life, I had plotted, schemed, maneuvered, manipulated, cozened, and, when the need arose, pleaded; and these are all mental activities, but by thinking I mean putting one fact against another and trying to measure the result. This kind of thinking is a very special thing.

The winter of 1929-1930 I worked at the public library in lower Harlem, at 203 West 115th Street. I was poorly paid—down to twenty-five cents an hour that winter—but I loved working in the library. The walls of books gave me a sense of history, of order, of meaning in this strange world, and I could easily pick up two, three, sometimes four hours of overtime in a week. I worked from four to nine, closing time, for five days and on Saturday from nine to one. Since we did checking and arranging on Saturdays, I could pick up the overtime there, and I could always slip down to the closed reference shelves in the basement to get my homework done. My wages averaged between seven and eight dollars a week, but in the shattered prices of deflation, that was decent money. The important thing was the world of books around me. I read everything without discrimination—psychology, astronomy, physics, history, and more history—and some of it I understood and some of it I didn't.

And I began to think.

The subway ride I took to my home was a nickel. At the uptown end of the subway, where I left the train, a man in a blue serge suit, jacket and vest and tie—a man of some fifty years—stood out on the street and sold apples for a nickel each. Every night on my way home I bought an apple, a large, shiny Washington State Delicious apple. I bought the apple because I was hungry, because the man touched something very deep inside of me, and because I had begun to think. This went on for several weeks. I was a kid with a job; he was a mature man, a businessman or an accountant or something of the sort to my guess. I thought of my father. Barney was a workingman; this was a middle-class educated man, and one night he stopped me.

"Hey, kid," he said, "what's your name?"

"Howard Fast."

"That's an odd name," he said. "Do they call you a fast worker?"

I stared at him without answering, and then I blurted out, "Do you have kids, mister?"

Now he stared at me, and then he began to cry. Tears—real tears. I don't know whether I had ever seen a grown man cry, and it remains in my memory as one of the most woeful moments of my life.

I grabbed my apple, pressed a nickel into his hand, and ran. I ran all the way home. He was gone the next day, and I never saw him again. There are theories that the level of consciousness varies from time to time and that most of our lives are lived at a very low level of consciousness, almost like a walking sleep. Memory is sharpest when it recalls the highest moments of consciousness; I believe this, and that moment scared my mind.

Other things were working on my personal mental schematic. I had seen my father on strike; I had seen him locked out; I had seen his head bloodied on a picket line. I had watched the economy of my own country collapse; I had seen the packing-crate villages grow on the riverfront. I did not have to be instructed about poverty or hunger; I had lived them both. I had fought and been beaten innumerable times, not because of my religion—Barney never imposed religion on us, for which I am eternally grateful—but because I was Jewish, and all of it worked together to create in my mind a simple plea, that somewhere, somehow, there was in this world an explanation that made sense.

That was my way. I never faulted the other ways. I knew kids who were arrested, who turned into thieves or ran with the gangs—it was the time of Prohibition—and I understood this, and often enough I said to myself, "There but for the grace of God goes Howard Fast." I was lucky. One of the kids ended up in the electric chair. Oh, I was damned lucky.

Jerry found a copy of *The Iron Heel* by Jack London. At that time, Jack London stood first among our literary heroes. Today, I find his prose flowery and too mannered, but our taste was less demanding then, and we read and reread every book of his on the library shelves—except for *The Iron Heel.* We never could find a copy in the library. The head librarian at 115th Street was a Mrs. Lindsay, a very dignified and tall woman, a distant relative I think of the man who was to become our mayor. I got up the courage to ask her why we didn't have *The Iron Heel,* and she informed me that it was considered a Bolshevik book. She had never read it, and she hoped I was not interested in such things.

Fast as candidate for Congress, twenty-third congressional district, New York City, 1952.

How could I not be interested? *Bolshevik* was a wild word at that time; it was not so long before that the Bolsheviks had burst into history. You couldn't pick up a copy of the *Daily News,* the *Mirror,* or the *Graphic* without having the infamies of the Bolsheviks scream at you from the front page. The word, Russian for "majority," has gone out of use today, but then it was the number one synonym for evil.

The Iron Heel was my first real contact with socialism; the book was passed around among the kids I knew at high school. If I had lived on the Lower East Side or in one of Brooklyn's immigrant enclaves, I would have had a taste of socialism with my mother's milk, but in this solidly Irish-Italian block there was no hint of it, and at that time George Washington High School was middle-class, filled with well-dressed boys and girls who had allowances and money for a decent lunch in the school cafeteria. Against this background, *The Iron Heel* had a tremendous effect on me. London anticipated fascism as no writer of the time did; indeed no historian or social scientist of the time had even an inkling of the blueprint Jack London laid out, which came into being a few decades after his death. In it, he drew the struggle against fascism by an underground socialist movement, and he did it so convincingly that we were not quite sure that what he wrote of had not already happened.

It was the beginning of my trying to understand why society was structured as I saw it to be structured. Communist bashing became so pervasive in the 1960s and 1970s that few people even attempted to understand or inquire into the forces that produced socialist thinking and, out of it, the Communist movement.

And then, one day, arranging books in the library, I came upon Shaw's *The Intelligent Woman's Guide to Socialism and Capitalism,* and the die was cast.

I think I read somewhere that Shaw had so named his book to excite the curiosity of men, and I had also heard that he believed women to be more intelligent than men—a belief I share. In any case, *The Intelligent Woman's Guide to Socialism and Capitalism* is the clearest exposition of the subject I know of. I was then sixteen, and the book provided me with a new way of thinking about poverty, inequality, and injustice. Shaw had opened an enormous Pandora's box, and never in my lifetime would I be able to close it. The book also set me off in a new direction in my reading, and in quick succession I read Thorstein Veblen's *The Theory of the Leisure Class,* Bellamy's *Looking Backward,* and Engels's *The Origin of the Family.* My mind exploded with ideas. I hurt dear Hallie Jamison, my wonderful high school English teacher, by engaging her in a discussion of whether any nation involved in World War One had been fighting a just war—her beloved having died on the western front—and I made a general nuisance of myself because of my obsession for knowing everything there was to know. In his novel *Martin Eden,* Jack London had stated unequivocally that a writer must have a total knowledge of science. I believed him and set out to gain just that, even reading a bit of Herbert Spencer—recommended by London—in the process. Still in high school, I found psychology, read the Watsonians and rejected them, read the Gestalt theorists and liked them a little better, read the Binet-Simon book on testing, gave intelligence tests to everyone I could corner, and thereby washed myself out of the process, for when it came time for me to be tested at

Recipient of the International Peace Prize, with daughter, Rachel, and wife, Bette, 1951.

school, I explained that I knew the tests forward and backward. Result—I never knew my own IQ and took comfort in that.

I decided to become a writer. There was no problem in making this decision. It was the only way of life I ever considered, from as far back as my memory goes. I decided to be a writer, to write stories and books, and to illustrate them myself. I had no desire to become an easel painter—only to be able to illustrate what I wrote in the manner of Howard Pyle and N. C. Wyeth. They were my idols; the marvelous illustrations they did for books and magazines constituted my approach to art.

We had pulled the family together and out of the wretched morass of poverty and misery. Jerry and I were earning enough to keep the family going on a decent basis even when Barney was out of work. You didn't need much to get by in the early thirties. Jerry rooted jobs out of everywhere and nowhere, and when I graduated from high school I was earning nine dollars a week as a page at the 115th Street library. The Morris Plan gave small loans on the strength of co-workers, without collateral. Their interest amounted to twenty-seven percent, but we somehow got Jerry through his first year of college and paid back the loan. I applied to both Cooper Union and the National Academy, then a sprawl of old-fashioned studio buildings at 110th Street, just east of the Cathedral of St. John the Divine. The waiting list at Cooper Union was years in length; the National Academy accepted me for immediate entrance.

I enrolled at the National Academy. By God, I had done it. I was seventeen years old, and I was alive and healthy, when by all the odds I should have been either dead or hopelessly weak and sick. With my brothers and my father, I had a clean, proper home, a bed without bedbugs—as a kid they had made my life in bed a nightmare—books of my own, shoes without holes, a warm winter overcoat, and above all, I was a scholarship student at what was then the most prestigious art school in America. And as yet, I had done no time in jail, and that was not the least of my accomplishments, for I was not a quiet or contemplative kid, but one of those irritating,

Bette Fast in sculpture studio, 1972.

impossible, doubting, questioning mavericks, full of anger and invention and wild notions, accepting nothing, driving my peers to bitter arguments and driving my elders to annoyance, rage, and despair. I probably had some good points as well.

And I was innocent—not simply unsophisticated, but innocent in the sense that I was free of hate. That applied to both of my brothers too; we were without hate. As far as sophistication was concerned, that was a quality you had to pick up along the way.

I had become a writer and I would remain a writer. The question of ever being anything else never entered my mind; there was only one thing I could be in this life and that was what I was. Each morning I arose at six and wrote. Two hours later, I left for the National Academy, where I practiced cast and figure drawing in the severe and tedious classical manner. I completed a story every few days and as promptly dispatched it to one magazine or another. It's hard to recall and believe in my own naïveté, for all those first stories were handwritten in ink, and my altered handwriting—I was left-handed—was not easily read. After sending out about a dozen stories, I happened to mention to one of the librarians what I was doing, and to my dismay she informed me that no magazine would bother to read a handwritten story. Either I typed out my stories or forgot the whole matter.

We had a family discussion. After all, since I read each story aloud to my brothers once it was done, they had a sort of vested interest, and it was agreed that we would put out $1.75 to rent a typewriter for a month. I had to learn to use it, and while I made a few attempts at touch typing, I soon gave that up and settled into the two-finger method, which I continue to use. I kept the typewriter for a second and then a third month, and then, incredibly, I sold a story.

Looking back, I find it astonishing; at the time, I felt it to be a miracle. It was not that I had no expectations of selling stories—I was supremely confident that one day I would—but it was a date in the indefinite future, and here, miracle of miracles, it had happened. The story was titled

"Wrath of the Purple," and the purchaser, for thirty-seven dollars in honest American money, was *Amazing Stories* magazine, the first of the science-fiction magazines.

In 1931, thirty-seven dollars was a substantial sum of money—at least at my level of society. I was still working at the library, going there directly from the academy, but the best I could do at the library, even with all the overtime I could squeeze out of the job, was nine dollars a week, and here one story had brought me more than a month's pay. Now that I had reached my full height of five feet, ten-and-one-half inches, my work at the library changed. Rather than rearranging books, putting returned books back on the shelves, and seeing that all the reference numbers read in proper sequence, I was put to the business of tracking down overdue books, going to the apartments of the people who had borrowed them, and reclaiming them—and if possible collecting the fines. The fine, I recall, was two cents per day per book.

I wrote my first novel when I was sixteen. I had never heard of anyone having a novel published at sixteen, but I said to myself, "Why not a first time?" I finished it, read it through, and decided that it was so bad the best thing I could do with it was consign it to the trash can. The second novel dealt with my year at the academy. It was titled "To Be an Artist." I brought it by hand to three publishers; each one asked me to come and get it—without comment. I was not deterred. I sold a story to a pulp magazine, and it brought me forty dollars.

I wrote my heart out every morning, and I went to work for the hatmaker. As the months passed, I discovered something that I had suspected for many years but had been unable to come to grips with: that the most wonderful, beautiful, and desirable of God's creatures was called a woman. To a boy of seventeen, this phenomenon is shrouded in frustration and ineptitude. I fell passionately in love with a girl named Marjorie. The problem was that, what with working at a job, writing, trying to educate myself, and sharing in the housekeeping, cleaning and cooking, of our male ménage, I had no time to deal with young love.

I learned about the bookstalls on lower Fourth Avenue (now Park Avenue South), hundreds of open stalls, thousands of books, and for forty cents I bought a battered copy of *Das Kapital* by one Karl Marx. Not too many years before, I had regarded books as things that existed only in the New York Public Library; now I was creating my own library, but as far as *Das Kapital* was concerned, I fought my way through two hundred pages or so and then surrendered. George Bernard Shaw did much better with explanation. *The Communist Manifesto,* which I bought for ten cents, a worn pamphlet, was full of brimstone and fire and much more to my taste. I fell in love with a girl named Thelma. I fell in love with a girl named Maxine.

When someone asks me how and why I became a Socialist and a Communist, the answer is always inadequate. Intellectuals deal with ideas and abstractions. Never having had enough education to become a proper intellectual, I have spent my life dealing with facts and events, and this journey has burned itself into my memory. I have tried to write these events as I experienced them, with no broader perspective than I had at the time and without giving them too much importance. I left home and spent a month wandering through the South, looking for work, seeing a land as different from New York City as night from day. I journeyed through a society in disintegration, saved from inner destruction by World War Two, still six years in the future. And through all this, I never whimpered or turned a thought against this land which I had come to love so, nor can I ever think of the South without recalling not the jails and the guns but the wonderful slow wagon ride through the Peedee Swamp, arguing the Civil War with the southern kids. But I had reached an age where the innocence, born not of faith but of intolerable poverty, was beginning to crumble and where I began to understand that society could be planned and function in another way, called socialism; and because I came to believe that the only serious socialist party in America was the Communist party, I was bitterly attacked and slandered for fifteen years of my life.

I went to work. I found work as a shipping clerk in a dress factory in the heart of the garment center, and I wrote, morning and evening, six, seven, eight hours a day. I had written three complete unpublished novels before I took off for the South. I wrote two more in the few months after I returned. Five novels—one a five-hundred-page opus. They are best unremembered. The sixth novel, which I called *Two Valleys,* found a publisher.

This first publisher was the old original Dial Press, and the man who accepted the book was the editor in chief of that distinguished publishing house, a gentleman by the name of Grenville Vernon. I received a one-hundred-dollar advance, and the book was sold to the British publishing house Michael Joseph. The fact that the author was not yet nineteen was made much of, and while the novel was no great work of art, it was a gentle and readable book, a love story set in Colonial times in the mountains of what is today West Virginia. The reviews were decent and kind, with many bows to my age, but sales were inconsequential because the owner of the company, Lincoln MacVeagh, had put the house up for sale. For all that, I was recognized as a bright new hope on the literary horizon. I was given a Bread Loaf Award, and I spent two weeks at that lovely spot in the Green Mountains eating marvelous food, learning the finer points in the use of knives and forks, watching the critic John Mason Brown and his colleagues drink more martinis than I had ever imagined human beings could consume and make sense, and falling moderately but romantically in love with Gladys Hasty Carroll, a very popular and beautiful writer of the time and about ten years older than I. I actually gathered the courage to tell her I loved her before the session finished, but that was as far as it went, and I never saw her again. She was very kind to me.

Suddenly everything dried up and I stopped writing. Months went by and I wrote nothing. I continued to work in the garment factory. I trundled trucks through the streets and packed cases and learned to use a pressing machine and a felling machine, and worked my way up to twelve and then fourteen dollars a week, and dated a beautiful girl who worked in a publishing house; we parted because beyond subway fare to work and back, a nickel each way, and fifteen cents more for lunch at the Automat, brown beans and coffee, I had nothing, not even a decent pair of pants. Jerry was in his third year of college—we managed that somehow—and Julius was in high school, and everybody worked, and our need to hold the family together, now that two of us were adults and my younger brother was pushing adulthood, was almost demonic. Barney could rarely get better than the lowest paid job, but we managed, with a kind of crazy pride that we took no welfare or outside help of any kind. Interestingly, my father, a loyal Democrat and for years a county commissioner who worshipped Al Smith, was always reminded by the local Democratic boss that if worse came to worst, the party would step in. I think of how many times he came around to check Pop's vote, have a shot of bootleg gin, and say to him, "You know, Barney, that the party will never let you or the kids go hungry." Well, there were times when we were hungry, but we never dunned the party, and Barney always rejected their annual turkey, with instructions that they give it to some poor family.

And then I went back to writing. Up each morning at six, dress, chew a sweet roll, drink a glass of milk, and write. Two more pulp stories were sold, and I paid a semester of Jerry's tuition. On and off, as I would hit a short-story sale, I would pay tuition. I fought for my writing now, so the two hours before I went to work were daily agony. More and more deeply aware of my own position, I struggled to write about myself. I put together a story about a little boy, living in the street I lived on, whom I called Ishky. I coined the name because it sounded very Jewish, and I had his mother speak only the most broken English; but when his mother's Yiddish was translated

The author in 1980.

Celebrating Louis Untermeyer's ninety-second birthday in Weston, Connecticut. Top row, from left: Bette, Jon, Howard Fast, and Untermeyer's son. Bottom row: Brynn Untermeyer, Louis Untermeyer, and Erica Jong Fast.

formally, it emerged as classical English, full of *thee*'s and *thou*'s. I got the idea from Henry Roth's wonderful book, *Call It Sleep.* Ishky had one friend, a little Italian boy, my friend then, who played the fiddle and who, because he was a shoemaker's son, we called Shoemake. The body of the story concerned the lynching of a black kid. My story would be called *The Children,* and I wrote and rewrote, and tore up what I had and wrote it again, and drank coffee and smoked. Drink had no allure for me; nicotine had.

But cigarettes cost money. The factory where I did my eight or nine hours of survival work each day had a solidly Jewish-immigrant working force—cutters, machine operators, everyone—and the chatter and gossip that never stopped were carried on in Yiddish. On my first day there, when I had to have orders translated, they named me *goy,* Yiddish for Gentile. I had picked up the cigarette habit from a waiter I worked with one summer, but brand cigarettes were twelve cents a pack—even the lowly Wings were eight or ten cents a pack, depending on where you bought them—and this cut into food money. Therefore I

bought one pack a week, treasured it at home as a crutch for writing, and depended on my bumming talents for daytime smoking. And since I never smoked more than two or three cigarettes during working time, and since practically everyone in the factory smoked, I could always find a butt. But only if I asked for it in Yiddish, and thereby my first Yiddish word was *papiros,* Yiddish for cigarette. Whatever my question, the workers would fling back at me, *"Freg mir in Yidish"* (Ask me in Yiddish).

Then a day came when I decided that *The Children* was as finished as it would ever be. My two published books and my handful of sold stories had persuaded a literary agency to accept me as one of its writers. The agency was McIntosh and Otis and was run by three pleasant ladies, Mavis McIntosh, Elizabeth Otis, and Mary Abbott. They were middle-class literary types, good agents, and to me characters out of an Edwardian novel. An additional attraction for me was that on the little table in their waiting room they kept a wooden box of cigarettes. I gave them *The Children*—forty-five thousand words of it—

and washed my hands of it. I decided that I would continue as a writer, but there would be no more about myself and my childhood. It was too close, too confusing, and too filled with pain.

Whit Burnett, publisher of *Story* magazine, bought *The Children* and published it. *Story* was the most distinguished magazine of the short story in America at a time when the short story was at its peak as an art form internationally and when American short stories were read and admired the world over—which says nothing for the finances of *Story.* Burnett paid fifty dollars for forty-five thousand words, by word count—still the practice at the time—one tenth of a cent per word. I was absolutely enraged when Mary Abbott telephoned to give me this offer, and I fumed and ranted until she convinced me that Whit Burnett published at a loss and that such was the reputation and distinction of *Story* that it could only profit me even if he paid me not a penny. Mary felt that it was a very good thing for young writers to struggle and make do, but the young writers she knew came from proper middle-class families and good universities with fallback. I had no fallback whatsoever. Nevertheless, she convinced me that *Story* was the proper place for the short novel I had written. I told her to go ahead, but it would have to be one hundred dollars. On and off, I had put a year into the book, and even as a newspaper delivery boy at the age of ten, I had not worked for two dollars a week. Also, since I had received an advance of one hundred dollars for each of my two published books, I might as well keep my price up. (That's a joke; I would not want it misunderstood.)

The Children was published in the March issue of *Story,* a year and a half after Bette, my wife to be, and I met. Since it was so long a piece, it took practically all of the magazine. James J. Fee, the police inspector of Lynn, Massachusetts, was put onto it, and he read the first copy of *Story* he had ever read, and probably the first book he had ever read. He proclaimed that *The Children* was "the rottenest thing I ever read!" Only two copies of *Story* went to the local news dealer, and Inspector Fee immediately confiscated them. The next day it was banned in Waterbury, Connecticut, and an order for six hundred extra copies promptly came in from news dealers in that town. Whit Burnett danced with delight, and Mary Abbott called to congratulate me, telling me that I was so lucky, since having a work banned was the best thing that could happen to sales, and if only it was banned in Boston, sales would skyrocket. It was banned in Boston and in six other New England cities, and *Story* had the largest press run in all its history. The book was hailed as a small masterpiece and lauded to the skies, and Whit Burnett said that *The Children* saved *Story,* at least for the time being. But saving Howard Fast was another matter, and when my agent suggested to Burnett that he let me share in the prosperity by adding another one hundred dollars to the sum he had paid, he turned her down flat.

A writer is a strange creature. He is a delicate sheet of foil on which the world prints its impressions, and he is self-serving and self-oriented and yet utterly vulnerable, and when I say "he," I mean "she" as well, and for a woman it holds true even more painfully, for whatever a man suffers, a woman suffers more and feels more deeply; and though everyone may believe that he or she can write, in these United States of over two hundred and fifty million people, only a handful can claim the title of writer in its highest sense. I married a gifted, beautiful woman who would one day be one of the finest sculptors we have, and she put aside her own need for my need. I don't know whether it was worth it, or how wise she was to follow me down the paths I took. If one grows old and a little bit wise, all the symbols of greatness and importance and glory shrivel to almost nothing.

By the time Bette and I married, I had finished *Place in the City,* and the book had been published with less than earthshaking results, selling perhaps five thousand copies; but now I was selling short stories for anywhere from five hundred to one thousand dollars each. Such sales every six months, though, did not pay the rent, and we filled in the low spots every way we could. We wrote term papers for college students who had money and no brains; I did pulp stories for fifty dollars each—anything, since once I married I gave up factory work to be a full-time writer.

Bette and I had invested in a 1931 Ford convertible, which cost us forty dollars. Not only did it run, but the clutch was so worn that no one else could start the car. A semimagical way of working clutch and gas pedal allowed me to put it into motion, and even though one of the tires had a hole the size of a fifty-cent piece, through which the inner tube protruded in a threatening bubble, we ran it for thousands of miles with no trouble. When something broke, it never cost more than a dollar to replace. We parked it on the street, and of course no thief in his right mind would have touched it.

We drove it everywhere, and on one of our journeys we went to Valley Forge in Pennsylvania and spent one afternoon there, moved deeply by the reconstruction of the old revolutionary war encampment. I decided then and there that I'd write a book about the army's winter in Valley Forge, and for the next six months I read American history and wrote the book I would call *Conceived in Liberty;* it became my first real breakthrough as a novelist.

With Sam Sloan, my editor, gone from Harcourt, Brace, and with his replacement there less than thrilled with the sales of *Place in the City,* Mary Abbott sent my new novel to Simon and Schuster. They accepted it immediately, published it, and sold fifteen thousand copies, a decent record for my writing. The book, which dealt with the American Revolution somewhat in the realistic manner of Erich Maria Remarque's novel *All Quiet on the Western Front,* about World War One—a treatment never before applied to our revolt—was received with great enthusiasm by the critics. James T. Farrell reviewed it for the *New York Times,* kindly and constructively, and I was unusually thrilled by his guess that when I got the "lightning bugs," as he called them, out of my writing, I might become a very important writer indeed.

During the years between 1937, when I got married, and 1942, when I took over the Voice of America at the Office of War Information, I withdrew completely from active political involvement. For the first time in my life, I was tasting financial security, minimal but actual. Our first year was difficult. I had read bits and pieces, never a full story, of the magnificent running battle and flight to freedom of Chief Little Wolf and his Cheyenne Indians. I wanted desperately to write about it, but the only way I

Howard and Bette Fast with two of their three grandchildren, Mollie and Benjamin, 1984.

could do so would be to go to Oklahoma, where the old Cheyenne reservation had been, and talk to some of the old Cheyennes still there. Also, in Norman, Oklahoma, at the university, there were Indian students and, on the faculty, a man named Stanley Vestal, who knew more about the Cheyennes than any white man in America. I told the story to Simon and Schuster and talked them into paying me one hundred dollars a month for an entire year. We had two hundred dollars in our bank account. Ninety dollars bought us an ancient Pontiac to replace our Ford, and with $110 to live on, we set off for Oklahoma. It was a wonderful trip; the Pontiac was fine as long as one didn't push it too hard, and the world of the Great Plains was an incredible change for this survivor of the city streets.

Back in New York, we were dead broke once again, but with the guarantee of one hundred dollars a month from Simon and Schuster. It took nine months for me to write *The Last Frontier,* and when I finished it, neither Bette nor I was particularly thrilled with the result. The editors at Simon and Schuster were less than thrilled, and they returned the manuscript with a note that cancelled the

unpaid two hundred dollars of my advance and let me understand that the prompt repayment of the ten months' stipend already spent would be expected. But none too soon, I assured them, since our next meal was the major problem.

Meanwhile, Sam Sloan's new publishing house, Duell, Sloan and Pearce, had begun to function, and when I told him that Simon and Schuster had dumped *The Last Frontier,* he asked to read the manuscript. He read it promptly and asked to see me, and the first thing he put to me was whether I knew how I went wrong. I didn't know, and then he explained, gently, that I had tried to tell the story from the Indians' point of view. "You can't," he said. "You can't get inside Little Wolf's head, and you can't translate Indian speech into English and make it believable." Then what to do with what I had? That was when Sam told me to throw it away and begin again and tell the story from the white man's point of view. When I explained that I had carfare home and not much more, he immediately gave me a check for two thousand dollars as an advance.

The publication of *The Last Frontier* marked the end of our time of poverty and intermittent small riches. Suddenly, Bette and I had enough money for all our modest desires, and I was hailed as a bright new star on the literary horizon. Carl Van Doren, writing a lead review of the book, said, *"The Last Frontier* is an amazing restoration and recreation. The characters breathe, the landscape is solid ground and sky, and the story runs flexibly along the zigzag trail of a people driven by a deep instinct to their ancient home. I do not know of any other episode of Western history that has been so truly and subtly perpetuated as this one. A great story has been found again, and as here told promises to live for generations."

Of course it was all too much. The literary world is never restrained in either its praise or its condemnation. There were no bad reviews, nor would there be any bad reviews for my next book, *The Unvanquished,* which I wrote and completed in the months between my giving the manuscript of *The Last Frontier* to Sam Sloan and its publication.

Years later, when I complained to my Zen teacher that my being a member of the Communist party had thrust me into literary obscurity and made me the hate target of the literary elite who ruled the weekly book section of the *New York Times* and other such reviews, he looked at me with contempt and said, "You dare to complain of something that saved your own soul!"

Perhaps he was right.

As for my books, they were reviled once I became a Communist, but they were read and read, and at no time during the fifty-six years that followed the publication of my first novel did efforts to suppress them actually succeed.

Pearl Harbor had happened, and the world was at war, and the United States joined the forces that faced Adolph Hitler and his fascist allies. It was 1942, and in the desperate rush by America to turn a peaceful nation into a war machine, many things were quickly if loosely put together. One of these was a propaganda and information center, something that the country had done well enough without in the past but that now was a necessity in this era of radio. This propaganda and information center, so hastily thrown together, was called the Office of War Information, or OWI; and feeling that the only available pool of talent to man it was in New York City, the government took over the General Motors Building at Fifty-seventh Street and Broadway. In the first few months after Pearl Harbor, the government set to it in a sort of frenzy to remake the building according to its needs, staff it, and somehow learn the art—if such it was—of war propaganda.

Howard Fast, meanwhile, was living the ultimate fulfillment of a poor boy's dream. At this point, 1942, I was sitting right on top of eighteen pots of honey. My novel *The Last Frontier,* published a year earlier, had been greeted as a masterpiece, praised to the skies by Alexander Woollcott and Rex Stout, and chosen as a selection by the esteemed Readers Club; and my new novel, *The Unvanquished,* just published, the story of the Continental army's most desperate moment, had been called by *Time* magazine, who found in it a parallel for the grim present, "the best book about World War Two." I was twenty-seven years old,

about to turn twenty-eight, and five years earlier I had married the wonderful blue-eyed, flaxen-haired Bette, an artist by every right, and still my wife and companion fifty-three years later. We had survived the first hard years nicely enough, and we had just put down five hundred dollars for an acre of land on the Old Sleepy Hollow Road near Tarrytown, in Pochantico Hills.

At Sears, Roebuck we purchased for twelve dollars a set of blueprints, and with a mortgage of eight thousand dollars and one thousand dollars in cash, we built a small, lovely two-bedroom cottage. Bette became pregnant, we acquired a wonderful mongrel named Ginger, and I finished writing a book I would call *Citizen Tom Paine.* I cleared the land myself, Bette learned to bake and cook and sew small clothes, and I saw a rewarding, gentle future, in which we would have many children and Bette would paint and I would write my books and earn fame and fortune. And then came the war, and it all turned to dust.

In quick succession, my father died; my younger brother, close to me and my dearest friend, enlisted in the army; I drew a low draft number; and Bette miscarried our first child and sank into gloom. The future that we had planned so carefully was cast aside; Ginger was given to my older brother and promptly ran away and disappeared; the house was put up for sale; we moved into a one-room studio in New York; and Bette, convinced that my orders would be cut in a matter of weeks at the most, leaving her to face the possibility of years alone, joined the Signal Corps as a civilian artist making animated training films.

When I argued with my wife that it made more sense for me to enlist, as my brother had, than to wait around for a summons by the draft board, she strenuously and angrily objected, guided by the sensible feminine hope that the board would somehow miss me. Then one midday, on West Fifty-seventh Street, I met Louis Untermeyer, and my life changed and nothing would ever again be what we had dreamed our lives might be. Whether it works that way, where a chance meeting can turn existence upside down, or whether what happened to me would have happened in any case, I don't know.

Louis Untermeyer, at that time in his middle fifties, had a national reputation as a poet and anthologist. His knowledge of poetry was encyclopedic, his critical sense wise and balanced, and his wit delightful. He would become a major figure in my life, a beloved friend as well as surrogate father, but at that time I knew him only slightly.

On this day in 1942 I greeted Louis Untermeyer as my savior and eagerly accepted his invitation to lunch. Any meal with Louis was a delight. He would bring a gourmet's appreciation to a boiled egg, and his wit was so much a part of him that he had no existence without it. During lunch I poured out my tale of boredom and frustration, and he offered a solution. The solution was the Office of War Information, and it was located down the street, two blocks from where we were eating.

Elmer Davis, newly appointed head of the Office of War Information, was trying to whip a massive, shortwave radio operation into shape, setting up speaking and translation units for every country of occupied Europe. The feeling at the State Department and the War Department was that we must somehow reach the medium-wave receivers in European households, and since the only part of the European community that was free and allied to us was Great Britain, our people cast their covetous eyes on the British Broadcasting Company. The British were none too happy at the thought of the Yanks putting their grubby fingers on the precious BBC, but their dependence on these same Yanks was enormous, so there was no way they could shunt our demands. Elmer Davis, a one-time correspondent for the *New York Times* and later a radio news commentator, was at that time the most respected man in the field of radio news transmission. Joseph Barnes, a veteran newspaperman, talented and respected, was brought in by Davis to work with him. Both of them understood the importance of medium wave as opposed to shortwave, and they persuaded our government to lean on the British; the result was that the British agreed to turn over their BBC medium-wave transmitters to us for four hours a day, from 2:00 A.M. to 6:00 A.M. our time, which was 7:00 A.M. to 11:00 A.M. London time. AT&T set up a triple transatlantic telephone transmission to London; it would take our voices across the ocean with practically no loss in quality.

So now we had it, a transmitting facility that would cover Europe with our propaganda and could be tuned in by every home on the continent. Now it remained only to find someone to prepare the basic fifteen-minute program that would be translated into eleven languages and repeated several times in French and German. My knowledge of what happened in this search came from John Houseman, who headed up the shortwave operation—dramatic radio propaganda—and whom I later came to know and like enormously. John—or Jack as we called him—had given up his work as a successful producer to come to the OWI, and according to him, three men were hired in succession to be BBC anchor writer, and each of the three served from a week to two weeks and then was fired. One was the head of the second-largest ad agency in New York; the other two were newspapermen.

During a meeting with Houseman on another subject, Davis and Barnes raised the question of whom to hire for the BBC and where to find him. They told Houseman how desperate they were and what a letdown the three candidates had been, all of them highly recommended and men of experience. There were other men—it was before the time when they might have turned to women—whom they wanted, men in good positions who would not give up their careers even for the OWI. Houseman asked Davis and Barnes exactly what they wanted, to which they answered someone who could write clean, straightforward prose, someone who was literate yet simple and direct.

To this, Houseman answered that he had just read the proofs of a book called *Citizen Tom Paine,* clean, colorful political writing by a kid name of Howard Fast. And how old was this kid? Twenty-seven or twenty-eight. And how do they get in touch with him? He's right here in this building, top floor, writing a pamphlet about the American Revolution. And what in hell was he or anyone else doing sitting up there and writing a pamphlet about the American Revolution? Didn't anyone up there understand that this was World War Two, and not the American Revolution? A few minutes after this discussion, the head of the pamphlet department came to my desk and told me that Elmer Davis, chief of the operation, wanted me downstairs in the radio section.

In Elmer Davis's office, Davis and Barnes and Houseman awaited me. I walked into the room, and the three cold-eyed, hard-faced men stared at me as if I were an insect on a pin, and then Elmer Davis asked, "Are you Fast?"

Of course, they were not hard-faced or cold-eyed, but I was scared and unsure of myself and convinced that I was to be fired for some awful foul-up in my pamphlet, which must have been brought to them as proof of my culpability. I can recall the conversation that followed fairly well, by no means exactly after all these years. Jack Houseman, my entry angel into this strange new world, began by spelling out the nature of what would be called from then on simply the BBC, how the deal with the British had come about, and what it was intended to do. Then Elmer Davis picked up and said to me, "That's why you're here, Fast. Jack says you can write."

They were all standing. Suddenly, they all sat down. No one asked me to sit down, so I remained standing. They kept looking at me as if I were distinctive in some way. I wasn't. I was five-feet, ten-and-a-half inches. I still had plenty of hair, and I had round cheeks that embarrassed the hell out of me because they turned pink at my slightest unease. Brown eyes and heavy, horn-rimmed glasses completed the picture.

"Do you follow me?" Davis asked.

I shook my head.

"What he means," Houseman said kindly, "is that he wants you to take over the BBC and write the fifteen-minute blueprint every day."

I shook my head again. If I had unclasped my hands, they would have been shaking like leaves. I was not being fired. This was worse.

"I can't do that," I said.

"Why not?"

"I just don't know how. I never wrote for radio. I never wrote for a newspaper."

"We're not asking for references," Barnes said. "Mr. Houseman here says you can write simply and well and that you can think politically. We're asking you to write a fifteen-minute news program that will tell people in occupied Europe how the war goes, what our army has done, and what our hopes and intentions are. We want you to do it plainly and honestly, to tell the truth and not mince words. You are not to lie or invent. You will have a pool of some twenty actors available, and you will choose three each night to speak your words for the English section. Other actors will speak the foreign translations."

"It's no use," I pleaded. "I'm going to be drafted. I have a low number."

Elmer Davis came to me and lifted off my glasses. Staring at them, he said, "You're technically blind in your right eye, aren't you?"

"Oh, no," I said. "No. I see quite well out of that eye."

"You won't be drafted," Elmer Davis said.

"Suppose I botch the whole thing?" I said.

"We'll give you a week, and if you botch it, we'll dump you."

"And if you're drafted," Barnes assured me, "you'll be back here in a uniform—unless we toss you out first."

They didn't fire me. The weeks stretched into months, and they didn't fire me. My number came up a few weeks after my BBC job began, and I was still of the belief that if you were going to fight fascism, the way to do it was with a gun in your hands. I wasn't worried about my bad right eye, because during the physical, standing on line to have my eyes examined, I simply memorized the chart. When my turn came and I handed my papers to the eye doctor, he studied them a bit longer than he had to and then consulted some notes on his desk.

"Fast?" He handed me a card to cover my right eye. No problem there. "The other eye now." I began to call off the chart, and the doctor grinned and held up three fingers.

"Forget the chart. How many fingers?"

I guessed two.

"Actually, three. Come on, mister—go back to where you were."

"They set me up, didn't they? Who was it? Barnes? Davis?"

I stomped out of there in a fury and went back to the nightmare that they called the American BBC—and a nightmare it was. I had never driven myself like that before or since, and I was no stranger to hard work, physical or mental. I would get into my office at eight in the morning, usually to find someone from some branch of the government waiting for me. The White House wanted to stress the numbers of tank production because the Germans were saying that in no way would we ever match their numbers. Or Whitehall wanted us to play down the invasion of the continent. Or why wasn't I putting more emphasis on food production? This gentleman is from the Department of Agriculture. I could plead that he didn't have to come up from Washington in person and kill a precious hour of my morning. The secretary so instructed him. The secretary felt that I did not understand that a war was fought with food as well as bullets. The people on the continent were starving. Did I understand what it meant for them to know that there would be ample food? Nobody made appointments with me; they just poured in. The Chamber of Commerce—how on earth did the U.S. Chamber of Commerce know what I was writing? No one publicized that we had four hours of

BBC each morning, but everyone appeared to know. Ordnance has this new carbine; eight in the morning, they're there with the carbine. What in hell am I to do with a carbine? How did I get here? I'm a kid, and I know practically nothing about anything. Ten P.M. I get back to my office, and a distinguished-looking gentleman tells me that he has been waiting two hours. He represents the shipyard owners of America. Do I know what shipyards mean in this war? Do I understand that without ships we would lose this war?

So much for the first thirty years of my life. As with any truncated autobiographical memoir, this account deals only with bits and snatches of my life. One searches one's memory for mileposts, so to speak, for moments of decision that point to one or another of the paths that might have been taken. My tenure with the Office of War Information was finished in 1944, when the entire operation of the new Voice of America, which I had created and brought to fruition, was moved to North Africa. I desperately wanted to go with it, but J. Edgar Hoover decided otherwise—by informing my superiors at the OWI that I was a Communist, which at that time I was not. I was offered another post in the organization, an assignment to write a pamphlet on American history. I refused it indignantly and resigned. I had only one purpose in mind, to go overseas and play some part in the war—if only to report on it.

My wife had become pregnant, and our first child, a daughter, was born that year. At the same time, I took two steps that were to change the course of my life. I joined the Communist party, and I went overseas to the China-Burma-India Theater of Operation as a correspondent for the magazine *Coronet* and for the newspaper *P.M.* My journey overseas and my experiences in North Africa, Saudi Arabia, and India resulted in little of major importance for either the war effort or the periodicals that had engaged me, but indeed they were very important in my education and

The Fast home in Connecticut.

development as a writer and observer of the tragedies and obscenities of the human race. I had a firsthand look at the waste and horror of war, and of the crime that mankind inflicts upon itself.

My part as a reporter overseas was short-lived; my membership in the Communist party, on the other hand, extended from 1944 to 1956. It changed my life, and even to the date of this writing, in April of 1993, almost forty years after leaving the party in sorrow and anger, its effects upon my career still continue. My reasons for joining the party are too complex to put down here. I have spelled them out in great detail in a memoir called *Being Red,* published by Houghton Mifflin in 1990. Suffice it to say that during my time at the OWI, I watched and wrote of the Soviet Union's struggle against the armies of Adolph Hitler. I worked with Communists, among others. I met Communists whom I admired. In the 1930s, almost every American writer or artist or musician whom I admired was either a member of the party or a friend of the party.

But for myself and my family, those twelve years became an unending parade of persecution and isolation. *Freedom Road,* a story of the struggle of the newly freed slaves after the Civil War, was the last book of mine to be published before it was generally known that I was a Communist. It appeared in 1944 to a chorus of critical praise such as few books have ever received. It sold more than a million copies worldwide, becoming during the next ten years perhaps one of the most widely read serious novels of the time. But that was the end of the critical praise. My next novel, *The American,* was denounced as Communist propaganda, the fate of book after book as the years of my party membership continued.

With the writing of *Spartacus,* things came to a head. The manuscript was submitted to my then publisher, Little, Brown and Company, welcomed and highly praised by my editor, Angus Cameron, then vice president of the company, and scheduled for publication. J. Edgar Hoover, head of the FBI, then decided to intervene personally, sending an agent to Little, Brown and Company with a decree that they were not to publish the book. Similar instructions were sent to every other publisher to whom the book was submitted. After seven leading publishers had declined the book, I published it myself. It sold forty thousand copies in hardcover and another million in paper reprint—but those reprint sales took place after I had left the party, as did the making of the motion picture.

In the course of those years in the party, every book I wrote was viciously attacked and denounced, a situation that reversed itself to a degree after I resigned from the Communist party in 1956.

In those Communist party years, I was sent to prison for three months for contempt of Congress, the act of refusing to surrender lists of names of people who had supported medical aid to Republican Spain.

In 1952, I was a candidate for Congress in the twenty-third congressional district in New York. I ran on the American Labor party ticket—a ticket denounced as pro-Communist—and I was soundly defeated.

When I look back on the years I spent as a member of the Communist party, I am torn between a sense of twelve years of frustration and repression, and a sense of twelve years of struggle and growth in social understanding. I don't regret them, but I deeply regret that I lacked the understanding that would have allowed me to balance my passion for social justice with a clearer judgement of the Communist party, which, instead of bringing us closer to socialism, turned a generation away from it.

When I left the party in 1956, after the monstrous revelations of Joseph Stalin's maniacal cruelties, I had a raging anger against a movement I felt betrayed by. I put some of my feelings into a bitter book called *The Naked God,* published in 1957, and subtitled *The Writer and the Communist Party.* But this feeling of rage and bitterness soon passed, eased by the fact that the world I once knew as a young writer opened up to me again. Two of my books, written under the shadow of my party membership, were immediately bought by film producers. *Spartacus* became not only an enormously successful film, but a best-selling novel ten years after its initial publication, and the novels written after leaving the party found a new generation and a new audience.

For my wife, my daughter, and my son, it was the beginning of a new life, a life without constant fear and persecution. In a nation where so much is easily forgotten, where history is almost meaningless, the years of the witch-hunt are hardly remembered at all, but they were agonizing years, not only for myself as an actual party member, but for liberals as well.

During the years of the blacklist, I decided to do what so many other blacklisted writers had done, to write under another name. My first attempt was a book called *The Fallen Angel,* which I published under the pseudonym of Walter Ericson. It was subsequently made into a film called *Mirage.* Later, my new agent, Paul Reynolds, suggested the name of E. V. Cunningham. I wrote twenty books under that name, published here and immensely successful in Europe.

Indeed, my release—it can be called that—from the party resulted in an explosion of repressed creativity on my part. Only the first of the E. V. Cunningham books was written during the blacklist; however, the pleasures of writing half-serious suspense stories became so captivating that I wrote, as I said, nineteen more. Nor did I limit myself to the novel. I had always loved California, and in 1974, we moved to Los Angeles, where my wife and I lived for six years. I did screenplays for three films, only one of which was produced. I turned my novel *Citizen Tom Paine* into a theatrical play, done first in Williamstown and eventually in Kennedy Center in Washington, D.C. I wrote a play based on the life of Jane Austen, called *The Novelist.* It was done at Williamstown, at Theater West in Springfield, Massachusetts, in Mamaroneck, and for a short run in New York.

While living in California, I decided to write a book about a woman whose life and experience would parallel my own, having her born the year and month of my own birth, namely November in 1914. I enjoy writing about women. I called her Barbara Lavette, and eventually the story of Barbara Lavette, from her birth to her sixty-eighth year, ran to five books that sold over ten million copies.

No matter what direction my writing took, I could never give up a social outlook and a position against hypocrisy and oppression. This has been a theme that runs through all of my writing. Some five years ago, I undertook a weekly column for the New York *Observer.* Selections from this column were published in a book of essays called *War and Peace.* The book was published by M. E. Sharpe.

All in all, I have lived the life of a writer, a man of letters, a life I chose and which I followed doggedly through the seventy-eight years of my life. I have been fortunate and unfortunate—but more fortunate than unfortunate. I have been married for fifty-six years to a wonderful woman, with whom I fell in love at the age of twenty. We have two children and three grandchildren, and we live very quietly in Connecticut, a place where we have lived for many years and which we love dearly.

I cannot close this short survey of my life as a writer without mentioning a book I wrote called *April Morning.* I wrote this book in 1960, the story of a young adolescent who was witness to the battles of Concord and Lexington at the beginning of the American Revolution. Quietly published by Crown Books, without fuss or fanfare, it went through almost fifty editions in hardcover and literally millions of copies in softcover, mass-market reprint. Generations of middle-school children have read this book, which is used as a text in most of the fifty American state school systems, and have taken from it a deep feeling of what America is and how it came into being.

[*Editor's note:* Portions of this essay are excerpted from the author's memoir, *Being Red.*]

Postscript (March, 1999)

A few days before my eightieth birthday, in 1994, my wife passed away after a seven-month struggle with cancer. We had been married more than fifty years, and her death was a terrible blow to me. I was plunged into gloom and acute depression, and for the following year I wrote almost nothing.

We then lived in a large house in Greenwich, most of it devoted to my wife's sculpture and painting and to my office space. The house was filled with her presence, her work, her paintings and sculpture. Wherever I turned, her work faced me. My wife had been a beautiful young woman, and the beauty stayed with her until her seventy-eighth year. To my mind, she was a great sculptor, and I still treasure much of her work.

Seven months after her death, when my son was looking for a house in Old Greenwich, I saw the small house where I live today. I had come only to advise him, but when I saw this house, I made my first step out of gloom and sorrow. I bid for it and bought it, and a few months later I moved into it, spreading my excess furniture among my children.

My emergence from depression was a slow and agonizing process. I was living alone, managing to write two columns a week for my local newspaper and the *Times-Mirror* wire. I needed help with research and other matters, but more than that, I found it almost impossible for me to live alone. Then, in April of 1996, I met a young woman—I say young because she was approaching fifty, and I was some thirty-two years older than she.

Her name is Mercedes O'Connor. She had been recently divorced and needed a job. I had been successful enough as a writer to afford her wages, and she took me up on my offer—and thereby gave me an entirely new creative life. She is a literate, well-read and remarkable woman, and within a week after the relationship began, I put aside the

gloom and began another book. This was to be called *An Independent Woman* and became the sixth and final book of the long series I had written about Barbara Lavette and the Lavette family.

To go back some years to 1974: it was then that I decided to write a book about a woman and her family. It became a very long project, and by the time I published the sixth and final book, it comprised almost two thousand pages. Each of the books became a best seller of sorts. An odd fact that I should note here is that this book, *An Independent Woman,* was published by Harcourt Brace, the same company that had published my first serious novel, *Place in the City,* some sixty years before.

My relationship with Ms. O'Connor not only took me out of depression, but evolved into a close and loving relationship. I was back at work now, doing the one thing I loved best, writing. A second novel, *Redemption,* was completed and will be published in July of 1999. *An Independent Woman* was published in June of 1997. And I am now in the process of completing still another novel to be called: *Greenwich, Connecticut,* and will probably be published in the year 2000.

Along with this, a screenplay of mine called *The Crossing* is in the process of filming as a television film by the Arts and Entertainment cable channel.

So you might say that I have begun another life of literary work at the rather ripe age of 81. I remain in good health, and so far my memory serves me well. I look forward cheerfully to the future. Certainly, it can be no worse than the past.

Writings

FOR YOUNG PEOPLE

The Romance of a People, Hebrew Publishing, 1941.

Tony and the Wonderful Door, Blue Heron, 1952, illustrated by Imero Gobbato, Knopf, 1968, published as *The Magic Door,* illustrated by Bonnie Mettler, Peace Press, 1979.

April Morning, Crown, 1961.

FOR ADULTS; NOVELS

Two Valleys, Dial, 1933.

Strange Yesterday, Dodd, 1934.

Place in the City, Harcourt, 1937.

Conceived in Liberty: A Novel of Valley Forge, Simon & Schuster, 1939.

The Last Frontier, Duell, 1941.

The Tall Hunter, Harper, 1942.

The Unvanquished, Duell, 1942.

Citizen Tom Paine, Duell, 1943.

Freedom Road, Duell, 1944.

The American: A Middle Western Legend, Duell, 1946.

The Children, Duell, 1947.

Clarkton, Duell, 1947.

My Glorious Brothers, Little, Brown, 1948.

The Proud and the Free, Little, Brown, 1950.

Spartacus, Blue Heron, 1951.

Silas Timberman, Blue Heron, 1954.
The Story of Lola Gregg, Blue Heron, 1956.
Moses, Prince of Egypt, Crown, 1958.
The Winston Affair, Crown, 1959.
Power, Doubleday, 1962.
Agrippa's Daughter, Doubleday, 1964.
Torquemada, Doubleday, 1966.
The Hunter and the Trap, Dial, 1967.
The Crossing, Morrow, 1971.
The Hessian, Morrow, 1972.
Max, Houghton, 1982.
The Outsider, Houghton, 1984.
The Call of Fife and Drum: Three Novels of the Revolution (contains *The Unvanquished, Conceived in Liberty,* and *The Proud and the Free*), Citadel, 1987.
The Dinner Party, Houghton, 1987.
The Pledge, Houghton, 1988.
The Confession of Joe Cullen, Houghton, 1989.
The Trial of Abigail Goodman, Crown, 1993.
Seven Days in June: A Novel of the American Revolution, Carol, 1994.

"THE IMMIGRANTS" SERIES

The Immigrants, Houghton, 1977.
The Second Generation, Houghton, 1978.
The Establishment, Houghton, 1979.
The Legacy, Houghton, 1980.
The Immigrant's Daughter, Houghton, 1985.

"AN INDEPENDENT WOMAN" SERIES

An Independent Woman, Harcourt and Brace, 1997.
Redemption, Harcourt, 1999.
Greenwich, Connecticut, Harcourt, forthcoming.

NOVELS; UNDER PSEUDONYM E. V. CUNNINGHAM

Sylvia, Doubleday, 1960.
Phyllis, Doubleday, 1962.
Alice, Doubleday, 1963.
Shirley, Doubleday, 1963.
Lydia, Doubleday, 1964.
Penelope, Doubleday, 1965.
Helen, Doubleday, 1966.
Margie, Morrow, 1966.
Sally, Morrow, 1967.
Samantha, Morrow, 1967, published as *The Case of the Angry Actress,* Dell, 1984.
Cynthia, Morrow, 1968.
The Assassin Who Gave Up His Gun, Morrow, 1969.
Millie, Morrow, 1973.
The Case of the One-Penny Orange, Holt, 1977.
The Case of the Russian Diplomat, Holt, 1978.
The Case of the Poisoned Eclairs, Holt, 1979.
The Case of the Sliding Pool, Delacorte, 1981.
The Case of the Kidnapped Angel, Delacorte, 1982.
The Case of the Murdered Mackenzie, Delacorte, 1984.
The Wabash Factor, Doubleday, 1986.

NOVELS; UNDER PSEUDONYM WALTER ERICSON

The Fallen Angel, Little, Brown, 1951, published as *The Darkness Within,* Ace, 1953, published as *Mirage* (as Howard Fast), Fawcett, 1965.

SHORT STORY COLLECTIONS

Patrick Henry and the Frigate's Keel and Other Stories of a Young Nation, Duell, 1945.
Departure and Other Stories, Little, Brown, 1949.
The Last Supper and Other Stories, Blue Heron, 1955.
The Edge of Tomorrow, Bantam, 1961.
The General Zapped an Angel: New Stories of Fantasy and Science Fiction, Morrow, 1970.
A Touch of Infinity: Thirteen New Stories of Fantasy and Science Fiction, Morrow, 1973.
Time and the Riddle: Thirty-one Zen Stories, Ward Ritchie Press, 1975.

NONFICTION

Haym Salomon, Son of Liberty, Messner, 1941.
Lord Baden-Powell of the Boy Scouts, Messner, 1941.
Goethals and the Panama Canal, Messner, 1942.
(With Bette Fast) *The Picture-Book History of the Jews,* Hebrew Publishing, 1942.
The Incredible Tito, Magazine House, 1944.
Intellectuals in the Fight for Peace, Masses & Mainstream, 1949.
Literature and Reality, International Publishers, 1950.
Tito and His People, Contemporary Publishers, 1950.
Peekskill, U.S.A.: A Personal Experience, Civil Rights Congress, 1951.
Spain and Peace, Joint Anti-Fascist Refugee Committee, 1952.
The Passion of Sacco and Vanzetti. A New England Legend, Blue Heron, 1953.
The Naked God: The Writer and the Communist Party, Praeger, 1957.
The Howard Fast Reader (includes *The Golden River*), Crown, 1960.
The Jews: Story of a People, Dial, 1968.
The Art of Zen Meditation, Peace Press, 1977.
Being Red (autobiography), Houghton, 1990.
The Novelist: A Romantic Portrait of Jane Austen, French, 1992.
War and Peace: Observations on Our Times, Sharpe, 1993.

PLAYS

The Hammer (produced in New York, 1950).
Thirty Pieces of Silver (produced in Melbourne, 1951), Blue Heron, 1954.
George Washington and the Water Witch, Bodley Head, 1956.
(With Dalton Trumbo) *Spartacus* (screenplay; motion picture directed by Stanley Kubrick, produced by Universal Studios, 1960).
The Crossing (produced in Dallas, Texas, 1962).
The Hill (screenplay), Doubleday, 1964.
David and Paula (produced by American Jewish Theater, New York, 1982).
Citizen Tom Paine: A Play in Two Acts (produced in Washington, D.C., 1987), Houghton, 1986.
The Novelist (produced in Williamstown, Massachusetts, 1987).
The Second Coming (produced in Greenwich, Connecticut, 1991).

OTHER

(With William Gropper) *Never Forget: The Story of the Warsaw Ghetto* (poetry), Jewish Peoples Fraternal Order, 1946.

Korean Lullaby (poetry), American Peace Crusade, n.d.

(Editor) *The Selected Works of Tom Paine,* Modern Library, 1946.

(Editor) *The Best Short Stories of Theodore Dreiser,* World Publishing, 1947.

(Contributor) Richard Burrill, *The Human Almanac: People through Time* (includes Fast's *The Trap*), Sierra Pacific Press, 1983.

More than ten of Fast's novels and stories have been adapted for production as motion pictures, including *Spartacus,* based on his novel of the same title, 1960; *Man in the Middle,* based on his novel *The Winston Affair,* 1964; *Mirage,* based on a story he wrote under the pseudonym Walter Ericson, 1965; *Penelope,* based on his novel of the same title, 1966; *Jigsaw,* based on his novel *Fallen Angel,* 1968; and *Freedom Road,* based on his novel of the same title, 1980. *The Immigrants* was broadcast as a television miniseries in 1979. *April Morning* was adapted as a television program, 1988. *The Crossing* (based on Fast's screenplay of the same title) was recorded on cassette, narrated by Norman Dietz, Recorded Books, 1988, and is being filmed for television by Arts and Entertainment Cable; *The Immigrant's Daughter* was recorded by Sandra Burr, Brilliance Corporation, 1991.

Author of the play *The Hessian,* based on his novel of the same name, 1971; and television scripts *What's a Nice Girl Like You...?,* 1971, based on his novel *Shirley; The Ambassador,* 1974; *21 Hours at Munich,* with Edward Hume, 1976. Author of introductions in Maxim Gorky's *Mother: The Great Revolutionary Novel,* Carol Publishing, 1992; Arthur J. Sabin's *Red Scare in Court: New York Versus the International Workers Order,* University of Pennsylvania Press, 1993; Bette Fast's *The Sculpture of Bette Fast,* M. E. Sharpe, 1995. Author of weekly column, *New York Observer,* 1989—, and columns for the *Daily Worker.*

Fast's work has been translated into eighty-two languages. His manuscripts are collected at the University of Pennsylvania, Philadelphia, and the University of Wisconsin, Madison.

FEDER, Robert Arthur 1909-1969 (Robert Arthur)

Personal

Born November 1, 1909 in New York, NY; died April 28, 1969, in Philadelphia, PA; married Joan Vatsek. *Education:* Attended University of Southern California.

Career

Oil operator, 1929-36; contributor of short stories to pulp fiction magazines; *Pocket Detective* (magazine), editor, 1936-37; Metro-Goldwyn Mayer Studios, screenwriter, beginning 1937. Producer of more than forty films, chiefly with Universal Studios, beginning 1947, including *Buck Privates Come Home,* 1947; *Abbott and Costello Meet Frankenstein,* 1948; *Francis,* 1950; *The Big Heat,* 1953; *The Long Gray Line,* 1955; *Man of a Thousand Faces,* 1957; *The Perfect Furlough,* 1958; *Operation Petticoat,* 1959; *The Great Impostor,* 1961; *Come September,* 1961; *Lover Come Back,* 1962; *That Touch of Mink,* 1962; *The Spiral Road,* 1962; *Father Goose,* 1964; *Bedtime Story,* 1964; *Shenandoah,* 1965; *Blindfold,* 1966; *A Man Could Get Killed,* 1966; *The King's Pirate,* 1967; *Hellfighters,* 1969; *Sweet Charity,* 1969; and *One More Train to Rob,* 1971. *Mysterious Traveler* (radio show), scriptwriter, beginning c. late 1940s; *Mysterious Traveler* (magazine), editor, 1951-52.

Awards, Honors

New Jersey Authors Award, 1967, for *Spies and More Spies.*

Writings

Somebody's Walking on My Grave, Ace, 1961.

Ghost and More Ghosts (stories), Random House, 1963.

Alfred Hitchcock and the Three Investigators in the Mystery of the Stuttering Parrot, Random House, 1964.

Alfred Hitchcock and the Three Investigators in the Mystery of the Green Ghost, Random House, 1965.

Alfred Hitchcock and the Three Investigators in the Mystery of the Whispering Mummy, Random House, 1965.

Alfred Hitchcock and the Three Investigators in the Mystery of the Vanishing Treasure, Random House, 1966.

Alfred Hitchcock and the Three Investigators in the Secret of Skeleton Island, Random House, 1966.

Mystery and More Mystery (stories), Random House, 1966.

Alfred Hitchcock and the Three Investigators in the Mystery of the Fiery Eye, Random House, 1967.

Alfred Hitchcock and the Three Investigators in the Mystery of the Silver Spider, Random House, 1967.

Alfred Hitchcock and the Three Investigators in the Mystery of the Screaming Clock, Random House, 1968.

Alfred Hitchcock and the Three Investigators in the Mystery of the Talking Skull, Random House, 1969.

Contributor of fiction to periodicals, including *Argosy, Wonder Stories, Thrilling Wonder Stories, Astonishing Stories, Astounding Science-Fiction, Unknown Worlds, A. Merritt's Fantasy Magazine, Detective Fiction Weekly, Popular Detective,* and *Weird Tales.* Author of stories for radio programs, including *Mysterious Traveler.*

Contributor to anthologies, including *Davey Jones' Haunted Locker: Great Ghost Stories of the Sea,* Random House, 1965; *Cloak and Dagger: 10 Thrilling Stories of Espionage,* Dell Mayflower, 1967; *Spies and More Spies,* Random House, 1967; *Thrillers and More Thrillers,* Random House, 1968; and *Monster Mix: Thirteen Chilling Tales,* Dell, 1968.

Uncredited editor for many of the "Alfred Hitchcock Presents" anthologies, including *Stories My Mother Never Told Me,* 1963, *Stories Not for the Nervous,* 1965, and (with Thomas Disch) *Stories That Scared Even Me,* 1967.

Adaptations

Arthur adapted many of his own short stories for *The Mysterious Traveler* and *Murder by Experts* radio programs.

Sidelights

The work of American writer and film producer Robert Arthur Feder (all of which appeared under his Robert Arthur byline) includes short stories, novels, anthologies, and books for young readers, many of them associated with radio, television, and other extraliterary media. Some of this work, including stories fleshed out from radio scripts and published in the *Mysterious Traveler* magazine in the 1950s, and the anthologies he compiled under the "Alfred Hitchcock Presents" imprimatur in the 1950s and 1960s, went uncredited.

Arthur began seeing his work published in pulp fiction magazines during the 1930s while holding down a job as an oil operator. His short story "The Terror from the Sea," in the February, 1931, issue of *Wonder Stories,* was the first of several dozen tales he published over the next three decades in leading science fiction and fantasy magazines, including *Thrilling Wonder Stories, Astonishing Stories, Astounding Science-Fiction, Unknown Worlds, A. Merritt's Fantasy Magazine,* and *Weird Tales.* Most of these stories are whimsical fantasies with clever twists, including his adventures of Murchison Morks, a member of an exclusive men's club who tells tall tales of postage stamps from imaginary countries that can magically transport letters there, obstinate men who disbelieve people and places out of existence, and similar improbabilities. Originally published in *Argosy* in the 1940s, the Morks stories garnered favorable comparisons to Lord Dunsany's tales of Jorkens and Arthur C. Clarke's *Tales from the White Hart,* and were praised by the editors of the *Magazine of Fantasy and*

In addition to his short stories, novels, anthologies, and books for young readers, Robert Arthur Feder produced more than forty films, including the 1948 classic **Abbott and Costello Meet Frankenstein.**

Science Fiction as fantasies that provide the reader with "a fresh imaginative frame for his own daydreams of escape." Arthur revised several for inclusion in *Ghosts and More Ghosts,* a collection of stories for young readers.

During the same interval, Arthur established an even stronger presence in the crime/mystery field with more than fifty short stories published in *Detective Fiction Weekly, Popular Detective,* and other detective and mystery fiction magazines. Anthony Boucher, writing in the *New York Times,* praised him as "one of the best puzzle-gimmick men in the business" when several of these stories were gathered in the collection *Mystery and More Mystery,* and found his first novel-length effort, the private-eye story *Somebody's Walking on My Grave,* "mildly disappointing" in part because it had "no suggestion of the inventive originality of Arthur's best shorts." Lavinia Russ also praised Arthur's mystery stories as "well-knit, well-told" in her review of *Mystery and More Mystery* for *Publishers Weekly.* The reviewer for *Library Journal* found them "competently plotted," and singled out their "touch of humor, rather unusual in this genre" for special notice.

Most of Arthur's fiction in the 1960s was written for pre-teen readers, notably his series of novels featuring the Three Investigators, which grew out of his association with the "Alfred Hitchcock Presents" anthologies spun off from the television show of the same name. The "Three Investigators" books are old-fashioned mystery adventures in the style of the "Hardy Boys" series, featuring Jupiter Jones, owner of Jones's Salvage Yard, and his young proteges, Bob and Pete, who help him solve complicated crimes and intrigues involving lost treasures, eccentric clients, evil criminals, and apparent supernatural menaces that prove to have a rational explanation.

"Entertaining and somewhat melodramatic adventures, enhanced as usual with the methods of real detective work," was how the reviewer for *Library Journal* described *Alfred Hitchcock and the Three Investigators in the Mystery of the Fiery Eye,* in which the trio helps a young friend decipher a cryptically worded will and claim a fabled jewel for his inheritance. Furthermore, the reviewer continued, appraising a plot built around the theft of an exotic royal family heirloom in *Alfred Hitchcock and the Three Investigators in The Mystery of the Silver Spider,* "this author has the knack of making the outrageous seem plausible." Even an "unlikely" tale such as *Alfred Hitchcock and the Three Investigators in the Mystery of the Vanishing Treasure,* in which the detectives solve a mystery involving an author of children's stories bedeviled by gnomes out of the illustrations for her books, impressed a *Library Journal* reviewer as "a competent formula job, amusing and strictly logical." The "Three Investigators" series was continued after Arthur's death by several writers, including William Arden, Marc Brandel, M. V. Carey, William McCay, G. H. Stone, and Nick West.

In addition to his anthologies for Alfred Hitchcock, Arthur also compiled anthologies of supernatural and suspense fiction aimed at younger readers, including *Davy Jones' Haunted Locker, Cloak and Dagger, Spies and More Spies,* and *Monster Mix.* Their eclectic blends of classic and contemporary fiction by writers that appealed to younger and mature readers alike prompted the reviewer of *Thrillers and More Thrillers* in *Publishers Weekly* to remark that "Arthur knows a good story when he sees it."

Works Cited

Boucher, Anthony, review of *Mystery and More Mystery, New York Times Book Review,* November 6, 1966, p. 68.

Boucher, Anthony, review of *Somebody's Walking on My Grave, New York Times Book Review,* March 26, 1961, p. 28.

Review of "Wilfred Weem, Dreamer," *Magazine of Fantasy and Science Fiction,* August, 1951, p. 15.

Review of *Mystery and More Mystery, Library Journal,* November 15, 1967, p. 4269.

Russ, Lavinia, review of *Mystery and More Mystery, Publishers Weekly,* November 7, 1966, p. 66.

Review of *Thrillers and More Thrillers, Publishers Weekly,* October 7, 1968, p. 54.

For More Information See

BOOKS

Ashley, Mike, *Who's Who in Horror and Fantasy Fiction,* Elm Tree Books, 1977.

Cook, Michael, *Mystery Detective and Espionage Magazines,* Greenwood Press, 1983.

International Motion Picture Almanac, Quigley, 1983.

Reginald, Robert, *Science Fiction and Fantasy Literature, Volume 1: A Checklist, 1700-1974,* Gale, 1979.

Tuck, Donald, *The Encyclopedia of Science Fiction and Fantasy,* Volume 1, Advent, 1974.

PERIODICALS

Library Journal, November 12, 1965, p. 5106; November 15, 1966, p. 5773.

Publishers Weekly, June 9, 1969, p. 46.

Teacher, October, 1978, p. 177.*

*   *   *

FILES, Meg 1946-

Personal

Born in 1946; raised in Michigan; married.

Addresses

Office—c/o Pima Community College, Tutoring Center, 2202 West Anklam Rd., Tucson, AZ 85709. *Agent*—c/o J. Daniel & Co., Box 21922, Santa Barbara, CA 93121.

Career

Author. Pima Community College, Tucson, AZ, Writing Lab director, c. 1988—; Ohio State University, Thurber House writer-in-residence.

Writings

Meridian 144, Soho Press (New York City), 1991.
Home Is the Hunter: And Other Stories, J. Daniel (Santa Barbara, CA), 1996.

Contributor of short stories and articles to periodicals, including *Writer's Digest* and *Rio Grande Review.*

Sidelights

Meg Files's debut novel *Meridian 144* blends an apocalyptic science-fiction scenario with one woman's forced journey of self-discovery. As the novel begins, Catherine "Kit" Manning is scuba-diving in the Pacific Ocean with her Air Force captain boyfriend when a nuclear strike occurs. She survives the shock waves that cause the death of her companion and makes it back to the island, breathing through her scuba equipment while she scavenges for food, finds her dog, and battles with escaped convicts and other sociopathic individuals who have survived. She also contemplates her life in flashback: a difficult childhood, unresolved conflicts with her mother, and an unhappy marriage that had recently ended. "Files spares us no detail of the horrors of the aftermath of a nuclear attack," noted *Booklist* reviewer Donna Seaman, who added: "Grim and stoical, this jolting debut novel dramatizes our complexity and destructiveness, weakness and strength, and capacity for good and evil." *School Library Journal* contributor Carolyn E. Gecan indicated that Manning's journey of "self-redemption" had put her in a position to take on an Eve-like role in a contemporary recasting of the Genesis creation story. "Grisly and poetic in turn," Gecan maintained, "[*Meridian 144*] should appeal to mature, thoughtful, and sensitive YAs."

Works Cited

Gecan, Carolyn E., review of *Meridian 144, School Library Journal,* April, 1992, p. 163.
Seaman, Donna, review of *Meridian 144, Booklist,* October 15, 1991, p. 406.

For More Information See

PERIODICALS

Kirkus Reviews, August 1, 1991, p. 950.
North American Review, March-April, 1997, pp. 43-45.
Publishers Weekly, August 16, 1991, p. 47.
Writer's Digest, June, 1995, pp. 80-81.*

G

GEEHAN, Wayne (E.) 1947-

Personal

Born September 20, 1947, in Hartford, CT; son of Edward, Jr. and Mary (maiden name, White) Geehan; married Susan E. Glendon (a bookkeeper), March 24, 1973; children: Greg, Jonathan, Douglas, Amy. *Education:* Attended Art Institute of Boston, 1965-69. *Hobbies and other interests:* Acrylic and oil painting, reading, genealogy, travel.

Wayne Geehan

Addresses

Home—34 Mohegan Rd., Acton, MA 01720. *Office*—741 Mount Auburn St., Watertown, MA 02472. *Electronic mail*—Geehan@ma.ultranet.com.

Career

American Publishing Corp., Watertown, MA, designer and illustrator, 1972-75; freelance illustrator, 1975—. Acton Commission on Disability, vice-president; Open Door Theater, Acton, set designer; community volunteer, 1986-92. *Military service:* U.S. Army, 1969-70; served in Vietnam. *Member:* Society of Children's Book Writers and Illustrators, Mystery Writers of America.

Awards, Honors

Honorary B.A., Art Institute of Boston, 1994.

Writings

CHILDREN'S BOOKS

Captain Blackwell's Treasure, self-illustrated, BePuzzled, 1993.
Computer Sleuths: Adventure Mystery for Kids Ages 8-12, illustrated by Suzanne Sullivan, BePuzzled, 1993.
Which Is Witch, BePuzzled, 1995.

ILLUSTRATOR

Howard Pyle, *Men of Iron,* retold by Earle Hitchner, Troll Associates (Mahwah, NJ), 1990.
Jules Verne, *Twenty Thousand Leagues under the Sea,* retold by Raymond James, Troll Associates, 1990.
Verne, *A Journey to the Center of the Earth,* retold by James, Troll Associates, 1990.
Rae Bains, *Jack London: A Life of Adventure,* Troll Associates, 1992.
Brownie Macintosh, *The Streamlined Double Decker Bus,* Covered Bridge Press, 1995.
Cindy Neuschwander, *Sir Cumference and the First Round Table: A Math Adventure,* Charlesbridge (Watertown, MA), 1997.

Neuschwander, *Sir Cumference and the Dragon of Pi: A Math Adventure,* Charlesbridge, 1999.

Sidelights

Wayne Geehan told *SATA:* "An illustrator wears lots of hats. That is what I usually tell children when I give presentations in their classrooms. One week I could be wearing the hat of a paleontologist: researching, learning about, then painting dinosaurs. The next week I could be wearing the hat of a historian: studying the homes, clothes, and lifestyles of people in the Middle Ages. Each book I illustrate is an exciting challenge and learning experience. Each book brings me to a new and fulfilling adventure.

"In my youth, I was an avid reader, spending hours in the library and bringing home stacks of books—books on sailing ships, pirates, ghosts, mysteries, adventure, and history. My imagination ran with the thirst for more knowledge, fact or fiction. It wasn't just the reading that stimulated my imagination; there were the illustrations—by Howard Pyle, N. C. Wyeth, Maxfield Parrish, Frank Schoonover, and many others. The classics were brought to life by their wonderful paintings. I am influenced today by many contemporary illustrators, such as Chris Van Allsburg, fantasy illustrators like Michael Whelan, Darrell Sweet, and the Hildebrant brothers, and far too many more to mention.

"I have often been asked by children if I had always wanted to be an artist. My first remembrance of what I wanted to do as a career was around the age of thirteen. I wanted to be an archaeologist. I loved history and science. I also loved to draw. Whenever I did a report or project, I would always have a drawing to accompany my work. However, at that time, I never thought that art would be my profession. When I got to high school, I knew that my weakness, mathematics, would keep me from a career in science and history, so I went with my strength—art.

"It is ironic that today, as an illustrator, I am still involved with history and science. It's even more ironic that I have been doing mathematics-adventure children's books for Charlesbridge Publishing."

*   *   *

GEESLIN, Campbell 1925-

Personal

Born December 5, 1925, in Goldthwaite, TX; son of Edward (an engineer) and Margaret Lee (Gaddis) Geeslin; married Marilyn Low (a teacher of English as a second language), 1951; children: Seth, Meg Melillo, Ned. *Education:* Columbia College, A.B., 1949; University of Texas, M.A., 1950.

Addresses

Home—209 Davis Ave., White Plains, NY 10605. *Agent*—Robert Lescher, 47 E. 19th St., New York, NY 10003.

Career

Houston Post, Houston, TX, began as reporter, became assistant managing editor, 1950-64; worked for Gannett Newspapers in Cocoa Beach, FL, White Plains, NY and Rochester, NY, 1964-68; *This Week,* New York City, managing editor, 1968-71; *Parade,* New York City, managing editor, 1970-71; New York Times Syndicate, New York City, editor, 1971-73; *Cue,* New York City, editor, 1973-75; *People,* New York City, senior editor, 1975-78; *Life,* New York City, text editor, beginning 1978. Trustee, White Plains Public Library. *Military service:* U.S. Navy, 1943-46.

Writings

The Bonner Boys: A Novel about Texas, Simon & Schuster, 1981, also published as *Whatever Became of the Bonner Boys?,* Simon & Schuster, 1981.
In Rosa's Mexico, illustrated by Andrea Arroyo, Knopf, 1996.
On Ramon's Farm: Five Tales of Mexico, illustrated by Petra Mathers, Atheneum, 1998.
How Nanita Learns to Make Flan, illustrated by Petra Mathers, Atheneum, 1999.

Author of a column on publishing for the *Authors Guild Bulletin.*

Sidelights

Campbell Geeslin began writing books shortly before his retirement from the world of print journalism, where he worked for more than three decades as a reporter and editor. Although he and his family were centered for many years in and around New York City, Geeslin distinctly recalled his youth in rural west Texas in the 1930s, and the vacations he and his family took to an even more exotic locale—across the border into Mexico.

Geeslin first wrote for an adult audience with his *Bonner Boys: A Novel about Texas.* The saga of five brothers who come of age on a west Texas ranch in the 1930s, the novel follows the siblings through the decisive experiences of World War II and its aftermath, as each must weigh a wide array of choices as he ponders his future. One becomes a musician, another an entrepreneur of questionable conduct, the third a journalist, and the last two a corporate executive and an attorney. All return to the Texas capital of Austin for a reunion and visit with their aged mother. A *Publishers Weekly* critic dubbed *The Bonner Boys* "a warm and satisfying novel" that solidly evokes life in the American Southwest of the 1930s.

Commenting on the success of *The Bonner Boys,* Geeslin told *SATA:* "The reviews were plentiful and kind, but sales were not." His next book, he further explained, had its origins simply as a labor of love. "After I retired from a job as an editor at *Life* magazine, I wrote and hand-printed from woodcuts an illustrated story for my twin granddaughters. An editor at Knopf wanted to buy the story, *In Rosa's Mexico,* but hired a professional illustrator to do the pictures."

"I grew up in west Texas and visited Mexico often on family vacations. That colorful country left indelible images that continue to feed my imagination." *In Rosa's Mexico,* with illustrations by Andrea Arroyo, is aimed at primary graders. The text and drawings present three tales centered on a little girl in Mexico and her encounters with fabled characters from Mexican folklore. In the first, "Rosa and El Gallo," she is distressed when volcanic ash has ruined the local violet crop; Rosa usually sells the flowers at the market to earn money for her impoverished family. As a result, the family plans to cook their rooster for food. To save himself, the Gallo begins to cough up lovely violet petals, which Rosa then sells at the market and earns enough to buy food for her family.

In the book's second tale, Rosa's beloved burro becomes sick. She rides up to the night sky and retrieves a remedy from "las estrellas"; the burro recovers and now wears the mark of heaven on his head. The final story centers on Rosa and her discovery of a missing wedding ring that had been stolen by a fox. Her honest actions save El Lobo, the wolf, who rewards her with a magic pillow. All of Geeslin's stories for *In Rosa's Mexico* are told in a limited vocabulary that incorporates many Spanish terms, but Arroyo's drawings provide easy clues to their meaning, and a glossary of a dozen Spanish words precedes the text as well. *New York Times Book Review* contributor Kathleen Krull termed the language and action "idiosyncratic [and] more than a little fantastic," adding that the spare prose works very well for the bilingual, magical-themed format. A *Publishers Weekly* assessment seconded this favorable appraisal, noting that Geeslin had crafted a "simply stated yet musical text." Most reviewers complimented the illustrations as well— images "enhancing the sense of a place and time more magical than mundane," as Janice M. Del Negro asserted in *Bulletin of the Center for Children's Books.*

Geeslin's second book for young readers, *On Ramon's Farm: Five Tales of Mexico,* follows a day in the life of a young boy as he goes about his farm chores. As he cleans up the barnyard and feeds its residents, Ramon is entertained by the friendly animals, and in return he creates poems about them. The animals speak Spanish to him, and again, a Spanish-English glossary of terms is provided. Geeslin told *SATA:* "My wife supplies the Spanish words when I need them. I visit schools and libraries whenever I'm invited and show how I print my own books."

Works Cited

Review of *The Bonner Boys, Publishers Weekly,* February 20, 1981, pp. 90-91.

Del Negro, Janice M., review of *In Rosa's Mexico, Bulletin of the Center for Children's Books,* January, 1997, p. 169.

Review of *In Rosa's Mexico, Publishers Weekly,* November 18, 1996, p. 74.

Krull, Kathleen, review of *In Rosa's Mexico, New York Times Book Review,* May 11, 1997, p. 24.

For More Information See

PERIODICALS

Booklist, May 1, 1981, p. 1186; November 15, 1996, p. 594.

Publishers Weekly, October 12, 1998, p. 75.

School Library Journal, December, 1996, p. 92.

*　　*　　*

GIOVANNI, Nikki 1943-

Personal

Born Yolande Cornelia Giovanni Jr., June 7, 1943, in Knoxville, TN; daughter of Gus Jones (a probation officer) and Yolande Cornelia (a social worker; maiden name, Watson) Giovanni; children: Thomas Watson. *Education:* Fisk University, B.A. (with honors), 1967; postgraduate studies at University of Pennsylvania School of Social Work and Columbia University School of Fine Arts, 1968.

Addresses

Office—English Department, Virginia Tech, Blacksburg, VA 24061.

Career

Poet, writer, lecturer. Queens College of the City University of New York, Flushing, assistant professor of black studies, 1968; Rutgers University, Livingston College, New Brunswick, NJ, associate professor of English, 1968-72; Ohio State University, Columbus, visiting professor of English, 1984; College of Mount St. Joseph on the Ohio, Mount St. Joseph, Ohio, professor of creative writing, 1985-87; Virginia Tech, Blacksburg, VA, professor, 1987—; Texas Christian University, visiting professor in humanities, 1991. Founder of publishing firm, NikTom Ltd., 1970; participated in "Soul at the Center," Lincoln Center for the Performing Arts, 1972; Duncanson Artist-in-Residence, Taft Museum, Cincinnati, 1986; Co-chair, Literary Arts Festival for State of Tennessee Homecoming, 1986; director, Warm Hearth Writer's Workshop, 1988—; appointed to Ohio Humanities Council, 1987; member of board of directors, Virginia Foundation for Humanities and Public Policy, 1990-93; participant in Appalachian Community Fund, 1991-93, and Volunteer Action Center, 1991-94; featured poet, International Poetry Festival, Utrecht, Holland, 1991. Has given numerous poetry readings and lectures worldwide and appeared on numerous television talk shows. *Member:* National Council of Negro Wom-

Nikki Giovanni

en, Society of Magazine Writers, National Black Heroines for PUSH, Winnie Mandela Children's Fund Committee, Delta Sigma Theta (honorary member).

Awards, Honors

Grants from Ford Foundation, 1967, National Endowment for the Arts, 1968, and Harlem Cultural Council, 1969; named one of ten "Most Admired Black Women," *Amsterdam News,* 1969; outstanding achievement award, *Mademoiselle,* 1971; Omega Psi Phi Fraternity Award, 1971, for outstanding contribution to arts and letters; Meritorious Plaque for Service, Cook County Jail, 1971; Prince Matchabelli Sun Shower Award, 1971; life membership and scroll, National Council of Negro Women, 1972; National Association of Radio and Television Announcers Award, 1972, for recording *Truth Is on Its Way;* Woman of the Year Youth Leadership Award, *Ladies' Home Journal,* 1972; National Book Award nomination, 1973, for *Gemini: An Extended Autobiographical Statement on My First Twenty-Five Years of Being a Black Poet;* "Best Books for Young Adults" citation, American Library Association, 1973, for *My House;* "Woman of the Year" citation, Cincinnati Chapter of YWCA, 1983; elected to Ohio Women's Hall of Fame, 1985; "Outstanding

Woman of Tennessee" citation, 1985; Post-Corbett Award, 1986; Woman of the Year, NAACP (Lynchburg chapter), 1989.

Honorary Doctorate of Humanities, Wilberforce University, 1972, and Fisk University, 1988; Honorary Doctorate of Literature, University of Maryland (Princess Anne Campus), 1974, Ripon University, 1974, and Smith College, 1975; Honorary Doctorate of Humane Letters, The College of Mount St. Joseph on the Ohio, 1985, Indiana University, 1991, Otterbein College, 1992, Widener University, 1993, Albright College, 1995, Cabrini College, 1995, and Allegheny College, 1997. Keys to numerous cities, including Dallas, TX, New York, NY, Cincinnati, OH, Miami, FL, New Orleans, LA, and Los Angeles, CA; Ohioana Book Award, 1988; Jeanine Rae Award for the Advancement of Women's Culture, 1995; Langston Hughes Award, 1996.

Writings

POETRY

Black Feeling, Black Talk, Broadside Press (Detroit), 1968, 3rd edition, 1970.
Black Judgement, Broadside Press, 1968.

Black Feeling, Black Talk/Black Judgement (contains *Black Feeling, Black Talk* and *Black Judgement*), Morrow, 1970, selection published as *Knoxville, Tennessee,* illustrated by Larry Johnson, Scholastic, 1994.
Re: Creation, Broadside Press, 1970.
Poem of Angela Yvonne Davis, Afro Arts (New York City), 1970.
Spin a Soft Black Song: Poems for Children, illustrated by Charles Bible, Hill & Wang (New York City), 1971, illustrated by George Martins, Lawrence Hill (Westport, CT), 1985, revised edition, Farrar, Straus, 1987.
My House, foreword by Ida Lewis, Morrow, 1972.
Ego-Tripping and Other Poems for Young People, illustrated by George Ford, Lawrence Hill (Chicago), 1973.
The Women and the Men, Morrow, 1975.
Cotton Candy on a Rainy Day, introduction by Paula Giddings, Morrow, 1978.
Vacation Time: Poems for Children, illustrated by Marisabina Russo, Morrow, 1980.
Those Who Ride the Night Winds, Morrow, 1983.
The Genie in the Jar, illustrated by Chris Raschka, Holt, 1996.
The Selected Poems of Nikki Giovanni (1968-1995), Morrow, 1996.
The Sun Is So Quiet, illustrated by Ashley Bryant, Holt, 1996.
Love Poems, Morrow, 1997.
Blues: For All the Changes: New Poems, Morrow, 1999.

Sound recordings by the author of her works include *Truth Is on Its Way,* 1971; *Like a Ripple on a Pond,* 1973; *The Way I Feel,* 1974; and *Legacies: The Poetry of Nikki Giovanni* and *The Reason I Like Chocolate,* both 1976.

OTHER

(Editor) *Night Comes Softly: An Anthology of Black Female Voices,* Medic Press (Newark, NJ), 1970.
Gemini: An Extended Autobiographical Statement on My First Twenty-Five Years of Being a Black Poet, Bobbs-Merrill (Indianapolis, IN), 1971.
(With James Baldwin) *A Dialogue: James Baldwin and Nikki Giovanni,* Lippincott (Philadelphia), 1973.
(With Margaret Walker) *A Poetic Equation: Conversations between Nikki Giovanni and Margaret Walker,* Howard University Press (Washington, DC), 1974.
(Author of introduction) *Adele Sebastian, Intro to Fine* (poems), Woman in the Moon, 1985.
Sacred Cows ... and Other Edibles (essays), Morrow, 1988.
(Editor, with C. Dennison) *Appalachian Elders: A Warm Hearth Sampler,* Pocahontas Press (Blacksburg, VA), 1991.
(Author of foreword) *The Abandoned Baobob: The Autobiography of a Woman,* Chicago Review Press, 1991.
Racism 101 (essays), Morrow, 1994.
(Editor) *Grand Mothers: Poems, Reminiscences, and Short Stories about the Keepers of Our Traditions,* Holt, 1994.
(Editor) *Shimmy Shimmy Shimmy like My Sister Kate: Looking at the Harlem Renaissance through Poems,* Holt, 1995.

(Editor) *Grand Fathers: Reminiscences, Poems, Recipes and Photos of the Keepers of Our Traditions,* Holt, 1999.

Contributor to numerous anthologies. Contributor of columns to newspapers. Contributor to magazines, including *Black Creation, Black World, Ebony, Essence, Freedom Ways, Journal of Black Poetry, Negro Digest,* and *Umbra.* Editorial consultant, Encore American and Worldwide News.

A selection of Giovanni's public papers is housed at Mugar Memorial Library, Boston University.

Adaptations

Spirit to Spirit: The Poetry of Nikki Giovanni (television film), 1986, produced by Corporation for Public Broadcasting, and Ohio Council on the Arts.

Sidelights

One of the best-known African American poets to reach prominence during the late 1960s and early 1970s, Nikki Giovanni has continued to create poems that encompass a life fully experienced. Her unique and insightful verses testify to her own evolving awareness and experiences as a woman of color: from child to young woman, from naive college freshman to seasoned civil rights activist, and from daughter to mother. Frequently anthologized, Giovanni's poetry expresses strong racial pride and respect for family. Her informal style makes her work accessible to both adults and children. In addition to collections such as *Re: Creation, Spin a Soft Black Song,* and *Those Who Ride the Night Winds,* Giovanni has published several works of nonfiction, including *Racism 101* and the anthology *Grand Mothers: Poems, Reminiscences, and Short Stories about the Keepers of Our Traditions.* A frequent lecturer and reader, Giovanni has also taught at Rutgers University, Ohio State University, and Virginia Tech.

Giovanni was born in Knoxville, Tennessee, in 1943, the youngest of two daughters in a close-knit family. Having gained an intense appreciation for her African American heritage from her outspoken grandmother, Louvenia Terrell Watson, Giovanni had a reputation for being strong-willed even as a child. "I come from a long line of storytellers," she once explained in an interview, describing how her family influenced her poetry through oral traditions. "My grandfather was a Latin scholar and he loved the myths, and my mother is a big romanticist, so we heard a lot of stories growing up." This early exposure to the power of spoken language would influence Giovanni's career as a poet, particularly her tendency to sprinkle her verses with colloquialisms such as curse words. "I appreciated the quality and the rhythm of the telling of the stories," she once commented, "and I know when I started to write that I wanted to retain that—I didn't want to become the kind of writer that was stilted or that used language in ways that could not be spoken. I use a very natural rhythm; I want my writing to sound like I talk."

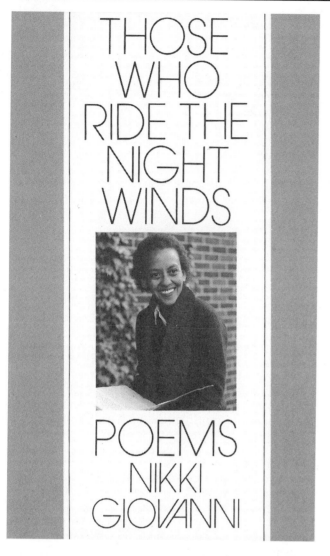

THOSE WHO RIDE THE NIGHT WINDS

POEMS NIKKI GIOVANNI

Dedicated to people who made a difference in the world, this book presents Giovanni's views on such influential figures as John Lennon, Billie Jean King, and Martin Luther King, Jr. (Cover photograph by Nancy Crampton.)

When Giovanni was a young child, she moved with her parents from Knoxville to a predominantly black suburb of Cincinnati, Ohio. She remained close to her outspoken grandmother, however, spending both her sophomore and junior years of high school at the family home in Knoxville. Encouraged by several schoolteachers, Giovanni enrolled at Fisk University, a prestigious, all-black college in Nashville, Tennessee. Unaccustomed to Fisk's traditions, the outspoken young woman inevitably came into conflict with the school's dean of women and was asked to leave. She returned to Fisk in 1964, however, determined to be an ideal student. She accomplished her goal, becoming a leader in political and literary activities on campus during what would prove to be an important era in black history.

Giovanni had experienced racism firsthand during her childhood in the South. Random violence that erupted in and near Knoxville "was frightening," she later recalled

in an autobiographical essay for *Contemporary Authors Autobiography Series* (*CAAS*). "You always felt someone was trying to kill you." Yet when Giovanni re-entered the freshman class at Fisk she was decidedly conservative in her political outlook. During high school she had been a supporter of Republican presidential candidate Barry Goldwater, as well as an avid reader of books by Ayn Rand, who was famous for her philosophy of objectivism (based on self-assertion and competition). The poet credits a Fisk roommate named Bertha with successfully persuading her to embrace revolutionary ideals. In the wake of the civil rights movement and demonstrations against U.S. involvement in the Vietnam conflict, demands for social and political change were sweeping college campuses around the country. "Bertha kept asking, 'how could Black people be conservative?,'" Giovanni wrote in *Gemini: An Extended Autobiographical Statement on My First Twenty-Five Years.* "'What have they got to conserve?' And after a while (realizing that I had absolutely nothing, period) I came around."

While Giovanni was at Fisk, a black renaissance was emerging as writers and other artists of color were finding new ways of expressing their distinct culture to an increasingly interested public. In addition to serving as editor of the campus literary magazine, *Elan,* and participating in the Fisk Writers Workshop, Giovanni worked to restore the Fisk chapter of the Student Non-Violent Coordinating Committee (SNCC). At that time, the organization was pressing the concept of "black power" to bring about social and economic reform. Giovanni's political activism ultimately led to her planning and directing the first Black Arts Festival in Cincinnati, which was held in 1967.

Later that year, Giovanni graduated magna cum laude with a degree in history. She decided to continue her studies at the University of Pennsylvania School of Social Work under a grant from the Ford Foundation, and then take classes at Columbia University's School of Fine Arts. This period was punctuated by tragedy, however, when Giovanni's beloved grandmother died. The loss "stirred in her a sense of guilt and shame both for the way in which society had dealt with this strong, sensitive woman, to whom she had been so close and who had deeply influenced her life, as well as for the way she herself had left her alone to die," according to Mozella G. Mitchell in *Dictionary of Literary Biography.*

Giovanni's first published volume of poetry grew out of her response to the assassinations of such figures as Martin Luther King Jr., Malcolm X, Medgar Evers, and Robert Kennedy. *Black Feeling, Black Talk* and *Black Judgement* display a strong, almost militant African American perspective as Giovanni recounts her growing political and spiritual awareness. These early books, which were followed by *Re: Creation,* quickly established Giovanni as a prominent new African American voice. *Black Feeling, Black Talk* sold more than ten thousand copies in its first year alone, making the author an increasingly visible and popular figure on the reading and speaking circuit. Because of Giovanni's overt activism, her fame as a personality almost preceded her critical acclaim as a poet. She gave the first public reading of her work at Birdland, a trendy New York City jazz club, to a standing-room-only audience. Mitchell described the poems Giovanni produced between 1968 and 1970 as "a kind of ritualistic exorcism of former nonblack ways of thinking and an immersion in blackness. Not only are they directed at other black people whom [Giovanni] wanted to awaken to the beauty of blackness, but also at herself as a means of saturating her own consciousness."

Critical reaction to Giovanni's early work focused on her more revolutionary poetry. Some reviewers found her political and social positions to be unsophisticated, while others were threatened by her rebelliousness. "Nikki writes about the familiar: what she knows, sees, experiences," Don L. Lee observed in *Dynamite Voices I: Black Poets of the 1960's.* "It is clear why she conveys such urgency in expressing the need for Black awareness, unity, solidarity.... What is perhaps more important is that when the Black poet chooses to serve as political seer, he must display a keen sophistication. Sometimes Nikki oversimplifies and therefore sounds rather naive politically." *Dictionary of Literary Biography* contributor Alex Batman heard in Giovanni's verse the echoes of blues music. "Indeed the rhythms of her verse correspond so directly to the syncopations of black music that her poems begin to show a potential for becoming songs without accompaniment," Batman noted.

Giovanni's first three volumes of poetry were enormously successful, taking into account the relatively low public demand for modern poetry. *Black Judgement* alone sold six thousand copies in three months, almost six times the sales level expected of a book of its type. As she traveled to speaking engagements at colleges around the country, Giovanni was often hailed as one of the leading black poets of the new black renaissance. The prose poem "Nikki-Rosa," Giovanni's reminiscence of her childhood in a close-knit African American home, was first published in *Black Judgement.* As it became her most beloved and most anthologized work, "Nikki-Rosa" expanded her appeal to an audience well beyond fans of her more activist poetry.

In 1969, Giovanni took a teaching position at Rutgers University. That year she also gave birth to her son, Thomas. Her decision to bear a child out of wedlock was understandable to anyone who knew her. Even as a young girl she had determined that the institution of marriage was not hospitable to women and would never play a role in her life. "I had a baby at twenty-five because I *wanted* to have a baby and I could *afford* to have a baby," she told an *Ebony* interviewer. "I did not get married because I didn't *want* to get married and I could *afford* not to get married."

Despite her success as a poet of the black revolution, Giovanni's work exhibited a shift in focus after the birth of her son. Her priorities had expanded and now

encompassed providing her child with the security of a stable home life. As she remarked to an interviewer for *Harper's Bazaar,* "To protect Tommy there is no question I would give my life. I just cannot imagine living without him. But I can live without the revolution." During this period Giovanni produced a collection of autobiographical essays, two books of poetry for children, and two poetry collections for adults. She also made several recordings of her poetry set against a gospel music backdrop. Reviewing these works, Mitchell commented that "we see evidence of a more developed individualism and greater introspection, and a sharpening of her creative and moral powers, as well as of her social and political focus and understanding."

In addition to writing her own poetry, Giovanni sought exposure for other African American women writers through NikTom, Ltd., a publishing cooperative she founded in 1970. Gwendolyn Brooks, Margaret Walker, Carolyn Rodgers, and Mari Evans were among those who benefited from Giovanni's efforts. Travels to other parts of the world, including the Caribbean, also filled much of the poet's time and contributed to the evolution

Giovanni's poetry collection explores issues specific to African-American young people, encouraging them to take pride in their cultural history. (Illustrated by George Ford.)

Bears store fat
chipmunks gather nuts
and I collect books
for the coming winter

Such wonders of childhood as tiptoeing through strawberry patches, licking chocolate-covered fingers, and snuggling under blankets are described in this collection of poetry for young children. (From The Sun Is So Quiet, *written by Giovanni and illustrated by Ashley Bryan.)*

of her work. As she broadened her perspective, Giovanni began to review her own life. Her introspection led to *Gemini: An Extended Autobiographical Statement on My First Twenty-Five Years of Being a Black Poet,* which earned a nomination for the National Book Award.

Gemini is a combination of prose, poetry, and other "bits and pieces." In the words of a critic writing in *Kirkus Reviews,* it is a work in which "the contradictions are brought together by sheer force of personality." From sun-soaked childhood memories of a supportive family to an adult acceptance of revolutionary ideology and solo motherhood, the work reflected Giovanni's internal conflict and self-questioning. "I think all autobiography is fiction," Giovanni once observed in an interview, expressing amazement that readers feel they learn something personal about an author by reading a creative work. "[T]he least factual of anything is autobiography, because half the stuff is forgotten," she added. "Even if you [write] about something terribly painful, you have removed yourself from it.... What you have not come to terms with you do not write." While she subtitled *Gemini* an autobiography, Giovanni denied that it offered a key to her inner self. The essays

contained in the volume—particularly one about her grandmother—were personal in subject matter and "as true as I could make it," she commented. But, as Giovanni noted in an interview several decades later, "I also recognize that there are [parts of] the book in which I'm simply trying to deal with ideas. I didn't want it to be considered *the definitive.* It's far from that. It's very selective and how I looked at myself when I was twenty-five."

In addition to writing for adults in *Gemini* and other works during the early 1970s, Giovanni began to compose verse for children. Among her published volumes for young readers are *Spin a Soft Black Song, Ego-Tripping and Other Poems for Young People,* and *Vacation Time.* Written for children of all ages, Giovanni's poems are unrhymed incantations of childhood images and feelings. *Spin a Soft Black Song,* which she dedicated to her son Tommy, covers a wealth of childhood interests, such as basketball games, close friends, moms, and the coming of spring. "Poem for Rodney" finds a young man contemplating what he wants to be when he grows up. "If" reflects a young man's daydreams about what it might have been like to participate in a historic event. In a *New York Times Book Review* article on *Spin a Soft Black Song,* Nancy Klein noted, "Nikki Giovanni's poems for children, like her adult works, exhibit a combination of casual energy and sudden wit. No cheek-pinching auntie, she explores the contours of childhood with honest affection, sidestepping both nostalgia and condescension."

Ego-Tripping and Other Poems for Young People contains several poems previously published in *Black Feeling, Black Talk.* Focusing on African American history, the collection explores issues and concerns specific to black youngsters. In "Poem for Black Boys," for example, Giovanni wonders why young boys of color do not play runaway slave or Mau-Mau, thereby identifying with the brave heroes of their own race rather than the white cowboys of the Wild West. "Revolutionary Dreams" and "Revolutionary Music" speak to the racial strife of the 1960s and 1970s and look toward an end to racial tension. Commenting on *Ego-Tripping,* a *Kirkus Reviews* contributor claimed: "When [Giovanni] grabs hold ... it's a rare kid, certainly a rare black kid, who could resist being picked right up."

Vacation Time contrasts with Giovanni's two earlier poetry collections for children by being "a much more relaxed and joyous collection which portrays the world of children as full of wonder and delight," according to Kay E. Vandergrift in *Twentieth-Century Children's Writers.* In *Vacation Time* Giovanni uses more traditional rhyme patterns than in *Spin a Soft Black Song.* Reviewing the work for the *Bulletin of the Center for Children's Books,* Zena Sutherland noted that the rhythms often seem forced and that Giovanni uses "an occasional contrivance to achieve scansion." Yet other critics praised the poet's themes. "In her singing lines, Giovanni shows she hadn't forgotten childhood adventures in ... exploring the world with a small person's sense of discovery," wrote a *Publishers Weekly* reviewer. Mitchell, too, claimed: "One may be dazzled by the smooth way [Giovanni] drops all political and personal concerns [in *Vacation Time*] and completely enters the world of the child and brings to it all the fanciful beauty, wonder, and lollipopping."

Giovanni's later works for children include *Knoxville, Tennessee* and *The Sun Is So Quiet.* The first work, a free-verse poem originally published in *Black Feeling, Black Talk, Black Judgement,* celebrates the pleasures of summer. Many of the warm images presented in the picture book again came directly from the author's childhood memories. Ellen Fader, writing in *Horn Book,* called *The Sun Is So Quiet* "a celebration of African-American family life for all families." Published in 1996, *The Sun Is So Quiet* offers a collection of thirteen poems, ranging in topics from snowflakes to bedtime to missing teeth. "The poems," wrote a *Publishers Weekly* reviewer, "hover like butterflies, darting in to make their point and then fluttering off."

Giovanni has found writing for children to be particularly fulfilling because she is a mother who reads to her son. "Mostly I'm aware, as the mother of a reader, that I read to him," she once observed in an interview. "I think all of us know that your first line to the child is going to be his parent, so you want to write something that the parent likes and can share." According to Mitchell, the children's poems have "essentially the same impulse" as Giovanni's adult poetry—namely, "the creation of racial pride and the communication of individual love. These are the goals of all of Giovanni's poetry, here directed toward a younger and more impressionable audience."

Throughout the 1970s and 1980s Giovanni's popularity as a speaker and lecturer increased along with her success as a poet and children's author. She received numerous awards for her work, including honors from the National Council of Negro Women and the National Association of Radio and Television Announcers. She was featured in articles for such magazines as *Ebony, Jet,* and *Harper's Bazaar.* She also continued to travel, making trips to Europe and Africa.

In *My House* Giovanni began to exhibit increased sophistication and maturity. Her viewpoint had broadened beyond a rigid black revolutionary consciousness to balance a wide range of social concerns. Her rhymes had also become more pronounced, more lyrical, more gentle. The themes of family love, loneliness, and frustration, which Giovanni had defiantly explored in her earlier works, find much deeper expression in *My House.* In a review for *Contemporary Women Poets,* Jay S. Paul called the book "a poetic tour through ... a place rich with family remembrance, distinctive personalities, and prevailing love." And in the foreword to *My House,* Ida Lewis observed that Giovanni "has reached a simple philosophy more or less to the effect that a good family spirit is what produces healthy communities, which is what produces a strong (Black) nation." Noting the focus on self-discovery throughout *My House,* critic John W. Conner suggested in *English Journal* that Giovanni "sees her world as an extension of herself ...

sees problems in the world as an extension of her problems, and ... sees herself existing amidst tensions, heartache, and marvelous expressions of love." "*My House* is not just poems," added Kalumu Ya Salaam in *Black World.* "*My House* is how it is, what it is to be a young, single, intelligent Black woman with a son and no man. It is what it is to be a woman who has failed and is now sentimental about some things, bitter about some things, and generally always frustrated, always feeling frustrated on one of various levels or another." *My House* contained the revelations of a woman coming to terms with her life. *The Women and the Men* continued this trend.

When Giovanni published *Cotton Candy on a Rainy Day,* critics viewed it as one of her most somber works. They noted the focus on emotional ups and downs, fear and insecurity, and the weight of everyday responsibilities. Batman also sensed the poet's frustration at aims unmet. "What distinguishes *Cotton Candy on a Rainy Day* is its poignancy," the critic maintained. "One feels throughout that here is a child of the 1960s mourning the passing of a decade of conflict, of violence, but most of all, of hope."

During the year *Cotton Candy* was published, Giovanni's father suffered a stroke. She and her son immediately left their apartment in New York City and returned to the family home in Cincinnati to help her mother cope with her father's failing health. After her father passed on, Giovanni and her son continued to stay in Cincinnati with her aging mother. She thus built the same secure, supportive, multigenerational environment for Tommy that she had enjoyed as a child.

The poems in *Vacation Time* reflect, perhaps, the poet's growing lightness of spirit and inner stability as she enjoys her family. Similarly, *Those Who Ride the Night Winds* reveals "a new and innovative form," according to Mitchell, who added that "the poetry reflects her heightened self-knowledge and imagination. *Those Who Ride the Night Winds* tends to echo the political activism of Giovanni's early verse as she dedicates various pieces to Phillis Wheatley, Martin Luther King Jr., and Rosa Parks. In *Sacred Cows ... and Other Edibles* she presents essays on a wide range of topics: African American political leaders, national holidays, and termites all come under her insightful and humorous scrutiny. Such essays as "Reflections on My Profession," "Four Introductions," and "An Answer to Some Questions on How I Write" are described by *Washington Post Book World* critic Marita Golden as "quintessential Nikki Giovanni—sometimes funny, nervy and unnerving with flashes of wisdom."

As Giovanni moved through her middle years, her works continued to reflect her changing concerns and perspectives. *The Selected Poems of Nikki Giovanni,* which spans the first three decades of her career, was heralded by *Booklist* critic Donna Seaman as a "rich synthesis [that] reveals the evolution of Giovanni's voice and charts the course of the social issues that are her muses, issues of gender and race." Twenty of the fifty-three works collected in *Love Poems* find the writer musing on subjects as diverse as friendship, sexual desire, motherhood, and loneliness, while the remainder of the volume includes relevant earlier works. "Funny yet thoughtful, Giovanni celebrates creative energy and the family spirit of African American communities," Frank Allen wrote of *Love Poems* in a *Library Journal* review.

Giovanni continues to supplement her poetry with occasional volumes of nonfiction. In *Racism 101* she looks back over the past thirty years as one who has influenced the civil rights movement and its aftermath. Characterized by a *Publishers Weekly* reviewer as "fluid, often perceptive musings that beg for more substance," this collection of essays touches on diverse topics. Giovanni gives advice to young African American scholars who are just starting an academic career, and she reflects on her own experiences as a teacher. She also provides a few glimpses into her personal life—for instance, she admits to being a confirmed "Trekkie." The book is a rich source of impressions of other black intellectuals, including writer and activist W. E. B. DuBois, writers Henry Louis Gates, Jr. and Toni Morrison, Supreme Court Justice Clarence Thomas, and filmmaker Spike Lee. "Giovanni is a shrewd observer and an exhilarating essayist," maintained Seaman in *Booklist*, "modulating her tone from chummy to lethal, hilarious to sagacious as smoothly as a race-car driver shifts gears." In addition to publishing original writings, Giovanni has edited poetry collections like the highly praised *Shimmy Shimmy Shimmy like My Sister Kate*. A compilation of works composed by African American writers during the Harlem Renaissance of the early twentieth century, *Shimmy* helps students of black writing to gain an understanding of the past.

"Most writers spend too much time alone; it is a lonely profession," Giovanni once explained. "I'm not the only poet to point that out. Unless we make ourselves get out and see people, we miss a lot." Teaching, lecturing, sustaining close family ties, and remaining active in her community have allowed the poet to balance the loneliness of writing with a myriad of life experiences. "[Teaching] enriches my life, I mean it keeps reminding all of us that there are other concerns out there," Giovanni said. "It widens your world . . . . I have certain skills that I am able to impart and that I want to, and it keeps me involved in my community and in a community of writers who are not professional but who are interested. I think that's good."

"Writing is . . . what I do to justify the air I breathe," Giovanni wrote, explaining her choice of a vocation in *CAAS*. "I have been considered a writer who writes from rage and it confuses me. What else do writers write from? A poem has to say something. It has to make some sort of sense; be lyrical; to the point; and still able to be read by whatever reader is kind enough to pick up the book." Giovanni believes one of her most important qualities is to have experienced life and to have been able to translate those experiences into her work— "apply the lessons learned," as she termed it in *CAAS*. "Isn't that the purpose of people living and sharing? So

that others will at least not make the same mistake, since we seldom are able to recreate the positive things in life." She continues to look back on her contributions to American poetry with pride. "I think that I have grown; I feel that my work has grown a lot," she once told an interviewer. "What I've always wanted to do is something different, and I think each book has made a change. I hope that the next book continues like that. Like all writers, I guess, I keep looking for the heart . . . ." She concluded, "human beings fascinate me. You just keep trying to dissect them poetically to see what's there."

Works Cited

Allen, Frank, review of *Love Poems, Library Journal*, February 1, 1997, p. 84.

Batman, Alex, *Dictionary of Literary Biography*, Volume 5: *American Poets Since World War II*, Part I: A-K, Gale, 1980.

Conner, John W., review of *My House, English Journal*, April, 1973, p. 650.

Review of *Ego-Tripping and Other Poems, Kirkus Reviews*, January 1, 1974, p. 11.

Fader, Ellen, review of *Knoxville, Tennessee, Horn Book*, September/October, 1994, p. 575.

Review of *Gemini: An Extended Autobiographical Statement on My First Twenty-Five Years of Being a Black Poet, Kirkus Reviews*, September 15, 1971, p. 1051.

Giovanni, Nikki, *Gemini: An Extended Autobiographical Statement on My First Twenty-Five Years of Being a Black Poet*, Bobbs-Merrill, 1971.

Giovanni, Nikki, interview in *Ebony*, February, 1972, pp. 48-50.

Giovanni, Nikki, interview in *Harper's Bazaar*, July, 1972, p. 50.

Giovanni, Nikki, essay in *Contemporary Authors Autobiography Series*, Volume 6, Gale, 1988, pp. 151-64.

Golden, Marita, review of *Sacred Cows . . . and Other Edibles, Washington Post Book Review*, February 14, 1988, p. 3.

Klein, Nancy, review of *Spin a Soft Black Song, New York Times Book Review*, November 28, 1971, p. 8.

Lee, Don L., "Nikki Giovanni," *Dynamite Voices I: Black Poets of the 1960's*, Broadside Press, 1971, pp. 68-73.

Lewis, Ida, introduction to *My House*, Morrow, 1972.

Mitchell, Mozella G., essay in *Dictionary of Literary Biography*, Volume 41: *Afro-American Poets since 1955*, Gale, 1985, pp. 135-51.

Paul, Jay S., "Nikki Giovanni," *Contemporary Poets*, St. James Press, 1996, pp. 390-91.

Review of *Racism 101, Publishers Weekly*, December 13, 1993, p. 54.

Salaam, Kalumu Ya, review of *My House, Black World*, July, 1974.

Seaman, Donna, review of *Racism 101, Booklist*, December 1, 1993, p. 658.

Seaman, Donna, review of *The Selected Poems of Nikki Giovanni (1968-1995), Booklist*, December 15, 1995, p. 682.

Review of *The Sun Is So Quiet, Publishers Weekly*, October 21, 1996, p. 83.

Sutherland, Zena, review of *Vacation Time, Bulletin of the Center for Children's Books,* October, 1980, p. 31.

Review of *Vacation Time, Publishers Weekly,* May 23, 1980, p. 77.

Vandergrift, Kay E., essay in *Twentieth-Century Children's Writers,* 4th edition, St. James Press, 1995, p. 388.

For More Information See

BOOKS

Contemporary Literary Criticism, Volume 64, Gale, 1991.

Dictionary of Literary Biography, Volume 5: *American Poets since World War II,* Gale, 1980; Volume 41: *Afro-American Poets since 1955,* Gale, 1985.

Evans, Mari, editor, *Black Women Writers, 1950-1980: A Critical Evaluation,* Doubleday, 1984.

Fowler, Virginia, *Nikki Giovanni,* Twayne, 1992.

Fowler, Virginia, editor, *Conversations with Nikki Giovanni,* University Press of Mississippi (Jackson), 1992.

Lystad, Mary, "Nikki Giovanni," *Twentieth-Century Young Adult Writers,* St. James Press, 1994, pp. 245-46.

Tate, Claudia, editor, *Black Women Writers at Work,* Crossroads Publishing, 1983.

PERIODICALS

Booklist, September 15, 1994, p. 122; December 15, 1995.

Bulletin of the Center for Children's Books, June, 1996, p. 334.

Jet, April 4, 1994, p. 29.

Kirkus Reviews, March 15, 1996, p. 447.

Library Journal, January, 1996, p. 103.

Publishers Weekly, December 18, 1995, pp. 51-52.

School Library Journal, April, 1994, p. 119; October, 1994, p. 152; May, 1996, p. 103.

Voice of Youth Advocates, December, 1994, p. 298; October, 1996, pp. 229-30.

*   *   *

GREENLAW, M. Jean 1941-

Personal

Born April 1, 1941, in St. Petersburg, FL; daughter of Hinckley and Dorothy (Ball) Greenlaw; married Shelton L. Root, Jr., September 11, 1971 (deceased, 1987). *Education:* Stetson University, B.A., 1962, M.A., 1965; Michigan State University, Ph.D., 1970. *Politics:* Republican.

Addresses

Home—2600 Sheraton Rd., Denton, TX 76201. *Office*—University of North Texas, College of Education, Denton, TX 76203. *Electronic mail*—greenlaw@coefs.coe.unt.edu.

Career

Elementary schoolteacher in Fort Lauderdale, FL, 1962-65; Harper & Row (publishers), New York City, elementary consultant, 1965-69; Michigan State University, East Lansing, graduate teaching assistant, 1969-70;

M. Jean Greenlaw

University of Georgia, Athens, assistant professor, 1970-74, associate professor, 1974-78; Southeast Technical Assistance, Team Right-to-Read, director, 1973-74. North Texas State University, Denton, associate professor, 1978-82; University of North Texas, Denton, professor of education, 1982-87, regents professor, 1987—, head of reading, 1990-96. Also served as visiting professor at Michigan State University and Columbia University, NY, both in 1987 and as a faculty member of National Faculty Atlanta, 1997-2003. Friends of the Denton Public Libraries, member, 1988—, president, 1992-94; City of Denton, Library Board, member, 1990-96, president, 1996; Keep Denton Beautiful Board, member, 1998—. *Member:* International Reading Association, 1965—; president of Denton area council, 1980-81; Children's Book Award Committee, 1983-85; Paul A. Witty Short Story Award committee, 1985-88. National Council of Teachers of English, 1965—; Books for Children Committee, 1970-75; National Nominating Committee, 1976, 1984; treasurer of Children's Literature Assembly (CLA), 1977-78; associate chair of CLA, 1977-78; advisory board member of CLA, 1975-78; chair of Literature for Adolescents Committee, 1978-80; Board of Directors, 1979-80, 1984-85, 1993-94; editor of newsletter, 1977-79; Commission on Literature, 1977-80; liaison with Association for Childhood Education International, 1977-81; chair of Elementary Section Nominating Committee, 1983; program chair of Spring Conference 1984, chair of CEE Commission on the Education of Teachers of Reading, 1983-86; Orbis Pictus Book Award Committee, 1989-90; Award for Excellence in Poetry for Children Committee, member, 1989-91, chair, 1991-94; National

Society for the Study of Education, 1968-91. American Library Association, 1970—; Newbery Award committee, 1980-82; chairperson of Batchelder Book Award committee, 1982-84; Notable Book Selection Committee, 1989-91. National Conference on Research in English (fellow), 1970—; National Reading Conference, 1970-80; Texas State Reading Association, 1978—; Texas Council of Teachers of English, 1978—; Texas Library Association. Phi Kappa Phi, 1970-95; vice-president for public relations, 1986-87. Phi Delta Kappa 1978—; vice-president for programs, 1981-82; president, 1982-83. Kappa Delta Pi 1961—; Delta Kappa Gamma, 1981-86.

Awards, Honors

Teacher of the Year, Broward County, FL, 1964; Award for Outstanding Teaching, International Kiwanis, 1964; New Model in American Education Award, National Education Association, 1964; Excellence in Teaching Citation, Michigan State University, 1970; Outstanding Leadership in Education Award, National Council of Teachers of English, 1976; named Outstanding Young Educator, Phi Delta Kappa, 1981; Arbuthnot Award, International Reading Association, 1992; named to "A Galaxy of Texas Stars," Texas Center for the Book, 1996; President's Council Service Award, University of North Texas, 1996; Distinguished Service Award, Texas State Reading Association, 1996; Distinguished Alumni Award, Stetson University, 1999.

Writings

FOR CHILDREN

Ranch Dressing: The Story of Western Wear, Dutton (New York City), 1993.
Welcome to the Stock Show, Dutton, 1997.

OTHER

(With Karla Hawkins Wendelin) *Storybook Classrooms: Using Children's Literature in the Learning Center,* Humanics (Atlanta, GA), 1984.
(With Margaret E. McIntosh) *Educating the Gifted: A Sourcebook,* American Library Association, 1988.

Editor of "Reading Today Goes to Class: For the Middle School Teacher," a column in *Reading Today,* 1987-90. Contributor to periodicals, including *Horn Book.* Member of editorial review board, *Reading Teacher,* 1988-90 and 1991.

Work in Progress

Women of the Wild Wild West and *Maine Event.*

Sidelights

M. Jean Greenlaw told *SATA:* "I was born in St. Petersburg, Florida, but grew up in Pennsylvania in a small town near Philadelphia. The oldest in a large family, with three sisters and two brothers, I always knew I wanted to be a teacher. After graduating from Stetson University in Florida, I taught in elementary grades in Fort Lauderdale. I received my master's degree from Stetson and my doctorate from Michigan State University. After teaching at the University of Georgia for eight years, I moved to Denton, Texas. I love living in Texas and plan to stay here forever! I share my home with the most wonderful dog in the world, a coal-black, miniature schnauzer named Sweetpea. She is feisty, funny, beautiful, and my constant companion."

Living in Texas has had an enormous influence on Greenlaw's writing. "Texas," she continued to *SATA,* "is my adopted state, and while living here I have been intrigued by the enduring nature of Western culture. My first book was a historical photographic essay, *Ranch Dressing: The Story of Western Wear.* I interviewed many people and did research in museums and libraries, and I unearthed a gold mine of priceless stories that needed to be told."

A *Kirkus Reviews* critic called *Ranch Dressing: The Story of Western Wear* "a title that's a candidate for most outrageous pun of the year." Included in this book are rarely told stories of key players in the western wear industry, like shirtmaker Jack A. Weil and the Justin family of boot fame. Combined with clear descriptions of authentic western attire, the tales form a source that is "not definitive," said the *Kirkus Reviews* critic, "but fun." *School Library Journal* reviewer Charlene Strickland recommended *Ranch Dressing* as "a useful source for reports."

Greenlaw's first successful experience writing a children's book inspired further creative efforts. "When *The Story of Western Wear* was published, I was hooked," she explained. "I realized that I wanted to write more books, and that I wanted most to write about the West. Because I love photography, I decided to continue to write photographic essays. For *Welcome to the Stock Show,* I followed three children for a year as they raised and showed their animals. I was at the barn with Daniel at four o'clock in the morning as he prepared his Jersey cows for showing. I watched Sarah help her goat give birth to twins in August and then went with her family to the State Fair of Texas, where one of the kids won her first blue ribbon. I also went to numerous shows with another Sarah, who won dozens of ribbons for her rabbits. The book features the experiences of these three children during a year of joy and hard work. Through their words, readers learn much about animals and about the inside workings of a stock show, whether it is a small community show or one of the huge shows in Fort Worth, Houston, or San Antonio."

Deborah Stevenson of *The Bulletin of the Center for Children's Books* commended *Welcome to the Stock Show* for its "absorbing details about show practices and conventions" as well as for the book's emphasis on "the responsibility and commitment of the young exhibitors and their families." Stevenson also approved of Greenlaw's subject matter, contending, "it's still hard to beat the animal/kid pairing as a topic." *School Library Journal* contributor Patricia Manning described *Wel-*

come to the Stock Show as "a Kuraltian slice of Americana."

Speaking of her next endeavor, Greenlaw said: "The book I am working on now is all about women who have been inducted into the National Cowgirl Hall of Fame. These are all women who truly made a difference in our culture. Learning about them has opened my eyes to how little we know about the women who settled the West and those who are still making a huge contribution."

Works Cited

Manning, Patricia, review of *Welcome to the Stock Show, School Library Journal,* September, 1997, p. 230.

Review of *Ranch Dressing: The Story of Western Wear, Kirkus Reviews,* December 1, 1993, p. 1523.

Stevenson, Deborah, review of *Welcome to the Stock Show, Bulletin of the Center for Children's Books,* October, 1997, pp. 51-52.

Strickland, Charlene, review of *Ranch Dressing: The Story of Western Wear, School Library Journal,* January, 1994.

For More Information See

PERIODICALS

Booklist, September 15, 1997, p. 225.
Bulletin of the Center for Children's Books, January, 1994, p. 154.

Autobiography Feature

Helen V. Griffith

1934-

I couldn't wait to learn to read. I used to open books and gaze at the pages, anticipating the excitement of seeing words appear out of those blocks of letters.

"When I start school," I told my brother (seventeen months younger), "I'll know so many words that when I talk, you won't understand what I'm saying." He seemed impressed, but not worried. Buddy didn't care about reading or big words. He just liked to play. His name was really John David, but my grandmother used to sing a little rhyme to him: Buddy Booster, riding on a rooster. For a while he was Buddy Booster; luckily, that didn't stick. Now most people call him Bud. Unfortunately, Buddy's first word was a breathy, "Ssiss," and I've been Sis ever since.

I was born in 1934 and grew up in Richardson Park, a suburb of Wilmington, Delaware. It was a nice place to live. Most of the families were first generation off-the-farm, and it seemed as if all the kids I knew had grandparents in the country to visit. I thought they were lucky.

My own parents had grown up in Wilmington, and my mother's mother lived in a dark rowhouse in town. There wasn't much to do when we visited, except to sit on the floor making houses out of playing cards. Actually, I enjoyed that. Another treat was my grandmother's friendly little dog, Tiny, that always greeted us by wetting on the rug.

I don't have many memories of my paternal grandmother's house, because she ran out of money when I was only a few years old. For the rest of her life she lived with one or another of her three children. She always wanted to have her own home again, but it never happened.

Everything in Richardson Park was in walking distance, which gave us some early independence. We could visit friends or go to the store or a movie without having to wait for someone to take us, and we could walk or ride our bikes home from school for lunch.

I was big on paper dolls and coloring books as a child, but I played outside a lot too. My favorite games were hopscotch and "jumpinrope." An older girl, bursting with secret knowledge, told me that someday I wouldn't feel like doing those things anymore. I tried not to believe her, but it was a chilling thought.

My parents had been married for ten years when I came along, and my mother, at thirty, considered herself a very old parent. She lived a long life, and over the years, especially the last ones, we spent a lot of time together. We talked so much and became so close that I began to feel that I had always known her. When I look at pictures now of my mother as a child, a teenager, a young woman, I recognize her as if I had been there. In fact, it's not like stages of a life. I see her whole life as one moment.

But when I was young, she was just my mother, too sociable and friendly in my opinion, usually out visiting or shopping or at the Richardson Park Women's Civic Club. (For years I thought it was "civvyclub.") She always managed to get home in time to cook supper for us though. My father used to pretend amazement, saying she could

Helen V. Griffith

swing into the driveway on two wheels and whip up a full meal in ten minutes. He told us she could always get a job as a short-order cook. She made the best things—corn fritters, fried tomatoes in milk gravy, oyster stew and clam chowder and baked shad. Good desserts too—chocolate pie and apple crisp and pineapple upside-down cake. One day she decided baking cakes wasn't worth the trouble; we ate them up too fast. That didn't make sense to me. I said, "What are they for, then?" but she didn't have an answer.

My mother was proud of us kids, and we knew she loved us, but not unconditionally. There were rules of behavior to be followed, and if they were broken, there were lectures. I used to think I'd rather be hit than have to hear those lectures. We knew that it was possible to go over the line with my mother, and that, if we did something she really disapproved of, forgiveness was not a sure thing. The knowledge didn't keep us from getting into trouble, but it did mean that we would go to any lengths to keep her from finding out when we did.

My mother's life didn't get off to a very good start. Her parents divorced when she was about eight, and her mother went to New York to try for an acting career. My mother lived with whatever relative would take her in for a while, but she wasn't wanted, and she knew it. Nobody had any money, which made matters worse. My mother told me that she decided very early that she was not going to be like the people around her. She wanted to be respectable and good, and she patterned her behavior on the most refined women she knew of, the heroines in silent movies. They must have been good role models, because anyone who remembers my mother tells me how cheerful and friendly she was, and how ladylike.

My father was something else again. As a teenager he had lived in a little railroad town called Atchee, Colorado, where he and his cousins rode horseback, hiked in the mountains, and started avalanches for fun. He loved fishing, hunting, and camping, and my mother said she always felt sorry that he had to give up that outdoor life when they married. There was no doubt he wanted to marry her though. He never knew she had saved his love letters and that, when I grew up, she showed them to me. They were so passionate they startled me, and so young, it hurt to read them.

My father probably should have stayed in Atchee. He didn't seem to fit in a house. Even as a child I was surprised at how reckless and rough he was. He was always sorry when he broke things, but he couldn't help it.

He also chain-smoked and was very careless with the cigarettes. There were burn marks on the kitchen counters, on tables and chair arms, and there were holes in the sheets, in his clothes, even in the cane headboard of their bed. He used the dogs' backs for ashtrays, and stubbed out his butts in his shirt pocket. Somehow he didn't burn down the house, but he came close many times. It wasn't rare for me to wake up to the sound of swearing and thumping as he beat out mattress and pillow fires.

My mother and I were always after him to stop smoking, not just because of the fires, but because his coughing in the morning was terrible to hear. Finally one day (he was in his seventies by then) he threw away his half-empty pack and just quit. He said, "I hope you women are satisfied," and from then on, when anybody asked him how he felt he said, "No good." But he didn't cough anymore.

I admired my father tremendously. He didn't graduate from high school, but he seemed to know everything. I learned not to ask him questions about my schoolwork, because he was always familiar with whatever subject we were studying and was ready to tell me more than I wanted to know. His spare time was spent reading, and his favorite books were about travel and explorations in foreign lands. At the supper table he talked about events in the news and told us the history behind what was happening now. I didn't always pay a lot of attention, but I believe I learned more history from my father than I learned in school.

He used to recite poetry sometimes, especially Poe and Robert Service. That was entertaining, but even better was his singing. I liked to sit on the cellar steps while he washed up after work and listen to "Bye Bye Blackbird," "Jada," and "Willie the Weeper." And it always made me laugh when he sang about Ramona from Barcelona who threw her bolero way up in the air-o.

My father was a machinist for the Pennsylvania Railroad. Although I had no idea what a machinist did, except that his clothes and hands were always black with grease, I remember being breathless with pride when I told people what my father's occupation was. His ways were my standard of the way a man should be. He never went to school functions, so I looked down on fathers who did. When we kids frustrated him, he would let out a stream of curses that would convulse me and my brother. His anger wasn't threatening, and to us it was very funny.

When I was in high school I was having trouble one night with a theme that was due the next day. It got late, and everyone was in bed when my father came downstairs

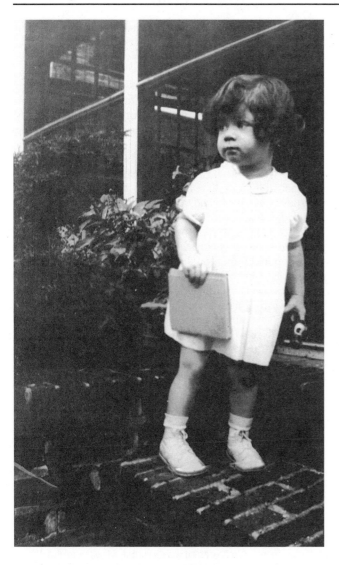

"Here I am with my Mother Goose *book."*

and handed me some papers. Thinking I didn't know what to write about, he had started a story for me. I didn't use it, but I kept it, and I have it still. I'm always surprised when I read that little story, because it sounds just like something I would write myself.

Except for a few years of battle when I started liking boys, my father and I were close. The older I get, the more like him I become, which may or may not be a good thing. We had the same sense of humor and could always make each other smile. I miss that.

The other member of our household was my grandfather, my mother's father. My brother and I loved him and were always respectful and polite to him, just as my parents were. He read all the time too, but, unlike my father, he read a lot of fiction. He took me to the library in Wilmington one day, the first time I had ever been there. Libraries were blessedly quiet then, and we sat at a round table while he looked over whatever it was he had come to read. He gave me a book too, an adult book with no pictures. I couldn't read yet, but I sat with the book open in front me, awed and happy and hoping people would notice.

My grandfather had had only five years of school, but he had taken correspondence courses in geometry and whatever other forms of mathematics are needed to become a tinsmith. By the time I appeared, he had a roofing and sheet-metal supply business. I work in that business today, and my brother is my boss.

My grandfather had a wonderful old set of Dickens that he often read, and he and my father would discuss the books at the supper table. I knew many Dickens plots and characters intimately, long before I could read them for myself. My mother was a fan too. She told me that she started reading *Dombey and Son* while she was carrying me, but she had to stop because it made her cry too much.

My brother, the only nonreader in the family, has no recollection of those dinner-table book talks at all. He says we talked about hunting and fishing. I don't remember that.

My brother doesn't recall our bedtime stories either. When we were very little, four or so, my grandfather would come into our bedroom after my mother had tucked us in and read from an enormous, ancient copy of *The Arabian Nights.* My brother usually fell right to sleep, but I liked lying there listening to those ghastly stories of death by scimitar and ogre and roc, although, as a Sunday School girl, I didn't always approve of the lifestyles of Sindbad and his associates.

I liked being read to so much that I got into the habit of calling my grandfather into our room in the middle of the night. That went on until my mother caught us and put a stop to it. He still read us the funny papers though, and the highlight of Sunday morning was sitting on his lap, my brother on one knee, and I on the other, while he read every single strip. I loved those times, and yet, as soon as I could read for myself, I gave them up without a thought.

There was no TV when we were growing up, but there was plenty of entertainment. We and everybody else went to lots of movies, often four or five in a week. We would just up and go, with no regard for the starting time, and then sit and watch and try to figure out what was going on. The last half or third or whatever was left of the movie would roll by, then news, a cartoon, previews, a "selected short subject," and then the feature would begin again. After a while there would be whispering. "This is where we came in. Do you want to leave? Shall we stay through to the end?" We often stayed, and I found it very interesting the way the plot began to make sense. To me now it seems like a strange way to go to the movies, but everybody did it, at least the people I knew.

You often read about the deep impressions those old movies made on people, and they certainly did on me. My brother and I still smile at how we ducked down in our seats in sheer terror when the Mummy walked out of the swamp or Frankenstein's Monster reared up from the operating table. We sat quietly through *The Maltese Falcon* and *Casablanca* with no clue as to what was happening. I remember Humphrey Bogart and Sidney Greenstreet talking and talking, but I only liked the parts when Peter Lorre was on. He was interesting.

My father took my brother and me to see *The Wizard of Oz.* For some reason, the scene when it starts to snow scared me, so we left. Later my mother took us to the same movie. When the snow scene came on, I got scared again and wanted to leave, but my mother said she'd paid to see the movie, and we were staying. Once I knew I had to stay,

I was fine. My mother was good at defusing situations. I was inclined to dramatize myself, but she wouldn't go along.

The radio was our other main family entertainment. There were kids' shows in the late afternoon that my brother and I and my grandfather listened to. My grandfather liked them even more than we did, just like the funny papers.

One show offered a disguise kit in exchange for labels and probably a quarter. I sent for it, but I was surprised when the disguise kit turned out to be a little box of makeup and a false mustache. I had fully expected a suitcase containing at least a ballet costume and a cape and some large hats, but I pretended to myself that I wasn't disappointed.

Even before I could read, I was familiar with the books in our bookcase. Very few were children's books, but there were enough to keep me happy. I had my thrilling Lois Lenski's *Mother Goose,* and now and then my grandfather, a haunter of used-book stores, would bring home a turn-of-the-century primer with pictures of serious-looking children dressed in complicated clothes. My grandfather and my parents read the stories to me so often that I knew them by heart and would sit reciting aloud, turning the pages at the appropriate places. Anyone watching assumed that I could read. I knew I couldn't and said so, but I think it was harder to believe that I could memorize all that material than that I could read it.

My grandfather had been a big vaudeville fan and used to tell me and my brother jokes that we didn't understand at all. We always laughed though. He was half Irish and loved funny stories about the Irish and songs like "Who Put the Overalls in Mrs. Murphy's Chowder?"

He liked to show me how he used to dance the Scotshoddie. I don't know how he really pronounced it, but that's how I heard it. One day he started to dance for me and wasn't able to do it. He made another attempt, but he simply couldn't remember the steps. I felt sorry, but I didn't know what to say. I don't think he ever tried again.

"The house in Richardson Park where I grew up."

A lady around the corner from us had a kindergarten in her house and I went there for a few months before I started first grade. It was very exciting. We made clocks out of paper pie plates and Easter baskets from oatmeal boxes. Each day before we went home we stood and swore never to drink or smoke or play cards and that we wouldn't drink tea or coffee before we were twenty-one. I felt slightly guilty about that pledge, because I had already done a little tea-drinking and card-playing, but I promised anyway.

I fully expected to learn to read in kindergarten, but I didn't. I was in first grade, almost six, when it happened, and then it wasn't like learning at all. The process was effortless, as if I had always known how, but the knowledge had just slipped my mind for a while. I understood the reasons for everything, grammar, spelling, punctuation; the whole system made perfect sense.

My poor brother, on the other hand, was in for years of torture. He just couldn't get it. We laugh now at the memories of his spelling lessons with my father, but at the time it wasn't funny to any of us. Buddy would be crying, my father swearing, I curled up with my fingers in my ears, aching with pity. He would usually remember the spellings long enough to pass his test, but no longer. My brother can read and write as well as anyone now, but his timetable was different from the school system's.

I first fell in love in first grade. His name was Edwin and he had rabbits. I had a rabbit myself, from Easter, and I proposed that we exchange pets as a sign of our feelings for each other. We did, and in no time his mother was at our door, outraged because our rabbit was wreaking havoc among their rabbits. It was a little confusing to my mother, since I hadn't thought to inform her of the switch, but soon the rabbits were returned to their own hutches. Not long after, Edwin and I drifted apart.

It was in my first year of school that I first learned I had had another brother. A classmate's mother told her to ask me if I was a sister of the boy who had drowned six years before. I said no, but when I mentioned it to my mother, she told me for the first time about my brother, David. From that time on, David's death was a central fact of my life. My mother had told me in the calmest, gentlest way, but I was still shocked. For a long time I tried to think that it was a mistake, that it was someone else's body they had found, and that David was still alive somewhere and would find his way back home.

Now and then over the years my mother told me little stories about David, how much fun he was and how grown up for his age. She said that after he died, no one mentioned his name anymore. The minister came to visit, and she told him how much she wanted to talk about David, and how nobody would listen. He just said, "No wonder, when you cry so much." My father wouldn't talk either. Except for going to work, he spent all of his time at the cemetery or in the cellar, smoking one cigarette after another. He told my mother he couldn't stand it and asked her how she could. She was sad telling me about it, years and years later. She said she just told him that there was nothing else to do.

David was nearly nine when he died, and I was born a few months later. My mother said she felt sorry about bringing a baby into such a grieving place as our home was then, but I'm glad I was on the way. I feel as if I fulfilled my purpose in the world just by being born. Having a new baby in the house forced my father back into the stream of life.

Still, my father never spoke of my brother, never said the word "drown," avoided saying the name "David," and would leave the room if we talked about a bad thing happening to a child. I always worried when we were with people and the conversation seemed to be heading that way. I cringed when the situation or dialogue in a movie touched on the death of a child.

Every Sunday we went to the cemetery, my brother and I and my father. My mother and grandfather rarely came along. Buddy and I played among the tombstones while my father filled vases and arranged flowers on David's grave. At Christmas, he trimmed a small tree with little red balls and lots of tinsel and took it to the cemetery for David. He had been doing this all my life, but I hadn't understood why before. I had just accepted it as something people did on Sundays.

One evening, when Buddy was about ten, he fell asleep in the bathtub. My father broke the door lock, pulled him out of the tub, and carried him to bed. Somehow, Buddy slept through the whole thing. Later, my mother told me she went downstairs during the night and found my father in the kitchen, shaking uncontrollably, trying to make a cup of coffee. She said there was coffee and water everywhere. That incident was never mentioned in front of my father, and the bathroom door was never fixed.

Years later, I asked my brother how those sad undercurrents in our lives had affected him. He didn't know what I meant; he had never felt them.

I think I was in second grade when my mother took me in to Wilmington to get a library card. Since I considered myself a reader now, I didn't want any books with pictures. I always checked out books that were much too difficult for me, but I read them anyway, as much as I was able. I developed what I later called my frozen vocabulary, words that I knew on the page and used in my thoughts, but couldn't pronounce. Some I didn't even recognize when I heard them spoken, especially French-derived ones. Ingenue, chic, naive, who could imagine their surprising pronunciations?

In the second grade I produced my one and only play. It came from a wonderful magazine I used to get called *Children's Activities* and was based on the story of "The Shoemaker and the Elves." I talked some classmates into playing the parts, made up a dance for the elves to do (cleverly casting twin girls in the roles), and the teacher let us perform it for our second grade class. I think it must have been very cute, but once it was over nobody ever mentioned it again. I wonder if anyone remembers it.

The first stories that I ever tried to write were inspired by *Children's Activities*. In fact, they were complete rip-offs. I found out early that plotting is not easy.

I wasn't very old when a condition surfaced that dogged me nearly all my life. I became shy. The first time I felt it was the year I was Queen of the May for Richardson Park. I was looking forward to being in the parade. I wore a white dress, and a Boy Scout pulled me down the main street in a wagon. Children in costumes followed us, and there were what seemed like hundreds of people lining the street, watching. I was holding a scepter with a star on the end, which I had planned to wave as I rode along. But when

Helen at nine in St. Petersburg, Florida.

I got out in front of the people, something happened to me. I felt very heavy, as if I couldn't lift my arms, and a weight on the back of my neck pushed my head toward my chest. I couldn't look up or smile or wave my wand as I had planned. Afterwards my mother said, "Why didn't you wave?" but I had no explanation. I didn't know anything about shyness at that point, but I had plenty of experience with it in the years to come.

Around the time the war started, my grandfather bought a farm, located just over the state line in Kaolin, Pennsylvania, about ten miles from our home. My mother said she had always dreamed of a little house in an orchard, but she never expected to be saddled with a huge stone barn and various collapsing outbuildings in the middle of seventy-six acres of neglected farmland. A long, axle-busting dirt lane led to a farmhouse that had been built in 1768 and showed no signs of being updated since. There was no electricity or plumbing, no closets, none of the comforts that were standard, even back in the forties.

We still had our home in Richardson Park, but now weekends were spent at the farm. Summers, my mother and brother and I stayed there all week too, and my father and grandfather came up in the evenings after work.

I loved the farm, loved being in the country, and was largely unaware of the drudgery my mother had had thrust upon her. She didn't think about it much at the time herself, she told me later. The work was there and had to be done. She ripped up old carpet strips and pulled hundreds of tacks from the floor. She set my brother and me to scraping paint off the walls, layers and layers of it. I hated doing it. Then we painted, and I hated that too. I just wanted to wander around outside and look at things.

The first summer we had the farm, my father used the horses and old machinery that came with the place to farm the old-time way, raising corn and cutting hay. He worked at the railroad all day and worked on the farm in the evenings and on weekends. My grandfather and brother and sometimes I worked along with him. Buddy was young, but he was willing and useful. I was practically no help at all.

My father bought pigs and became so attached to them that it took firmness and threats from my mother before he finally took them off to be butchered. He gave them all names and histories and used to tell me of the conversations they would have on winter nights when he drove up to the farm to feed them. I wish I could remember the things he told me. It was wartime and I recall that the pigs had differing views of the situation. I knew my father was making the stories up, but sometimes he half-convinced me that they were true. I asked him if the pigs were worried about being eaten, and he said no, that they were proud of their destiny. He asked me if I didn't wish I knew my own destiny. I didn't quite know what he meant, but I remember telling people that our animals knew their destiny and were proud.

When I was eight, I was diagnosed with rheumatic fever. I had been getting thinner and weaker for more than a year, but the doctor said I was just nervous. Finally one day in school I put my head down on my desk, and the teacher told me to go home and tell my mother I was sick. I argued, but she insisted. My mother took me to a different doctor that day, and he sent me to bed. I had to stay there for weeks, and I wasn't allowed to run for a year. I have a permanent void where that year's arithmetic should be, but I got a lot of reading done.

Somebody gave me Felix Salten's *Bambi,* and it really became a part of me. I loved the story and the realistic view of nature that was presented in the book. Later my grandfather took me to see the movie, but I was disappointed in it because it was a cartoon. The book was so real to me; I wanted to see real deer.

There was a little book on our bookshelf that I had always ignored, because it didn't look interesting. It was small and old, with a tiny faded picture of a landscape on the front. One day I flipped through the pages and saw that it was about a horse. Of course, I read it then. It was the first time I had heard of *Black Beauty.*

I was a very critical reader. I approved of the writing in *Black Beauty* and *Bambi,* but I complained that the Nancy Drew books were empty. I didn't know what I meant; I just

Helen with her grandfather, mother, father, and brother.

"I was about thirteen when this was taken."

knew something was missing. That didn't stop me from reading every one.

I was very particular about my comic books too. I was delighted by what I considered the sophisticated humor in Donald Duck and Little Lulu, and Captain Marvel won my approval among the action heroes. (I was an adult before I discovered that I had been pronouncing "Shazam" with the accent on the wrong syllable.) I would have loved to compare literary opinions with the neighbor kids, and in fact I tried, but I only got blank stares. They read comics for the action, not the writing.

My very favorite books were about horses and dogs. When I said my prayers at night I would always pray aloud for a Doberman pinscher and a pony, until my father asked me if I was praying to God or Santa Claus.

When I was nine my mother took me and my brother to Florida. Since my father worked at the railroad, we could ride cheaply, but my parents hadn't realized how the war had affected travel. We ended up spending more than a month in St. Petersburg because we couldn't get tickets home. That was fine with me, but it meant another blank in my math education. Since I was good at reading, everyone assumed I was smart. I probably thought so too, at the time. I was rarely asked to make up work I missed, so it was missed forever.

One of my most lasting impressions from that Florida trip was the view from the train window. It was March, turning more and more springlike as we rode south. Along the track were small houses with long porches, and in the fields men were plowing with mules. It seemed like an idyllic life. I wanted a house by a railroad track. I wanted a mule.

In real life, I didn't find field work nearly so enchanting. Although my father never farmed after that first summer, he always planted a large vegetable garden, his "truck patch," every year, and we helped to plant and weed, my brother with a good will, I reluctantly. My mother complained that we never went anywhere anymore because of the farm, and it was true. The work necessary to keep the place fairly habitable was endless. I have mental images of my grandfather walking around carrying a ladder or buckets of cement, my father hoeing in the truck patch, my brother helping whichever man wanted him, my mother cooking, while I sat on the porch reading, writing, or drawing. My father called me "Silk Pillow Sis," because he said all I wanted from life was to sit on a silk pillow and do nothing. It made me mad when he said that, because there was a lot of truth in it.

The last summer of my father's life, when he was eighty-one, we got one last garden planted. My father had to work lying on the ground, but he was determined to have a garden, even if it was just a few tomato and pepper plants.

A few years later I wrote a book that I called *Georgia Music,* about a little girl and her grandfather working in a garden. I liked it, but no one wanted to publish it at that time, so I put it away for awhile. When I came across the story and read it some years later, I surprised myself by starting to cry. I had thought, while I was writing the book, that my inspiration came from my long-ago train ride through the south. Now I could see that the characters in *Georgia Music* were really me and my father. I wouldn't purposely have chosen to write something so personal. For one thing, it would have hurt too much to dwell on that memory. Yet I could write a book about it and not notice what I was doing. That's something to sit and think about someday.

When I was in high school my grandfather brought home a collection of poems by Robert Frost. I had two or three old poetry books that I enjoyed reading, English books filled with references to Cook and the nursery and tea time, but I had never seen anything like the Frost poems, the way they didn't rhyme and the way they were about country things. I sat right down and wrote my own Robert Frost poem. It was called "Barns." I showed it to my English teacher and she liked it so much she had me submit it to the *Atlantic Monthly.* They sent me a very nice letter explaining what they thought it lacked, so my teacher, Miss Kramer, had me send it to a teen magazine, *Calling All Girls.* They paid me ten dollars and published it. That should have been the beginning of my writing career, and maybe if I'd had Rita Kramer pushing me, it would have been. As it was, I never submitted another manuscript until I was nearly forty years old.

I still have some of the writing I did in my high school English classes, and I'm surprised at how good it sounds to me. In fact, sometimes I have the uncomfortable feeling that I'm really no better a writer now than I was at seventeen.

The old farmhouse.

I entered the University of Delaware after high school, majoring in agriculture. I liked the agriculture, but hated everything else about college. I really don't know why. I dropped out after one semester and went to business school, where I was much happier. I learned to work a comptometer, a type of office machine now extinct, and went to work in an office. I used to enjoy playing office when I was little (although it was hard to get anyone to play it with me), and I found real office work just as much fun. I had no ambition at all and no desire for any responsibility. I liked being able to go home when the day was over and not think about work until the next morning.

All this time I wasn't writing anything or even thinking about writing. In fact, I didn't seem to be thinking about anything at all. Then, just for a change I suppose, I decided to give college another try. This time I went to Ohio State, but after one semester I quit again, leaving my parents shaking their heads. (My father: There's something radically wrong with that girl.) I went back to work, and then, on an impulse, just from seeing some irresistible pictures in a travel magazine, I quit my job to take a trip to England. My father didn't see anything radically wrong with that; he was all for it. I traveled around the country in buses and trains, found the house where my grandmother was born, visited the Bronte parsonage, Jane Austen's home, and, thrill of thrills, Thomas Hardy country.

When I returned home, I went to business school again, this time to learn typing and shorthand. They were fun, especially shorthand, a special little code that only I could read. I got another undemanding job, and spent some of my evenings taking courses in things like pottery, classical guitar, and painting. Then, for no particular reason, I enrolled in something called Writing for Magazines, and the lights went on. I had thought it was a course on how to write, but it wasn't that at all. It was about selling. For the first time, I heard about *Writers' Market,*

and query letters, and how a manuscript is typed, all the most basic of information, but news to me.

During the ten weeks of the course, our assignment was to choose a nonfiction topic, query an editor, interview someone, write an article, submit it, and see what happened. I did all those things and sold the article to a local magazine. It seemed so easy. I sold another one to the same magazine. Then the magazine changed editors, and the new editor apparently didn't like my ideas. Maybe it wasn't so easy after all.

It was just as well. I liked being published, but I wasn't crazy about writing nonfiction. I was much too shy to be a good interviewer, and the subjects that were of interest to magazines didn't seem that interesting to me. I wrote a couple of humorous articles and sold them to newspapers, and then one day I had an idea for a children's mystery story. I hadn't considered writing for children before, but I went ahead with it and found a feeling of freedom in doing fiction that I hadn't felt with other kinds of writing. There I was, all by myself, inventing a world, solving problems, directing lives. That's how it seemed to me, and it was exhilarating. I hadn't felt so confident of my abilities since I learned to read.

I called the story "The Owl Tape," sent it to a children's magazine I found listed in *Writers' Market,* and it was accepted and published. The money was nothing, so I never considered quitting my job to write. I did it in my spare time, just because I liked seeing my imagination in print.

I sent my first few stories to children's and teen magazines, because magazines were what I had learned about in my course. Then I wrote a story that I called "John and His Strange Pets." I thought it was good, but I couldn't sell it. I sent it to every possible children's magazine listed in *Writers' Market,* one by one, carefully recording the date I sent it out and the date (months later) when it came back.

After three years, *Writers' Market* had run out of magazines for me to try, but I still liked the story. I wondered if it could possibly be a picture book. My course hadn't covered picture book manuscripts, but *Writers' Market* told me what to do. That book was my Bible. I asked for a copy for Christmas every year.

I retyped my little story, which was now a picture book, and sent it off. When it was returned, I was neither surprised nor discouraged. I just kept sending it out. Again and again.

Then one day it came back with a letter from Susan Hirschman at Greenwillow Books. She said the story wasn't quite right, but if I had anything else, she'd look at it. I really didn't have anything else, but I changed the parts of the story that had bothered her and sent it back. It wasn't long before Susan called and told me that Greenwillow would publish my book, and they did, with the title *Mine Will, Said John.*

I was happy at having a book published, of course, but it was my mother who was overjoyed. Through the years, she derived far more pleasure from my writing than I ever did. She loved Susan Hirschman, she loved Greenwillow Books, and she told me that our trips to New York to "see my publisher" were the best times of her life.

I put off visiting Greenwillow as long as I could. For one thing, I felt kind of old to be a beginning writer; I was forty-five. I knew I would be clumsy and say foolish things.

Another obstacle was that my mother wanted to go with me. I really didn't want to appear at my publisher's with a mother. I was afraid of what those sophisticated New York people would think. My father said, "The hell with them," so I gave in, took my mother, and everyone at Greenwillow was lovely to her, even when she offered to send them copies of the poems I had written as a child. Now, when I remember how happy that visit made her and how wholeheartedly glad she was for my success, I'm grateful that I listened to my father and took her along.

After Greenwillow took my first book, I really wanted to be able to interest them in another one, but I had no idea what to write. At last it occurred to me to read some children's books and see what was being done. I happened on Arnold Lobel's Frog and Toad books and was surprised at the format—several little stories in one book, with one mild but appealing adventure unfolding in each story. I decided to try doing my own little stories.

My innocent young dog, Whippet, and a barn cat that had seen it all were just the characters I needed. It wasn't hard to imagine a relationship between them.

I had been raised on books where animals talked in a European fairy-tale style or like well-brought-up English children, and that was fine, but I wanted my characters to sound American. I wanted them to speak in a way that was informal and modern, with American sentence construction, but not crude or slangy, and not so up-to-the-minute that the language would soon seem dated. After pages of false starts and feeling-my-way writing, I finally came up with something that felt right. I doubt if anyone noticed the American accent that was so important to me, but Greenwillow published the book.

I called it *Whippet and the Cat* originally, but the illustrations were very un-whippety. There was no real reason, as far as the story was concerned, for the dog to be a whippet, but I had imagined it as one, so I changed the name of the dog in the book to Alex and the title of the book to *Alex and the Cat.* Later, the books *More Alex and the Cat* and *Alex Remembers* were illustrated by Donald Carrick, with a dog that, although not a whippet, was very appealing. Then, some years later, the Alex stories were combined into one book, and Sonja Lamut came the closest yet, with a very cute puppy that is just about the real thing.

I was living at the farm when I started writing books. I had chickens and barn cats, along with Whippet the Whippet, Misty the Weimeraner (who kept the cat population down in ways better not described), and a stray dog that skulked in the fields during the day and came nosing around for food at night. I called her Foxy, but it wasn't until I found her puppies that we actually made contact. They were hiding in a groundhog hole, and when I picked

"The first writing I ever sold was a poem about this barn."

"Foxy was a stray who gave me the ideas for three books."

one up, the dog's protective instinct was stronger than her fear. She ran to my side, not to fight, but to stare up at me with dark, imploring eyes. After that encounter, Foxy became my shadow. She needed somebody to trust, and I was it.

Whatever had happened to Foxy before she appeared at my farm made her unable to relate to people in a normal doggy way. It was hard on her, but handy for me. Her fragile personality gave me three books.

When I wrote the first book, *Foxy,* I plotted myself into a corner. It's the only time I had to physically go to the scene of the action before I could work out the book's ending. Since the story took place in the Florida Keys, my research trip wasn't exactly a hardship.

The second book, *Plunk's Dreams,* came from watching Foxy sleep. I wondered what dreams could cause such snarling and growling from an animal that, when awake, never even barked. I named the Foxy character Plunk after a dog my father had when he was a boy. I wish I had thought to ask him where that name came from.

When Foxy grew old and weak, I sometimes sat on the floor beside her, hoping that my nearness might be a comfort to her. She didn't seem to dream anymore, and I used to wonder what was in her mind now. Did she remember being young and active, able to run and jump? Did she miss being able to chase cats and groundhogs? Gradually, the story *Dream Meadow* formed in my mind. There's an old lady in the story and my mother said,

suspiciously, "That's not me, is it?" That made me laugh, because the thought never entered my mind. My mother grew old, but she never seemed like an old woman to me, and she certainly was nothing like the frail old lady in Nancy Barnet's illustrations.

I wonder if my mother would recognize herself in Nickel, the young boy in my novel, *Cougar.* I wasn't thinking of her at all when I began to plot the story, but as I got into the book, I began to see similarities between Nickel's background and my mother's. His character came to life for me when I gave him her instinct for self-preservation, her urge to rise above her surroundings, her ability to recognize a helping hand and take it.

After the book was completed and published, I noticed something else. My mother used to insist that she had a guardian angel. I always scoffed, but she wasn't kidding. She said that she could feel a presence that comforted her when she was sad or afraid. I suppose it would be possible to think of Cougar as Nickel's guardian angel, although I haven't been able to go that far yet.

It's only lately that I've begun to see that most of what I write relates somehow to my early life, an unnerving realization. The most trivial events loom large in my memory and show up here and there in my plots. Long-ago conversations pop up in the dialogue.

For instance, I've only just become aware that the boys in *Dinosaur Habitat* are very much like my brother and me at that age. I remember being extremely protective of him and at the same time feeling superior because I was older and got good grades without trying. And I remember how my brother just enjoyed doing the things he liked to do, without worrying about what other people were doing or thinking. I thought I was giving those attributes to the characters of Nathan and Ryan because it was what the story called for. Now I don't know what to think.

I still haven't recognized anyone in *Emily and the Enchanted Frog.* It seems to be just three funny stories about nobody in particular. I closely observed a hermit crab so that I could write one of the stories, *Emily and the Mermaid,* but it didn't have any discernible personality, so I think I can credit my imagination, not my memory, for the story.

The book that gave me the hardest time was *Journal of a Teenage Genius.* That's because I had written it as a short story, complete in itself, but I couldn't sell it. One day, in my usual state of no ideas, I sent it to Susan Hirschman. I knew it wasn't a book. I don't know what I was hoping. That it would grow in the mail. That Susan would be looking for a ten-page novel. After she read it, she said, "This is a very good first chapter." That would have been nice to hear if I'd had any idea at all how to go on with the book.

The idea for a fairy tale, *Nata,* came from someplace, giving me an excuse to put *Genius* aside for what turned out to be a couple of years. Nata was the name I gave the little fairy that the story was about, but I had no idea what she looked like until Nancy Tafuri's illustrations showed me.

When I got around to trying *Journal of a Teenage Genius* again, I amazed myself by coming up with enough ideas to finish the book. It took a lot of thinking, and I still wonder how I did it. Of course, I wonder that about most of my books. Each one could only have been written when it was written, not earlier or later. My brain keeps changing.

One day I was musing about talking dolls. I thought how ironic it would be to have such a wonderful thing and then not be able to get along with it. The idea of a girl not speaking to her doll struck me as a funny situation, so I worked out a story about the personality conflict between a girl named Caitlin and her annoying talking doll, Holiday. I called it *Caitlin's Holiday.* Susan Condie Lamb drew amusing pictures for it, as she had done for *Plunk's Dreams* and *Emily and the Enchanted Frog.*

Not long after the book was published, I visited a school in New Jersey where the librarian, Carol Hurd, had gotten the students excited over the story. Even the boys had joined in making pictures and displays relating to the book. The children were so caught up in the plot that they almost looked on the characters as real people. They wanted to know what had become of Jodi, one of the dolls in the story. To tell the truth, I barely remembered Jodi, but the children remembered very well, and they wanted her to become alive the way Holiday was. I took their advice and wrote *Doll Trouble.* Without Mrs. Hurd and the students at Hillside School, I would never have thought of that book.

How Many Candles? was never intended to be a book at all. When Greenwillow Books had their tenth anniversa-ry, I wrote a little joking story, using the *Alex and the Cat* characters, and sent it to them as a sort of anniversary card. It was years later when Susan Hirschman, cleaning out some files, came across the story and read it to the writer Kevin Henkes. I have him to thank for suggesting to Susan that it would make a picture book, although at the time I didn't see how it could possibly work. Susan thought differently, and I'm surprised at how well it turned out. The illustrations by Sonja Lamut have a lot to do with that.

I'm often surprised after I finish a book to realize how different it is from what I intended. *Georgia Music* was going to be about a band of musical insects. *Foxy* was to take place in Pennsylvania, but I never got the characters out of Florida. I first thought of *Cougar* as a funny book about a talking bike. And of course *Georgia Music* was just a story about a man and his granddaughter on a southern farm.

I never expected to start a series when I wrote *Georgia Music.* When I couldn't sell it, I tried to revise it, but I stopped because I didn't like what was happening. In my revisions I felt myself losing the story I was trying to tell and going in another direction. I gave up my attempts, because I really did like the story the way it was. It wasn't until some time later, after *Georgia Music* had finally been published, that I came across the pages of revision and read them with new eyes. I saw possibilities now which I hadn't

The author with Whippet, the inspiration for her Alex books.

Author Helen V. Griffith with Rose, her future inspiration.

been able to see when I was working on the original book. I used those ideas to write another book about the same characters, but in a very different mood.

I called that book *Grandaddy's Place,* and later when I had some other thoughts about the same characters, I wrote *Grandaddy and Janetta* and *Grandaddy's Stars.* James Stevenson illustrated all four of the books, getting the characters and sense of place just right

My father never got to see the Grandaddy books. I wonder if he would have seen himself and me in the characters of Grandaddy and Janetta.

When my father died, I left the farm and went back to live with my mother. I was still taking evening courses, fewer crafts now and more university classes. The University of Delaware is in Newark, Delaware, not far from Wilmington, and they have a campus in Wilmington, too. It occurred to me that since I was taking so many courses, I might as well matriculate. Then, if I collected enough credits, I would be able to graduate. I decided to major in English, hoping I would be guided to great books that I didn't know anything about. Sometimes that actually happened. Of course I also had to study subjects that I would never have chosen on my own and, somewhat to my surprise, I found everything interesting. I enjoyed every class I took, loved the lectures, thrived on the work (although I think I may have complained a time or two). I would come home from class and lecture my mother. She was interested too. She had wanted to go to college, but it

wasn't in the cards for her. During what turned out to be the last year of her life, we started studying Chinese together. There was something very endearing about the sight of this ninety-one-year-old lady sitting across from me at the kitchen table, carefully drawing each character as she counted in Chinese from one to ten.

It took me about fifteen years of evening classes before I graduated. Some semesters I took two or three classes, others none at all. I wasn't in any hurry. As I saw the credits mounting up and graduation looming, I thought it would be nice to be the oldest member of the class of '98, but several other old duffers beat me out of that honor.

I seem to have gone through my whole life without a plan, and I don't believe that's the way it should be done. I've just drifted from job to job and from hobby to hobby, always taking the path of least resistance, and somehow along the way I got lucky and became a writer. I have trouble thinking of myself as a real writer though; I don't feel like one. I know there are published books out there with my name on them, but I'm still not convinced. Strangely enough, even after all this time, I have no idea how the publishing business works. I was too shy to ask questions in the beginning, and now it seems too late.

Sometimes I decide that I'm not serious enough about the business of writing. During those moods, I try to come up with goals. I even resolve to write every day. Then the mood passes.

But just because I'm not serious about the business doesn't mean I'm not serious about my writing. I work hard to make each book interesting and well-written and worth reading. This means rewriting everything several skillion times. It also means not liking to read a book once it's published, because I see too many things I want to change.

I'm very grateful for the people and pleasures that writing has brought into my life. My mother used to say that her women's club gave her a lifetime interest and purpose. She remained active and involved in the club until her death. I hope it works out that way with me and my writing.

Writings

FOR CHILDREN

"Mine Will," Said John, illustrated by Muriel Batherman, Greenwillow, 1980, published with illustrations by Joseph A. Smith, 1992.

Alex and the Cat (see below), illustrated by Joseph Low, Greenwillow, 1982.

Alex Remembers (see below), illustrated by Donald Carrick, Greenwillow, 1983.

More Alex and the Cat (see below), illustrated by Donald Carrick, Greenwillow, 1983.

Foxy (novel), Greenwillow, 1984.

Nata, illustrated by Nancy Tafuri, Greenwillow, 1985.

Georgia Music, illustrated by James Stevenson, Greenwillow, 1986.

Journal of a Teenage Genius (novel), Greenwillow, 1987.

Grandaddy's Place, illustrated by James Stevenson, Greenwillow, 1987.

Emily and the Enchanted Frog, illustrated by Susan Condie Lamb, Greenwillow, 1989.

Caitlin's Holiday, illustrated by Susan Condie Lamb, Greenwillow, 1990.

Plunk's Dream, illustrated by Susan Condie Lamb, Greenwillow, 1990.

Doll Trouble, illustrated by Susan Condie Lamb, Greenwillow, 1993.

Grandaddy and Janetta, illustrated by James Stevenson, Greenwillow, 1993.

Dream Meadow, illustrated by Nancy Barnet, Greenwillow, 1994.

Grandaddy's Stars, illustrated by James Stevenson, Greenwillow, 1995.

Alex and the Cat (contains *Alex and the Cat, Alex Remembers,* and *More Alex and the Cat*), illustrated by Sonja Lamut, Greenwillow, 1997.

Dinosaur Habitat, illustrated by Sonja Lamut, Greenwillow, 1998.

Cougar (novel), Greenwillow, 1999.

How Many Candles?, illustrated by Sonja Lamut, Greenwillow, 1999.

GROVES, Maketa 1950-

Personal

Born June 1, 1950, in Detroit, MI; daughter of Levi C. and Louise (Bunley) Smith; separated; children: Lee Michael Smith, Donald Roy Groves. *Education:* Attended Wayne State University; Antioch University West, San Francisco, B.A., 1976.

Addresses

Home—2125 West Royal Palm Rd., No. 2103, Phoenix, AZ 85021. *Office*—4212 West Cactus Rd., Suite 1110-35, Phoenix, AZ 85029.

Career

World of Difference, San Francisco, CA, project manager and special education administrator; Southwest Education Center, Glendale, AZ, special education teacher. Headlands Center for the Arts, Sausalito, CA, artist in residence, 1992; Cultural Competency Focus Group, Washington, DC, member.

Awards, Honors

Josephine Mills Award, PEN Oakland, 1998, for *Red Hot on a Silver Note.*

Writings

Red Hot on a Silver Note (poems), Curbstone Press (Willimantic, CT), 1997.

Image and Imagination, Freedom Voices Press, 1997.

Work represented in anthologies, including *Adam of Ife,* Lotus Press, 1992. Contributor to magazines, including *Left Curve* and *Morena.*

Work in Progress

A novel, tentatively titled *Ronny and Juneau;* a poetry manuscript, tentatively titled *Sinner.*

Sidelights

Maketa Groves told *SATA:* "I was born on June 1, 1950, in Detroit, Michigan. I grew up in the inner city, listening to Motown, country music, and the poetry and rhythm of my neighborhood's unique dialects.

"The primary influences on my writing have been my father and uncle. When I was eight or nine years old, my father introduced me to the poetry of Edgar Allan Poe. While I found much of Poe's subject matter frightening, I fell in love with the effortless flow and perfect rhyme of his words. Though unusual for the times, my father and uncle were far-thinking 'feminist' men, who taught me to seek experiences that were out of the mold for women. My aunts (on my father's side) were also women of independent thinking and action, and they were clearly in charge of their lives. From all of them, I learned to be independent and to believe in my powers of observation. The lessons I learned from my family have helped me develop as a poet. Though my childhood included some of what is known as shadow-side or 'dark' experiences, my father taught me that these also have a place in the scheme of life, and that they make interesting subject matter.

"As human beings, we are full of unique experiences. What I try to do when I write is welcome my listeners into a world they had not previously explored. Hopefully the listening or reading audience will find some knowledge there that will be illuminating. As a writer, I like to explore what lies under the surface of actions, reactions, and 'realities.' I like to expose contradictions (my own as well as those of others) and explore volatile forces. I also believe that the written (and spoken) word is a viable force for positive social change. Some of the

Maketa Groves

social action causes I like to explore in my writing are war, homelessness, and prejudice.

"I believe that writers should be true to what they know and write about what they know, without regard for popular sentiment on the subject. I would advise all young writers to open themselves to experience and to try and always be honest in written explorations of experience.

"Within five years, I hope to be able to dedicate myself completely to the craft of writing. By 'completely,' I mean that my work would be writing, and I would have no need to seek any other. That would be my ideal, perfect existence."

Groves's debut collection of verse, *Red Hot on a Silver Note,* draws inspiration from all reaches of her personal experience: pumping gas as a summer job, watching her exhausted mother scrub the floor, or listening with wonder to the music of Miles Davis. Critics have applauded Groves's poetic voice and style. *Bay Guardian* contributor Jennifer Joseph called Groves's poetry "immediately engaging" and asserted: "Her subject matter is personal and complex yet presented in a simple and straightforward way. Her language possesses a musical quality and rhythm." Jessica English, writing in the *Weekly Alibi,* maintained: "Long and slender, [Groves's] poems wind outward like sinewy wrinkled and fascinating fingers until—wham—they hit some gnarled knuckle bone of truth."

Works Cited

English, Jessica, review of *Red Hot on a Silver Note, Weekly Alibi,* October 22-28, 1997, p. 31.

Joseph, Jennifer, review of *Red Hot on a Silver Note, Bay Guardian,* November, 1997, p. 12.

For More Information See

PERIODICALS

Chiron Review, spring, 1998, p. 47.

H

HAMMOND, Winifred G(raham) 1899-1992

OBITUARY NOTICE—See index for *SATA* sketch: Born June 22, 1899, in Covington, IN; died January 14, 1992, in Walnut Creek, CA. Teacher and writer. Hammond received her A.B. degree from Indiana University, and her A.M. degree from the University of California, Berkeley. She began her career as a high school science and mathematics teacher, but she is best remembered as the author of a popular series of science books for young people. Her first work, published in 1959, was *Elephant Cargo,* followed by *Rice: Food for a Hungry World* (1961), *Plants, Food, and People* (1964), *The Riddle of Seeds* (1966), *Sugar from Farm to Market* (1967), *Cotton from Farm to Market* (1968), *Wheat from Farm to Market* (1970), *The Riddle of Teeth* (1971), *Corn from Farm to Market* (1972), and *The Story of Your Eye* (1975).

—*Robert Reginald and Mary A. Burgess*

*   *   *

HARTER, Debbie 1963-

Personal

Born August 14, 1963, in High Wycombe, Buckinghamshire, England; daughter of John (a management consultant) and Sarah Miller (a travel publicist; maiden name, Logan; present surname, Stroud) Harter. *Education:* Attended Islington Institute for Adult Education and Blackheath School of Art. *Hobbies and other interests:* Dancing, music, riding, walking.

Addresses

Home—54 Aberdeen Rd., London N5 2XB, England.

Career

Freelance illustrator and designer. Designer of gift card and wrapping paper designs for Whistling Fish and Robot Designs; designer of ceramics for English Country Pottery; also designer and creator of jewelry and textiles. *Member:* National Geographic Society.

Awards, Honors

Shortlisted for English 4-11 Award, best children's picture book, 1998, for *Walking through the Jungle.*

Writings

AUTHOR AND ILLUSTRATOR

Walking through the Jungle, Barefoot Books (Bath, England), 1997, Orchard Books, 1997.

ILLUSTRATOR

Stella Blackstone, *Who Are You?,* Barefoot Books, 1996, Abbeville Press (New York City), 1996.
Blackstone, *Where Is the Cat?,* Barefoot Books, 1996, Abbeville Press, 1996.
Blackstone, *Can You See the Red Balloon?,* Barefoot Books, 1997, Orchard Books, 1998.
Blackstone, *Bear in a Square,* Barefoot Books, 1998.
Blackstone, *Bear on a Bike,* Barefoot Books, 1998.
Herb the Vegetarian Dragon, Barefoot Books, 1999.

Illustrator of children's books on world history.

Work in Progress

Illustrations for *Bear's Busy Family.*

Sidelights

Debbie Harter told *SATA:* "I have loved fairytales and stories since I was very young. As a child I used to write and illustrate my own books. As I grew older, I became more interested in contemporary design. I began my career in this field, with a stall at Camden Lock Market. Although I always wanted to do children's books, the design side of my work took off, and through my greeting card designs I got many different design commissions. However, I began to feel constricted by the work I was doing, so I started painting in bright watercolors. This led to a new range of cards which, in turn, led to my first work for Barefoot Books, *Who Are You?*

"I work in watercolors. I love the flexibility and intensity of the colors. I use very thick paper, because I load it with water. I never know quite how it's going to turn out until the paint has dried completely.

"I think children's picture books are very important. They stimulate a child's imagination, and they also open the door to the world of the subconscious. They are a very powerful teaching tool. My aim is to write as well as illustrate, and I hope to do this for the rest of my life. My advice to any aspiring illustrators is—never, never, ever give up!"

For More Information See

PERIODICALS

Child Education, October, 1997, p. 70.
Publishers Weekly, August 31, 1998, p. 74.*

* * *

HELMAN, Andrea (Jean) 1946-
(Andy Helman)

Personal

Born September 15, 1946, in Columbus, OH; daughter of Sam (a business proprietor) and Adelle Helman. *Education:* Ohio University, B.S.J. (Bachelor of science, journalism), 1968. *Politics:* Independent. *Religion:* Jewish.

Addresses

Home—10710 35th Ave. S.W., Seattle, WA 98146.

Career

WOUB Radio, Athens, OH, writer, talent, producer, 1964-68; *Columbus Citizens Journal,* Columbus, OH, city desk reporter, 1966; *Jewish Chronicle,* Pittsburgh, PA, reporter, 1968; Halle Brothers (retail chain), Cleveland, OH, advertising copy writer, 1970; KDKA-TV, Pittsburgh, public affairs assistant director, 1970-72; Entertainment Services, Inc., Columbus, promotions director, 1973-74; freelance writer for print, broadcast, and industrial video, 1974—; Warner-Amex QUBE, Columbus, writer, talent, producer, 1977-81; WCMH-TV, Columbus, writer, talent, producer, 1982-83; KING-TV, Seattle, WA, writer, talent, producer, 1983-86; University of Washington, television executive producer, 1990-95. *Member:* Pacific Northwest Writers Conference (trustee), American Federation of Television and Radio Artists.

Andrea Helman and photographer Art Wolfe teamed to create a unique counting book featuring flora and fauna from the Pacific Northwest.

Awards, Honors

Nominee, National Academy of Television Arts and Sciences (Emmy), Outstanding Achievement, individual craft, writing, for *P.M. Magazine* series; N.C.T.A. Ace Award; ABC Building Blocks Catalogue selection, Young Hoosier Picture Book list, 1997-98, nominee, Washington Children's Choice Picture Book, 1998, all for *O Is for Orca;* Kids Pick of the Lists, *Bookselling This Week,* and Top 10 Science Books for Youth, *Booklist,* both 1998, both for *Northwest Animal Babies.*

Writings

O Is for Orca: A Pacific Northwest Alphabet Book, Sasquatch, 1995.
1, 2, 3 Moose: A Pacific Northwest Counting Book, Sasquatch, 1996.
Northwest Animal Babies, Sasquatch, 1998.

Articles and essays published in journals, including *McCalls, Redbook,* and *Christian Science Monitor.*

Sidelights

Andrea Helman is a writer who has enjoyed a versatile career in the field of print and broadcast journalism. A graduate of Ohio University, Helman worked variously as a news reporter, copywriter, scriptwriter, broadcaster, and producer at a number of newspapers and television and radio stations in Ohio and Pennsylvania before moving to the state of Washington in the early 1980s. In 1995 she published the first of her books for children. Offering an exploration of her Pacific Northwest home, *O Is for Orca,* an alphabet book, and *1, 2, 3 Moose,* a counting book, garnered praise for their informative, nature-centered texts, which render them good science books for preschoolers in the estimation of many critics. *O Is for Orca,* illustrated with color photographs by Art Wolfe, highlights the land, animals, and native people of the Pacific Northwest. Helman's text "helps youngsters to identify the ecology, habitats, and geography" of the region, according to *School Library Journal* contributor Mollie Bynum. A reviewer for *Publishers Weekly* praised *O Is for Orca,* citing its "piquant regional flavor" while asserting that the book's "appeal shouldn't be limited to a single corner of the country." *1, 2, 3 Moose* focuses on the wildlife and other natural features of Helman's adopted home, celebrated both in the author's text and in Wolfe's accompanying photographs. In this work, "the counting often takes a backseat to science," according to *Booklist* reviewer Lauren Peterson, as the author describes the ecology of the region, habits of its wild creatures, and the distinct characteristics of its plant life. The result, Peterson claimed, is a counting book that will be just as useful in teaching science to young children.

Works Cited

Bynum, Mollie, review of *O Is for Orca, School Library Journal,* February, 1996, p. 95.
Review of *O Is for Orca, Publishers Weekly,* October 2, 1995, p. 73.
Peterson, Lauren, review of *1, 2, 3 Moose, Booklist,* November 1, 1996, p. 503.

For More Information See

PERIODICALS

Canadian Children's Literature, spring, 1998, pp. 84-85.

*   *   *

HELMAN, Andy
See HELMAN, Andrea (Jean)

*   *   *

HENRY, Ernest 1948-

Personal

Born August 25, 1948, in London, England; son of Maurice Samuel (in advertising) and Sylvia (a singer; maiden name, Handel) Henry; married Nadine Aroyo (a promotions director), October 17, 1978; children: Nicholas, Rupert. *Education:* Attended Guildhall School of Music. *Religion:* Jewish.

Addresses

Home—23 Hornby Close, London NW3 3JL, England.

Ernest Henry

Career

Writer and performer. Mad Tour (solo show), performer throughout England and Scotland, beginning in 1998; guest on media programs, including *Fully Booked,* on British Broadcasting Corporation (BBC)-TV.

Writings

The Adventures of Phil and Lill, illustrated by Keith Smith, Bloomsbury (London, England), 1996.
Poems to Shout Out Loud … and Some to Whissssssper, Bloomsbury, 1996.
Not More Poems to Shout Out Loud, illustrated by Paul Daviz, Bloomsbury, 1996.
Rub-a-Dub-Dub: New and Best Loved Poems for Babies, illustrated by Joanna Walsh, Bloomsbury, 1997.
New Improved Limericks, Limerick Books (London, England), 1997.
The New Adventures of Phil and Lill, illustrated by Keith Smith, Limerick Books, 1998.
More Adventures of Phil and Lill, illustrated by Smith, Limerick Books, 1998.
Wishes for My Baby, Element, 1998.
Dora Dee and the Magical Smile, Health Education Authority, 1998.

Some books are available in spoken-word or musical versions. Creator of *The Phil and Lill Colouring Book.* Author of columns for *Girl Talk* and *Young Telegraph.*

Work in Progress

Christmas at Cozy Warm, a Phil and Lill story, which is also scheduled to be produced as a musical play; two more "New Improved" comedy books; *Bunge,* a black comedy; humorous poetry for children; a novel for young teenagers.

For More Information See

PERIODICALS

School Librarian, November, 1997, p. 209.

*   *   *

HOLBROOK, Kathy 1963-

Personal

Born July 23, 1963, in Anchorage, AK; daughter of Richard (an artist and business owner) and Wilma (Wintz) Morton; married Don Holbrook (an artist), September 4, 1990. *Politics:* "Conservative." *Religion:* Roman Catholic. *Hobbies and other interests:* "Training my German shepherd dog for tracking, obedience, and protection work."

Addresses

Home—2223 Wolfangle Rd., Cincinnati, OH 45244. *Electronic mail*—tmgrafix@aol.com.

Career

Wagner Repro, Cincinnati, OH, manager of computer department, 1993-94; Trademark Stationery, Cincinnati, owner and designer of stationery, 1994—. Freelance artist and illustrator. *Member:* Eastfork Schutzhund Club.

Illustrator

Susan Knauss, *Tempe and Her Horse: A Story of Revolutionary Times,* Research Triangle Publishing (Fuquay Varina, NC), 1996.
Chi Sun Rhee, *Under the Aruban Sun,* Research Triangle Publishing, 1996.
Charles Langley, *Catherine and Geko: The Adventure Begins,* Research Triangle Publishing, 1996.
Donna York Gilbert, *On the Road with Thibadeau Ya-Ya: In North and South Carolina,* Research Triangle Publishing, 1997.
Charles Langley, *Catherine, Anna, and Geko Go to the Beach,* Research Triangle Publishing, 1998.
Ethel Pochocki, *More Once upon a Time Saints,* Bethlehem Books (Warsaw, ND), 1998.
Doris D. Smith, *A Daughter's Return to Her Roots,* Bookmasters, 1998.
James H. Nelson, *Khmer Warrior,* Research Triangle Publishing, 1998.
Roland Taylor, *Mabrey Bass's Tarboro,* Research Triangle Publishing, 1998.

Kathy Holbrook's pictures provide a vibrant backdrop for Ethel Pochocki's collection of tales about the lives of lesser-known saints. (From More Once Upon a Time Saints, *illustrated by Holbrook.)*

Work in Progress

Developing a line of children's activity books.

Sidelights

Kathy Holbrook told *SATA:* "I'm a country girl with little formal training. My father and his father were artists, and so it runs in the family naturally! I was raised in a very religious Catholic family and loved to read stories of the saints. I devoured the stories quickly. Soon there was little left to read. I began writing and illustrating my own stories, and a career was born.

"Although most of my time has been spent illustrating what others have written, I am working on my own line of books, written expressly for children. I don't want children to run out of material as I once did. My work is from a Catholic perspective, in a most traditional style. This is my specialty, I think."

HUGHES, Ted 1930-1998

OBITUARY NOTICE—See index for *SATA* sketch: Born Edward James Hughes, August 17, 1930, in Mytholmroyd, Yorkshire, England; died of cancer, October 28, 1998, in Devon, England. Poet, editor, children's book author. Britain's poet laureate from 1984 until his death, Ted Hughes was considered one of the finest poets of the twentieth-century, although, particularly in the United States, his poetic reputation was overshadowed by his early marriage to fellow-poet Sylvia Plath. The son of a carpenter, Hughes grew up in rural Yorkshire, attended Cambridge University, and worked odd jobs part-time to support his writing in the early 1950s. He met and married Plath, an American, in 1956, and the following year published his first book of poems, *The Hawk in the Rain,* to significant acclaim. The volume is seen as a watershed moment in the history of twentieth-century English poetry for its elemental, often harsh, and mythical treatment of nature, in direct contrast to the restraint that prevailed in poetry at that time. Hughes went on to write more than thirty volumes of poetry, though his finest books are considered those composed at the beginning and at the end of his career, as well as a number of plays, translations, and several books for children. He also edited numerous volumes of poetry, including several collections by Plath. In the fulfillment of his post as executor of Plath's literary estate, Hughes drew the ire of many in the literary community when he rejected requests for quotes from his late wife's works. In the decade after her death, Plath was taken up by some as a symbol of suppressed female genius, and in this scenario Hughes was often cast as the villain. Further complicating matters, the married woman for whom he left Plath killed herself, and the daughter she had had by Hughes, in the same manner as Plath. His readings were disrupted by cries of "murderer!" and his surname, which appears on Plath's gravestone, was repeatedly effaced. Hughes's unpopular decisions regarding Plath's writings, over which he had total control after her death, were often in service of his definition of privacy; he also refused to discuss his marriage to Plath after her death. Thus it was with great surprise that, in 1998, the literary world received Hughes's intimate portrait of Plath in the form of his *Birthday Letters,* a collection of prose poems covering every aspect of his relationship with his first wife.

Hughes's books for children are noted for the same brevity of writing, strong imagery, and imagination that he brought to his adult works. They contain a lightening of, but not a departure from, his explanation of the intensity of the forces both within and outside of man which order his place in the natural world and the universe. In addition to the Order of the British Empire, and the Order of Merit, which Hughes received from the Queen of England, he was awarded numerous literary prizes during his lengthy career, including the Forward Prize for Poetry for *Birthday Letters,* and the Whitbread Book of the Year Award, for his *Tales from Ovid* (1997). For his children's works, Hughes received a number or prestigious honors, including Signal Poetry Awards for *Moon-Bells and Other Poems* (1978), *Under the North Star* (1981), and *What is the Truth? A Farmyard Fable for the Young* (1984), which also received a Guardian Award in 1985. Before his death, Hughes worked with Michael Morpurgo to create the Children's Laureate, which Morpurgo describes as "an honour to be awarded biannually to a children's writer or illustrator, to focus awareness of the best of children's books, amongst adults and children alike . . . ." Morpurgo added: "Ted Hughes was indeed a children's champion. He touched young lives, making readers and writers of so many of us. He opened our eyes, he taught us to fly."

OBITUARIES AND OTHER SOURCES:

PERIODICALS

Books for Keeps, January, 1999, p. 12.
Carousel, spring, 1999, p. 37.
Chicago Tribune, October 30, 1998, sec. 1, p. 13.
Los Angeles Times, October 30, 1998, pp. A1, A12.
New York Times, October 30, 1998.
Times (London), October 30, 1998.
USA Today, October 29, 1998.
Washington Post, October 30, 1998, p. B6.

K–L

KIRK, Daniel 1952-

Personal

Born May 1, 1952, in Elyria, OH; son of Donald (a puppeteer) and Connie (a puppeteer; maiden name, Porch) Kirk; married Julia Gorton (an author and illustrator), 1986; children: Ivy, Raleigh, Russell. *Education:* Ohio State University, B.A. (summa cum laude), 1974. *Politics:* Left Democrat. *Religion:* "Nature worship."

Addresses

Home and office—207 Baldwin St., Glen Ridge, NJ 07028.

Career

Author and illustrator. *Exhibitions:* Storyopolis Gallery, Los Angeles, CA.

Awards, Honors

Kirk has received various awards from the American Institute of Graphic Arts and the Society of Illustrators.

Writings

AUTHOR AND ILLUSTRATOR

Skateboard Monsters, Rizzoli, 1992.
Lucky's Twenty-Four Hour Garage, Hyperion, 1996.
Trash Trucks!, Putnam, 1997.
Breakfast at the Liberty Diner, Hyperion, 1997.
Bigger, Putnam, 1998.
Hush, Little Alien, Hyperion, 1999.
The Snow Family, Hyperion, 1999.
Moondogs, Putnam, 1999.

ILLUSTRATOR

Maida Silverman, *Dune: Pop-Up Panorama Book,* Grosset & Dunlap, 1984.
Santa Claus the Movie Pop-Up Panorama Book, Grosset & Dunlap, 1985.
Michael Lipson, *How the Wind Plays,* Hyperion, 1994.
Margaret Wise Brown, *The Diggers,* Hyperion, 1995.
Kevin Lewis, *Chugga-Chugga Choo-Choo,* Hyperion, 1998.

Work in Progress

Humpty Dumpty, for Putnam.

Daniel Kirk

Sidelights

Author and illustrator Daniel Kirk told *SATA* that he knew at the age of five that he would one day be an artist. Fittingly, he found in his own kids the inspiration to fulfill his childhood dream. "I started writing stories when my children were very small," he recalled, "and I get lots of good ideas for books based on the funny things my kids say and do. I have always been a painter, and I used to write a lot of songs, but I never thought of putting my writing and my picture-making together until I spent a lot of time reading books to my own children. Now I try all my ideas out on my two sons and daughter, and get their feedback on which of my characters are interesting, how I should end stories, and which of my stories are worth writing down."

One story that was well worth writing down is Kirk's self-illustrated debut book, *Skateboard Monsters,* in which a group of playing children rush to get out of the way as a gang of zany monsters on skateboards takes over the sidewalk. In a *Booklist* review, Ilene Cooper praised the book's "in-your-face artwork that uses unusual perspectives, elongated shapes, and the boldest of colors to match the feverish, skateboarding mood." *School Library Journal* contributor Carolyn Noah commended Kirk's illustrations, which "[burst] off the pages with energy and wild good cheer," and his text, "jet-propelled verse [that] is graphically integrated."

Kirk told *SATA* that he likes to try different techniques when he paints. "My books *Breakfast at the Liberty Diner* and *Lucky's Twenty-Four Hour Garage* are both set in the 1930s," he said, "so I chose a painting style that looks reminiscent of art from that time period." *Booklist* reviewer Ilene Cooper commented favorably on Kirk's approach, noting that *Breakfast at the Liberty Diner* "captures the [1930s] feeling in both the subject matter and the style of the art." Bobby and his family are waiting for Uncle Angelo at the Liberty Diner when they are surprised by a visit from President Roosevelt. "Filled with bustling, sipping, munching, smiling people, the scenes at the Liberty Diner come alive," remarked a *Kirkus Reviews* critic. *Lucky's Twenty-Four Hour Garage* tracks the customers and cars that visit a 1939 New York City garage in the wee hours of the morning. A *Publishers Weekly* contributor called the book "a captivating slice of Americana." In a review for *Booklist,* Ilene Cooper declared, "Kirk's art ... is absolutely terrific. The glowing oils that fill the pages bring you right into the 24-hour world of Lucky's garage." Cooper concluded: "this is artwork that will delight both [young] listeners and the adults who read to them."

Kirk employs another medium for his artwork in *Trash Trucks!,* which tells of Kim and Pete's adventures helping out on garbage day. "I used collage and mixed media technique, and a much wilder design style," he explained, "because the story is about wild and fanciful garbage trucks who come to life and roam around." "Sesame Street's Oscar would be hard pressed to match the enthusiasm that Kirk ... shows for garbage collection," a *Publishers Weekly* critic remarked in a review of the book. "Kirk portrays the trucks as urban heroes," the reviewer continued, "and his rhythmic rhyming tale has all the flash of a Broadway musical." A *Kirkus Reviews* critic noted that "the bright colors, inventive design, and in-your-face perspective present a diverting visual cacophony." The same commentator added that the "big, bold images make the book an irresistible read." Michael Cart of *Booklist* maintained that "Kirk's singsong, rhyming text is infectious ... but the main attraction is the rambunctious art."

Compared to his earlier efforts, "*Bigger* is a very straightforward kind of book," said Kirk, "and the pictures are direct to match the text." *Bigger* follows one boy's development inch by inch, from embryo to school age. *School Library Journal* contributor Jody McCoy asserted that Kirk's "writing is appropriately simple and utilitarian," and "point of view is handled beautifully." A reviewer for *Publishers Weekly* declared: "The stylized pictures match the idealized account of growing up, which bubbles with satisfaction and wonder."

In addition to illustrating his own texts, Kirk has also provided the pictures for works by other children's authors. Notable among these efforts is his artwork for a reinterpretation of Margaret Wise Brown's *The Diggers,* originally published in 1960 with illustrations by Clement Hurd. In a *Booklist* review, Carolyn Phelan praised the "large, brilliantly colored oil paintings [done] in a heroic style that romanticizes man and his machines." Kirk also illustrated Michael Lipson's *How the Wind Plays,* of which Anna Biagioni Hart, writing in *School Library Journal,* remarked, "this personification of wind will be fascinating to youngsters and a boon to creative teachers or librarians." Reviewing the work for *Booklist,* Ilene Cooper called attention to Kirk's versatility of technique, noting that his oil paintings "combine a 1930s style with a modern airbrushed look that's eye-catchingly fresh."

Kirk told *SATA* that his work on children's books has been "the most fulfilling work I have ever done. The more I write, the more ideas occur to me. I was worried that I might just have a handful of stories inside me, but now it seems like there is a bottomless sea of great stories out there, and I just have to go fishing for them.

"The most difficult part of my job is getting used to the fact that a picture book takes me four or five months to paint. That is a long, boring time for me, because once I have written the book and drawn the sketches, I feel ready to leave the project behind, and move on to something new and challenging. But people seem to like the way I paint, so I must slog on through all the pictures and try to be patient.

"I do not have a particular writing style that I always use. I feel that the story dictates the way it should be told, and sometimes that will be in rhyme, sometimes in prose, sometimes with lots of verbal details or dialogue, and sometimes very spare. Sometimes it is best to let the pictures tell the story themselves. There are authors who have a particular way of writing, and each book they write is instantly recognizable as their book. That would be boring for me. I like to try something a little different each time! The only constants are that I like bright colors; simple shapes; rounded, dimensional characters; and atmospheric lighting.

"I think picture books are very important to children. I hope that the books I do will encourage imagination, curiosity, playfulness, love of words and artwork, and get kids to think about things that are important to them. I love books that are unconventional and nonconformist, and in my own writing, I don't like to preach. Morals are sometimes useful, and they always help a book sell, but I feel that my job is primarily to create a sense of wonder and fun, to entertain, to suggest different ways of thinking about things; and sometimes, if it fits, teach a lesson, too!"

Works Cited

Review of *Bigger, Publishers Weekly,* April 27, 1998, p. 65.

Review of *Breakfast at the Liberty Diner, Kirkus Reviews,* August 15, 1997, p. 1307.

Cart, Michael, review of *Trash Trucks!, Booklist,* May 15, 1997, p. 1579.

Cooper, Ilene, review of *Breakfast at the Liberty Diner, Booklist,* November 1, 1997, p. 482.

Cooper, review of *How the Wind Plays, Booklist,* May 1, 1994, p. 1609.

Cooper, review of *Lucky's Twenty-Four Hour Garage, Booklist,* September 1, 1996, p. 143.

Cooper, review of *Skateboard Monsters, Booklist,* January 15, 1993, p. 921.

Hart, Anna Biagioni, review of *How the Wind Plays, School Library Journal,* May, 1994, p. 99.

Review of *Lucky's Twenty-Four Hour Garage, Publishers Weekly,* August 26, 1996, p. 97.

McCoy, Jody, review of *Bigger, School Library Journal,* May, 1998, p. 118.

Noah, Carolyn, review of *Skateboard Monsters, School Library Journal,* February, 1993, p. 73.

Phelan, Carolyn, review of *The Diggers, Booklist,* May 1, 1995, pp. 1576-77.

Review of *Trash Trucks!, Kirkus Reviews,* May 1, 1997, p. 723.

Review of *Trash Trucks!, Publishers Weekly,* May 12, 1997, p. 75.

For More Information See

PERIODICALS

Bulletin of the Center for Children's Books, June, 1998, p. 367.

Horn Book, March-April, 1999, p. 193-94.

Kirkus Reviews, August 1, 1996, p. 1154; March 15, 1998, p. 406.

New York Times Book Review, December 22, 1996, p. 16; May 17, 1998, p. 28.

Publishers Weekly, October 27, 1997, p. 74, March 15, 1999, p. 59.

School Library Journal, July, 1995, pp. 54-55.

LAVIGNE, Louis-Dominique

Personal

Education: Attended the Conservatoire d'Art Dramatique, Montreal, and studied under Giovanni Poli and Augusto Boal.

Addresses

Office—c/o Theatre Department, University of Quebec a Montreal, Case Postale 8888, Succursale Centre-Ville, Montreal, Quebec H3C 3P8, Canada.

Career

Writer, director, and actor for film and television. Founding member of several contemporary theater troupes, including Theatre de Quartier. Teacher of creative writing, University of Quebec.

Awards, Honors

Governor General's Award (Canada), theatre, 1992, for *Les petits orteils* (translated as "Ten Tiny Toes").

Writings

PLAYS FOR CHILDREN

On est capable (title means "You Can Do It"), Quebec/ Amerique (Montreal), 1981.

Parasol, VLB Editeur (Montreal), 1988.

Le sous-sol des anges, VLB Editeur (Montreal), 1991.

Les petits orteils, produced at Theatre de Quartier, 1998, translation published as *Ten Tiny Toes,* 1998.

Tu peux toujours danser, produced at Theatre Le Clou, 1998.

OTHER PLAYS

As-tu peur des voleurs?, translation by Henry Beissel published as *Are You Afraid of Thieves?,* Simon and Pierre Publishing (Toronto), 1978.

Rosemonde, translation by Mark Bromilow, produced at Santa Fe Stages Festival (Quebec), 1997.

Also author of plays written with Jean Debefve, including *Le voyage de Petit Morceau, L'Arche de Noe, La soupe au crapaud, Le piano sauvage, L'Ornithorynque, Desordres, La grande maison, Kobold!,* and *Les Papas.*

Sidelights

For more than a quarter century, French-Canadian writer, director, actor, and educator Louis-Dominique Lavigne has been a driving force behind French-language theater in Quebec, particularly children's theater. In addition to helping establish several theater groups in Quebec, such as the Theatre de Quartier, Lavigne has written more than thirty scripts, including *On est capable.*

Lavigne's play *On est capable* (title means "You Can Do It") is geared for primary graders. This work centers on a group of children who solve the problem of a lack of playground space. In a review of several plays for children in *Canadian Children's Literature*, Louise Filteau discussed *On est capable:* "These pieces give children a mirror image of their personal reality, both of the family and of society. Watched or read by children and adults together, they will lend themselves to interesting and perhaps educational discussions for both parties." One of Lavigne's primary collaborators on projects for young people has been Jean Debefve, of the Theatre de Galafronie in Brussels, Belgium. The two have produced plays for children of various ages that have been a staple of that theater's repertoire. In *Les Papas* (title means "The Fathers"), both Lavigne and Debefve took to the stage in the title roles.

Works Cited

Filteau, Louise, review of *On est capable, Canadian Children's Literature,* 1982, pp. 60-67.

* * *

LEVY, Elizabeth 1942-

Personal

Born April 4, 1942, in Buffalo, NY; daughter of Elmer Irving and Mildred (Kirschenbaum) Levy; married George R. Vickers (a professor of sociology), January 26, 1979. *Education:* Brown University, B.A. (magna cum laude), 1964; Columbia University, M.A.T., 1968.

Career

Writer, 1971—. American Broadcasting Co., New York City, editor and researcher in news department, 1964-66; Macmillan Publishing Co., Inc., New York City, assistant editor, 1967-69; New York Public Library, New York City, public-relations writer, 1969; JPM Associates (urban affairs consultants), New York City, staff writer, 1970-71. *Member:* Authors Guild, Authors League of America, Mystery Writers of America, PEN.

Awards, Honors

Outstanding Book of the Year, *New York Times,* 1977, for *Struggle and Lose, Struggle and Win: The United Mine Workers;* Charlie May Simon Children's Book Award, Arkansas Department of Education, 1995, for *Keep Ms. Sugarman in the Fourth Grade.*

Writings

FOR CHILDREN; FICTION

Nice Little Girls, illustrated by Mordicai Gerstein, Delacorte, 1974.

Lizzie Lies a Lot, illustrated by John Wallner, Delacorte, 1976.

(With Earl Hammond and Liz Hammond) *Elephants in the Living Room, Bears in the Canoe,* Delacorte, 1977.

Frankenstein Moved in on the Fourth Floor, illustrated by Mordicai Gerstein, Harper, 1979.

The Tryouts, illustrated by Jackie Hann, Four Winds Press, 1979.

Running Out of Time, illustrated by W. T. Mars, Knopf, 1980.

Running Out of Magic with Houdini, illustrated by Blanche Sims, Knopf, 1981.

Dracula Is a Pain in the Neck, illustrated by Mordicai Gerstein, Harper, 1983.

The Shadow Nose, illustrated by Mordicai Gerstein, Morrow, 1983.

The Computer That Said Steal Me, Four Winds Press, 1983.

Cold as Ice, Morrow, 1988.

Keep Ms. Sugarman in the Fourth Grade, illustrated by Dave Henderson, HarperCollins, 1992.

Gorgonzola Zombies in the Park, illustrated by George Ulrich, HarperCollins, 1993.

Cleo and the Coyote, illustrated by Diana Bryer, HarperCollins, 1996.

Wolfman Sam, illustrated by Bill Basso, HarperCollins, 1996.

My Life as a Fifth-Grade Comedian, HarperCollins, 1997.

Third Grade Bullies, illustrated by Tim Barnes, Hyperion, 1998.

FOR CHILDREN; "SOMETHING QUEER" MYSTERY SERIES; ILLUSTRATED BY MORDICAI GERSTEIN

Something Queer Is Going On, Delacorte, 1973.

. . . *at the Ballpark,* Delacorte, 1975.

. . . *at the Library,* Delacorte, 1977.

. . . *on Vacation,* Delacorte, 1980.

. . . *at the Haunted School,* Delacorte, 1982.

. . . *at the Lemonade Stand,* Delacorte, 1982.

. . . *in Rock 'n' Roll,* Delacorte, 1987.

. . . *at the Birthday Party,* Delacorte, 1990.

. . . *in Outer Space,* Hyperion, 1993.

. . . *in the Cafeteria,* Hyperion, 1994.

. . . *at the Scary Movie,* Hyperion, 1995.

. . . *in the Wild West,* Hyperion, 1997.

FOR CHILDREN; "JODY AND JAKE MYSTERY" SERIES

The Case of the Frightened Rock Star, Pocket Books, 1980.

The Case of the Counterfeit Race Horse, Pocket Books, 1980.

The Case of the Fired-Up Gang, Pocket Books, 1981.

The Case of the Wild River Ride, Pocket Books, 1981.

FOR CHILDREN; "FAT ALBERT AND THE COSBY KIDS" SERIES

The Shuttered Window, Dell, 1981.

Mister Big Time, Dell, 1981.

Take Two, They're Small, Dell, 1981.

Spare the Rod, Dell, 1981.

Mom or Pop, Dell, 1981.

The Runt, Dell, 1981.

FOR CHILDREN; "MAGIC MYSTERIES" SERIES; ILLUSTRATED BY ELLEN EAGLE

The Case of the Gobbling Squash, Simon & Schuster, 1988.

The Case of the Mind Reading Mommies, Simon & Schuster, 1989.

The Case of the Tattletale Heart, Simon & Schuster, 1990.

The Case of the Dummy with Cold Eyes, Simon & Schuster, 1991.

FOR CHILDREN; *"BRIAN AND PEA BRAIN" MYSTERY SERIES; ILLUSTRATED BY GEORGE ULRICH*

School Spirit Sabotage, HarperCollins, 1994.

Rude Rowdy Rumors, HarperCollins, 1994.

A Mammoth Mix-Up, HarperCollins, 1995.

FOR CHILDREN; *"INVISIBLE INC." MYSTERY SERIES; ILLUSTRATED BY DENISE BRUNKUS*

The Schoolyard Mystery, Scholastic, 1994.

The Mystery of the Missing Dog, Scholastic, 1995.

The Snack Attack Mystery, Scholastic, 1995.

The Creepy Computer Mystery, Scholastic, 1996.

The Karate Class Mystery, Scholastic, 1996.

Parents' Night Fright, Scholastic, 1998.

FOR YOUNG ADULTS; FICTION

Come Out Smiling, Delacorte, 1981.

Double Standard, Avon, 1984.

The Dani Trap, Morrow, 1984.

Night of Nights, Ballantine, 1984.

All Shook Up, Scholastic, 1986.

Cheater, Cheater, Scholastic, 1993.

The Drowned, Hyperion, 1995.

"THE GYMNASTS" SERIES

The Beginners, Scholastic, 1988.

First Meet, Scholastic, 1988.

Nobody's Perfect, Scholastic, 1988.

The Winner, Scholastic, 1989.

The Trouble with Elizabeth, Scholastic, 1989.

Bad Break, Scholastic, 1989.

Tumbling Ghosts, Scholastic, 1989.

Captain of the Team, Scholastic, 1989.

Crush on the Coach, Scholastic, 1990.

Boys in the Gym, Scholastic, 1990.

Mystery at the Meet, Scholastic, 1990.

Out of Control, Scholastic, 1990.

First Date, Scholastic, 1990.

World Class Gymnast, Scholastic, 1990.

Nasty Competition, Scholastic, 1991.

Fear of Falling, Scholastic, 1991.

The New Coach, Scholastic, 1991.

Tough at the Top, Scholastic, 1991.

The Gymnast Gift, Scholastic, 1991.

Go for the Gold, Scholastic, 1992.

NONFICTION

The People Lobby—The SST Story, Delacorte, 1973.

Lawyers for the People: A New Breed of Defenders and Their Work, Knopf, 1974.

By-Lines: Profiles in Investigative Journalism, Four Winds Press, 1975.

(With cousin, Robie H. Harris) *Before You Were Three: How You Began to Walk, Talk, Explore, and Have Feelings,* photographs by Henry E. F. Gordillo, Delacorte, 1977.

(With Mara Miller) *Doctors for the People: Profiles of Six Who Serve,* Knopf, 1977.

(With Tad Richards) *Struggle and Lose, Struggle and Win: The United Mine Workers,* photographs by Henry E. F. Gordillo, Four Winds Press, 1977.

(With Mara Miller) *Politicians for the People: Six Who Stand for Change,* Knopf, 1979.

If You Lived When They Signed the Constitution, illustrated by Richard Rosenblum, Scholastic, 1987.

PLAYS

(Co-author) *Croon* (one-act), first produced in New York City at Performing Garage, March 28, 1976.

(Co-author) *Never Waste a Virgin* (two-act), first produced in New York City at Wonderhorse Theatre, December 3, 1977.

Lizzie Lies a Lot (based on Levy's novel of the same title), first produced by the Cutting Edge, 1978.

OTHER

(Adaptor) *Marco Polo: The Historic Adventure Based on the Television Spectacular,* Random House, 1982.

Father Murphy's First Miracle (novelization of the television series *Father Murphy*), Random House, 1983.

Return of the Jedi (adaptation from the screenplay by Lawrence Kasdan and George Lucas), Random House, 1983.

The Bride (based on the film of the same title), Random House, 1985.

Adaptations

Something Queer at the Library was adapted for film by Mitchell Seltzer Productions/Bosustow Productions, 1978.

Sidelights

From children's chapter and picture books to young adult novels and mystery series, Elizabeth Levy's works encompass a wide range of reading levels and genres. Levy once told *SATA*, "as a child I read all the time and omnivorously. I read everything from *Nancy Drew* to *War and Peace*. My mother recalls coming into my room when I was twelve years old and finding *Winnie-the-Pooh*, *War and Peace*, *Peyton Place*, and a *Nancy Drew* mystery scattered on my bed. My eclectic reading habits haven't changed much since then, which accounts in part for the variety of books I write."

One of Levy's first works of fiction for younger readers, *Lizzie Lies a Lot,* confronts the issue of honesty when a young girl realizes that her lies threaten a friendship. Lizzie lies to her parents to make them think she is a good dancer, and to her friend Sara to entertain her. Eventually tiring of telling lies, Lizzie realizes that she must change. *Lizzie Lies a Lot* "is the most autobiographical of my books," Levy explained to *SATA*. "I did lie a lot as a child, and I can distinctly remember what it felt like when I knew I was lying and no one else did. Like Lizzie in my novel, I told my mother I had been asked to perform in a school assembly and I kept up that lie for months.

"Oddly enough, my first published work was a lie. When I was in third grade, a newspaper published my poem 'When I Grow Up I Want to Be a Nurse All Dressed in White.' I didn't want to be a nurse. If I wanted to be anything, I wanted to be a writer, but the idea of being a writer seemed a fantasy. I grew up without any concrete ambitions, but with an entire card catalog of fantasies.... I think about my own childhood a lot, and when I write about a certain age I have very vivid memories of what it felt like then. I think that memories from childhood are like dreams. It's not important to remember all of them, but what you do remember is important."

Although Levy draws upon her childhood for many of her plots, she also bases her books on what interests her today. "When I write for children," she told *SATA*, "I am really writing about things that seem funny or interesting to me now. I don't think writing a good book for children is very different from writing one for teenagers or adults. The emotions we have as children are in many ways as complex as those we have as adults. The best children's writers know this and are not tempted to oversimplify."

Among Levy's most popular works for children are the adventures of the Bamford brothers, Sam and Robert. The pair's escapades, which begin in *Frankenstein Moved in on the Fourth Floor* and *Dracula Is a Pain in the Neck,* are continued in Levy's 1993 book, *Gorgonzola Zombies in the Park*. In this story, Sam and Robert's eight-year-old cousin, Mabel, has come to New York for a visit. Annoyed by her constant teasing, the boys convince Mabel that the statues in Central Park were once living things, changed to statues by a zombie with breath that smells as bad as Gorgonzola cheese, one of Mabel's favorite foods. When someone smears the smelly cheese on the statues, the cousins embark on a search for the culprit. Bonnie Siegel praised the book's "strong characters and snappy dialogue" in a *School Library Journal* review, and *Booklist*'s Stephanie Zvirin asserted that the plot "will win over middle-grade readers, especially those who have enjoyed the brothers' previous comic adventures." In *Wolfman Sam,* another installment in the chronicles of the Bamford boys, Sam is chosen as the school's disc jockey, and adopts the name Wolfman Sam. Robert, jealous of all the attention Sam is getting, finds a list of the identifying characteristics of werewolves, which scares Sam into thinking he might really be a werewolf. Robert's scheme sets off a series of humorous episodes in what *School Library Journal* contributor Suzanne Hawley called "a light-hearted and believable story." Stephanie Zvirin, writing for *Booklist,* observed that "the relationship between the brothers is solidly grounded."

Levy's series of easy-to-read chapter books for children, the "Brian and Pea Brain" mysteries, includes the 1994 book *Rude Rowdy Rumors*. In this work, seven-year-old Brian is a star soccer player, and a jealous teammate is stirring up trouble by spreading wild lies about him. Accompanied by his younger sister Penny, affectionately known as Pea Brain, Brian sets out to discover the

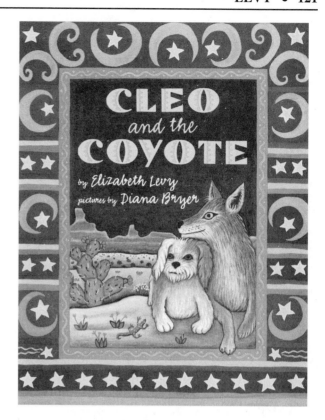

Elizabeth Levy explores themes of loyalty and ownership in her picture book about a city dog named Cleo who befriends a lonely coyote while on a camping trip with her master. (Cover illustration by Diana Bryer.)

source of the hurtful rumors. Blair Christolon, in a review for *School Library Journal,* noted that "Levy presents a straightforward tale using basic vocabulary and simple sentence structure," adding that the mystery "ends on a clever, humorous note that will leave readers chuckling." *Booklist* critic Lauren Peterson praised the book's "fast-paced plot" and called Brian an "appealing, likable protagonist."

A departure from Levy's series work is her collaboration with illustrator Diana Bryer on the picture book *Cleo and the Coyote*. An abandoned dog named Cleo, who has just found a home with a boy and his mother, finds herself on a plane to Utah to visit the boy's sheep-rancher uncle. The story chronicles Cleo's adventures in her new desert surroundings, including her relationship with a coyote. Susan Powers, writing in *School Library Journal,* declared, "everything about this book is warm.... Levy departs boldly and successfully from her dog-meets-boy story and extends the breadth of this tale."

Many of Levy's other works for children employ the mystery-series format. The "Invisible Inc." mysteries chronicle the adventures of three young sleuths: Chip, who is invisible; Justin, who is hearing impaired and a lip reader; and Charlene, the leader of the group. In *Parents' Night Fright,* the prize-winning story that Charlene is supposed to read at Parents' Night disappears, and the trio follows a trail of suspects and clues before apprehending the thief. In a *School Library Journal* review, Pam Hopper Webb maintained: "This fast-paced contemporary story grabs readers' attention much like a prime-time sitcom." *Booklist*'s Stephanie Zvirin noted that "the interactions between the characters have solid appeal, and the meaty text ... gives children a good opportunity to practice their reading skills."

Among Levy's most popular works have been the "Something Queer" books, featuring the girl sleuths Gwen and Jill, who solve puzzling mysteries at school and in their neighborhood. In *Something Queer at the Haunted School,* they track down what may be a real ghost. In *Something Queer on Vacation,* they discover who has been knocking down sand castles at the beach. Among the most engaging aspects of the series, a reviewer for the *Bulletin of the Center for Children's Books* believes, are a "light style, active girl detectives, humor, and a gratifying solution to the mystery."

Jill and Gwen discover that pictures are missing from their library books about special dogs in Levy's mystery **Something Queer at the Library,** *one in a series of works about the amateur sleuths. (Illustrated by Mordicai Gerstein.)*

Levy finds that she takes a different approach when she writes a mystery. "I find writing mysteries very different from writing novels," she told *SATA*. "The great pleasure of writing a mystery is that I know how the book will end. Before I begin a mystery, I have to figure out who did it and why. I know that by the end of the book my detectives will expose the character. Usually I do not know the path my detectives will take to make this discovery. I have to go back and on the second and third drafts I must change significant parts of the book to lay clues that develop towards the end of the book.

"However, the end is always in place. I think that is why we like mysteries. People who don't read mysteries can never understand how I can read them at night before I go to sleep. 'Don't they keep you up?' friends ask. I find mysteries comforting. I read them when I'm tired or upset. Unless the writer is a cheat, I know the book will have a satisfactory ending. The bad will be punished and the characters I like will survive to live in another book. I only like mystery 'series.'

"Novels are completely different. Usually I write a novel about a conflict that I remember from my own childhood or something that I have experienced recently but believe that I also experienced when I was younger. I believe that the gift of a novel is to let others know that they are not alone, and that our secrets are usually far more shameful if kept hidden than if allowed out in the open."

Levy's novels for middle graders and young adults deal with a wide variety of themes. *Cheater, Cheater* explores the difficulties of middle-school life. Seventh grader Lucy Lovello cheats at a friend's bowling party in order to impress a boy, and as a result must deal with the consequences of being labeled a cheater. Jana R. Fine, writing in *School Library Journal,* asserted that in *Cheater, Cheater,* "all of [Levy's] characters show realistic idiosyncrasies associated with young teens," and dubbed the book "a well-tempered portrayal of young adolescent life." A *Kirkus Reviews* critic praised the book's "natural, smooth dialogue leading to a thought-provoking resolution."

The Drowned incorporates supernatural and horror-story elements. The book's protagonist, Lily, is spending the summer in Atlantic City, where her father drowned a few years earlier, leaving her with a fear of the ocean. Lily and a mysterious friend decide to make some money by leading a tour of spooky Atlantic City sights, including the house of a boy who drowned. Lily becomes ill at the house and is cared for by the boy's mother, at which point the story takes a scary and surprising turn. Deborah Stevenson of *Bulletin of the Center for Children's Books* noted that the story has "an enticing blend of local atmosphere and classic supernatural horror motifs," as well as a "straightforward and accessible style." *Booklist* critic Janice Del Negro asserted that "this supernatural potboiler will be an easy booktalk."

In danger of being sent to a school for kids with "behavior problems," class clown Bobby redeems himself when he is offered the chance to organize a school-wide comedy competition.(Cover illustration by Mark Elliott.)

My Life as a Fifth-Grade Comedian is the humorous story of class clown Bobby, whose constant shenanigans annoy everyone and threaten his relationship with his family and his success in school. Finally Bobby's teacher, Mr. Matous, gives Bobby the job of organizing a school-wide comedy competition, and the boy has a chance to turn his comedic energy into something productive. A *Kirkus Reviews* critic called *My Life as a Fifth-Grade Comedian* "hard to put down," while Darcy Schild praised its "realistic setting" and "believable emotions" in a *School Library Journal* review.

Works Cited

Review of *Cheater, Cheater, Kirkus Reviews,* July 15, 1993, p. 936.

Christolon, Blair, review of *Rude Rowdy Rumors, School Library Journal,* January, 1995, pp. 88-89.

Del Negro, Janice, review of *The Drowned, Booklist,* December 1, 1995, pp. 620-21.

Fine, Jana R., review of *Cheater, Cheater, School Library Journal,* October, 1993, p. 126.

Hawley, Suzanne, review of *Wolfman Sam, School Library Journal,* April, 1997, p. 113.

Review of *My Life as a Fifth-Grade Comedian, Kirkus Reviews,* June 15, 1997, p. 952.

Peterson, Lauren, review of *Rude Rowdy Rumors, Booklist,* January 1, 1995, pp. 820-21.

Powers, Susan, review of *Cleo and the Coyote, School Library Journal,* May, 1996, p. 94.

Schild, Darcy, review of *My Life as a Fifth-Grade Comedian, School Library Journal,* September, 1997, p. 219.

Siegel, Bonnie, review of *Gorgonzola Zombies in the Park, School Library Journal,* December, 1993, p. 91.

Something about the Author, Volume 31, Gale, 1983, pp. 115-18.

Review of *Something Queer in Rock 'n' Roll, Bulletin of the Center for Children's Books,* December, 1987.

Stevenson, Deborah, review of *The Drowned, Bulletin of the Center for Children's Books,* December, 1995, p. 131.

Webb, Pam Hopper, review of *Parents' Night Fright, School Library Journal,* September, 1998, p. 176.

Zvirin, Stephanie, review of *Gorgonzola Zombies in the Park, Booklist,* December 1, 1993, p. 691.

Zvirin, Stephanie, review of *Parents' Night Fright, Booklist,* July, 1998, p. 1890.

Zvirin, Stephanie, review of *Wolfman Sam, Booklist,* November 15, 1996, p. 588.

For More Information See

BOOKS

Fifth Book of Junior Authors and Illustrators, H. W. Wilson, 1983, pp. 193-95.

PERIODICALS

Booklist, October 1, 1993, p. 330; August, 1997, pp. 1901-02; April 15, 1998, pp. 1445-46.

Bulletin of the Center for Children's Books, January, 1998, p. 164.

Kirkus Reviews, January 15, 1996, p. 137.

School Library Journal, December 15, 1995, p. 131; July, 1998, p. 78.

Voice of Youth Advocates, December, 1993, p. 294.

*   *   *

LODGE, Bernard 1933-

Personal

Born October 19, 1933, in Chalfont, St. Peter, Buckinghamshire, England; son of William (an electrical engineer) and Olive (a nurse; maiden name, Green) Lodge; married Maureen Roffey (an illustrator), April 19, 1956; children: David, Josephine, Katherine. *Education:* Attended Dover and Canterbury Art Schools, 1951-54, and Royal College of Art, London, 1956-59.

Addresses

Home—Surrey, England.

Career

BBC-Television, London, England, graphic designer, 1960-67, 1969-77; graphic designer for television advertising, 1977—. *Military Service:* British Army, 1954-56; served in Royal Artillery.

Awards, Honors

Recipient of three Silver Awards for BBC-TV title sequences from Design and Art Direction (London), for "Dr. Who," 1968, for "The British Empire," 1973, and for "The Mind, Beyond," 1976; Kate Greenaway Medal, Highly Commended, 1976, for *Tinker, Tailor, Soldier, Sailor: A Picture Book.*

Writings

PICTURE BOOKS; FOR CHILDREN

(With Maureen Roffey) *The Grand Old Duke of York,* illustrated by Maureen Roffey, Bodley Head, 1975, Merrimack Book Service, 1978, Whispering Coyote Press, 1993.
Tinker, Tailor, Soldier, Sailor: A Picture Book, illustrated by Roffey, Bodley Head, 1976, Merrimack Book Service, 1978.
Rhyming Nell, illustrated by Roffey, Bodley Head, 1979, Lothrop, Lee & Shepard, 1979.
Door to Door: A Picture Book, illustrated by Roffey, Lothrop, Lee & Shepard, 1980, published as *Door to Door: A Split-Page Picture Book,* Whispering Coyote Press, 1993.

SELF-ILLUSTRATED PICTURE BOOKS

There Was an Old Woman Who Lived in a Glove, Whispering Coyote Press, 1992, Houghton Mifflin, 1999.
(Reteller) *Prince Ivan and the Firebird: A Russian Folk Tale,* Whispering Coyote Press, 1993.
The Half-Mile Hat, Whispering Coyote Press, 1995.
Tanglebird, Heinemann, 1997, Houghton Mifflin, 1997.
Mouldylocks, Heinemann, 1998, Houghton Mifflin, 1998.

ILLUSTRATOR

Maureen Roffey, *Let's Have a Party,* Bodley Head, 1974, Merrimack Book Service, 1978.
Stella Blackstone, *My Granny Went to Market: A Round-the-World Counting Rhyme,* Barefoot Books, 1995, published in the U.S. as *Grandma Went to Market: A Round-the-World Counting Rhyme,* Houghton Mifflin, 1996.
Nikki Siegen-Smith (compiler) *Songs for Survival: Songs and Chants from Tribal Peoples around the World,* Dutton, 1996.
Pippa Goodhart, *Noah Makes a Boat,* Heinemann, 1997, Houghton Mifflin, 1997.

Adaptations

The Grand Old Duke of York has been adapted for audio cassette by Spoken Arts, 1994.

Sidelights

Bernard Lodge is a British author and illustrator of children's books who has blended his book writing with a successful career as a graphic designer in animation for television programming and advertising. Working with his wife, Maureen Roffey, he wrote texts for award-winning titles such as *Tinker, Tailor, Soldier, Sailor.* In addition to illustrating for other authors, he has also produced popular self-illustrated titles including *There Was an Old Woman Who Lived in a Glove, Tanglebird,* and *Mouldylocks.* Lodge told *Something about the Author* (*SATA*), after publication of his first few titles, that the "story of my career as an author could be engraved on the head of a pin except that it would need padding." Such understatement is a Lodge signature in his books as well as in his life.

Lodge's first efforts as a writer of children's books were in collaboration with his wife. Their initial title, *The Grand Old Duke of York,* proved popular enough to encourage further joint efforts. A counting verse book, *Tinker, Tailor, Soldier, Sailor,* followed. The four familiar characters of the title plan a party with "Jelly, pies and pickled beef." A counting sequence from one to eight is blended into these preparations. *Growing Point* reviewer Margery Fisher called this book a "good joke, carried through most professionally," while a reviewer for *The Junior Bookshelf* described the effort as a "cheerfully expanded nursery jingle, which develops into a cumulative counting story" from this gifted pair.

A further collaborative effort was *Door to Door,* in which a split-page layout reveals the happenings inside and outside twelve different houses along a road. "The verses are quite simple and pleasant for children to learn," noted a reviewer for *The Junior Bookshelf. Publishers Weekly* called Lodge's verse "playful jingles." Everybody in the block is very busy doing something or other: "At Number One / Old Joe's begun / To load the beds / and chairs. / Mum says good-bye / And has a cry / As she lingers on / the stairs." Writing in *School Library Journal,* Carolyn Jenks noted that Roffey's pictures "are full of detail and activity" and that satisfying "the universal curiosity about what happens in other people's homes is a good theme." Ruth M. Stein of *Language Arts* called *Door to Door* a "clever picture book" and noted especially the "brilliant use" of the double view design that allows the reader to see what is going on inside each house as well as the "humorous verse and graphics."

Lodge ended a lengthy hiatus from his involvement in the creation of children's picture books with the publication of his self-illustrated *There Was an Old Woman Who Lived in a Glove.* In this story, a takeoff from the old nursery rhyme "There Was an Old Woman Who Lived in a Shoe," Lodge tells the story of a white-haired lady and her dove, Albert, as the pair set off to see the world. *Booklist*'s Ilene Cooper called Lodge's verse "clever though sometimes thin." At one point the old woman goes in the tracks of a postman: "She followed a postman / Who lived with a snail / That was helping /

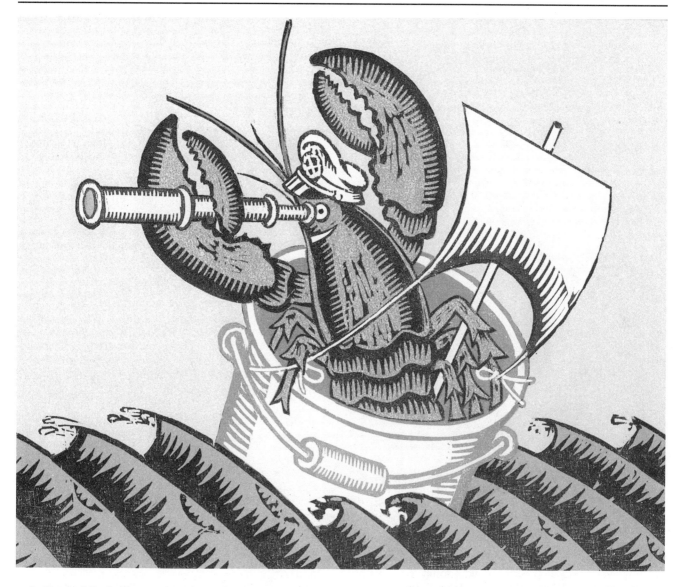

In Bernard Lodge's engaging picture book, a woman who lives in a glove surveys the equally unlikely homes, including a bucket and a bowler hat, of other creatures. (From There Was an Old Woman Who Lived in a Glove, *written and illustrated by Lodge.)*

Slowly deliver the mail." Cooper maintained that it is "the attractive artwork that really makes the book a cut above." Lodge created woodcut illustrations for this book, printed them on an antique handpress, and then assembled the prints into collages. Of course it takes a trip to make the old woman realize that her glove is actually the perfect place for her. "Expressive, boldly colored woodcuts give a sense of life, action and playfulness to each house," observed Ronald Jobe in *School Library Journal.* Jobe also commented that the text in rhyme is "fun."

Lodge turned to a classic Russian folktale for his next solo effort, *Prince Ivan and the Firebird.* In this retelling, he used a mid-nineteenth-century version of the quest tale, "enlivened by [his] exuberant folk-art-inspired illustrations," according to a writer for *Publishers Weekly.* Denise Anton Wright in *School Library Journal* praised Lodge's "natural integration of the white

of the pages into his designs," full of onion domes and Cossack-inspired apparel. Wright concluded that though there are many versions of this tale, "few are as imaginative."

A giant with an expensive straw hat informs Lodge's *The Half-Mile Hat,* a "fanciful story," according to *Publishers Weekly,* with "illustrations as diverting to look at as his tall (or wide) tale is to read." For *Tanglebird,* Lodge once again chose woodcuts as illustrations, this time done in soft pastels. When the other birds ridicule Tanglebird, who has a difficult time making a tidy nest, he flies off to the city. There, unfortunately, he makes similar messes with yarn and kite string in an attempt to fashion a nest. Befriended by a little girl, he learns how to tie shoelaces and to weave, and back home in the woods again, he makes the most beautiful nests imaginable. A *Kirkus Reviews* commentator observed that although the lesson is a bit "manipu-

Tanglebird flew out over the rooftops of the city towards the distant woods.

With the help of a little girl, the title character in Lodge's self-illustrated book **Tanglebird** *transforms his tangled nest into a neatly woven, beautiful home that becomes the envy of the other birds.*

lated," nevertheless "children will like Tanglebird's triumph over those who once mocked him." *Booklist*'s Cooper noted that Lodge's illustrations have their "own look that both kids and adults will respond to," and concluded that the book is a "great story-hour choice." A *Publishers Weekly* critic also praised the illustrations in *Tanglebird,* commenting that "Lodge's merry, rustic prints have moments of slapstick humor, and make wonderful use of pattern, subtly flattening foliage, clothing and freeways." Writing in *School Library Journal,* Lisa S. Murphy observed that the little girl who befriends Tanglebird, Gina, "subtly molds Tanglebird's weakness into strength, without compromising his free spirit." Murphy also noted that the woodcut/pastel artwork made the book "as appealing as its message."

With *Mouldylocks,* Lodge tells the story of the eponymous witch and her birthday. Mouldylocks receives a new broomstick first thing in the morning which whisks her away to a surprise party. There she receives all sorts of gifts, from a book of magic spells to a Snakes and Ladders game with *real* snakes. When things get out of hand, Mouldylocks uses magic spells to set everything right before the arrival of the birthday cake. *Booklist*'s GraceAnne A. DeCandido described Mouldylock's hair as "acid-green vermicelli," and noted that the woodcut

illustrations in general "have a fiendish charm." DeCandido concluded that the book is "fine Halloween storytime fodder."

Lodge has also illustrated several picture books for other authors, including *Grandma Went to Market, Songs for Survival,* and *Noah Makes a Boat.* The first title tells the story of a grandmother who shops till she drops. Reviewing that title, Hazel Rochman noted in *Booklist* that "Lodge's line-and-color paintings show a nice English lady in a big hat with a shopping cart, surveying the sweet wonders of the world." *Publishers Weekly* called the illustrations in that same title "cheerful art," while Marianne Saccardi noted in *School Library Journal* that "Lodge depicts characteristic landscapes or architecture in brightly colored gouache illustrations stretching across a page and a third."

Songs for Survival is an anthology of songs and chants from the tribal peoples of six continents, and Lodge's illustrations for this book are "in a unified style," according to a *Publishers Weekly* commentator, "lino-cuts that seem generally primitivist but are specific to no one culture." *School Library Journal* contributor Renee Steinberg noted that Lodge's "vibrantly colored illustrations offer a celebration of life." The story of the Flood and of Noah's efforts to save two of each on his ark is

and Wizard Twittle gave her a pop-up book of spells.

At her own birthday celebration, a little witch must summon all her magic powers to restore order after the party games get out of hand. (From Mouldylocks, *written and illustrated by Lodge.)*

retold by Pippa Goodhart in *Noah Makes a Boat.* Cooper, writing in *Booklist,* noted that there have been many versions of the old Bible story. "What makes this one a winner are Lodge's robust lino cut illustrations," Cooper observed. She went on to note that Lodge's illustrations "provide the perfect medium to convey the particulars of Noah's work." *Publishers Weekly* noted that the author's simple straightforward style "allows Lodge free reign for his full-bleed spreads of animals running rampant in pairs as they ready themselves for the ark-bound parade."

Whether illustrating his own distinctive titles, or working in collaboration with other authors of children's books, Lodge has created his own style—a blend of whimsy and solid graphic skills—and has ultimately disproved his own self-effacing judgment of his work. The "head of the pin" upon which he once ironically commented that his career could be etched has grown significantly in both size and stature.

Works Cited

Cooper, Ilene, review of *There Was an Old Woman Who Lived in a Glove, Booklist,* October 15, 1992, pp. 434-35.

Cooper, Ilene, review of *Noah Makes a Boat, Booklist,* October 1, 1997, p. 323.

Cooper, Ilene, review of *Tanglebird, Booklist,* March 1, 1997, p. 1172.

DeCandido, GraceAnne A., review of *Mouldylocks, Booklist,* September 1, 1998, p. 133.

Review of *Door to Door, Junior Bookshelf,* December, 1980, p. 285.

Review of *Door to Door, Publishers Weekly,* November 21, 1980, p. 59.

Fisher, Margery, review of *Tinker, Tailor, Soldier, Sailor, Growing Point,* January, 1977, p. 3050.

Review of *Grandma Went to Market: A Round-the-World Counting Rhyme, Publishers Weekly,* February 5, 1996, p. 881.

Review of *The Half-Mile Hat, Publishers Weekly,* January 9, 1995, p. 64.

Jenks, Carolyn, review of *Door to Door, School Library Journal,* February, 1994, p. 89.

Jobe, Ronald, review of *There Was an Old Lady Who Lived in a Glove, School Library Journal,* February, 1993, pp. 84-85.

Lodge, Bernard, *Tinker, Tailor, Soldier, Sailor,* Bodley Head, 1976.

Lodge, Bernard, *Door to Door,* Whispering Coyote Press, 1980.

Lodge, Bernard, *There Was an Old Woman Who Lived in a Glove,* Whispering Coyote Press, 1992.

Murphy, Lisa S. review of *Tanglebird, School Library Journal,* April, 1997, p. 113.

Review of *Noah Makes a Boat, Publishers Weekly,* August 25, 1997, p. 65.

Review of *Prince Ivan and the Firebird, Publishers Weekly,* August 9, 1993, p. 479.

Rochman, Hazel, review of *Grandma Went to Market: A Round-the-World Counting Rhyme, Booklist,* February 1, 1996, p. 936.

Saccardi, Marianne, review of *Grandma Went to Market: A Round-the-World Counting Rhyme, School Library Journal,* April, 1996, p. 99.

Review of *Songs for Survival: Songs and Chants from Tribal Peoples around the World, Publishers Weekly,* June 3, 1996, p. 84.

Stein, Ruth M., review of *Door to Door, Language Arts,* April, 1981, p. 474.

Steinberg, Renee, review of *Songs for Survival: Songs and Chants from Tribal Peoples around the World, School Library Journal,* July, 1996, p. 96.

Review of *Tanglebird, Kirkus Reviews,* March 1, 1997, p. 384.

Review of *Tanglebird, Publishers Weekly,* February 24, 1997, p. 90.

Review of *Tinker, Tailor, Soldier, Sailor, The Junior Bookshelf,* April, 1977, p. 80.

Wright, Denise Anton, review of *Prince Ivan and the Firebird, School Library Journal,* November, 1993, p. 100.

For More Information See

PERIODICALS

Kirkus Reviews, August 1, 1998, p. 1120.

Publishers Weekly, July 20, 1998, p. 218.

New York Times Book Review, August 31, 1997, p. 13.

School Librarian, August, 1997, p. 131.

School Library Journal, September, 1997, p. 182; October, 1998, pp. 106-07.

Times Educational Supplement, July 18, 1997, p. 35.*

—Sketch by J. Sydney Jones

M–N

MacLACHLAN, Patricia 1938-

Personal

Born March 3, 1938, in Cheyenne, WY; daughter of Philo (a teacher) and Madonna (a teacher; maiden name, Moss) Pritzkau; married Robert MacLachlan (a clinical psychologist), April 14, 1962; children: John, Jamie, Emily. *Education:* University of Connecticut, B.A., 1962.

Patricia MacLachlan

Addresses

Home—Williamsburg, MA. *Office*—Department of Education, Smith College, Northampton, MA 01063.

Career

Bennett Junior High School, Manchester, CT, English teacher, 1963-79; Smith College, Northampton, MA, visiting lecturer, 1986—; writer. Lecturer; social worker; teacher of creative writing workshops for adults and children. Children's Aid Family Service Agency, board member, 1970-80.

Awards, Honors

Golden Kite Award, Society of Children's Book Writers, 1980, for *Arthur, for the Very First Time;* Notable Children's Trade Book, National Council for Social Studies and the Children's Book Council, 1980, for *Through Grandpa's Eyes,* 1982, for *Mama One, Mama Two,* and 1985, for *Sarah, Plain and Tall; Boston Globe-Horn Book* Award, 1984, for *Unclaimed Treasures;* Golden Kite Award, Scott O'Dell Historical Fiction Award, Best Books, *School Library Journal,* and Notable Children's Books, *New York Times,* all 1985, Newbery Medal, American Library Association, Jefferson Cup Award, Virginia Library Association, Christopher Award, and Children's Books of the Year, Child Study Association of America, all 1986, Garden State Children's Book Award, New Jersey Library Association, and International Board on Books for Young People Honor List nominee, both 1988, all for *Sarah, Plain and Tall; Parents' Choice* Award, Parents' Choice Foundation, 1988, and *Horn Book* Fanfare citation, 1989, all for *The Facts and Fictions of Minna Pratt; Arthur, for the Very First Time, Cassie Binegar, Sarah, Plain and Tall,* and *Seven Kisses in a Row* were all named Junior Library Guild selections. MacLachlan was honored with a University of Southern Mississippi Medallion for her body of work.

Writings

PICTURE BOOKS

The Sick Day, illustrated by William Pene du Bois, Pantheon, 1979.

Through Grandpa's Eyes, illustrated by Deborah Ray, Harper, 1980.

Mama One, Mama Two, illustrated by Ruth Lercher Bornstein, Harper, 1982.

Seven Kisses in a Row, illustrated by Maria Pia Marrella, Harper, 1983.

Three Names, illustrated by Alexander Pertzoff, HarperCollins, 1991.

What You Know First, illustrated by Barry Moser, Harper-Collins, 1995.

JUVENILE NOVELS

Arthur, for the Very First Time, illustrated by Lloyd Bloom, Harper, 1980.

Moon, Stars, Frogs, and Friends, illustrated by Tomie de Paola, Pantheon, 1980.

Cassie Binegar, Harper, 1982.

Tomorrow's Wizard, illustrated by Kathy Jacobi, Harper, 1982.

Unclaimed Treasures, Harper, 1984.
Sarah, Plain and Tall, Harper, 1985.
The Facts and Fictions of Minna Pratt, Harper, 1988.
Journey, Delacorte Press, 1991.
Baby, Delacorte Press, 1993.
Skylark, HarperCollins, 1994.
All the Places to Love, illustrated by Mike Wimmer, HarperCollins, 1994.

Also author of teleplays for *Sarah, Plain and Tall* and *Skylark.* Contributor to *Newbery Award Library II,* edited by Joseph Krumgold, Harper, 1988.

Adaptations

Arthur, for the Very First Time was adapted as a filmstrip with cassette, Pied Piper, 1984; *Sarah, Plain and Tall* was adapted as a filmstrip with cassette, Random House, 1986, and as a Hallmark Hall of Fame television film starring Glenn Close and Christopher Walken, Columbia Broadcasting System (CBS), 1991; *Mama One, Mama Two, Through Grandpa's Eyes,* and *The Sick Day* were recorded on audio cassette, Caedmon, 1987. *Through Grandpa's Eyes* was adapted as a motion picture and videorecording, Grey Haven Films, 1987; *Skylark* and *Journey* were adapted as Hallmark Hall of Fame presentations, 1993 and 1995, respectively.

Sidelights

Patricia MacLachlan is known for her award-winning picture books and novels for children, which include *The Sick Day; Arthur, for the Very First Time; Sarah, Plain and Tall;* and *The Facts and Fictions of Minna Pratt.* Populated by eccentric, endearing characters and often focusing on family relationships, MacLachlan's works are considered tender, humorous, and perceptive. Although she usually concentrates on the realities of everyday life in her books, MacLachlan has also penned more fanciful tales such as *Tomorrow's Wizard* and *Moon, Stars, Frogs, and Friends.* Reviewers generally praise MacLachlan's work, indicating that her graceful, lucid prose is particularly suitable for reading aloud and that her warm, optimistic stories both enlighten and entertain young readers.

Born in Wyoming and reared in Minnesota, MacLachlan was an only child. Although she had no siblings for companionship, she enjoyed a strong relationship with her parents and benefited from an active imagination. MacLachlan's parents were teachers and encouraged her to read; her mother urged her to "read a book and find out who you are," the author related in her Newbery acceptance speech published in *Horn Book.* MacLachlan read voraciously, sometimes discussing and acting out scenes in books with her parents. She wrote in *Horn Book,* "I can still feel the goose bumps as I, in the fur of Peter Rabbit, fled from the garden and Mr. McGregor— played with great ferocity by my father—into the coat closet . . . . Some days I would talk my father into acting out the book a dozen times in a row, with minor changes here and there or major differences that reversed the plot."

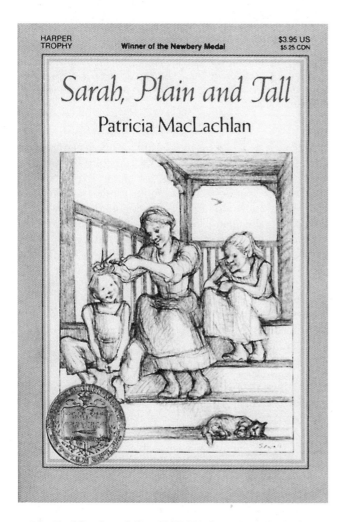

MacLachlan based her 1985 Newbery Award-winning book about a mail-order bride on her mother's memories. (Cover illustration by Marcia Sewall.)

MacLachlan was also kept company by her imaginary friend, Mary, "who was real enough for me to insist that my parents set a place for her at the table," the author recalled. "Mary was a free spirit. She talked me into drawing a snail on the living room wall, larger and larger, so that the room had to be repainted.... My parents tolerated Mary with good humor, though I'm sure it was trying. Mary was ever present. 'Don't sit there,' I'd cry with alarm. 'Mary's there!' One of my early memories is of my father, negotiating with Mary for the couch after dinner."

Though she was creative enough to invent a friend and concoct elaborate fantasies, MacLachlan did not write stories as a child. The author remembers being intimidated by the intensely personal nature of writing and the belief that "writers had all the answers." Remembering a school assignment, she continued: "I wrote a story on a three by five card. I still have it: 'My cats have names and seem happy. Often they play. The end.' My teacher was not impressed. I was discouraged, and I wrote in my diary: 'I shall try not to be a writer.'"

Indeed, MacLachlan did not begin to write until years later, at the age of thirty-five. Married with children of her own, she kept busy by working with foster mothers at a family services agency and spending time with her family. As her children grew older, though, she "felt a need to do something else—go to graduate school or go back to teaching, perhaps," she told *SATA.* "It dawned on me that what I really wanted to do was to write. How would I ever have the courage, I wondered. It was very scary to find myself in the role of student again, trying to learn something entirely new."

MacLachlan started her successful writing career by creating picture books. Her first, *The Sick Day,* details how a little girl with a cold is cared for by her father. In a *Bulletin of the Center for Children's Books* review, Zena Sutherland called *The Sick Day* a "read-aloud story told with a polished ease that belies the fact that this is MacLachlan's first book for children." Another work, *Through Grandpa's Eyes,* explores how a young boy is taught by his blind grandfather to "see" the world through his other senses. "The book makes you want to slow the pace of life to appreciate the beauties we so often take for granted," enthused Ruth W. Bauer in *Children's Book Review Service.*

Mama One, Mama Two takes a frank yet comforting look at mental illness and foster parenting. In the story a girl is taken in by "Mama Two" while waiting for her natural mother, "Mama One," to recover from psychological problems. MacLachlan, praised for the simplicity and sensitivity she brings to these stories, is especially noted for her deft handling of unconventional subject matter. While there have been other books that have explored foster parent and child relationships, "this is the nicest yet," declared Zena Sutherland in *Bulletin of the Center for Children's Books.*

Encouraged by her editor, MacLachlan also started to write novels intended for a slightly older audience. She

As the years pass and a family grows in size, its members cherish the special places on their farm and carry out such loving traditions as carving the names of newborns on rafters in the barn. (Cover illustration by Mike Wimmer.)

commented to *SATA* on the differences between the two genres: "It is more difficult to write a picture book than a novel. A good picture book is much like a poem: concise, rich, bare-boned, and multi-leveled.... When I want to stretch into greater self-indulgence, I write a novel." MacLachlan's first novel, *Arthur, for the Very First Time,* tells of a young boy's emotional growth during the summer he spends with his great-uncle and great-aunt. In an interview with Ann Courtney in *Language Arts,* MacLachlan commented that she particularly enjoyed writing *Arthur.* "At the time *Arthur* was an intensely personal thing. I knew I was writing about a lot of me, a lot of my family, a lot of what I was thinking about at the time."

Evaluations of *Arthur* were favorable, as critics commended MacLachlan's realistic characters and her sincere yet entertaining look at childhood problems. "Fine characterization, an intriguing mix of people and problems, and the author's remarkable knack for leaving between the lines things best unsaid are some of the strengths of the novel," maintained *Booklist* reviewer Judith Goldberger. Zena Sutherland echoed the sentiment in her review of *Arthur* in *Bulletin of the Center for Children's Books,* asserting: "The story has a deep tenderness, a gentle humor, and a beautifully honed writing style."

MacLachlan again addresses a child's resistance to change in her second novel, *Cassie Binegar.* Part of a large, somewhat disorganized, but happy family, Cassie finds herself longing for the serenity found in her friend Mary Margaret's home. Growing up is suddenly a much more difficult task, as Cassie begins to self-consciously compare herself and her family with others around her. And at the core of most of her problems is a fear of change, a fear that comes to the fore when the family moves and Cassie's aging grandmother, among other relatives, comes to stay with the Binegars. *Horn Book* reviewer Ann A. Flowers described MacLachlan's writing in *Cassie Binegar* as "elegant and evocative." *School Library Journal* contributor Wendy Dellett found the characters in the novel "pleasant and kindly" and the author's writing "luminous and readable."

A character in *Arthur, for the Very First Time* provided the seed for MacLachlan's best-known work, *Sarah, Plain and Tall.* Aunt Mag in *Arthur* was a mail-order bride (a woman who meets her husband by answering a newspaper advertisement) as was a distant relative of MacLachlan's. In *Sarah, Plain and Tall* the title character answers a newspaper advertisement and as a result goes to visit a lonely widower and his children on a midwestern prairie. When Sarah arrives, the children take to her immediately and hope she'll stay and marry their father. Considered a poignant and finely wrought tale, *Sarah, Plain and Tall* garnered widespread critical acclaim; MacLachlan received a Newbery Medal for the novel in 1986. "A near perfect miniature novel that fulfills the ideal of different levels of meaning for children and adults," said Betsy Hearne in *Booklist.* Margery Fisher of *Growing Point* deemed *Sarah, Plain and Tall* a "small masterpiece."

"My mother told me early on about the real Sarah," stated MacLachlan in her Newbery Medal acceptance speech, "who came from the coast of Maine to the prairie to become a wife and mother to a close family member. . . . So the fact of Sarah was there for years, though the book began as books often do, when the past stepped on the heels of the present; or backward, when something *now* tapped something *then.*" Shortly before two of her children were to leave for college, MacLachlan's parents took the family on a trip to the prairie where they, and MacLachlan, were born. This trip made the connection between the past and the present more evident to both MacLachlan and her mother, who was beginning to lose her memory because of Alzheimer's disease.

"When I began *Sarah,*" continued MacLachlan in her speech, "I wished for several things and was granted something unexpected. Most of all I wished to write my mother's story with spaces, like the prairie, with silences that could say what words could not . . . . But books, like children, grow and change, borrowing bits and pieces of the lives of others to help make them who and what they are. And in the end we are all there, my mother, my father, my husband, my children, and me. We gave my mother better than a piece of her past. We gave her the same that Anna and Caleb and Jacob received—a family."

Critics praised *Sarah, Plain and Tall* for its simplicity, its driving emotional force, and its strong characterizations and descriptions. "It is the simplest of love stories expressed in the simplest of prose," maintained Martha Saxton in the *New York Times Book Review,* adding: "Embedded in these unadorned declarative sentences . . . are evocations of the deepest feelings of loss and fear, love and hope." Trev Jones, writing in *School Library Journal,* asserted: "Through a simple sentence or phrase, aspects of each character's personality . . . are brought to light." And Margery Fisher contended in *Growing Point* that "not a word is wasted, not a nuance missed in the quiet tenor of a narrative which creates, seemingly without any effort, the family's world of sky and prairies and Sarah's remembered world of sea and sand."

MacLachlan's first novel after winning the Newbery was *The Facts and Fictions of Minna Pratt.* Eleven-year-old Minna, teetering on the edge of adolescence, finds herself confronted with numerous changes as she strives to develop a vibrato. While she practices her cello to attain this dream, Minna also longs for her eccentric mother, a writer, to be more like a "mother." And in the midst of all this appears Lucas Ellerby, a violinist who has the quiet and peaceful home Minna desires. Lucas, on the other hand, is fascinated with the unusual ways of Minna's family, and the two experience their first romance. "Patricia MacLachlan has created a wonderfully wise and funny story with such satisfying depths and unforgettable characters that one is reluctant to let it go," praised a *Horn Book* reviewer. Heather Vogel Frederick, writing in the *New York Times Book Review,* declared: "If writers of children's fiction were organized into a guild, the title of master craftsman would be bestowed upon Patricia MacLachlan. Her crisp, elegant prose and superb storytelling ability . . . grace her newest novel, *The Facts and Fictions of Minna Pratt.*"

MacLachlan continued to hone her realistic storytelling skills with two tales of loss—*Journey* and *Baby.* The former concerns a young boy named Journey who must come to terms with having been abandoned by his mother. Journey and his sister Cat have always lived with their grandparents, but it is only recently that their mother has left them. Each member of the family copes with the abandonment differently, and piecing together some old photographs of his mother enables Journey to feel the love that he seeks. Nancy Bray Cardozo wrote in the *New York Times Book Review:* "The language Ms. MacLachlan uses is beautiful, emotionally articulate. Journey speaks as though an eloquent adult is reminiscing about a childhood tragedy, the sadness still keenly remembered." *Baby* is also about a family dealing with tragedy. Shortly after twelve-year-old Larkin's infant brother dies, his family finds a baby girl, Sophie, abandoned on their driveway. Once the members of the family break down and let Sophie into their hearts, despite the fact that her mother will be coming back for her, they are finally able to grieve for their recent loss.

"MacLachlan's style remains masterly," concluded a *Publishers Weekly* commentator. "It is difficult to read her sentences only once, and even more difficult to part from her novel."

The heartwarming story of the prairie family and their mail-order mother that was introduced in *Sarah, Plain and Tall* is continued in *Skylark*. Published in 1994, *Skylark* finds Sarah and her new family facing a seemingly unending drought. Not yet fully familiar with life on the prairie, Sarah starts to feel pressure, and after the family's barn burns she takes the children to stay with her aunts in Maine. Although the children are fascinated by the sea, they miss their father terribly, and all are excited when he arrives in Maine with news that rain has fallen. Sarah, too, has news, and when the family returns to the prairie Sarah writes her name in the dirt of her true home. MacLachlan's writing "neatly presents a very real setting and enormously powerful characters," claimed a *Publishers Weekly* contributor, concluding: "There are worlds in MacLachlan's words."

As with the mail-order bride in *Sarah, Plain and Tall*, MacLachlan often gleans elements of her stories from personal experience. She explained to *SATA* that "my books derive chiefly from my family life, both as a child with my own parents as well as with my husband and kids. *The Sick Day* ... could happen in almost any family. *Mama One, Mama Two* comes from my experiences with foster mothers and the children they cared for." MacLachlan also noted in *Horn Book* that "the issues of a book are the same issues of life each day. What is real and what is not? How do you look at the world? How do I?" Sometimes the influence of the author's life on her work is unconscious; scenes from her childhood appear on her pages, episodes that she thought she had invented but that had actually happened. Once, she described an unusual tablecloth in one of her books, thinking she had made up the cloth's design; she later discovered that her mother had used a virtually identical tablecloth when MacLachlan was a child. Referring to such an instance in *Junior Library Guild*, MacLachlan commented, "I realized that this is the magic. When you write you reach back somewhere in your mind or your heart and pull out things that you never even knew were there."

MacLachlan is heartened by children's reactions to her work; she noted to *SATA* that "it's hugely gratifying to know that kids all over read what I write." Affirming the importance of encouraging young writers, the author visits schools to speak with students and give writing workshops. "In my experience, children believe that writers are like movie stars. I am often asked if I arrived in a limousine," MacLachlan remarked in *SATA*. "I admit that sometimes I'm a little flattered at the exalted idea kids have about writers. But more importantly, I feel it's crucial that kids who aspire to write understand that I have to rewrite and revise as they do. Ours is such a perfectionist society—I see too many kids who believe that if they don't get it right the first time, they aren't writers."

When asked what advice she would have for beginning writers, MacLachlan commented in *Language Arts*, "I would certainly say only write books for children if you really love children's books and want to do it. Writing for children is special because I think children read with a great true belief in what they're reading. The other thing is to read. One must understand the far reaches of children's books because they're really about many of the same subjects as adults are concerned with. Don't be condescending. I hate the didacticism that sometimes comes through in children's books. I would read and read and read. There is no better model than a good book."

Works Cited

Review of *Baby, Publishers Weekly*, August 16, 1993, p. 104.

Bauer, Ruth W., review of *Through Grandpa's Eyes, Children's Book Review Service*, April, 1980, p. 84.

Cardozo, Nancy Bray, review of *Journey, New York Times Book Review*, March 22, 1992, p. 25.

Courtney, Ann, interview with Patricia MacLachlan, *Language Arts*, November, 1985, pp. 783-87.

Dellett, Wendy, review of *Cassie Binegar, School Library Journal*, September, 1982, p. 124.

Review of *The Facts and Fictions of Minna Pratt, Horn Book*, July-August, 1988, pp. 495-96.

Fisher, Margery, review of *Sarah, Plain and Tall, Growing Point*, March, 1987, p. 4750.

Flowers, Ann A., review of *Cassie Binegar, Horn Book*, February, 1983, pp. 45-46.

Frederick, Heather Vogel, review of *The Facts and Fictions of Minna Pratt, New York Times Book Review*, January 8, 1989, p. 36.

Goldberger, Judith, review of *Arthur, for the Very First Time, Booklist*, October 15, 1980, pp. 328-29.

Hearne, Betsy, review of *Sarah, Plain and Tall, Booklist*, May 1, 1985, pp. 1254, 1256.

Jones, Trev, review of *Sarah, Plain and Tall, School Library Journal*, May, 1985, p. 171.

MacLachlan, Patricia, "Arthur, for the Very First Time," *Junior Library Guild*, September, 1980.

MacLachlan, Patricia, "Facts and Fictions," *Horn Book*, January-February, 1986, pp. 19-26.

MacLachlan, Patricia, "Newbery Medal Acceptance," *Horn Book*, July-August, 1986, pp. 407-19.

Review of *Skylark, Publishers Weekly*, November 29, 1993, p. 65.

Sutherland, Zena, review of *Arthur, for the Very First Time, Bulletin of the Center for Children's Books*, September, 1980, pp. 15-16.

Sutherland, Zena, review of *Mama One, Mama Two, Bulletin of the Center for Children's Books*, April, 1982, pp. 153-54.

Sutherland, Zena, review of *The Sick Day, Bulletin of the Center for Children's Books*, September, 1979, pp. 11-12.

For More Information See

BOOKS

Children's Literature Review, Volume 14, Gale, 1988, pp. 177-86.

*   *   *

MacPHERSON, Winnie 1930-

Personal

Born March 15, 1930; married Robert MacPherson, August 4, 1951; children: Richard. *Education:* Attended Drake Business College (Elizabeth, NJ), 1949, and Cittone Institute (Edison, NJ), 1983.

Addresses

Home—231 Bradford Ave., Linden, NJ 07036.

Career

Jersey Mortgage Co., Elizabeth, NJ, clerk typist, 1966-73; Pamarco, Inc., Roselle, NJ, executive secretary, 1973-82; Rockwell International, Cranford, NJ, executive secretary, 1983-92.

Writings

Cheetahs for Kids, NorthWord Press (Minnetonka, MN), 1998.

Work in Progress

Writing "The Happy Chair" and "School Cat"; research on small cats, including the caracal, sand cat, serval, and fishing cat.

Sidelights

Winnie MacPherson told *SATA:* "Although my education and past employment were not geared to a writing career, it was always in the back of my mind. Bringing up two children, running a home, and working full-time did not leave much room for another career. Now that my children are grown and my grandchildren are teenagers, there is time to pursue new interests. Writing and illustrating were at the top of the list, so off I went to writing workshops at a local college. I chose to write for children because I enjoy being with them. Children are so open to learning new things and enjoying life. Classroom visits are a fun way to talk with my readers in person.

"*Cheetahs for Kids* is my first book to be published. It is exciting and interesting to see the work of the author, publisher, illustrator, and printer all come together to create the book. I have not had any illustrations published yet. I'm still working on that.

"When writing about animals, I am sharing my love for them with the children. My hope is that, upon learning

Winnie MacPherson

more about a particular animal, they will come to love it, too. So many animals in the wild today are in danger of extinction. The fate of these animals will be the children's concern in the future. There are children who never heard of a cheetah. They may never visit a zoo or safari park. Books and television may be their only sources of information.

"When I get an idea for a story or drawing, I gather everything I can find about the subject—pictures, books, articles, et cetera. If it is a book I am planning, all of this goes into a zippered three-ring notebook. At this point, I do any necessary research. It is fun to me because I am always researching something I love. When all this information is put in the notebook, I am ready to begin writing.

"I usually have more than one project in process at a given time. If one gives me a 'problem,' I switch to one of the others. If I'm lucky, while working on a second project, the answer to the problem on the first one may come to me. My advice to any aspiring writer is: Don't give up. If you believe in what you are writing, keep on writing and submitting. Don't let the rejections get you down.

"My hobbies are varied but usually of a creative nature. I recently built a doll house. Though frustrating at times, when windows didn't fit and so forth, I enjoyed every minute. My family appreciates the quilts I have made.

But writing and artwork remain at the top of my list of favorite things to do."

*　　*　　*

MAMMANO, Julie (Lynn) 1962-

Personal

Born July 2, 1962, in Lynwood, CA; daughter of Louis George (a retired beauty-supply sales-representative) and Judith Alice (Cornett) Mammano. *Education:* Biola University, B.A., 1984. *Politics:* "I always make sure to vote!" *Religion:* Christian. *Hobbies and other interests:* Surfing, snowboarding, hiking, travel.

Addresses

Home and office—La Mirada, CA. *Agent*—Elizabeth Harding, Curtis Brown Ltd., 10 Astor Pl., New York, NY 10003.

Career

Day Spring Greeting Cards, Siloam Springs, AR, designer and illustrator, 1984-86; Focus on the Family, Pomona, CA, assistant designer, 1987-91; freelance illustrator and writer, 1991—. Works as jewelry designer, greeting card illustrator, and illustrator for various paper products and publications. Public speaker at schools, libraries, and special events. *Member:* Society of Children's Book Writers and Illustrators, Southern California Council on Literature for Children and Young People, SCCBA, Montage.

Awards, Honors

Parents' Choice Award for Children's Books, Parents Choice Foundation, and International Design Competition Merit Winner, *HOW* magazine, both 1996, both for *Rhinos Who Surf;* Certificate of Merit for greeting-card illustration, Society of Illustrators.

Writings

AUTHOR AND ILLUSTRATOR

Rhinos Who Surf, Chronicle (San Francisco, CA), 1996.
Rhinos Who Snowboard, Chronicle, 1997.
Rhinos Who Skateboard, Chronicle, 1999.

Work in Progress

Another "rhino" book, introducing a female character; stories based on the author's childhood experiences.

Sidelights

Julie Mammano told *SATA:* "I'm living proof that God has a sense of humor. As a kid I didn't like reading or writing, so what did I end up becoming as an adult? A children's book author and illustrator! Now I enjoy reading and writing, so there's hope for those reluctant readers.

Julie Mammano

"I always had a natural talent for drawing. My parents encouraged me in my artwork and kept me in line doing my schoolwork, especially reading, writing, and math. I had a hard time learning to read. My parents' support and encouragement will always be appreciated. Various teachers and friends also helped me.

"My first 'art' job was that of a paste-up artist for a local city newspaper, while in high school. After graduating from college I was hired as a staff designer and illustrator for a greeting card company in Arkansas. Then I was a children's-magazine designer when I returned to California. Children's books always appealed to me, but for some reason it never crossed my mind to pursue children's-book illustration. I guess it seemed too far out of reach.

"Then in 1992 my friend Nikki Grimes (author of many wonderful children's books) encouraged me to give children's book illustration a try. She got me a badge to attend a meeting of the American Booksellers Association, which was held locally that year. I took my portfolio to all the publishers I could, and it was actually fun. I had nothing to lose, so it was like a big hunt. My art received lots of positive feedback, but no one was able to find any manuscripts that would fit with my artistic style. Some editors and art directors even told me that my art would *not* work for children's books. So, after many rejections, I decided I would have to write my own story to illustrate.

"Now my problem was deciding what to write about. A few months later, an idea came to me while surfing with friends. When the name 'Griff' was mentioned in a conversation, while we were sitting on our surfboards waiting for a wave, I thought it sounded like the type of name a rhino would have. That gave me an idea for a story, and [eventually] *Rhinos Who Surf* was published. *Rhinos Who Snowboard* came next, and as a result of this book, I learned how to snowboard. Now I hope to attempt skateboarding. When I visit schools to talk about being an author and illustrator, the kids love the idea that I actually do what I write about. I will draw the line, though, if the rhinos go bungee-jumping!

"Becoming an author and illustrator of children's books has been an unexpected thing in my career. It has been an enjoyable and rewarding journey. I'm so glad that this new world opened before me. I hope to be an encouragement and inspiration to others, especially to kids who struggle with reading and writing. Never give up!"

For More Information See

PERIODICALS

L.A. Times, December 6, 1998.
L.A. Times Book Review, February 14, 1999.
Parenting Magazine, June, 1996.
Publishers Weekly, May 20, 1996, p. 258.
School Library Journal, July, 1996, p. 69; March, 1998, p. 184.
Surfing Magazine, June, 1996, p. 62.

*   *   *

McKEE, David 1935-

Personal

Full name David John McKee; born January 2, 1935, in Devon, England; son of Richard William (an agricultural machine representative) and Violet (Easton) McKee; married Barbara Patricia Enuss; children: Chantel Patricia, Chuck Richard, Brett William. *Education:* Plymouth College of Art, N.D.D., 1956; Hornsey College of Art, A.T.C., 1959. *Religion:* Church of England.

Addresses

Home—8 Spencer Mansions, Queens Club Gardens, London W14 9TL, England; also resides in France, Italy, and Spain. *Agent*—c/o Andersen Press, 62-65 Chandos Place, Covent Garden, London WC2N 4NW, England.

Career

Author and artist, illustrator, cartoonist, and filmmaker. Founder of animation company King Rollo Films. *Military service:* British Army, Royal Army Educational Corps, instructor, 1956-58; became sergeant.

Awards, Honors

Deutscher Jugendliteraturpreis, 1987, for *Two Monsters;* Children's Choice selection, International Reading Association-Children's Book Council, 1997, for *Elmer and Wilbur,* and 1999, for *Elmer Takes Off.*

Writings

FOR CHILDREN; AUTHOR AND ILLUSTRATOR

Bronto's Wings, Dobson, 1964.
Two Can Toucan, Abelard (London, England), 1965.
(Reteller) *Hans in Luck,* Abelard, 1967.
Mark and the Monocycle, Abelard, 1968.
Six Men, Nord-Sud Verlag (Switzerland), 1971, A. & C. Black (London), 1972.
(Reteller) *The Man Who Was Going to Mind the House: A Norwegian Folk-Tale,* Abelard, 1972.
Lord Rex, the Lion Who Wished, Abelard, 1973.
The Day the Tide Went Out—and Out—and Out—and Out—and Out, Abelard (London), 1975, Abelard (New York), 1976.
Two Admirals, Andersen, 1977, Houghton, 1977.
Tusk Tusk, Andersen, 1978, Barron's (Woodbury, NY), 1979.
Not Now, Bernard, Andersen, 1980.
I Hate My Teddy Bear, Andersen, 1982, Clarion (New York), 1984.
The Hill and the Rock, Andersen, 1984, Clarion, 1985.
Two Monsters, Andersen, 1985, Bradbury (New York), 1986.
The Sad Story of Veronica Who Played the Violin: Being an Explanation of Why the Streets Are Not Full of Happy Dancing People, Andersen, 1987, Kane/Miller (Brooklyn, NY), 1991.
Snow Woman, Andersen, 1987, Lothrop, 1988.
Who's a Clever Baby Then?, Andersen, 1988, published in the United States as *Who's a Clever Baby?,* Lothrop, 1988.
The Monster and the Teddy Bear, Andersen, 1989.
Annabelle Pig and the Travellers [and] *Benjamin Pig and the Apple Thiefs,* Macmillan (London), 1990.
Zebra's Hiccups, Andersen, 1991, Simon & Schuster, 1993.
The Schoolbus Comes at Eight O' Clock, Andersen, 1993, Hyperion (New York), 1994.
Isabelle's Noisy Tummy, Andersen, 1994.
Charlotte's Piggy Bank, Andersen, 1996.
Prince Peter and the Teddybear, Andersen, 1997, published in the United States as *Prince Peter and the Teddy Bear,* Farrar, Straus, 1997.

"EXTRAORDINARY ADVENTURES OF MR. BENN" SERIES

Mr. Benn, Red Knight, Dobson (London), 1967, McGraw, 1968.
123456789 Benn, McGraw, 1970.
Mr. Benn Annual, Argus Press, 1972.
Big Game Benn, Dobson, 1979.
Big Top Benn, Dobson, 1980.
Caveman, Hodder and Stoughton (London), 1993.
Diver, Hodder and Stoughton, 1993.
Red Knight (based on the television series), Hodder and Stoughton, 1993.

Spaceman (based on the television series), Hodder and Stoughton, 1993.

"ELMER" SERIES; SELF-ILLUSTRATED PICTURE BOOKS

Elmer: The Story of a Patchwork Elephant, McGraw, 1968, revised edition, Andersen (London), 1989.
Elmer Again and Again, Dobson, 1975.
Elmer Again, Andersen, 1991, Lothrop, 1992.
Elmer on Stilts, Andersen, 1993.
Elmer and Wilbur, Andersen, 1994, Lothrop, 1996.
Elmer and the Snow, Andersen, 1994, published in the United States as *Elmer in the Snow,* Lothrop, 1995.
Elmer's Day (board book), Andersen, 1994, Lothrop, 1994.
Elmer's Colours (board book), Andersen, 1994, published in the United States as *Elmer's Colors,* Lothrop, 1994.
Elmer's Friends (board book), Andersen, 1994, Lothrop, 1994.
Elmer's Weather (board book), Andersen, 1994, Lothrop, 1994.
Elmer's Pop-Up Book, Andersen, 1996, published in the United States as *I Can Too!,* Lothrop, 1997.
Elmer and the Wind, Andersen, 1997, Lothrop, 1998.
Elmer Plays Hide-and-Seek, Andersen, 1998, published in the United States as *Hide-and-Seek Elmer: An Elmer Lift-the-Flap Book,* Morrow, 1998.
Elmer Takes Off, Lothrop, 1998.
Elmer and the Lost Teddy, Andersen, 1998, published in the United States as *Elmer and the Lost Teddy Bear,* Lothrop, 1999.

"MELRIC THE MAGICIAN" SERIES; SELF-ILLUSTRATED, EXCEPT AS NOTED

The Magician Who Lost His Magic, Abelard, 1970.
The Magician and the Sorcerer, Abelard, 1974, Parents Magazine Press (New York), 1974, published as *Melric and the Sorcerer,* Methuen (London), 1987.
The Magician and the Petnapping, Abelard, 1976, Houghton, 1976.
The Magician and the Balloon, Abelard, 1978, published as *Melric and the Balloon,* Peter Bedrick, 1986, Methuen, 1988.
The Magician and the Dragon, Abelard, 1979, Peter Bedrick, 1986, published as *Melric and the Dragon,* Methuen, 1987.
The Magician and Double Trouble, illustrated by David Hope, Abelard, 1981.
The Magician's Apprentice, Blackie (London), 1987, published as *Melric's Apprentice,* Methuen, 1988.
The Magician and the Crown, Blackie, 1988.
Tales of Melric the Magician, Treasure (London), 1991.

"KING ROLLO" SERIES

King Rollo and the Birthday, Andersen, 1979, Little, Brown, 1979.
King Rollo and the Bread, Andersen, 1979, Little, Brown, 1979.
King Rollo and the New Shoes, Andersen, 1979, Little, Brown, 1979.
King Rollo and the Balloons, Andersen, 1980, Creative Company, 1982.
King Rollo and the Tree, Andersen, 1980, Creative Company, 1982.
King Rollo and the Dishes, Andersen, 1980.
King Rollo and the Search, Andersen, 1981, Creative Company, 1982.
King Rollo and the Bath, Andersen, 1981, Creative Company, 1982.
King Rollo and King Frank, Andersen, 1981, Creative Company, 1982.
King Rollo and the Breakfast, Creative Education, 1982.
King Rollo and the Dog, Creative Education, 1982.
King Rollo and the Masks, Creative Education, 1982.
King Rollo and the Playroom, Creative Education, 1982.
Further Adventures of King Rollo (includes *King Rollo and the Dishes, King Rollo and the Balloons, King Rollo and King Frank,* and *King Rollo and the Search*), Andersen, 1983.
King Rollo's Playroom and Other Stories (includes *King Rollo and the Masks, King Rollo and the Playroom, King Rollo and the Breakfast,* and *King Rollo and the Dog*), Andersen, 1983.
The Adventures of King Rollo (includes *King Rollo and the Bread, King Rollo and the Birthday, King Rollo and the New Shoes,* and *King Rollo and the Tree*), Andersen Press, 1983.
King Rollo and the Letter, Andersen, 1984.
King Rollo's Letter and Other Stories, Andersen, 1984.
King Rollo's Spring, Andersen, 1986, Viking, 1987.
King Rollo's Autumn, Andersen, 1986, Viking, 1987.
King Rollo's Summer, Andersen, 1986, Viking, 1987.
King Rollo's Winter, Andersen, 1986, Viking, 1987.
King Rollo and Santa's Beard, Andersen, 1990.
King Rollo's Christmas, Red Fox, 1992.

ILLUSTRATOR; ALL WRITTEN BY KURT BAUMANN

Joseph, the Border Guard, Parents Magazine Press, 1972.
Joachim the Dustman, English text by Margaret Baker, A. & C. Black, 1974.
Joachim the Policeman, translated from the original German manuscript, A. & C. Black, 1975.

ILLUSTRATOR; ALL COMPILATIONS BY ALVIN SCHWARTZ

Tomfoolery: Trickery and Foolery with Words, Pan Books, 1975.
Witcracks: Jokes and Jests, Pan Books, 1975.
A Twister of Twists, a Tangler of Tongues: Tongue Twisters, Pan Books, 1976.

ILLUSTRATOR; "SUPER GRAN" SERIES; ALL WRITTEN BY FORREST WILSON

Super Gran, Puffin, 1978.
Super Gran Rules O.K.!, Puffin, 1981.
Super Gran Superstar, Puffin, 1982.
Super Gran Is Magic, Puffin, 1983.
The Television Adventures of Super Gran (based on television scripts by Wilson and Jenny McDade), Puffin, 1984.
More Television Adventures of Super Gran (based on television scripts by Wilson and McDade), Puffin, 1984.
Super Gran on Holiday, Puffin, 1987.
Super Gran at the Circus (based on television scripts by McDade), Puffin, 1987.
Super Gran to the Rescue, Puffin, 1987.
Super Gran Abroad, Puffin, 1988.

ILLUSTRATOR; COMPILATIONS BY ROSEMARY DEBNAM

A Book of Pig Tales, Kaye & Ward, 1979.
A Book of Bears, Kaye & Ward, 1981.
A Book of Cats, Kaye & Ward, 1983.
Stories for a Prince, Kaye & Ward, 1983.
A Book of Mice, Heinemann (United Kingdom), 1987.

ILLUSTRATOR; ALL WRITTEN BY HAZEL TOWNSON

The Speckled Panic, Andersen Press, 1982.
The Choking Peril, Andersen Press, 1985, Chivers North America (Hampton, New Hampshire), 1996.
One Green Bottle, Andersen Press, 1987.
Gary Who?, Andersen Press, 1988.
Hot Stuff, Andersen Press, 1991, Chivers North America, 1997.
Who's Afraid of the Evil Eye, Andersen Press, 1993.
Disaster Bag, Andersen Press, 1994.
The One-Day Millionaires, Andersen Press, 1995.
Rumpus on the Roof, Andersen Press, 1995.
Break-in, Andersen Press, 1997.
The Coughdrop Calamity, Andersen Press, 1998.

ILLUSTRATOR; "PADDINGTON FIRST BOOKS" SERIES; ALL WRITTEN BY MICHAEL BOND

Paddington and the Knicker-Bocker Rainbow, Collins, 1984, published in the United States as *Paddington and the Knickerbocker Rainbow,* Putnam, 1985.
Paddington at the Zoo, Collins, 1984, Putnam, 1985.
Paddington at the Fair, Collins, 1985, Putnam, 1986.
Paddington's Painting Exhibition, Collins, 1985, published in the United States as *Paddington's Art Exhibition,* Putnam, 1986.
Paddington at the Palace, Collins, 1986, Putnam, 1986.
Paddington Minds the House, Collins, 1986, published in the United States as *Paddington Cleans Up,* Putnam, 1986.
Paddington and the Marmalade Maze, Collins, 1987.
Paddington's Busy Day, Collins, 1987.
Paddington's Magical Christmas, Collins, 1988.

ILLUSTRATOR; "DINNER LADIES" SERIES; ALL WRITTEN BY DAVID TINKLER

The Scourge of the Dinner Ladies, Andersen, 1987, Chivers North America, 1995.
The Dinner Ladies Clean Up!, Andersen, 1990.
Revenge of the Dinner Ladies, Andersen, 1991.

ILLUSTRATOR; "TROUBLE" SERIES; ALL WRITTEN BY MICHAEL HARRISON

Bags of Trouble, Andersen, 1988.
Trouble Abroad, Andersen, 1990.
Trouble in Store, Andersen, 1991.

OTHER ILLUSTRATED WORKS

Walter Kreye, *The Poor Farmer and the Robber-Knights,* Abelard, 1969.
John Briston, *The Pegasus Book of Plastics,* Dobson, 1969.
(With Ann Reynolds) Hilary Schuard, George Corston, and K. G. O. Watts, *Mathematics Everywhere,* edited by E. M. Williams, Longmans, 1969.
Frank Moore, *Hector's House Annual* (from BBC-TV series written and directed by Regine Artarit and Georges Croses), British Broadcasting Corporation, 1969-73.
Liane Smith, *Bertha the Tanker,* British Broadcasting Corporation, 1970.
Elizabeth Hull Froman, *Mr. Drackle and His Dragons,* Watts, 1971.
Heloise Lewis and others, *Vamos Amigos: A Caribbean Spanish Course,* Longman, 1971-73.
Elizabeth Holt and Molly Perham, *Kids' London,* Abelard, 1972.
Deborah Manley and Peta Ree, *Piccolo Book of Parties and Party Games,* Pan Books, 1973.
Pamela Schaub, *Fire!* ("Breakthrough Continuation Reader"), Puffin, 1973.
Schaub, *The Day We Went to the Seaside* ("Breakthrough Continuation Reader"), Puffin, 1973.
Christine Pullein-Thompson, *The Follyfoot Pony Quiz Book,* Pan Books, 1974.
Sydney Paulden, *Yan and the Gold Mountain Robbers,* Abelard, 1974.
Mary Archard, *Cook for Your Kids!: A Strategic Guide to Family Feeding,* Allen & Unwin (Australia), 1975.
Christine Nostlinger, *Fiery Frederica,* Abelard, 1975.
Caroline Moorehead, *Helping: A Guide to Voluntary Work,* Macdonald & Jane's, 1975.
Beatrice Harrop, compiler, *Okki-Tokki-Unga: Action Songs for Children,* A. & C. Black, 1976.
Sydney Paulden, *Yan and the Firemonsters,* Abelard, 1976.
Katie Wales, compiler, *A Book of Elephants,* Parents Magazine Press, 1977.
Gordon Snell, *The King of Quizzical Island,* A. & C. Black, 1978.
Rosemary Weir, *Albert's World Tour,* Abelard, 1978.
David Ingram, *Out and About* ("Startline" series), Longman for the Schools Council, 1978.
Ingram, *Getting It Right* ("Startline" series), Longman for the Schools Council, 1978.
David Mackay, *What in the World,* Longman, 1979.
Ursula Moray Williams, *Jeffy, the Burglar's Cat,* Andersen, 1981.
David Gadsby and Harrop, compilers, *Harlequin: 44 Songs Round the Year,* Black, 1981.
Robert Alan Smith, compiler, *Blue Bell Hill Games,* Penguin, 1982.
L. Frank Baum, *The Wizard of Oz,* Puffin, 1982.
Baum, *The Marvellous Land of Oz,* Puffin, 1985.
Ursula Moray Williams, *Spid,* Andersen, 1985.
Christopher Schenk, *Hands On: Hands Off,* A. & C. Black, 1986.
Shirley Isherwood, *Something New for Bear to Do,* Hutchinson, 1986.
Beverley Mathias and Jill Bennett, compilers, *Pudmuddle Jumps In: Poems,* Methuen, 1987.
Shirley Isherwood, *A Special Place for Edward James,* Hutchinson, 1988.
Jose Luis Olaizola, *Uncle Ambrosio's Helper,* Andersen, 1989.
David Mackay, Brian Thompson, and Patricia Schaub, *After School,* Longman for the Schools Council, 1989.
Mackay, Thompson, and Schaub, *Big and Little,* Longman for the Schools Council, 1989.
Chuck McKee, *The Mystery of the Blue Arrows,* Andersen, 1990.

Elizabeth Hawkins, *Henry's Most Unusual Birthday,* Andersen, 1990.

Valerie Stillwell, *The Toffees from Zongaba,* Andersen, 1992.

Hiawyn Oram, *Out of the Blue: Stories and Poems about Colour,* Andersen, 1992, published in the United States as *Out of the Blue: Poems about Color,* Hyperion, 1993.

Robert Swindells, *Rolf and Rosie,* Andersen, 1993.

Joan Cass, *A Book of Dragons,* Mammoth, 1993.

Roger Collinson, *Willy and the Semolina Pudding and Other Stories,* Andersen, 1994.

The Book Project, *Our Favourite Nursery Rhymes,* Longman, 1994.

Roger Collinson, *Willy and the UFO and Other Stories,* Andersen, 1995.

Violet McKee, *Macaroni,* Andersen, 1998.

Contributor of illustrations to newspapers and to *Punch* magazine.

OTHER

Also author of screenplay, *Greenback Hell,* 1974, and of television plays for the *Mr. Benn* series. *King Rollo* has been adapted into films and television programs by McKee's animation company; the films featuring the character have been shown in forty countries. McKee is also the illustrator of *Abracadabra Guitar!* by Hilary Bell, 1980, and *Game-Songs with Professor Dogg's Troupe,* edited by Harriet Powell, 1983. Several of his books have been translated into Spanish and Welsh.

Adaptations

Tusk Tusk was dramatized as a school play in Nottingham, England, and performed at the Royal Albert Hall, London.

Work in Progress

Illustrations for *Time,* Gallimard Jeunesse, for Scholastic.

Sidelights

Called "the contemporary master of the children's parable" by William Henry Holmes in the *Listener* and an "acknowledged master of the [picture book] genre" by Irene Babsky in *School Librarian,* David McKee is a prolific, popular author and illustrator whose works are considered unusual, amusing, and thought-provoking. McKee has written and illustrated picture books, stories, and retellings and has illustrated picture books, fiction, and nonfiction; all of his works are directed to preschoolers and primary graders. In addition, he has written scripts for two television series based on his characters as well as a teleplay. McKee is perhaps best known as the creator of series books featuring Mr. Benn, an unassuming banker who becomes involved in fantastic adventures when he tries on different suits of clothes; Elmer, a jovial elephant with a patchwork hide; Melric the Magician, a sorcerer who struggles to maintain his position in a medieval court; and King Rollo, a childlike monarch. The author is also well known for individual picture books such as *Not Now, Bernard* and *I Hate My Teddy Bear* that are sometimes considered controversial for their satiric views and surrealistic art. As an illustrator, McKee is recognized for providing the pictures for series of books by such authors as Michael Bond, Hazel Townson, and David Tinkler as well as titles by L. Frank Baum, Christine Nostlinger, Ursula Moray Williams, and Robert Swindells, among others. He has also illustrated books by his wife Violet and son Chuck.

McKee's works reflect what Stephanie Nettell of *Books for Keeps* has called "his own quirkily surreal vision of life." Characteristically, the author blends reality and fantasy in stories featuring human, animal, and imaginary protagonists that show how quickly ordinary life can become extraordinary. Although his works are filled with humor and topics with child appeal, McKee addresses serious issues, such as the futility of war; the importance of communication, equality, tolerance, and emotional warmth; the development of self-knowledge and self-reliance; and respect for individuality. He is often praised for creating moral tales that demonstrate his insight into both childhood and the human condition. The tone of McKee's books ranges from gentle and lighthearted to darkly humorous and absurdist. The author also ends several of his works with sudden ironic twists that playfully skew the concept of the happy ending. As a prose stylist, McKee writes in language considered simple yet subtle. As an artist, he is considered a virtuoso whose style—influenced by such artists as Saul Steinberg and Andre Francois—is both recognizable and accessible. McKee's illustrations, which are done as colorful paintings and line art, range from delicate drawings to detailed double-page spreads. The artist, who is often lauded for the harmonious integration of his texts and pictures, is commended for his graphic, contemporary style, his varied use of perspective, and the originality and beauty of his work. Although some critics have found McKee's books too idiosyncratic and sophisticated for children, most observers acknowledge him as a gifted writer, artist, and humorist whose works are both entertaining and substantive. Gillian Klein of *Twentieth-Century Children's Writers* called McKee's work "direct and appealing to children. He is on their side." A reviewer in the *Junior Bookshelf* claimed, "No one does a funny picture-story better than David McKee," while a critic in another issue of the same periodical concluded that "few authors today give such direct and unalloyed pleasure."

Born in Devon, England, McKee received a degree from the Plymouth College of Art before entering the British Army; he served as an instructor in the Royal Army Educational Corps and earned the rank of sergeant. In 1959, McKee received a second degree from the Hornsey College of Art and became a freelance painter and illustrator. He began his career by doing cartoons for newspapers and for the satirical magazine *Punch.* In 1964, he published the first of his books for children, *Bronto's Wings,* the story of a dinosaur who yearns to fly so that he can join the migrating birds going south for

Elmer's friends are all different,   but they all love Elmer.

A patchwork elephant presents the concept of friendship in this installment in the popular "Elmer" series. (From Elmer's Friends, *written and illustrated by McKee.)*

the winter. Writing in *Growing Point,* Margery Fisher noted that the "eccentric illustrations ... are most impressive ... and there are plenty of the tiny details children like to search for in picture books." In 1967, McKee published the first of his books about Mr. Benn, which are collected under the series title "The Extraordinary Adventures of Mr. Benn." This introductory work, *Mr. Benn, Red Knight,* is often considered one of the most outstanding titles in the series. The story describes how Mr. Benn is transported back in time when he tries on a suit of armor at a costumier's shop. After rescuing a dragon and riding him triumphantly, he goes home to dream of more adventures. A reviewer in the *Junior Bookshelf* called *Mr. Benn, Red Knight* "a most exciting and unusual book," while Gertrude B. Herman of *School Library Journal* claimed that McKee's "marvelously inventive illustrations" place him "firmly among modern English artists such as Burningham, Ambrus, Stobbs, Rose, and Wildsmith." In his next book about the character, *123456789 Benn,* McKee describes how Mr. Benn finds himself in prison after trying on a convict's uniform. Noting the gloom of the prison and the sad state of its inmates, Mr. Benn—with the help of head convict Smasher Lagru—transforms the prison into a happier place with the prison's paint and the cooking skills of its inmates. Writing in the *New York Times Book Review,* Selma G. Lanes noted, "The experience, wholly engrossing and humanizing, makes for a refreshingly novel tale." A reviewer in *Publishers Weekly* stated, "The story is such inspired silliness that it could brighten the viewpoint of the most pragmatic computerizer—it could even blow his mind." In *Big Game Benn,* Mr. Benn is transported to the African jungle when he tries on a hunter's clothes. Posing as a guide, he thwarts a group of hunters by appealing to their vanity, having them exchange their guns for cameras. Writing in *Growing Point,* Margery Fisher called *Big Game Benn*

"a comic statement about conservation" before concluding that McKee lightens his message with his "subtly teasing colour-range and odd perspectives and the offhand brilliance with which he suggests a jungle atmosphere."

In 1968, McKee published *Elmer: The Story of a Patchwork Elephant,* the first of his series of works about the lovable pachyderm. In this story, Elmer decides that he wants to be like the other elephants in his herd. When he dyes his multicolored patchwork grey, the other elephants don't recognize him; he also notices that they are not as cheerful without his colorful skin and jokes. After a rain storm washes off the dye, Elmer decides that he is happy in—and with—his own skin, and the other elephants declare a holiday. A reviewer in *Publishers Weekly* noted, "McKee's gentle humor and love of irony are in full force in this celebration of individuality and laughter," while J. A. Cunliffe of *Children's Book News,* claiming that McKee's colors "have the jostling brilliance of a fairground," concluded that "children from about three to six will delight in [*Elmer*]." In *Elmer Again,* Elmer paints all of the other elephants to look just like him before realizing the importance of individuality. Writing in the *School Librarian,* Carol Hill stated, "Just to open this book is to be confronted with a kaleidoscope of shape and colour.... [*Elmer Again*] is so delightful that it will be read again and again." In 1994, McKee published four board books featuring Elmer—*Elmer's Colours, Elmer's Day, Elmer's Friends,* and *Elmer's Weather*—that he directed to the very youngest children. These works, which introduce language and other concepts, are noted for their humor and for the brightness of their pictures. In her review of the titles in *School Library Journal,* Linda Wicher noted that *Elmer's Friends,* "the most sophisticated of the four, leaves readers with the message that we can be different and still get along." In 1997, McKee created *Elmer's Pop-Up Book,* published in the United States as *I Can Too!* In this book, Elmer meets a variety of jungle animals who insist that they possess specific talents that he lacks, such as flying, flapping, stretching, and swinging. By good-naturedly reinterpreting the definitions of these skills, Elmer proves the other animals wrong. In her review of what she called "this cleverly crafted pop-up book" in *School Library Journal,* Lucy Rafael stated that its "message is clear: anything is possible when one thinks positively."

In 1970, McKee published *The Magician Who Lost His Magic,* the first of his series of books about Melric, a magician who serves an impetuous, childish king and who learns lessons as he attempts to retain his job. In this initial offering, Melric loses his powers, until he learns that magic must be used for sensible purposes. In her review in the *School Librarian,* Gabrielle Maunder stated, "David McKee has two great gifts which will be familiar to those who have seen his former books . . . ; these are his ability to tell a ridiculous story with an absolutely straight face, and the other his talent to make each spread interesting by the way in which he divides it into sections." Mary B. Mason of *School Library Journal* added that *The Magician Who Lost His Magic* is an "effectively told story" with illustrations that are "characterized by expressive, comic detail." In *The Magician and the Sorcerer,* Melric is confronted by Sondrak, an evil and ambitious sorcerer; recognizing the power of laughter, Melric defeats Sondrak by making people laugh at him. A reviewer in *Times Literary Supplement* noted that "the illustrations offer all kinds of comic detail to delight the mind and eye," while Edward Hudson of *Children's Book Review,* calling McKee "a man full of ideas and with a sense of humour which enables him to convert them into words and pictures which will appeal to young children," predicted that the Melric series could become "as popular as *Pugwash* or *Noggin the Nog.*" *The Magician and the Balloon,* published in the United States as *Melric and the Balloons,* outlines how Melric saves his country from his king's meddling. Writing in the *Junior Bookshelf,* Marcus Crouch commented, "If you want proof that the ideal illustrator of a picture book is the author, then David McKee provides it." Moira Small of *Books for Keeps* concluded, "Children who know Melric will always want to know what he's up to . . . . Introduce Melric to a child today and you'll both be delighted."

The King Rollo series features a chubby, ingenuous king who, despite his beard, is truly childlike. Because of his position, King Rollo does adult things that children often wish they could. He approaches all of his activities with innocence and curiosity. According to Annette Curtis Klause of *School Library Journal,* the king "rolls, bounces, waves, and prances through his small world, always with a sense of true delight and discovery." Other members of Rollo's kingdom include Queen Gwen, Rollo's competent partner; Cook, who is a bit fearsome but always ready to give the king some sage advice; the Magician, who has great respect for the correct use of magic and is as afraid of Cook as King

King Rollo was in the garden.

"I'm going to climb that tree," he said.

"Don't climb the tree, you'll get your hands dirty," said the magician.

"I'm still going to climb that tree," said King Rollo.

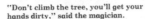

Four previously published books about King Rollo and his friends have been collected in a single, delightful volume. *(From* The Adventures of King Rollo, *written and illustrated by McKee.)*

Rollo; and Hamlet the cat, who is both observant and always ready for adventure. McKee published his first three books about Rollo—*King Rollo and the Birthday, King Rollo and the Bread,* and *King Rollo and the New Shoes*—in 1979. In these works, which are produced in a small format designed to fit the hands of preschoolers and early readers, Rollo attempts to tie his shoes, makes a birthday cake for his queen, and tells the Magician to change a farmer's loaf of bread into a variety of dishes. A critic in *Kirkus Reviews* noted that the stories contain "some slight, raffish charm and varying amounts of substance—varying, that is, from almost none to as much as one might expect (except perhaps from Sendak), given the format." Writing in *School Library Journal,* Bessie Condon Egan concluded, "A good series for lower elementary-age beginning readers and good bedtime fare to share with pre-schoolers, King Rollo is bound to be a hit with American audiences."

Produced in a larger format than the earlier books, *King Rollo's Playroom and Other Stories* contains four new stories about the little king. In the title story, Cook advises the king to clean up his many toys; when Rollo steps on some of his toys and breaks them, he realizes he should have listened to Cook. "The simple storyline and the clear, attractive pictures make these an excellent first series for very young children finding out about their world," concluded a reviewer in *Books for Keeps.* Writing in the *Times Educational Supplement,* Naomi Lewis commented: "Zany as they may seem, the King

Rollo books have more in them than you would think." Noting that *King Rollo's Playroom* is "as before, at once witty and childlike," the reviewer concluded by advising, "Don't wait to enter the glorious Rollo world if you're four or less." Writing in *British Book News Children's Books* about the series, Audrey Laski noted that McKee's "most popular books are probably the King Rollo picture-strips .... King Rollo is Everychild, doing things children like to do, supported by Queen and cat, enjoying life even when things go wrong; these are cheerful and reassuring books." As with the character of Mr. Benn, King Rollo has achieved additional popularity through the animated films and television shows created by McKee's studio, King Rollo Films.

McKee has received much attention for a trio of individual titles that he wrote in the late 1970s and early 1980s—*Tusk Tusk; Not Now, Bernard;* and *I Hate My Teddy Bear.* In *Tusk Tusk,* the author describes a time when the elephants of the world were either black or white. Hating each other for their color, the elephants fought to death, except for a few pacifists from both groups who fled to the jungle; later, their peaceful descendants emerge as grey. The book ends on an ironic note: the grey elephants discover that they once again fall into two groups—those with little ears and those with big ears. Writing in the *Times Educational Supplement,* Carolyn O'Grady commented, "The illustrations are especially ingenious: trunks become guns, revolvers,

In David McKee's self-illustrated picture book, the noises that Isabel's tummy makes are a source of amusement to her classmates but an embarrassing nuisance to her, until the day they visit a zoo and the sounds of her stomach become surprisingly helpful.

and hands to point an accusing finger. The colours are especially lovely .... " Elaine Moss of the *Times Literary Supplement* added, "Like Michael Foreman, David McKee can use humour and his considerable talents as an artist to make young people think about current issues." Writing in *School Library Journal,* Ruth M. McConnell noted, "The moral is muddled as a final cameo shows elephants with medium ears clasping trunks ..., while the ironic caption of '*Viva la difference*' under the opening cameo of a pachyderm-punch-out will also be lost on small fry." In an interview with Audrey Laski in *British Book News Children's Books,* McKee denied that his postscript is bleak: he views it as a message "to the adult that the child will be" and as a remembrance that "we have to live with all the differences." He also noted that some teachers have banned *Tusk Tusk* from their classrooms as racist. Laski commented that this "is a dotty response to a book whose overriding impulse is passionately anti-war and one that is actually no more about race than about any other divider."

I Hate My Teddy Bear is often considered McKee's signature work as well as his most surrealistic. In this book, two small children, Brenda and John, are sent outside while their mothers have tea. After leaving their "hated" bears—toys so familiar that they have become boring—under a tree, they play a game of one-upsmanship, boasting that their teddies can do things like fly, sing, and count backwards. The bears carry on a conversation of their own, finally agreeing that they are equally talented. At the end of the story, the children carefully retrieve their bears, demonstrating, in the words of Margery Fisher of *Growing Point,* "all the time the happiest of alliances." McKee's watercolor illustrations tell a separate story, depicting a background where adults move heavy loads of huge hands and feet and perform activities like palm-reading, painting, conjuring, and spying. The final illustration shows all the giant pieces being mounted as statues for a sculpture exhibition. Writing in the *Times Educational Supplement,* Naomi Lewis called *I Hate My Teddy Bear* "a most remarkable book" and "a brilliant foray into the surreal—or far more likely, a demonstration of the real: that the centre of any happening is never where we think." Mary Butler Nickerson of *School Library Journal* commented, "Although activity is portrayed ..., it is surreal, unexplained, and gratuitous and overwhelmed by the preponderance of isolated sad-faced children who sit and stare. The sense of dislocation and desolation is strong. This is a book for children?" Gillian Klein of *Twentieth-Century Children's Writers* claimed, "The divergence of text and picture in *I Hate My Teddy Bear* is practically subversive." In her review in *Picture Books for Young People 9-13,* Elaine Moss quotes author Russell Hoban, who said of the book that it "will help any child to get a grip on the ungraspable." Moss added, "Make of this surrealist picture book what you wish, but don't miss it so long as you don't mind not being sure what it's all about." Speaking about *I Hate My Teddy Bear* to Audrey Laski of *British Book News Children's Books,* McKee commented, "Primarily, it's a love-story."

In *Not Now, Bernard,* McKee features a child whose self-absorbed parents answer his every statement with the refrain of the title. Throughout the book, his parents never look at Bernard, not even when he tells them that there is a monster in their garden ready to eat him. Not even after the monster devours Bernard and takes his place in the family do his parents change their response. At the end of the story, Bernard's mother puts the monster to bed in Bernard's room, despite the creature's claim that he is a monster. Writing in the *Times Educational Supplement,* Carolyn O'Grady predicted, "A lot of adults, I'm sure, will hate David McKee's *Not Now, Bernard.* Kids love it.... [E]ven very young children see the joke and apparently couldn't care a jot about poor Bernard, transferring their affections immediately to the lovable gruesome monster." Aidan Warlow of the *School Librarian* said of the book, "As a satirical comment on neglectful parents, it works. As a picture book for infants, it doesn't." A reviewer in *Publishers Weekly* concluded that *Not Now, Bernard* is "a bizarre, negative picture book that should be for grownups. 'Taint funny, McKee." Noting McKee's comment that children relate first to Bernard and then to the monster, Audrey Laski of *British Book News Children's Books* concluded, "Presumably, they understand instinctively ... that Bernard has cheerfully become, rather than been engulfed by, this rather engagingly ugly violet-coloured beast."

McKee defends the right of a picture book for children to be, as he told Audrey Laski, "another art medium." He says of his work, "You start with a clean piece of paper, you make a mark on it and immediately it's wrong—you spend the rest of the time trying to put it right." Of the inspiration for his books, McKee said, "It's not as if you write them at all, it's as if you listen to them being told." He concluded, "Most of us have got more than we realize.... I really enjoy life and I *know* I enjoy it." McKee appears to feel the same about his films for children, several of which are based on characters from his books. He told Frances Farrer of the *Times Educational Supplement,* "Everybody wants different things from children's films. They want them to have morals, or to teach things, or to be full of action—by which they mean violence. Luckily what we want is often what kids want. They want magicians and dragons." When Farrer noted that success without compromise is a major achievement, McKee and animator Leo Beltoft responded, "Basically we just do it because we enjoy it. There wouldn't be any point otherwise."

Works Cited

Babsky, Irene, review of *The School Bus Comes at Eight O'Clock, School Librarian,* May, 1994, p. 56.

Crouch, Marcus, review of *The Magician and the Balloon, Junior Bookshelf,* April, 1979, p. 98.

Cunliffe, J. A., review of *Elmer: The Story of a Patchwork Elephant, Children's Book News,* November-December, 1968, pp. 311, 313.

Egan, Bessie Condon, review of *King Rollo and the Birthday* and others, *School Library Journal,* August, 1980, p. 54.

Review of *Elmer: The Story of a Patchwork Elephant, Publishers Weekly,* September 8, 1989, p. 68.

Review of *Elmer Again, School Librarian,* August, 1991, p. 102.

"Enticing Ingredients," *Times Literary Supplement,* September 20, 1974, p. 1011.

Farrer, Frances, "Scrambling to the Top of the Tree," *Times Educational Supplement,* December 18, 1981, p. 22.

Fisher, Margery, review of *Bronto's Wings, Growing Point,* July, 1964, p. 345.

Fisher, Margery, review of *Big Game Benn, Growing Point,* November, 1979, pp. 3607-08.

Fisher, Margery, review of *I Hate My Teddy Bear, Growing Point,* January, 1983, p. 4016.

Herman, Gertrude B., review of *Mr. Benn, Red Knight, School Library Journal,* March, 1969, p. 144.

Hudson, Edward, review of *The Magician and the Sorcerer, Children's Book Review,* winter, 1974-75, p. 145.

Hudson, William Henry, review of *Two Monsters, Listener,* November 7, 1985, p. 32.

Review of *King Rollo and the Birthday* and others, *Kirkus Reviews,* June 15, 1980, p. 777.

Review of *King Rollo's Spring, King Rollo's Summer, King Rollo's Autumn,* and *King Rollo's Winter, Books for Keeps,* September, 1988, p. 6.

Klause, Annette Curtis, review of *King Rollo's Autumn* and *King Rollo's Summer, School Library Journal,* March, 1988, pp. 170-71.

Klein, Gillian, essay on McKee in *Twentieth-Century Children's Writers,* fourth edition, edited by Laura Standley Berger, St. James Press, 1995, pp. 650-52.

Lanes, Selma B., review of *123456789 Benn, New York Times Book Review,* November 8, 1970, p. 51.

Laski, Audrey, "Enjoying Life: An Interview with David McKee," *British Book News Children's Books,* March, 1986, pp. 2-5.

Lewis, Naomi, "Feather, Fur, and Fantasy," *Times Educational Supplement,* June 3, 1983, p. 44.

Lewis, Naomi, "Once Upon a Line," *Times Educational Supplement,* November 19, 1982, p. 32.

Mason, Mary B., review of *The Magician Who Lost His Magic, School Library Journal,* December 15, 1970, pp. 36-37.

Maunder, Gabrielle, review of *The Magician Who Lost His Magic, School Librarian,* December, 1970, p. 502.

McConnell, Ruth M., review of *Tusk Tusk, School Library Journal,* January, 1980, p. 59.

Moss, Elaine, "Going to the Pictures," *Times Literary Supplement,* September 29, 1978, p. 1087.

Moss, Elaine, review of *I Hate My Teddy Bear, Picture Books for Young People 9-13,* edited by Nancy Chambers, Thimble Press, 1985, p. 13.

Review of *The Magician and the Sorcerer, Times Literary Supplement,* September 20, 1975, p.1011.

Review of *Mr. Benn, Red Knight, Junior Bookshelf,* April, 1968, p. 95.

Nettell, Stephanie, review of *Charlotte's Piggy Bank, Books for Keeps,* May, 1996, p. 25.

Nickerson, Mary Butler, review of *I Hate My Teddy Bear, School Library Journal,* August, 1984, p. 62.

Review of *Not Now, Bernard, Publishers Weekly,* April 3, 1981, p. 74.

O'Grady, Carolyn, "Horrors," *Times Educational Supplement,* June 20, 1980, p. 44.

O'Grady, Carolyn, "Paradise Lost and Found," *Times Educational Supplement,* June 23, 1978, p. 21.

Review of *123456789 Benn, Junior Bookshelf,* October, 1970, p. 276.

Review of *123456789 Benn, Publishers Weekly,* August 17, 1970, p. 50.

Rafael, Lucy, review of *I Can Too!, School Library Journal,* January, 1998, p. 89.

Review of *The Sad Story of Veronica Who Played the Violin, Junior Bookshelf,* October, 1987, pp. 214-15.

Small, Moira, review of *Melric and the Balloon, Books for Keeps,* September, 1988, p. 9.

Warlow, Aidan, review of *Not Now, Bernard, School Librarian,* September, 1980, p. 252.

Wicher, Linda, review of *Elmer's Colors* and others, *School Library Journal,* January, 1995, p. 90.

For More Information See

BOOKS

Children's Literature Review, Volume 38, Gale, 1996, pp. 153-82.

PERIODICALS

Books for Keeps, November, 1997, p. 20.
International Review of Children's Literature and Librarianship, volume 7, no. 1, pp. 11-18.
Junior Bookshelf, August, 1996, p. 142.
Kirkus Reviews, April 15, 1999, p. 633.
Magpies, May, 1999, pp. 26-27.
Publishers Weekly, June 16, 1997, p. 58.
School Librarian, August, 1996, p. 107; August, 1997, p. 131; spring, 1999, p. 19.*

—*Sketch by Gerard J. Senick*

*   *   *

MIKAELSEN, Ben(jamin John) 1952-

Personal

Born November 24, 1952, in La Paz, Bolivia; son of John (a radio engineer) and Luverne (Wold) Mikaelsen; married Melanie Troftgruben (a critical care nurse), June, 1980. *Education:* Attended Concordia College, Moorhead, MN, 1971-72, and Bemidji State University, Bemidji, MN, 1975-79. *Hobbies and other interests:* Horseback riding, parachute jumping, motorcycle travel, sled dog racing, flying airplanes, scuba diving, camping, music, and study and raising of bears.

Addresses

Home and office—233 Quinn Creek Rd., Bozeman, MT 59715. *Agent*—Sandra Choron, 4 Myrtle St., Haworth, NJ 07641. *Electronic mail*— ben@benmikaelsen.com.

Ben Mikaelsen

Career

Owner of awards and office supplies business, Bozeman, MT, 1980-84; owner of woodworking business, Bozeman, MT, 1984-85; writer, 1985-1992. *Military service:* U.S. Army, 1973-75, Arlington, VA; corporal; received Joint Service Commendation Medal. *Member:* Society of Children's Book Writers and Illustrators, Hellgate Writers, Montana Authors' Coalition.

Awards, Honors

Spur Award, Western Writers of America, 1992, Children's Book Award, International Reading Association, 1992, Golden Sower Award, Nebraska Library Association, 1995, California Young Reader Medal, California Reading Association, 1995, Indian Paintbrush Award, Wyoming Library Association, 1995, Flicker Tale Book Award, North Dakota Library Association, 1998, all for *Rescue Josh McGuire;* California Young Reader Medal, California Reading Association, 1997, for *Sparrow Hawk Red;* Maryland Children's Choice Book Award, Maryland International Reading Association Council, 1998, for *Stranded;* Notable Books for Children, American Library Association, 1999, and Golden Spur Award for Best Western Juvenile Fiction, Western Writers of America, 1999, both for *Petey.*

Writings

Rescue Josh McGuire, Hyperion, 1991.
Sparrow Hawk Red, Hyperion, 1993.
Stranded, Hyperion, 1995.
Countdown, Hyperion, 1996.
Petey, Hyperion, 1998.

Rescue Josh McGuire has been translated into Danish and French.

Work in Progress

In September of 1998, Mikaelsen completed a research trip to Alaska for his next book, tentatively called *Touching Spirit Bear.* Mikaelsen returned from a four-month trip to do general research and photo work in February of 1999. On that trip, he and his wife drove 15,000 miles, from Bozeman, Montana, to the southern tip of South America, the Terra Del Fuego.

Sidelights

Ben Mikaelsen's award-winning first novel, *Rescue Josh McGuire,* was widely praised for its fast-paced adventure, its detailed depictions of the Montana wilderness, and its engaging portrait of a wild bear cub. Mikaelsen, who says he draws the "soul" of each of his novels from real experience, is no stranger to bears, the wilderness, or adventure. The author has had the unique experience of raising a six-hundred-pound black bear named Buffy at his home in the mountains of Bozeman, Montana. Additionally, Mikaelsen told *SATA* that over the years he has been involved in many adventures, including "a sixteen-hundred-mile cross-country horseback trip from Minnesota to Oregon, numerous parachute jumps, racing sled dogs, playing horse polo, building a log house, private and commercial pilot training, extensive scuba diving, and worldwide travel." Although his personal adventures have entailed courage and endurance, and his fiction is engaging for its action and suspense, Mikaelsen's adventure stories are not of the rugged "man versus nature" variety. Rather, they make an appeal for peaceful coexistence between the natural and social worlds. In *Rescue Josh McGuire,* to be kind and gentle in a sometimes inhumanely bureaucratic society is the greatest act of courage.

Mikaelsen recalls his childhood from the viewpoint of a social outsider. In his early youth he lived in Bolivia, where "being raised as a minority helped me understand the self-doubt and desperate lack of self-worth many children face while growing up." Because his parents worked too far from the schools for their six children to commute, Mikaelsen and a younger brother were placed in a boarding school apart from their older siblings, permanently weakening the family bonds, according to the author. Mikaelsen told *SATA* that his boarding school was a rigid place, where "English matrons held a solid seat of law, all the way down to strappings if you didn't do things right." When Mikaelsen returned to the United States at the age of twelve, he found that schoolmates could be equally harsh and demanding. "In Bolivia," he said, "we wore uniforms—saddle shoes with high bobby socks and leather knickers with a kind of blouse-type shirt. So the first day of school in the United States, I dressed up in my best go-to-school clothes. I learned early how cruel kids can be."

Although he felt like an outsider throughout high school, Mikaelsen now recognizes that the ways he coped with his childhood trials resulted in some positive outcomes. "Being ostracized," he said, "contributed to writing in the sense that a piece of paper became my friend. I was one of those kids that laid awake at night dreaming *before* I went to sleep. By the next morning, I would always forget the things I had been dreaming about, so I realized that if I was to capture them, I would have to put them on paper. I never thought of myself as a writer, but I enjoyed writing poetry. Back then if you were a male writing poetry you were a sissy, so I never showed anybody. That was just my own secret. A lot of my writings for many, many years came that way."

Despite his feelings of self-doubt within the social world, Mikaelsen was an adventurer, even as a child. "I was always the kid that took the dare, always the one that would climb up the telephone pole or the flag pole. I remember once when my group of friends was cliff-diving, rather than take the chance of failing in front of other kids, I swam across the lake and, all by myself, I got up the courage and dived off this cliff. Somebody heard that Ben dove off that twenty-foot rock, and that just led from one thing to another. Pretty soon it was twenty-five feet, then thirty feet, then thirty-five feet, and then it was heights no other kid would even jump off of. All of a sudden it struck me that this was the very, very first time in my life when somebody said, 'gosh, that's neat.' My whole body had a hunger for that attention, so I started doing other things . . . ."

By the time he was in college, Mikaelsen was skydiving. "I was able to parachute into the homecoming game and bring in the game football and things like that. Kids would say, 'wow, that's pretty neat,' and I felt like a hero, with more positive attention than I'd ever received in my life." In college Mikaelsen also received encouragement about his writing for the first time. "My preferred language was Spanish," Mikaelsen said. "At five years old I could not speak English very well. I always had trouble with grammar, with spelling, with word mechanics. I was always told that that was what writing was, and because I was so poor at these things, I thought I could not be a writer." Mikaelsen recalled that in his first year of college his English professor called him to the front of the room to comment on a paper he had written, telling him immediately that his grammar skills were those of a seventh or eighth grader. With much fear, Mikaelsen asked his professor if he should drop the class. Mikaelsen remembers the professor's words: "'Oh no, no, no. I just finished reading two hundred and fifty essays, and out of them only one made me laugh and cry, and that was yours. You're a writer.'" Mikaelsen said: "That was the first time that somebody let me know that this was something special. Then I was anxious to sit down with the tutor and work on grammar and word mechanics, although I'm still terrible with that."

Being a writer, Mikaelsen soon discovered, required just as much courage as being an adventurer. "There is so much more to writing than I ever dreamed," he said. "I know when I first sat over the cliff at twenty feet above the water with nobody around, I looked down, and this monster was facing me, saying 'you can't do it.' I said 'I can' and I jumped into the monster's face. It's the same monster that looked at me when I wanted to make my first parachute jump, and the same one I saw later when we made a cross-country horseback trip from Minnesota to Oregon in 1976. Now, when I'm writing at two o'clock in the morning, halfway through a book, I'm doubting my premise for the book, I'm doubting my story line, I'm doubting myself. It's that same identical monster that I have to jump in the face of. I began, finally, to realize that being a successful writer isn't just putting the good words down, it's facing that monster."

Mikaelsen, whose childhood home in Bolivia had been high upon a fourteen-thousand-foot plateau in the Andes mountain range between Bolivia and Peru, grew up with a deeply ingrained love of mountains. Consequently, in 1980, he and his wife moved to the mountains of Bozeman, Montana. In 1984, the couple adopted Buffy, a declawed black bear cub, from a wild game farm. The adoption entailed a huge commitment. Mikaelsen told *SATA:* "We have probably twenty-thousand dollars invested in Buffy's facility with its pond, playground and eating area, denning area, and waste area. I spend about three to four hours a day with him when he's out of hibernation, and a half hour or forty-five minutes a day when he's in hibernation, and that's still not enough time. Buffy gets better care than most children—that's what an animal needs, and that's the only reason Buffy and I have the relationship we do, because of that tremendous amount of time."

Mikaelsen learned quickly that keeping a wild animal in captivity is not like raising a household pet. Buffy had been used in laboratory research before Mikaelsen adopted him. "I don't know what had been done with him in research," Mikaelsen said, "but it hadn't been good. He was very, very distrusting and insecure. One minute he would cuddle with me and hug my side as if I was the only thing he had in life, and the next minute a car horn or something would scare him and he would turn around and bite me as hard as he could. The first couple of months I had started raising him like you would a dog, and I wasn't having any luck. He was getting more independent and more angry. So then I started raising him like a child. I would give him his food in a bottle instead of a dish, and cuddle him in my arms as he drank it. I would go out and put him to bed every night and let him fall asleep in my lap. If I heard him crying then I would go out and sleep with him the rest of the night. When I started doing that I immediately had luck.

"I learned a real important lesson with Buffy, and that's that you never tame a wild animal. Buffy is not a tame animal. If something threatens him, he is a six-hundred-and-some pound very, very dangerous animal. My wife and I are the only two people that can come into his facility. If a stranger were to come into his facility without me along, he would most likely attack him. But when Buffy comes into the house (and he comes into the house a lot), he's visiting. A stranger could come in the house, and Buffy would just be as friendly as all get out. But even after a half hour of playing with him in the house, if the stranger went into Buffy's facility, he'd lay his ears back. You're dealing with really deep instincts.

"I used to think I owned Buff, that I was his master, and he should do what I said. Having that attitude almost got me killed. He would get violent when I tried to rule him. Then I finally said, 'Hold it, I'm not his master, neither is he mine, but we're friends, we're going to coexist.' According to Mikaelsen, learning to understand and respond to Buffy's needs rather than to try to control him was a big lesson in life. A former bear hunter himself, Mikaelsen realized while raising Buffy that he had previously been enjoying wildlife from a very limited perspective. "Any appreciation I had of a wild animal ceased at the moment I killed it. Now I feel like I've come to appreciate and understand and be amazed by the complexity of Buffy's existence." Among Mikaelsen's dedications in *Rescue Josh McGuire*, is one to "'Buffy,' a 500-pound black bear who taught me to have respect and be gentle."

When it became known that Mikaelsen was successfully raising Buffy, the Fish and Game Department in Bozeman brought him other orphaned black bear cubs. Mikaelsen took care of some of these orphans while the department decided what to do with them. Since there were few viable alternatives, the orphaned cubs sometimes had to be destroyed. Although Montana has laws against shooting a mother bear with a cub, the laws are unenforceable. Mikaelsen blames spring bear hunting for the hundreds of cubs orphaned in Montana every season, and he has become an activist for more sportsmanlike hunting laws in his state. The strength of his feelings about this issue triggered his first published novel. "There was one pair of cubs," he told *SATA,* "I spent probably a week trying to save their lives, staying up all night to bottle feed them. They ended up being destroyed because they couldn't find a good home. I think that was the point when I said, 'Hold it, let's make it the premise of a book.'"

Rescue Josh McGuire begins with the senseless killing of a mother bear by thirteen-year-old Josh's alcoholic father, Sam. Although Sam will not admit that the bear he shot was a mother, Josh, who witnesses the killing, goes back to the scene during the night and finds the orphaned cub. Bringing the cub, whom he names Pokey, back home with him, Josh sets up a room for him in the barn and, despite Pokey's unpredictable biting, the two develop a very close and affectionate relationship. Relations in Josh's home, on the other hand, are severely strained. The previous year, Josh's brother, Tye, was killed in a car accident. Sam, devastated by the loss, has taken to heavy drinking and, while drunk, is abusive to his wife and his surviving son. Pokey, who is a reminder to Sam of his unacknowledged error in killing the mother bear, is doomed to almost certain death when Sam notifies the game warden of his existence. Sam tells Josh that there is no alternative but for Pokey to be delivered into the hands of medical researchers.

After thinking it over, Josh decides he cannot accept the fate that adults have devised for Pokey. Borrowing his brother's motocross cycle, he rides off in the night—with Pokey in a box on the cycle rack and his dog, Mud Flap, on the cycle's gas tank—to the mountains north of Yellowstone Park, seventy miles from his home. Josh leaves behind a note: "I can't let Pokey die so I'm running away. I'll come home when I can keep Pokey and when nobody can hunt bears anymore." After they arrive on the mountain trail, a ferocious summer blizzard breaks out, severely testing the boy's survival skills. In the days that follow, the three experience extremes of cold, deprivation, loneliness, and danger, as well as some triumphs and happy times together.

Much of the novel is divided between Josh's adventures in the mountains and the initially unsuccessful efforts of the search and rescue team to find him. When Mud Flap is badly wounded in a bear attack, Josh must overcome his distrust of the adult world in order to contact his friend Otis for help. Otis is a gruff ex-wildlife biologist who had become so frustrated with the bureaucracies intended to protect wildlife that he became a recluse, spending most of his time tending to wounded wild animals. Otis agrees to help Mud Flap, but when he drives out to pick her up, he is unknowingly followed by the police, leading to Josh's eventual rescue.

After getting into a serious motorcycle accident in the night, Josh stands in need of rescue, but, thinking that he has been deceived by his friend, he continues to try to elude the search and rescue party. Unbeknownst to Josh, his disappearance has raised the interest of the media, bringing national coverage to his call for more stringent wildlife laws. By the end of the story, Josh, a fairly naive boy who only wants to do what is right, has effectively countered the injustices of hypocritical bureaucracies, a complacent social world, and even his father's alcoholism.

Josh's point of view is limited, as any child's would be, and at the same time, clear and optimistic. Mikaelsen told *SATA* that he had written half of *Rescue Josh McGuire* before he could find a way to save Pokey's life. "It was a problem I was not able to solve as an adult.... I needed a child's point of view. From Josh's point of view, Pokey is just this precious little life that's going to end if I don't do something—it's just that simple. An adult character would have had to let the cub go and let it get killed." Josh's youthful naivete actually tempers the character Otis's adult cynicism. Otis had fought city hall for many years and had finally given up. Seeing the integrity with which young Josh takes on powerful forces, however, spurs Otis back into action.

Josh, Pokey, Mud Flap, and Otis all encounter some extremely harsh and unfair experiences. Although the outcome of the novel is highly positive, Mikaelsen does not paint a particularly rosy picture of the American way. "I am one of those people who believes that if you don't reveal the world's shortcomings, you slam the door on learning. If we try to teach kids that all bureaucracy is right and not questionable, then we eliminate any chance of improving upon the deficiencies that bureaucracies have. Likewise with parents. If a child can never look at a parent and say, 'Maybe my parent is wrong, maybe what they're doing isn't right,' then the parents' ways can never be improved upon."

Mikaelsen did a great deal of research for *Rescue Josh McGuire.* "When I write about issues, I get an overwhelming sense of responsibility. If I write about an issue wrongly, I do as much harm as I do good. So when I decided that I was going to take on spring bear hunting and alcoholism—gosh! I spent time with people who were in rehab; I went up to the part of the country where much of the novel takes place and, with my wife, spent the whole week camping there, laying it all out for authenticity. I also went down to the Bozeman Search and Rescue Department. I knew some of the members, and they actually sat down with me and drew a format and helped me choreograph Josh's rescue."

For Mikaelsen, writing takes place in life and experience as well as in an author's mind. Living his books by actively entering into the adventures he writes about is, according to the author, "a fun way to keep from getting to be a mole. I think writers tend to get reclusive. I don't find the actual writing of a book healthy. I have to spend too many hours by myself. Whenever I finish a rough draft, I just clear out and head down to some waterfall somewhere and sit, trying to get away from the computer terminal, away from being a human mole."

Mikaelsen continued: "My next book, *Sparrow Hawk Red,* is an adventure story about a young boy who lives among the homeless in Mexico. Now, how in the world was I going to know what it's like to be homeless in Mexico living up here in Montana? So I actually went down and spent several weeks in a variety of places all the way from Tucson to Tijuana to Ensenada to Nogales to Mexicali. There was one point where I was standing around looking at the homeless children, thinking, 'this is really good for me to stand around and look at the homeless and feel guilty.' And then I thought, 'Baloney, I have no more idea of what it's like to be hungry and cold than the man on the moon.' One afternoon I was getting a taco; I pulled my billfold out and thought, 'those homeless children don't have a billfold.' So I put it away, and the next day I came back with no billfold, just a T-shirt and jeans. For the next three days I just lived among the homeless, and I got very hungry. At first, I wasn't willing to eat out of a garbage can the way I saw a lot of them do, but I did eat some pretty wretched food. Finally, I did resort to eating from a garbage can, and I did get sick. I also slept on gravel in the alleys at night with a piece of cardboard over me. I was fortunate that three days later I could just walk back across the border to a motel and my clean clothes and a hot shower. I had a feeling at that point what it was like to be homeless—at least I've seen that look in their eyes and I can write about it."

The realistic way in which Mikaelsen was able to portray Mexican street life won him unanimous appreciation from reviewers of *Sparrow Hawk Red*. In the novel, Ricky Diaz, a thirteen-year-old flying ace, discovers that his mother's death was not just an accident, but an act of retribution taken by drug smugglers against his father, who used to work for the Drug Enforcement Agency. Avenging her death requires that Ricky take on the drug cartel in a mission that has been turned down by even the most seasoned of Drug Enforcement Agents— his father. Across the border in Mexico, Ricky goes undercover as a *ratero* (a homeless street kid), and luckily receives some tips from a street-smart *ratera* named Soledad. *School Library Journal* contributor Pat Katka offered a favorable assessment of the novel, asserting that "the characterization is strong, the depiction of street life realistic, and the theme timely." A

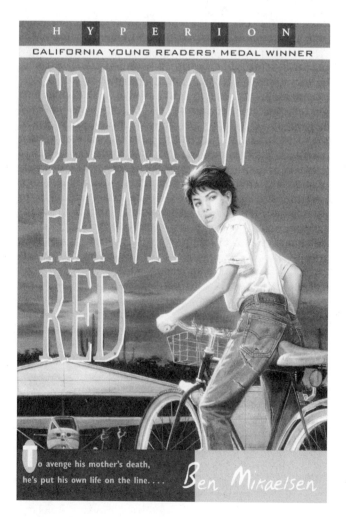

In Mikaelsen's award-winning adventure novel, thirteen-year-old Ricky Diaz attempts to avenge his mother's murder by crossing the border into Mexico to steal an airplane from the drug smugglers responsible for her death. (Cover illustration by Eric Velasquez.)

reviewer for *Quill and Quire* commented: "Soledad changes his [Ricky's] views of street kids, whom he will never again dismiss or despise." *Booklist's* Chris Sherman also noted Ricky's growth as a result of his relationship with Soledad, which taught him "the importance of his heritage and the dignity inherent in all people." Appreciative of "the pace and the chase," Roger Sutton of the *Bulletin of the Center for Children's Books* deemed the book "tremendously exciting." *Sparrow Hawk Red* is, according to Sherman, "a dynamite story, certain to appeal to even hard-core nonreaders."

Commenting further about his hands-on approach to research, Mikaelsen told *SATA*: "I can go to libraries and get a lot of my research, but I've never found the soul of my story in a library—not until I was awake at four o'clock in the morning trying to bottle-feed a cub that was almost starved to death. In that struggle—the little critter struggling for life—I discovered the soul of my novel. Or when I was among the homeless, and I saw that look of hopelessness in some little kid who hadn't had a decent meal in three years and was almost naked except for his dirty underpants. When I actually felt the hunger and cold and looked into his eyes, that's where I found the soul for that story. For my next book, I worked for a month at a dolphin facility. I went out and helped find a dolphin who was caught in a shrimp net, and I also got involved in a whale stranding. That was when I found the soul of my story."

Mikaelsen's experience at the dolphin facility led him to write *Stranded*, a book that draws parallels between a twelve-year-old girl's search for independence and a pair of beached dolphins' quest for freedom. The novel's heroine, Koby, lives with her feuding parents on a sailboat in the Florida Keys. Having lost her right foot in a bicycling accident four years earlier, Koby feels exasperated by her parents' smothering attitude at home, and self-conscious among her peers at school. When swimming in the ocean or motoring her dinghy through the Keys, though, Koby is at her free-feeling best. One day, while enjoying the water, Koby comes to the aid of a birthing dolphin caught in a net. She later encounters the dolphin and its calf in dangerously shallow water and makes a heroic effort to rescue them. Hearing of Koby's special talents, peers and parents alike begin sensing and reinforcing in Koby a new feeling of competence.

Roger Sutton of the *Bulletin of the Center for Children's Books* thought Koby a "seaworthy heroine who makes things happen . . . . Girls don't often feature in such fast-paced fare," Sutton continued, "so this is definitely welcome." *Voice of Youth Advocates* contributor Ann C. Sparanese credited Mikaelsen with creating "another winning young character willing to take on adult-size adventure and triumph over impossible odds." With nothing but praise for the book, she called *Stranded* "a heartwarming story, believable and at the same time grist for fantasies of heroism and wonderful deeds." *Kliatt* contributor Cecilia Swanson recommended the story to "animal lovers and readers who are dealing with their own struggle to be independent."

While issues and settings are important to Mikaelsen, he also sees merit in interacting with his child protagonists. "I try to imagine a child walking through the real world beside me. Then that character comes alive for me. What's wonderful then, is that it's just like having a best friend—you can never predict what your best friend will do next. In *Rescue Josh McGuire,* for instance, the part of the book where Josh had his motorcycle accident was not in my plans. While I was writing, Josh did just what Josh would do in the circumstances: he rode his cycle too fast in the dark. I put my cursor back and erased two paragraphs and I tried to write him continuing up the hill. But again, he went into the ditch, this time getting hurt even worse, and I realized that my character had come alive, and I had to let him do what he wanted to do. And it made a much better end."

For all of his talents in children's literature, Mikaelsen did not set out to become a children's writer. *Rescue Josh McGuire* was written as an adult novel; it was his publisher who suggested it be targeted to young adults. Mikaelsen said that this "taught me a real good lesson, that there is no difference in an adult book and a children's book except that the main character is a child. I realized that I can write what I want, as complexly and to whatever issues I wish. In fact, I can do anything I want, looking through a child's point of view."

Mikaelsen, who has not forgotten the challenges he faced as an insecure teenage boy, seeks to empower the children with whom he has contact. "Now I go into a school system as an author-in-residence, and I realize that every kid gets teased for something. Sometimes it's just that they live on a farm and still have the smell of manure on their shoes, or sometimes their parents cut their hair funny. When I talk to the kids I say, 'Okay, the differences aren't a weakness, the differences are what make you special. That's what has made me an author; that's what has made me able to write a book. So what you do is take your differences and highlight them.'"

Mikaelsen's books also aim at offering children new possibilities. In the novel *Countdown,* the two fourteen-year-old heroes, Vincent and Elliot, are raised by fathers who expect them to follow in their own career paths. Vincent, living in an outlying village of Kenya, is supposed to become a traditional Masai warrior, while Elliot is expected to work on the family ranch in Montana. Despite their fathers' wishes, Vincent longs to learn of the world beyond his village by going to school, and Elliot dreams of becoming an astronaut. Both boys have the chance to widen one another's horizons through their experiences as well as their unlikely relationship via shortwave radio. *Voice of Youth Advocates* contributor Brenda Moses-Allen wrote that "Mikaelsen provides a fascinating scenario of Elliot's nine months' training to become a payload specialist (one-mission astronaut)," citing the author's use of "vivid and exciting detail." *School Library Journal* reviewer Joel Shoemaker also appreciated Mikaelsen's "careful research [which] allows integration of details that lend authenticity to the tale." In another favorable assessment of *Countdown,* Chris Sherman of *Booklist* stated, "Mikaelsen weaves a provocative message through his novel and blends two fast-paced stories into a single, powerful whole."

Mikaelsen told *SATA:* "In all my writing I try to help children discover that they count. I want to take a child on a journey that changes their emotions, attitudes, and perspective. Children are the future. Children's literature offers a sobering but exciting chance to effect that future, environmental or social. For this reason I enjoy writing to issues."

In his novel *Petey* Mikaelsen explores attitudes toward people with disabilities and the ways those attitudes have evolved in the last century. Petey, the title character, was born in 1920 with cerebral palsy, but he was misdiagnosed as mentally retarded and sent to a mental institution. For the next fifty years, Petey experiences one loss after another, as the caretakers he has befriended move on without him. "Step by institutional step," wrote *School Library Journal* contributor Joel Shoemaker, "readers see how this tragedy could happen. More importantly, readers feel Petey's pain, boredom, hope, fear, and occasional joy." In 1977, Petey finally receives an accurate diagnosis, only to be taken away from everything and everyone familiar, and transferred to a nursing home. While at the home, Petey is defended from a group of teenage bullies by Trevor, a lonely eighth-grader facing his own personal challenges. Petey and Trevor become friends, and Trevor's transformative experiences with Petey comprise the second half of the novel. "[T]his book is much more than a tearjerker," proclaimed Shoemaker, "its messages—that all people deserve respect; that one person can make a difference; that changing times require new attitudes—transcend simplistic labels." GraceAnne A. DeCandido of *Booklist* also applauded *Petey's* message, noting, "there's a real strength here in the depiction of the person inside a disability and the dignity that is a divine right."

Concluding his remarks to *SATA,* Mikaelsen revealed: "The secret to happiness has been described to me as doing whatever you do with a passion, to the best of your ability, and for others. Writing has given me this happiness."

Works Cited

DeCandido, GraceAnne A., review of *Petey, Booklist,* November 1, 1998, pp. 484-85.

Katka, Pat, review of *Sparrow Hawk Red, School Library Journal,* May, 1993, p. 127.

Mikaelsen, Ben, telephone interview with Sonia Benson for *Something about the Author,* conducted October 9, 1992.

Moses-Allen, Brenda, review of *Countdown, Voice of Youth Advocates,* June, 1997, p. 112.

Sherman, Chris, review of *Countdown, Booklist,* January 1, 1997, p. 856.

Sherman, Chris, review of *Sparrow Hawk Red, Booklist,* August, 1993, p. 206.

Shoemaker, Joel, review of *Countdown, School Library Journal,* March, 1997, p. 188.

Shoemaker, Joel, review of *Petey, School Library Journal,* November 1, 1998, p. 124.

Sparanese, Ann C., review of *Stranded, Voice of Youth Advocates,* December, 1995, p. 306.

Review of *Sparrow Hawk Red, Quill and Quire,* May, 1993, p. 37.

Sutton, Roger, review of *Sparrow Hawk Red, Bulletin of the Center for Children's Books,* June, 1993, p. 324.

Sutton, Roger, review of *Stranded, Bulletin of the Center for Children's Books,* May, 1995, p. 317.

Swanson, Cecilia, review of *Stranded, Kliatt,* January, 1997, p. 9.

For More Information See

PERIODICALS

Booklist, December 15, 1991, p. 758; August, 1995, p. 1949.

Bulletin of the Center for Children's Books, December, 1991, p. 100; November, 1996, p. 107.

Junior Bookshelf, December, 1992, pp. 258-59.

Kirkus Reviews, March 15, 1993, p. 377.

Publishers Weekly, October 5, 1998, p. 91.

School Librarian, February, 1993, p. 30.

School Library Journal, February, 1992, p. 108; June, 1995, p. 112.

OTHER

Web site: http://benmikaelsen.com.

*   *   *

Gerald Morris

MORRIS, Gerald 1963-
(Gerald Paul Morris)

Personal

Born October 29, 1963, in Riverside, WI; son of Russell A. (a missionary) and Lena May (a missionary; maiden name, Phillips) Morris; married Rebecca Hughes (a registered nurse), August 2, 1986; children: William, Ethan, Grace. *Education:* Oklahoma Baptist University, B.A., 1985; Southern Baptist Theological Seminary, M.Div., 1989, Ph.D., 1994. *Politics:* Democrat. *Religion:* Baptist.

Addresses

Home—624 North 16th Ave., Wausau, WI 54401. *Office*—P.O. Box 2014, Wausau, WI 54401-2014. *Electronic mail*—fbcw@pcpros.net.

Career

Southern Baptist Theological Seminary, Louisville, KY, adjunct professor of Hebrew and biblical interpretation, 1994-95; Ouachita Baptist University, Arkadelphia, AR, assistant professor of biblical studies, 1995-96; teacher at Christian school in Arkadelphia, 1997; HortCo Landscaping, Norman, OK, contract laborer, 1997-98; First Baptist Church, Wausau, WI, pastor, 1998—. *Member:* Society of Biblical Literature, American Academy of Religion, Society of Children's Book Writers and Illustrators, Minnesota-Wisconsin Baptist Convention.

Writings

(As Gerald Paul Morris) *Prophecy, Poetry, and Hosea,* Sheffield Academic Press, 1996.

(Old Testament editor) *Life and Times Historical Reference Bible,* Thomas Nelson (Nashville, TN), 1998.

The Squire's Tale (novel), Houghton, 1998.

The Squire, His Knight, and His Lady (novel), Houghton, 1999.

Work in Progress

The Savage Damsel and the Dwarf, for Houghton, publication expected in 2000; *Dear DJ,* a "contemporary semi-epistolary novel," completion expected in 2000; *Parsifal's Page,* an Arthurian novel, completion expected in 2001; research on narrative techniques in the biblical books of I and II Kings.

Sidelights

Gerald Morris told *SATA:* "I began my first novel when I was in the eighth grade. It was a perfectly dreadful western in which sharp-eyed gunslingers squinted into the sun and tough-as-boot-leather oldtimers called people 'young 'un' and spat into the dust. The early chapters were, providentially, lost.

"I returned to writing novels when I went to graduate school. Writing fiction was an antidote to the gaseous prose I was churning out for my professors. Maybe because I wrote as a sort of simplifying exercise, I chose to write for children and adolescents. A child's world is no simpler than an adult's, but children often see their world with clearer eyes. These first attempts at children's novels received some very fine, preprinted rejection cards in a variety of pretty colors. Pastels were big in the late 1980s. Then my first child, William, was born, to be followed two years later by Ethan, then Grace. Life was busier then, so I put the novels aside.

"Then, for a while, I was an academic. I finished my doctorate and became a professor of Hebrew and biblical interpretation for a couple of years. When my last academic contract ended, I was rather at loose ends, and so I decided to rework some of those old novels. This time, one was accepted—*The Squire's Tale.* Encouraged, I kept writing. Meanwhile, I tutored Greek, taught middle schoolers, taught English as a second language, did some substitute teaching, and worked for a landscaper. At the end of that time, I became the pastor of the First Baptist Church of Wausau, Wisconsin. So now, I suppose, I write children's novels as an antidote to my own sermons."

In his first book for children, *The Squire's Tale,* Morris uses the Arthurian Legends as inspiration for his story about a young medieval lad who serves as squire for Sir Gawain. Uncertain of his parentage, fourteen-year-old Terence decides to leave the wizard who raised him and join Sir Gawain on his quest to become The Maiden's Knight. As he follows the adventures of the future Knight of the Round Table, Terence not only discovers who his real parents are, but also what his destiny will be. In the novel, Morris offers a different view of Sir Gawain as he is seen through the eyes of Terence, a perspective that *School Library Journal* reviewer Helen Gregory claimed was "both original and true to the legend of Gawain." She went on to suggest that "readers who savor swashbuckling tales of knighthood will enjoy this adventure." *Horn Book* critic Ann A. Flowers praised Morris's characters, saying: "Both Sir Gawain and Terence are remarkably engaging figures, holding our attention and affection." Shelle Rosenfeld noted in a *Booklist* review that in addition to being a "well-written, fast read," *The Squire's Tale* also offers readers "well-drawn characters, excellent, snappy dialogue, detailed descriptions of medieval life, and a dry wit."

Terence and Gawain continue their adventures in *The Squire, His Knight, and His Lady,* a sequel to *The Squire's Tale* that was dubbed by a *Kirkus Reviews* critic

"an ideal follow-up to the first book and just as full of characters who are brave, loyal, and admirably human." In this story, Sir Gawain accepts a challenge in King Arthur's stead to meet the Knight of the Green Chapel, and sets out to find him with the assistance of his young squire Terence. The two are joined in their quest by Lady Eileen, whom they rescue from her evil uncle. Together, the trio encounter a cannibal hag, a sea Monster, the treacherous Marquis of Alva, and the Green Knight in disguise at an enchanted castle. "Laced with magic, humor, and chivalry," noted *Horn Book* reviewer Anne St. John, "this reworking of 'Sir Gawain and the Green Knight,' in which Gawain learns humility and Terence discovers his true place in the world, provides an engaging introduction to the original tale." A *Publishers Weekly* commentator asserted: "Morris retells various medieval legends with plenty of action, tongue-in-cheek humor and moments of keen perception.... For those who like their adventures fast and flip, this questing comedy is good sport."

Morris went on to tell *SATA:* "My faith is important to me. (This is good. We pastors are *encouraged* to believe something, after all.) All the same, I don't see myself as a 'Christian novelist.' I am, rather, a novelist who is a Christian, and a pastor, and a teacher, and a landscaper."

Works Cited

Flowers, Ann A., review of *The Squire's Tale, Horn Book,* July-August, 1998, p. 492.

Gregory, Helen, review of *The Squire's Tale, School Library Journal,* July, 1998, p. 97.

Rosenfeld, Shelle, review of *The Squire's Tale, Booklist,* April 15, 1998, pp. 1436-37.

St. John, Anne, review of *The Squire, His Knight, and His Lady, Horn Book,* March-April, 1999, p. 210.

Review of *The Squire, His Knight, and His Lady, Kirkus Reviews,* April 1, 1999, p. 536.

Review of *The Squire, His Knight, and His Lady, Publishers Weekly,* March 15, 1999, p. 60.

For More Information See

PERIODICALS

Kirkus Reviews, March 1, 1998, p. 342.
Publishers Weekly, April 27, 1998, p. 67.
School Library Journal, May, 1999, pp. 128-29.

*   *   *

MORRIS, Gerald Paul
See MORRIS, Gerald

Cindy Neuschwander

NEUSCHWANDER, Cindy 1953-

Personal

Born October 27, 1953, in San Diego, CA; daughter of Max (a teacher) and Carol (a homemaker) Grazda; married Bruce Neuschwander (a corporate controller), May 26, 1973; children: Tim Neuschwander, Seth Neuschwander. *Education:* Willamette University, B.A., 1975; Stanford University, M.A., 1976. *Politics:* "Registered as not affiliated with any party." *Religion:* Christian. *Hobbies and other interests:* Travel, skiing, beach bodysurfing.

Addresses

Office—Frederiksen Elementary School, 7243 Tamarack Dr., Dublin, CA 94568.

Career

Teacher, writer. Frankfurt International School, Oberursel, Germany, teacher, 1989-92; American Community School, London, England, teacher, 1992-93; Tracy Unified School District, Tracy, CA, teacher, 1993-96; Dublin Unified School District, Dublin, CA, teacher, 1996—. *Member:* Society of Children's Book Writers and Illustrators, National Council of Teachers of Mathematics.

Writings

Sir Cumference and the First Round Table: A Math Adventure, illustrated by Wayne Geehan, Charlesbridge (Watertown, MA), 1997.

Amanda Bean's Amazing Dream: A Mathematical Story, with activities by Marilyn Burns, illustrated by Liza Woodruff, Scholastic, 1998.

Sir Cumference and the Dragon of Pi: A Math Adventure, illustrated by Wayne Geehan, Charlesbridge, 1999.

Work in Progress

The Great Knight of Angleland, a book about lines and angles.

Sidelights

Cindy Neuschwander told *SATA:* "I am a native Californian. I was born in San Diego, CA, but have lived in many places, including Germany, England, Austria, Hawaii, and the East Coast. I received a B.A. in International Studies from Willamette University and an M.A. in Education from Stanford University. I have been teaching since 1976, both at the high school and elementary school levels.

"I currently teach third grade in Dublin, CA, where I'm a mathematics education specialist. I also enjoy reading children's literature. An interest in both of these areas led me to write children's stories with mathematics-based themes.

"In 1992, while living in England, I began working on my first book, *Sir Cumference and the First Round Table.* Prior to submitting it for publication, I took a writing class through the University of California at Berkeley. Since then I have had two other books published, *Amanda Bean's Amazing Dream* and *Sir Cumference and the Dragon of Pi.*

"In my spare time, I enjoy activities with my family. I have been married to my husband, Bruce, for more than twenty-five years. We have two sons: Tim, a junior at Dartmouth College in Hanover, New Hampshire, and Seth, a sophomore at Foothill High School in Pleasanton, CA. Seth is an excellent soccer player and Bruce and I spend much of our time at his soccer practices and matches.

"My family and I also enjoy traveling. We recently visited Quebec City in eastern Canada. The entire family has spent time on five of the earth's seven continents. Only Australia and Antarctica remain unvisited. We also love to ski in the winter and body surf and backpack in the summer. We are active in our local church and are a committed Christian family."

For More Information See

PERIODICALS

Booklist, September 15, 1998.
Kirkus Reviews, July 1, 1998, p. 970.
School Library Journal, September, 1998, p. 178.

P

PAIGE, Robin
See ALBERT, Susan Wittig

*   *   *

PETERS, Andrew Fusek 1965-

Personal

Born July 2, 1965, in Hildesheim, Germany; son of Frederick Maxwell (a geologist) and Vera Anna Fusek (an actress) Peters; married Polly Anne Peters (a drama teacher and writer), July 13, 1991; children: Rosalind Jana Peters. *Education:* Attended Corpus Christi College, Oxford University, 1984. *Politics:* Liberal. *Religion:* "Open minded."

Addresses

Home—Old Chapel, Lydbury North, Shropshire, SY7 8AU.

Career

Creative writing tutor, 1987—; author, 1992—. Broadcaster, musician. Has been a presenter and writer for national radio (BBC Radio 4) and television (BBC1 poetry series *Wham Bam Strawberry Jam* among other programs). Currently writing/presenting poetic/historical documentaries for Carlton & Central TV. *Member:* Poetry Society, National Association of Writers in Education, Society for Storytelling, Performing Rights Society, and MCPS.

Awards, Honors

West Midland Arts Valuing the Arts Award, 1996; BBC Radio 4 Write Out Loud Award, 1997; West Midland Arts Creative Ambition Award, 1998; Arts Council Translation Award, 1999, for *Sheep Don't Go to School.*

Andrew Fusek Peters

Writings

Word Whys (poetry for children), Sherbourne (Oswestry, England), 1992.

(Reteller) *Salt Is Sweeter Than Gold* (picture book), illustrated by Zdenka Kabatova-Taborska, Barefoot Books (Bath, England), 1994.

(With Mark Peters) *May the Angels Be with Us* (poetry), Shropshire County Council Education Services, 1994.

The House That Learned to Swim, Ginn, 1996.

The Goat Eared King and Other Czech Tales, Collins Educational, 1996.

The Weather's Getting Verse: The Stomping and Storming Poems of Andrew Peters, illustrated by Alan Larkins, Sherbourne, 1996.

(Reteller) *The Barefoot Book of Strange and Spooky Stories,* Barefoot, 1997, published as *Strange and Spooky Stories,* illustrated by Zdenka Kabatova-Taborska, Millbrook, 1998.

When I Come to the Dark Country: Poems of Land, Love and Loss (adult poetry), illustrated by Jackie Astbury, Abbotsford (Lichfield, England), 1997.

The Moon Is on the Microphone: The Wild and Wacky Poems of Andrew Fusek Peters, illustrated by Danny Bradford, Sherbourne, 1997.

(Editor) *Sheep Don't Go to School: Mad and Magical Children's Poetry,* illustrated by Marketa Prachaticka, Bloodaxe, 1999.

(Editor) *The Upside Down Frown* (collection of shape poems), Wayland/Young McDonald Books, 1999.

Also author of *A Pint of Unleaded Please* (poetry for children); poems published in anthologies, including *Jugular Defences,* Oscar's Press, 1993, *Custard Pie,* Macmillan, 1995, *A Faber Book of First Verse,* Faber & Faber, 1995, *The Young Poetry Pack,* Radio 4 and the Poetry Society, 1995, and *Friends,* Macmillan (in press), and in journals, including *Heart Throb* (WMArts Literary Magazine), 1993. Articles published in *Junior Education.*

OTHER

Colour People-Didjeridu (sound recording), Sonoton, 1990.

Also *Tales from under the Puddle* (sound recording), with Sue Harris, 1992.

Work in Progress

Poems with Attitude, a book of adolescent poems written with Polly Anne Peters for Wayland Books. Also: "A book of poems about my family's Czech history, their life before the war, during the communist regime and how they fled—and how personal history intertwines with the social history of this century."

Sidelights

Andrew Fusek Peters told *SATA:* "What interests me as a writer? That language is a craft and we have to serve our apprenticeship. It is something that takes time, patience and much work and it is a job. I used to get asked *but what is your day job?* as if writing were some kind of hobby—my books dashed off in a couple of hours! I am very much a perfectionist as I draft, whether it is stories, poems, or a piece for television. In poetry, as well as writing free verse, I love traditional forms— sonnet, sestina, roundel and fitting modern day language into these historical structures. I have even written a *Garland of Sonnets!*

Peters's collection of spine-tingling, sinister stories features such oddities as a talking skull, a wooden doll that becomes larger than life, and a boy who is not allowed to let his feet touch the ground. (Illustrated by Zdenka Kabatova-Taborska.)

"I mainly write for children. As an author and performer, I love to entertain, and write a lot of material that has a surreal sense of imagination, as well as throwing in the odd piece about bogies or kissing. But I am aware that children are sophisticated humans with the whole range of human emotions. Children's publishers often shy away from any of the big issues—such as grief, bullying, falling in love, etc.—yet this is the material that has often gone down well with readers and critics. I have been reading and admiring a lot of American children's poetry recently—and though I love the zany use of language, some of it seems to play safe. When my brother died of AIDS in America, in 1993, I put together a book of his and my poems for teenagers that was successfully published. It dealt with all the joy of growing up together, and the fights, and the illness, and death and finally the healing of time. As a collection, it had a huge response in Britain, with features in the *Guardian, The Times Educational Supplement* and on the Radio Four arts program *Kaleidoscope,* as well as support from actors such as Sir Ian McKellan and well known children's poet Brian Patten. Poetry, in this instance, became a powerful medium to express a universal message of loss, and the book reached out to all those who had lost a loved one in whatever circumstances.

"My wife and I have recently completed a collection of adolescent poems. I do a lot of work with this age group, performing and running writing workshops. It seems that there is very little published work that deals with their experiences of growing up, especially not in poetry. You could say there was a gap in the market, or that once again, publishers have been reluctant to tackle a difficult area. The poems we have written deal with bullying, drug addiction, dysfunctional families, abuse, alcoholism, sex, sexuality and falling in love—issues that affect many young people these days. Trialling these poems has been a joy. To see tough kids from an inner city area who normally hate poetry fall completely silent as I read the poems showed me that I had touched a nerve. Poetry doesn't just have to be about swaying trees! It will be interesting to see the response when the collection is published.

"My other interest as a writer is how to get across the sense of the magical and lyrical to my audience. My collection of *Strange and Spooky Stories* is a collection of traditional tales gleaned from my mother's Czech upbringing, and from storytellers worldwide. There is something very powerful about traditional tales, the repeated motifs, events happening in threes, the impossible becoming everyday and good triumphing over bad. In a sense, they are poetry in narrative form. The trick is to convey an atmosphere in your words that carries the reader for a while far from this world, to the place where imagination sings."

Peters is a poet and storyteller whose interest in Czechoslovakian folk tales was kindled by the history of his mother's family. His picture book *Salt Is Sweeter Than Gold* retells a traditional Czech fairy tale about an old king who asks his daughters to express their love for him. While the older two flatter him with extravagant claims, the youngest announces only that she loves her father more than salt. The king angrily banishes the girl, asserting that he will welcome her return only when salt becomes more valuable than gold. *School Librarian* critic David Lewis noted similarities between these opening scenes and Shakespeare's play *King Lear*. The young princess finds a home with an old wise woman in the forest, who helps the princess become reunited with her father. "This picture book will appeal to children seeking 'princess books,'" predicted *Booklist* reviewer Carolyn Phelan.

Peters also includes a traditional tale from Czechoslovakia in his compilation of nine *Strange and Spooky Stories*. Also included are legends from North America, the British Isles, and Central Europe, each with an element of the magical in them. Reviewers were quick to distinguish between the content and style of these stories, which were published in Great Britain under the title *The Barefoot Book of Strange and Spooky Stories,* and the kind of tales usually presented to American children as "scary." A *Children's Book Review Service* contributor maintained: "Readers will be captured by the strange, silly and spooky tales." "Peters writes in a simple, almost conversational style that should appeal to storytellers," observed Julie Corsaro in *Booklist*. A *Times Educational Supplement* commentator similarly asserted: "Andrew Fusek Peters's skill as an oral

storyteller is evident in his retellings.... [You] could read these stories aloud in the classroom with enormous pleasure."

Works Cited

Review of *The Barefoot Book of Strange and Spooky Stories, Times Educational Supplement,* January 30, 1998, p. 15.

Corsaro, Julie, review of *Strange and Spooky Stories, Booklist,* February 1, 1998, p. 916.

Lewis, David, review of *Salt Is Sweeter Than Gold, School Librarian,* November, 1994, p. 147.

Phelan, Carolyn, review of *Salt Is Sweeter Than Gold, Booklist,* January 1, 1995, p. 824.

Review of *Strange and Spooky Stories, Children's Book Review Service,* February, 1998, pp. 78-79.

*   *   *

PINKNEY, Jerry 1939-

Personal

Born December 22, 1939, in Philadelphia, PA; son of James H. (a general contractor) and Williemae Pinkney; married Gloria Jean Maultsby, 1960; children: Troy Bernadette, Jerry Brian, Scott Cannon, Myles Carter. *Education:* Attended Philadelphia Museum College of Art (now University of the Arts), 1957-59. *Hobbies and other interests:* "I am a lover of music, with a large music collection. I enjoy all kinds of music: jazz, classical, rock, and pop."

Addresses

Home and studio—41 Furnace Dock Rd., Croton-on-Hudson, NY 10520.

Career

Painter, illustrator, author, designer, and educator. Worked as a designer/illustrator for Rustcraft Greeting Card Co., Dedham, MA, and Barker-Black Studio, Boston, MA, and helped found the Kaleidoscope Studio before opening his own studio, Jerry Pinkney, Inc., Croton-on-Hudson, NY, in 1971. Rhode Island School of Design, visiting critic, 1969-70, member of visiting committee, 1991; Pratt Institute, Brooklyn, NY, associate professor of illustration, 1986-87; University of Delaware, distinguished visiting professor, 1986-88, associate professor of art, 1988-92; University of Buffalo, NY, visiting artist, 1989; Syracuse University, NY, guest faculty, 1989; Fashion Institute of Technology, NY, art mentor, 1989; State University of New York at Buffalo, visiting professor, 1991-92; guest lecturer at numerous schools and universities; served on judging committees for numerous art and illustration shows. United States Postal Service, Stamp Advisory Committee, 1982-92, Quality Assurance Committee, 1986-92; served on the NASA Artist Team for the space shuttle Columbia. Designer of commemorative stamps for the United States Postal Service "Black Heritage" series, the

Jerry Pinkney

Help End Hunger and United Way commemorative stamps, and the "Honey Bee" commemorative envelope. Lecturer in elementary schools, colleges, universities, art schools, and in museum literature conferences across the United States. *Exhibitions:* Pinkney has exhibited his works in twenty-four one-man and numerous group shows throughout the United States and in Japan, Italy, Czechoslovakia, Russia, Taiwan, and Jamaica, including shows at the Brooklyn Museum; the National Center of Afro-American Artists, Boston; the Air and Space Museum, Washington, D.C.; the Boston Museum of Fine Arts; the Cedar Rapids (IA) Museum of Art; and the California African American Museum at Los Angeles. *Member:* Society of Illustrators, Society of Children's Book Writers and Illustrators.

Awards, Honors

New Jersey Institute of Technology Award, 1969, for *Babushka and the Pig;* Council on Interracial Books for Children Award, 1973, Children's Book Showcase selection, 1976, and Jane Addams Book Group Award, 1976, all for *Song of the Trees;* Jane Addams Book Group Award, *Boston Globe-Horn Book* Honor Book, and National Book Award finalist, all 1977, and Young Readers Choice award, 1979, all for *Roll of Thunder,*

Hear My Cry, which also won the Newbery Medal in 1977 for its text by Mildred D. Taylor; American Institute of Graphic Arts Book Show selections, 1980, for *Childtimes: A Three Generation Memoir* and *Tonwe-ya and the Eagles, and Other Lakota Indian Tales; Boston Globe-Horn Book* Award (nonfiction honor) and Carter G. Woodson Award (outstanding merit), both 1980, both for *Childtimes: A Three-Generation Memoir;* Outstanding Science Book Award, National Association of Science Teachers, 1980, Carter G. Woodson Award, and Coretta Scott King Award runner-up, both for *Count on Your Fingers African Style;* Christopher Award and Coretta Scott King Award, both 1986, both for *The Patchwork Quilt; Redbook* Award, 1987, for *Strange Animals of the Sea;* Parents Choice Award, 1987, for *The Tales of Uncle Remus;* Coretta Scott King Award, 1987, for *Half a Moon and One Whole Star;* Reading Magic Award, 1988, and Notable Book, American Library Association (ALA), both for *More Tales of Uncle Remus;* Parents Choice Award, 1988, for *Rabbit Makes a Monkey Out of a Lion;* Coretta Scott King Award, 1988, Notable Book, ALA, and Caldecott Honor Book, 1989, all for *Mirandy and Brother Wind;* Irma S. and James H. Black Award, Bank Street College of Education, and Parents Choice Award, both 1989, Caldecott Honor Book and Coretta Scott King Honor

Book, both 1990, and Golden Sower Award, 1992, all for *The Talking Eggs;* Golden Kite Award, Society of Children's Book Writers and Illustrators, 1990, for *Home Place;* Parents Choice Award, 1992, for *Further Tales of Uncle Remus;* Parents Choice Award (picture book), 1992, for *Back Home;* Caldecott Honor Book and *Boston Globe-Horn Book* Award for illustration, both 1995, both for *John Henry;* Coretta Scott King Award and Christopher Award, both 1997, both for *Minty: A Story of Young Harriet Tubman;* Ten Best Illustrated Books, *New York Times,* for *The Hired Hand.* Pinkney has also received numerous awards from the Society of Illustrators; Certificates of Achievement from the NAACP in 1979 and from the Urban League in 1980; and a designation as Citizen of the Year from Kappa Alpha Psi Fraternity in 1980. In addition, he has received seven awards for his body of work, including a citation for children's literature from Drexel University, 1992; Philadelphia College of Art and Design Alumni Award, 1992; David McCord Children's Literature Citation from Framingham State College, Massachusetts, 1992; the Irma S. and James H. Black Award, Bank Street College of Education, 1995, for excellence in children's literature; Children's Literature Festival Award, Keene State College, Keene, NH, 1996; Hope Dean Award, Foundation for Children's Books, Boston, MA 1997; and Virginia Hamilton Literary Award, Kent State University, Kent, OH, 2000.

Illustrator

Joyce Cooper Arkhurst, reteller, *The Adventures of Spider: West African Folk Tales,* Little, Brown, 1964.

Adeline McCall, *This Is Music,* Allyn & Bacon, 1965.

V. Mikhailovich Garshin, *The Traveling Frog,* McGraw, 1966.

Lila Green, compiler, *Folktales and Fairytales of Africa,* Silver Burdett, 1967.

Ken Sobol, *The Clock Museum,* McGraw, 1967.

Harold J. Saleh, *Even Tiny Ants Must Sleep,* McGraw, 1967.

John W. Spellman, editor, *The Beautiful Blue Jay, and Other Tales of India,* Little, Brown, 1967.

Ralph Dale, *Shoes, Pennies, and Rockets,* L. W. Singer, 1968.

Traudl (pseudonym of Traudl Flaxman), *Kostas the Rooster,* Lothrop, 1968.

Cora Annett, *Homerhenry,* Addison-Wesley, 1969.

Irv Phillips, *The Twin Witches of Fingle Fu,* L. W. Singer, 1969.

Fern Powell, *The Porcupine and the Tiger,* Lothrop, 1969.

Ann Trofimuk, *Babushka and the Pig,* Houghton, 1969.

Thelma Shaw, *Juano and the Wonderful Fresh Fish,* Addison-Wesley, 1969.

Ken Sobol, *Sizes and Shapes,* McGraw, 1969.

Francine Jacobs, adapter, *The King's Ditch: A Hawaiian Tale,* Coward, 1971.

J. C. Arkhurst, *More Adventures of Spider,* Scholastic Book Services, 1972.

Adjai Robinson, *Femi and Old Grandaddie,* Coward, 1972.

Mari Evans, *JD,* Doubleday, 1973.

A. Robinson, *Kasho and the Twin Flutes,* Coward, 1973.

Berniece Freschet, *Prince Littlefoot,* Cheshire, 1974.

Beth P. Wilson, *The Great Minu,* Follett, 1974.

Mildred D. Taylor, *Song of the Trees,* Dial, 1975.

Cruz Martel, *Yagua Days,* Dial, 1976.

Mildred D. Taylor, *Roll of Thunder, Hear My Cry,* Dial, 1976.

Phyllis Green, *Mildred Murphy, How Does Your Garden Grow?,* Addison-Wesley, 1977.

Eloise Greenfield, *Mary McLeod Bethune,* Crowell, 1977.

Verna Aardema, *Ji-Nongo-Nongo Means Riddles,* Four Winds Press, 1978.

Lila Green, reteller, *Tales from Africa,* Silver Burdett, 1979.

Rosebud Yellow Robe, reteller, *Tonweya and the Eagles, and Other Lakota Indian Tales,* Dial, 1979.

Eloise Greenfield and Lessie Jones Little, *Childtimes: A Three-Generation Memoir,* Crowell, 1979.

Virginia Hamilton, *Jahdu,* Greenwillow, 1980.

Claudia Zaslavsky, *Count on Your Fingers African Style,* Crowell, 1980.

William Wise, *Monster Myths of Ancient Greece,* Putnam, 1981.

Barbara Michels and Bettye White, editors, *Apples on a Stick: The Folklore of Black Children,* Coward, 1983.

Valerie Flournoy, *The Patchwork Quilt,* Dial, 1985.

Crescent Dragonwagon, *Half a Moon and One Whole Star,* Macmillan, 1986.

Barbara Gibson, *Creatures of the Desert World and Strange Animals of the Sea,* edited by Donald J. Crump, National Geographic Society, 1987.

Nancy White Carlstrom, *Wild, Wild Sunflower Child Anna,* Macmillan, 1987.

Julia Fields, *The Green Lion of Zion Street,* Macmillan, 1988.

Pat McKissack, *Mirandy and Brother Wind,* Knopf, 1988.

Verna Aardema, *Rabbit Makes a Monkey of Lion,* Dial, 1989.

Robert D. San Souci, *The Talking Eggs: A Folktale from the American South,* Dial, 1989.

Marilyn Singer, *Turtle in July,* Macmillan, 1989.

Crescent Dragonwagon, *Home Place,* Macmillan, 1990.

Jean Marzollo, *Pretend You're a Cat,* Dial, 1990.

Arnold Adoff, *In for Winter, Out for Spring,* Harcourt, 1991.

Zora Neale Hurston, *Their Eyes Were Watching God,* University of Illinois Press, 1991.

Sonia Levitin, *The Man with His Heart in a Bucket,* Dial, 1991.

Gloria Jean Pinkney, *Back Home,* Dial, 1992.

Virginia Hamilton, *Drylongso,* Harcourt, 1992.

Colin T. Eisler, *David's Songs: His Psalms and Their Stories,* Dial, 1992.

Nancy Willard, *A Starlit Somersault Downhill,* Little, Brown, 1993.

Thylias Moss, *I Want to Be,* Dial, 1993.

Johanna Hurwitz, *New Shoes for Silvia,* Morrow, 1993.

Gloria Jean Pinkney, *The Sunday Outing,* Dial, 1994.

Rudyard Kipling, *The Jungle Book: The Mowgli Stories,* Morrow, 1995.

Valerie Flournoy, *Tanya's Reunion,* Dial, 1995.

Jane Yolen, *Fever Dream,* HarperCollins, 1996.

Alan Schroeder, *Minty: A Story of Young Harriet Tubman,* Dial, 1996.

Robert D. San Souci, *The Hired Hand: An African-American Folktale,* Dial, 1997.

Rudyard Kipling, *Rikki-Tikki-Tavi,* Morrow, 1997.

Barbara Diamond Goldin, *Journeys with Elijah: Eight Tales of the Prophet,* Harcourt, 1998.

(And reteller) *The Ugly Duckling,* Morrow, 1999.

(And reteller) *The Little Match Girl,* Phyllis Fogelman Books, 1999.

ALL WRITTEN BY JULIUS LESTER; RETELLINGS, EXCEPT AS NOTED

The Tales of Uncle Remus: The Adventures of Brer Rabbit, Dial, 1988.

More Tales of Uncle Remus: Further Adventures of Brer Rabbit, His Friends, Enemies, and Others, Dial, 1988.

Further Tales of Uncle Remus: The Misadventures of Brer Rabbit, Brer Fox, Brer Wolf, the Doodang, and All the Other Creatures, Dial, 1990.

The Last Tales of Uncle Remus, Dial, 1994.

John Henry, Dial, 1994.

Sam and the Tigers: A New Telling of Little Black Sambo, Dial, 1996.

Black Cowboy, Wild Horses: A True Story (biography), Dial, 1998.

OTHER

Contributor of cover art to *The Planet of Junior Brown* by Virginia Hamilton and *Rainbow Jordan* by Alice Childress and of illustrations to *On the Wings of Peace,* Houghton Mifflin, 1995, and *Read-to-Me,* DIANE Publishing Company, 1996. Also illustrator of Helen Fletcher's *The Year Around Book,* and of a series of limited edition books for adults published by Franklin Library that includes *Gulliver's Travels, Tom Jones, Wuthering Heights, The Flowering of New England, The Education of Henry Adams, The Winthrop Covenant, Early Autumn, Selected Plays, These Thirteen, The Covenant, Cat on a Hot Tin Roof, Rabbit Run, Rabbit Redux,* and *Lolita.* Contributor of illustrations to textbooks and to magazines, including *Boys' Life, Contact, Essence, Seventeen,* and the *Saturday Evening Post.*

Adaptations

The Patchwork Quilt, Half a Moon and One Whole Star and *Yagua Days* were presented on the PBS television program *Reading Rainbow;* the video *Meet the Caldecott Illustrator: Jerry Pinkney* was released in 1991; *Mirandy and Brother Wind* and *The Talking Eggs* were released on video in 1992 and 1993 respectively; *John Henry* was released on video in 1998.

Work in Progress

Aesop's Fables, for North South Books.

Sidelights

Called an "artist nonpareil" by Michael Cart in *Booklist* and a "master of color" by Ruth Ann Smith in *Bulletin of the Center for Children's Books,* Jerry Pinkney is regarded as one of the most gifted contemporary American illustrators for children. He is also credited with being instrumental in bringing multicultural subjects, especially those regarding African Americans, to the picture book genre. Praised for the realism and technical excellence of his art, Pinkney is also acclaimed for the beauty, drama, and authenticity of his pictures as well as for the way he both complements and enhances the texts he illustrates. He has provided pictures for works by such authors as Virginia Hamilton, Mildred D. Taylor, Eloise Greenfield, Arnold Adoff, Verna Aardema, Patricia McKissack, Robert D. San Souci, Nancy Willard, Zora Neale Hurston, his wife, Gloria Jean Pinkney, and Julius Lester. With Lester, the artist has shared in the creation of retellings of the Uncle Remus stories and Helen Bannerman's *Little Black Sambo*—works often considered offensive to African Americans—that provide contemporary readers and viewers with a fresh perspective. Pinkney is the illustrator of several books of folklore—stories, riddles, and verses—as well as animal tales and books dealing with family life and childhood play. Although he specializes in African American subjects, his works are generally considered universal; he has portrayed white characters in his books and has illustrated titles featuring both Native and Hispanic Americans. Pinkney has also illustrated Barbara Diamond Goldin's *Journeys with Elijah: Eight Tales of the Prophet,* a compilation of tales of Elijah in Jewish communities throughout the world.

As an artist, Pinkney characteristically uses watercolor and pencil as his primary mediums; he also uses pastels, colored pencils, and cray-pas to create his drawings and paintings, which range from small inserts to large double-page spreads. Viewing the pages of his picture books as a stage for dramatic action, Pinkney attempts to tell stories visually, much like the director of a play or film. The artist, who likes to reveal the personality of his characters through action, often uses his family, his friends, and himself as the models for his pictures; in fact, he often takes photographs of his subjects before beginning his illustrations. The result is works that are considered immediate and dynamic, and the artist is often lauded for creating lush, well-designed pictures that reflect a full range of emotions. Although some reviewers fault his art as overly static due to its photographic style, most critics laud Pinkney as a distinctive artist who creates impressive, evocative pictures and who has contributed greatly to the development of multicultural literature. Writing in *Children's Literature Association Quarterly,* Anthony L. Manna commented, "As Jerry Pinkney has coursed his way through more than three dozen books he has increasingly counterbalanced his technical skill with an emotional depth.... In Pinkney's case, the drama inherent in narrative has served him as a guiding consciousness that both accommodates his discovery of an inner text that deals in universals, and spurs him to spin his own compelling tale in visual terms." Michael Cart of *Booklist* concluded that Pinkney "brings the best kind of talent to his collaborative work as an illustrator: he consistently demonstrates not only a sympathetic intellectual grasp of an author's material, but also an empathetic understanding of its emotional content."

In **The Patchwork Quilt,** *illustrator Pinkney collaborated with author Valerie Flournoy to convey the close bond between Tanya, her mother, and her grandmother as they work together on a quilt that tells the story of their life as a family.*

Born in Philadelphia into a family of six, Pinkney was a middle child. He describes his family, who lived in an all-black block of the Germantown section of the city, as close, loving, and supportive. Several of his siblings—three girls and two boys—were interested in art. Writing in *Children's Books and Their Creators,* Pinkney commented, "I started drawing as far back as I can remember, at the age of four or five. My brothers drew, and in a way I was mimicking them. I found I enjoyed the act of putting marks on paper. It also gave me a way of creating my own space and quiet time, a way of expressing myself." In his essay for *Something about the Author Autobiography Series (SAAS),* Pinkney noted, "My first recollection of feeling that art would play an important part in my life was early in elementary school. I found that by using a drawing for a project, my teachers soon realized this was something other children weren't doing, and that there was potential talent in my work. Two things happened: I was able to solve certain class projects in a unique way, and I enjoyed the response that I got and the encouragement from teachers and fellow students. So I knew then that expressing myself with marks on a paper was going to be a part of my life." In his acceptance speech for the *Boston Globe-Horn Book* Award in 1995, Pinkney noted, "Growing up

in a small house in Philadelphia, there were few books [about people of color] for me and my five siblings to read and few stories told. There were, however, three that I remember: *Little Black Sambo,* 'Tales of Uncle Remus,' and 'John Henry' .... Little Black Sambo, Brer Rabbit, and John Henry—these heroes from my childhood gave support and comfort in a world where almost all heroes in literature were white." Later, Pinkney would illustrate all of these tales in retellings written by Julius Lester.

Pinkney attended Hill Elementary School, an African American grade school in Philadelphia. Although he claimed in *SAAS* that he "was not a terrific speller or a fast reader" and that he sometimes wrestled with self-doubts and conflicts over whether to draw or to be social, Pinkney graduated with the top male honors in his class. He noted in *Children's Books and Their Creators,* "Drawing helped me feel good about myself." At Roosevelt Junior High, Pinkney became friends with both black and white students; at Roosevelt, he commented, "the spark for my curiosity about people was lit. This interest and fascination with people of different cultures appears throughout my work." When Pinkney was twelve, he met John Liney, the creator of the popular comic strip "Little Henry." Liney, who noticed Pinkney sketching at a newsstand where he worked, invited the young artist to visit his studio. "There," Pinkney noted, "I learned about the possibility of making a living creating pictures." Writing in *SAAS,* Pinkney stated, "In many ways [Liney] was the first person to plant a seed of the possibilities of making a living as an artist." Pinkney's formal art training started at Dobbins Vocational Art School, an institution where he majored in commercial art. At Dobbins, Pinkney recalled, "for the second time I started to get some idea of how to make a living by making marks on paper." His first instructor, Samuel Brown, was African American. In his senior year, Pinkney met his future wife, Gloria Jean Maultsby. After completing an intensive three-year program, Pinkney won a scholarship to the Philadelphia College of Art; he became the first member of his family to go to college.

At PCA, Pinkney majored in advertising design and immersed himself in abstract painting and self-expression; he also took printing, drawing, and paintmaking and began going to museums and art galleries. Writing in *SAAS,* he recalled, "I began to change my thinking in terms of moving from representational interpretation to more expressionistic works." Pinkney once told *Something about the Author (SATA),* "Art school introduced me to art on a level I had never experienced—an awareness of what my particular talents were." At the beginning of his junior year, Pinkney married Gloria Jean Maultsby; after their first child—a daughter, Troy Bernadette—was born, Pinkney left school and began freelancing. He did calligraphy for a department store and worked in a prestigious florist shop, first as a driver and later as a flower arranger, the florist shop winning several contests for their floral designs. After an adjunct professor at PCA told him about a position at Rustcraft Greeting Card Company in Massachusetts, Pinkney put together a portfolio and, after being hired as a studio-card designer, moved his family to Boston. While at Rustcraft, Pinkney designed and illustrated posters for the studio card department, in addition to greeting cards. He recalled in his autobiographical essay that this "was a valuable time for me and, again, a widening of my experience as an artist." Pinkney told *SATA* that while at Rustcraft, "I always had one foot in design and one in illustration. Though I hadn't had much formal training in illustration, I had the desire to illustrate." During his time at Rustcraft, Pinkney and his wife had three more children: Jerry Brian, who has become a successful illustrator under the name Brian Pinkney; Scott Cannon; and Myles Carter, who has begun illustrating children's books with photographs. Pinkney left Rustcraft to take a position at Barker-Black Studio, a Boston illustration house where he stayed for two years. Before leaving Barker-Black, Pinkney illustrated his first children's book, *The Adventures of Spider: West African Folk Tales* by Joyce Cooper Arkhurst. In her review in *Horn Book,* Priscilla L. Moulton noted that *The Adventures of Spider,* which contains six tales about the trickster hero, includes "strikingly modern illustrations, many in bold color."

While at Barker-Black, Pinkney met two other young artists, Joe Vino and Rob Howard, with whom he would start the design house Kaleidoscope Studios. After two years, Pinkney left to start his own business, Jerry Pinkney Studio, working mainly in advertising and as an illustrator for textbooks and magazines; he also designed book jackets and record album covers. Pinkney became involved with the Boston Action Group, a civil rights organization, and volunteered as a graphic designer at the National Center of Afro-American Artists in Boston. In 1970, the artist moved his family to New York; although he concentrated on freelancing for advertisers, Pinkney was still able to illustrate one or two books per year, many with multicultural subjects and themes. As he noted in *Children's Books and Their Creators,* "The late 1960s and early 1970s brought about an awareness of the need for African American writers. Publishers sought out African American illustrators for this work. And there I was." Among other projects, Pinkney provided the pictures for a series of limited edition books for the Franklin Library and an African American historical calendar for Seagrams that is now considered a collector's item. He also created nine postage stamps for the Black Heritage Series issued by the U.S. Postal Service as well as stamps for the United Way and the Help End Hunger campaign. Pinkey created a poster of the Carver National Monument for the U.S. Parks Department and a portrait of Jesse Jackson for the U.S. Information Agency; in addition, he provided the illustrations for a *National Geographic* article on the Underground Railroad and a 1992 article for the same periodical, entitled "The African Slave Trade." He wrote in *SAAS,* "I was trying to use these projects as vehicles to address the issues of being an African American and the importance of African American contributions to society." In the early 1980s, Pinkney was invited by the U.S. Postal Service to serve on the Citizens' Stamp Advisory Committee, a position he still holds. "At the

time," he noted in *SAAS,* "I was not thinking consciously about this whole thing of becoming a role model, but when I think back on it, it was probably there. I wanted to show that an African American artist could certainly make it in this country on a national level in the visual graphic arts. And I wanted to show my children the possibilities that lay ahead for them. That was very important. I wanted to be a strong role model for my family and for other African Americans."

While contributing to a variety of fields, Pinkney continued to develop his style as an illustrator of children's books. In the beginning of his career, Pinkney specialized in providing the pictures for books of folktales from a variety of cultures; at the time, his illustrations were line drawings in black and white. His pictures for two books by Adjai Robinson—*Femi and Old Grandaddie* in 1972 and *Kahso and the Twin Flutes* in 1973—are considered a turning point in Pinkney's direction and focus. These works, drawings for African tales from Sierra Leone, are credited with reflecting a new depth of emotion, a new consciousness of the human figure, and a new emphasis on African American subjects. *Kasho and the Twin Flutes* is also the first book

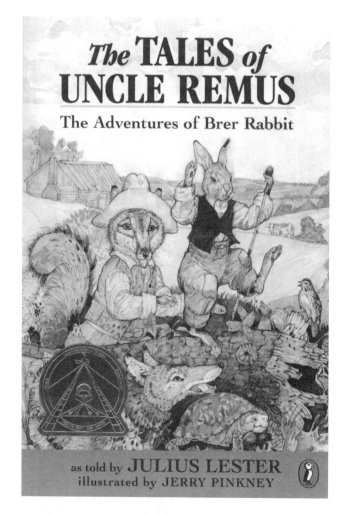

Julius Lester gives a modern sensibility to his retelling of the timeless tales of Brer Rabbit and friends. (Cover illustration by Pinkney.)

in which Pinkney used photographs of models as part of his art. Assessing *Femi and Old Grandaddie,* a critic in *Kirkus Reviews* noted, "The more dramatic moments ... are heightened by Jerry Pinkney's fluid pencil drawings. His wonderfully expressive faces, semi-abstract landscapes and draperies, and clever use of perspective and pose keep the reader in the middle of the action." In her review of *Kasho and the Twin Flutes* in *Library Journal,* Helen Gregory commented that Pinkney's sketches "capture the humor of the story and the humanity of the characters." In his interview in *SATA,* Pinkney called *Tonweya and the Eagles, and Other Lakota Indian Tales,* a collection of Native American folktales by Rosebud Yellow Robe, "my favorite book at that time. It came at a time when I had gained confidence in my drawings. *Tonweya* answers all the questions I was confronting in my work." Writing about the book in the *Christian Science Monitor,* Robert Gish concluded that Pinkney "adds immeasurably to making the make-believe believably real."

In 1985, Pinkney provided his first full-color illustrations for *The Patchwork Quilt,* a picture book by Valerie Flournoy that describes how the year-long completion of a quilt brings a family together. Writing in *Horn Book,* Hanna B. Zeiger stated that Pinkney's paintings of the family "glow with as much warmth and vibrancy as the loveliest of quilts," while Betsy Shea of the *New York Times Book Review* asserted, "There is warmth and intimacy in the richly detailed watercolor illustrations .... One doesn't need words to sense the affection among family members or the pride they feel in their

Overshadowed by her spoiled sister Rose, hard-working Blanche is catapulted into a fantastical world in this Caldecott Honor Book, in which talking eggs convey lessons about inner beauty and goodness. (From The Talking Eggs, *written by Robert D. San Souci and illustrated by Pinkney.)*

achievement, a beautiful patchwork quilt." Pinkney often depicts African American children in pictures accompanying texts that are nonspecific about the race of the main characters. For example, in *Half a Moon and One Whole Star,* a picture book by Crescent Dragonwagon that depicts the nighttime activities that occur while young Susan sleeps, Pinkney makes the character a black child. A critic in *Kirkus Reviews* noted that this element "adds an interesting dimension and should broaden the range of readership," while a reviewer in *Bulletin of the Center for Children's Books* called the paintings "among the best work that Pinkney has done."

In 1987, Pinkney began his partnership with African American author Julius Lester on a series of retellings of the Uncle Remus stories. Originally retold by Joel Chandler Harris, a white author, in the latter part of the nineteenth century, the stories feature anthropomorphic animal characters—most notably the clever Brer Rabbit—in tales that come from African American folklore. In Harris's versions of the tales, he has Uncle Remus, a black ex-slave, tell the tales in dialect to a small white boy. Although considered classics, Harris's versions of the tales have been criticized for containing racial stereotypes. Lester's retellings of the tales are credited with excising the offensive elements while making the stories accessible to contemporary readers, especially children. Pinkney provided the illustrations for four volumes of Uncle Remus stories, beginning with *The Tales of Uncle Remus: The Adventures of Brer Rabbit.* Critics generally praised Pinkney for creating illustrations that capture the personalities of the animals without losing their animal natures. In her review of the first volume in the *New York Times Book Review,* June Jordan maintained: "Every single illustration by Jerry Pinkney is fastidious, inspired, and a marvel of delightful imagination." In her review in the *School Librarian,* Irene Babsky commented that Pinkney's illustrations "are distinguished by warmth and sensitivity, and achieve that rare attainment in the illustrators' art of adding a dimension of their own yet being entirely in harmony with the text." In her review of *More Tales of Uncle Remus* in *Horn Book,* Mary M. Burns concluded that the book "offers a tale for any audience. The illustrations are equally remarkable for their energy and synchronization with the spirit as well as with the words of the text." Reviewing *Further Tales of Uncle Remus,* Betsy Hearne of the *Bulletin of the Center for Children's Books* claimed, "Pinkney's watercolor compositions have loosened up considerably, with more flexible lines, satisfying tonal blends, and generous textural variations." In a review of the final "Uncle Remus" book, *The Last Tales of Uncle Remus,* in another issue of the same periodical, Hearne noted, "Pinkney's drafting has relaxed, smoothed out, and mellowed just as a good story does over time, and he manages to underscore Lester's sly tone by treating the cast of characters with seriously deadpan respect."

In his acceptance speech for the *Boston Globe-Horn Book* Award for *John Henry* in 1995, Pinkney commented, "When the Uncle Remus tales were read to me, Brer Rabbit and I became friends and have remained so—

even through the labor of creating over one hundred illustrations for the four volumes of Brer Rabbit tales retold by Julius Lester. I welcomed the chance to bring life to characters who shaped my growing-up years and who helped shape my interest in telling stories through pictures."

In 1994, Pinkney and Lester collaborated on *John Henry,* a picture book that retells the tall tale about the legendary African American strongman. Writing in *Bulletin of the Center for Children's Books,* Elizabeth Bush commented that "the earthy, craggy watercolors capture the sober, thoughtful side of Henry's story—his tenuous relationship with his surroundings as both larger-than-life hero and smaller-than-nature mortal." *New York Times Book Review* contributor Jack Zipes called Pinkey's illustrations "exquisite," and concluded that the pictures "employ a subtle blend of colors to bring out the interconnections of the man with nature and his society." Michael Cart of *Booklist* commented that Pinkney's watercolors "are so beautiful that they summon their own share of smiles and tears. But more importantly, the realism of style and the artistic skill that are Pinkney's signature lend authenticity to legend, while his affection for his subject brings humanity and heart to a tall-tale hero who, in other versions of the legend, has been only ... well, tall. Here he is every inch the folk hero." In his acceptance speech for the *Boston Globe-Horn Book* Award for *John Henry,* Pinkney noted, "The vision of how best to portray John Henry came from the warm and rich feelings that I carried from my childhood into my adulthood.... For with this book we strove to create an African American hero that would inspire all."

As they did with the Uncle Remus stories, Pinkney and Lester published a revised version of another controversial children's classic, *Little Black Sambo,* in 1996. Called *Sam and the Tigers: A New Telling of Little Black Sambo,* the volume deletes the questionable images and character names of Helen Bannerman's tale of a century ago while placing the story in a fantasy land that echoes the American South of the 1920s. Focusing on the resourcefulness of the main character—now renamed—and the humor of the tale, Lester and Pinkney are credited with revitalizing an essentially enjoyable story. Writing in *Bulletin of the Center for Children's Books,* Betsy Hearne claimed, "Helen Bannerman could ask for no sharper successors than Julius Lester and Jerry Pinkney.... Pinkney's tigers are perfectly proportioned, and their expressive faces and postures outstrip an already colorful cast." A reviewer in *Publishers Weekly* added, "Pinkney's lavish illustrations—a feast of figures, color, expressions, and detail—pick up and run with the expansive mood of the text."

Pinkney and Lester have also collaborated on the picture book *Black Cowboy, Wild Horses: A True Story,* a tale based on an incident in the life of African American cowboy Bob Lemmons. A former slave, Lemmons possessed the unique ability to bring in a herd of wild mustangs by himself by becoming one with them. In *Black Cowboy, Wild Horses,* Pinkney and Lester de-

In this Caldecott Honor Book illustrated by Pinkney, Julius Lester depicts African-American folk hero John Henry as a miracle of nature whose strength and quickness amaze people and animals alike.

scribe how Lemmons and his stallion Warrior track a wild herd until, after Bob defeats the mustang leader, they are accepted. Calling the book "essential for anyone interested in the Wild West," a reviewer in *Publishers Weekly* noted, "The fluid brushwork of Pinkney's watercolors seem tailor-made for the flow of muscle, mane, and tail of wild mustangs galloping across the prairie." *Horn Book* reviewer Lauren Adams concurred, stating that Pinkney's "magnificent earth-toned paintings bring to life the wild beauty of the horses and the western plains, the dark drama of a nighttime thunderstorm, the fierce battle of the stallions." Writing in *School Library Journal,* Ruth Semrau stated that throughout the book "both text and pictures emphasize the blending of all life." Noting that the aim of the authors was to recast their childhood love of cowboys and the Old West with more recent research on the contributions of black and Hispanic cowboys, Semrau concluded, "They have done that, and achieved something else as well: youngsters will reflect on the relationships between humans and other animals."

In addition to his work as an illustrator, Pinkney wrote his first text for an adaptation of the Hans Christian Andersen tale *The Ugly Duckling* in 1999. He has also spent thirty years as an educator and visiting artist at such institutions as the Rhode Island School of Design, Pratt Institute, Fashion Institute of Technology, Syracuse University, the University of Delaware, the University of Buffalo, and the State University of New York at

Buffalo. "[As] a teacher," Pinkney stated in *Horn Book*, "it is my hope to influence others as I have been." Writing about his approach to his art in the same essay, Pinkney stated, "I think of all the drawings for a book as one piece of art. That's a conflict, because I'm trying to get the reader to turn the page. I'm trying to get him or her to look at the page and then be curious about turning it. So I'm trying to hold you and make you move at the same time." Concluding his comments in *Children's Books and Their Creators*, Pinkney reflected: "It still amazes me how much the projects I have illustrated have given back to me—the personal as well as the artistic satisfaction. They have given me the opportunity to use my imagination to draw, to paint, and to travel through the voices of the characters in the stories—and, above all else, to touch children."

Works Cited

Adams, Lauren, review of *Black Cowboy, Wild Horses: A True Story, Horn Book*, July-August, 1998, pp. 477-78.

Babsky, Irene, review of *Tales of Uncle Remus: The Adventures of Brer Rabbit, School Librarian*, May, 1988, p. 77.

Burns, Mary M., review of *More Tales of Uncle Remus, Horn Book*, September-October, 1988, pp. 639-40.

Bush, Elizabeth, review of *John Henry, Bulletin of the Center for Children's Books*, October, 1994, p. 54.

Cart, Michael, "Carte Blanche: Invisible No Longer," *Booklist*, February 15, 1995, p. 1069.

Review of *Femi and Old Grandaddie, Kirkus Reviews*, November 15, 1972, p. 1303.

Gish, Robert, review of *Tonweya and the Eagles, Christian Science Monitor*, October 15, 1979, p. B3.

Gregory, Helen, review of *Kasho and the Twin Flutes, Library Journal*, December 15, 1973, p. 3702.

Review of *Half a Moon and One Whole Star, Bulletin of the Center for Children's Books*, May, 1986, p. 164.

Review of *Half a Moon and One Whole Star, Kirkus Reviews*, February 15, 1986, p. 301.

Hearne, Betsy, review of *Further Tales of Uncle Remus: The Misadventures of Brer Rabbit, Brer Fox, Brer Wolf, the Doodang and Other Creatures, Bulletin of the Center for Children's Books*, May, 1990, pp. 218-19.

Hearne, Betsy, review of *Sam and the Tigers: A New Telling of Little Black Sambo, Bulletin of the Center for Children's Books*, July-August, 1996, p. 378.

Jordan, June, "A Truly Bad Rabbit," *New York Times Book Review*, May 17, 1987, p. 32.

Manna, Anthony L., "Reading Jerry Pinkney Reading," *Children's Literature Association Quarterly*, winter, 1991-92, pp. 269-75.

Moulton, Priscilla L., review of *The Adventures of Spider: West African Folk Tales, Horn Book*, October, 1964, pp. 496-97.

Pinkney, Jerry, "The Artist at Work: Characters Interacting with the Viewer," *Horn Book*, March-April, 1991, pp. 171-79.

Pinkney, Jerry, essay in *Children's Books and Their Creators*, edited by Anita Silvey, Houghton Mifflin, 1995, p. 527.

Pinkney, Jerry, "John Henry," *Horn Book*, January-February, 1996, pp. 32-34.

Pinkney, Jerry, interview in *Something about the Author*, Volume 41, Gale, 1985, pp. 164-74.

Pinkney, Jerry, essay in *Something about the Author Autobiography Series*, Volume 12, Gale, 1991, pp. 249-66.

Review of *Sam and the Tigers, Publishers Weekly*, August 5, 1996, p. 441.

Semrau, Ruth, review of *Black Cowboy, Wild Horses: A True Story, School Library Journal*, June, 1998, p. 113.

Shea, Betsy, review of *The Patchwork Quilt, New York Times Book Review*, October 20, 1985, p. 18.

Zeiger, Hanna B., review of *The Patchwork Quilt, Horn Book*, September-October, 1985, p. 546.

Zipes, Jack, "Power Rangers of Yore," *New York Times Book Review*, November 13, 1994, p. 30.

For More Information See

BOOKS

Children's Literature Review, Volume 43, Gale, 1997, pp. 144-76.

Holtze, Sally Holmes, essay on Pinkney in *Children's Books and Their Creators*, edited by Anita Silvey, Houghton Mifflin, 1995, pp. 526-28.

Sixth Book of Junior Authors and Illustrators, edited by Sally Holmes Holtze, Wilson, 1989, pp. 225-27.

PERIODICALS

American Artist, May-June, 1982.

American Visions, April, 1989, pp. 46-9.

Graphis, July-August, 1993, p. 89.

Horn Book, January-February, 1996, pp. 42-49.

Kirkus Reviews, March 1, 1999, p. 380; April 1, 1999, p. 533.

Publishers Weekly, February 22, 1999, p. 93.

School Library Media Activities Monthly, February, 1998, pp. 46-47.

Wilson Library Bulletin, April, 1989, pp. 92-93.

—*Sketch by Gerard J. Senick*

* * *

POWERS, Tim 1952-

Personal

Born February 29, 1952; son of Richard (an attorney) and Noel (Zimmerman) Powers; married Serena Batsford (a legal secretary), 1980. *Education:* California State University at Fullerton, B.A., 1976. *Religion:* Roman Catholic.

Addresses

Agent—Russell Galen, Scott Meredith Literary Agency, 845 Third Ave., New York, NY 10022.

Career

Writer.

Awards, Honors

Philip K. Dick Memorial Award, 1984, and Prix Apollo, c. 1984, both for *The Anubis Gates;* Locus Award, 1996, for *Expiration Date.*

Writings

FICTION

The Skies Discrowned, Laser, 1976, revised edition published as *Forsake the Sky,* Tom Doherty Associates, 1986.

An Epitaph in Rust, Laser, 1976, revised edition, NESFA Press (Cambridge, MA), 1989.

The Drawing of the Dark, Del Rey, 1979.

The Anubis Gates, Ace Books, 1983, limited edition illustrated by Mark Bilokur and Arnie Fenner, introduction by Ramsey Campbell, published by Mark V. Ziesling (Shingletown, CA), 1990.

Dinner at Deviant's Palace, Ace Books, 1985.

(With James P. Blaylock) *Axolotl Double A-1,* Axolotl, 1986.

Night Moves, introduction by Blaylock, Axolotl, 1986.

On Stranger Tides, Ace Books, 1987.

The Stress of Her Regard, Ace Books, 1989.

Last Call, Morrow, 1992.

Expiration Date, Tor, 1996.

Earthquake Weather, Tor, 1997.

OTHER

(With Richard B. Isaacs) *The Seven Steps to Personal Safety: How to Avoid, Deal with, or Survive the Aftermath of a Violent Confrontation,* illustrated by D. F. Bach, Center for Personal Defense Studies (New York), 1993.

Also author of the introduction to *The Selected Letters of Philip K. Dick, 1975-76,* six volumes, Underwood Books, 1992; author of introduction to *Sudden Fear: The Horror and Dark Suspense Fiction of Dean R. Koontz,* edited by Bill Munster, Borgo Press, 1988.

Sidelights

A two-time winner of the Philip K. Dick Memorial Award, science fiction and fantasy novelist Tim Powers writes surreal, quick-paced fantasy and science fiction novels with interesting young adult characters that appeal to teen readers. In many of his novels, including *The Anubis Gates* and *The Stress of Her Regard,* Powers deals with time travel, and these historical fantasies are often populated by authentic figures. He also favors fantastic episodes featuring supernatural and mythical characters and exhibits a penchant for the horrific, adventurous, and grotesque. "A Tim Powers science fiction novel never fails to titillate and elucidate with the dark and the bizarre," Sue Martin remarked in the *Los Angeles Times Book Review,* "and all with such original, eccentric color and style."

Powers won his first Dick award for his action-packed science fiction mystery and horror thriller *The Anubis Gates.* The novel details the adventures of Brendan Doyle, a twentieth-century English professor who travels to 1810 London to attend a lecture given by Samuel Taylor Coleridge, the English Romantic poet. When he is kidnapped by gypsies and consequently misses his return trip to 1983, the mild-mannered Doyle is forced to become a street-smart con man, escape artist, and swordsman, in order to survive in the dark and treacherous London underworld. He defies bullets, black magic, murderous beggars, freezing waters, imprisonment in mutant-infested dungeons, poisoning, and even a plunge back to 1684. Coleridge himself and Lord Byron make appearances in the novel, which also features a poor tinkerer who creates genetic monsters and a werewolf that inhabits others' bodies when his latest becomes too hairy.

The Anubis Gates met with an enthusiastic critical reception. Reviewers commended Powers's inventive and lively storyline and applauded his finesse in managing the twisting and jam-packed plot. In addition, critics praised his characters, especially his roguish beggars, whom they compared to some of the wretched characters of English novelist Charles Dickens. "Plotted with manic fervour, executed with exhilarating dexterity at breakneck speed," lauded Colin Greenland in the *Times Literary Supplement,* "*The Anubis Gates* is a virtuoso performance, a display of marvelous fireworks that illuminates everything in flashes, with scant afterglow."

Powers followed *The Anubis Gates* with *Dinner at Deviant's Palace,* a post-nuclear holocaust fantasy set in Los Angeles, California. The novel centers on a powerful "psychic vampire"—commandant of the foul nightclub Deviant's Palace—and his followers, who brainwash Los Angeles inhabitants and seize control of the entire city. Gregorio Rivas is a "redeemer," a member of a group out to reclaim the city, who sets out to save his former lover from the cult's sinister grasp. He barely escapes with his life after he encounters its alien, bloodthirsty demon leader. Radioactive wastelands and monstrous creatures, along with dark, underworld characters and spirits, round out the fantastic elements of *Dinner at Deviant's Palace.*

With his imaginative *On Stranger Tides,* Powers returned to historical fantasy. This novel traces the high-sea adventures of an eighteenth-century fortune-seeking young man, John Chandagnac. While traveling to the West Indies on a mission to retrieve his father's stolen inheritance, Chandagnac is shanghaied by the notorious pirate Blackbeard— now plagued with voodoo ghosts— and forced to join his band of zombie pirates. Captured too is a sorcerer with a fixation for matriarchs and a crazed widower who totes his wife's severed head in a box. With Chandagnac as gourmet chef, this motley crew ventures through the Caribbean and to a treacherous Florida swamp in search of the legendary Fountain of Youth. Their swashbuckling adventures lead them to encounters with ghosts, beach-strolling corpses, dancing

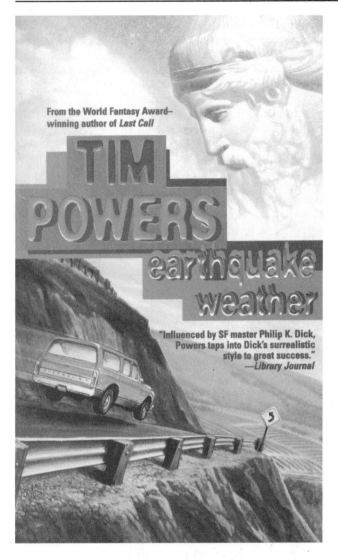

The final installment in Tim Powers's trilogy,
Earthquake Weather *blends elements of mysticism and
the supernatural as Janis Cordelia Plumtree and Koot
Hoomie attempt to reunite the body and spirit of the
dead Scott Crane. (Cover illustration by Michael
Koelsch.)*

dead chickens, animated plants, and finally to a watery
reservoir used to resurrect the dead. "Tim Powers has
written across the entire range of the literature of the
fantastic," declared Orson Scott Card in his *Washington
Post Book World* review, "but he is at his best when
writing gonzo historical novels ... like *On Stranger
Tides.*"

Powers's 1992 novel *Last Call* introduces the adolescent
hero Koot Hoomie Parganas, who is also featured in two
sequels, *Expiration Date* and *Earthquake Weather.* As
Expiration Date begins, "Kootie," as he is known,
breaks a statue in his parents' home. Inside he finds an
odd vial, sniffs it, becomes clairvoyant, and has a vision
that his birth parents were actually murdered by a man
named Sherman Oaks. Kootie runs away to Los Angeles
to find Oaks, a homeless person. Oaks and other
members of Los Angeles's secret addict community of

"ghost-eaters," who inhale disembodied spirits, want
Kootie's vial, which holds the ghost of Thomas Edison.
One of these spirit-junkies is Loretta deLarava, whose
late husband, a film producer, was murdered. Her two
adult stepchildren—one of them an electrical engineer
with several questions he would like to pose to Edison—
become involved in the quest for the valuable vial.

In his pursuit of Oaks, Kootie is tailed by Loretta, who
wishes to cover up the murder of her husband. Meanwhile, Edison's ghost retains a "spirited" personality,
and Kootie channels his voice when he ingests the
contents. Powers incorporates interesting details about
this fantastical spirit world and the human addicts who
delve into it, echoing some of *Alice in Wonderland*
author Lewis Carroll's novelistic devices. Powers's
ghosts adore palindromes, for instance—a word, phrase,
or even sentence that reads the same backwards as it
does left to right. Several suspenseful chase scenes are
followed by a showdown at the *Queen Mary,* a historical
ocean liner docked at Long Beach. Kevin S. Beach,
writing in *Voice of Youth Advocates,* asserted that
Powers's "creativity and originality are abundantly
apparent in this tale." *Booklist* reviewer Carl Hays
maintained: "Powers's quirky vision may baffle fans of
more conventional fantasy, but his colorful characters
and delightful sense of the absurd should continue to
attract new readers."

In *Earthquake Weather,* readers find the hero Kootie
nearing adulthood but confined indoors with a mysterious wound that will not heal. The wound could be a sign
that he is destined to succeed the Fisher King of the
West, the late Scott Crane, whose death was chronicled
in *Last Call.* Two mental-hospital escapees arrive at
Kootie's home, bringing him the well-preserved body of
Crane. One of the visitors, Janis Plumtree, is occasionally possessed by Crane's killer, Omar Salvoy, though she
is ostensibly diagnosed with multiple-personality disor-
der. Salvoy has the power to instigate earthquakes.
Plumtree is accompanied by Sid "Scant" Cochran, a
wealthy vintner incarcerated in the psychiatric hospital
after finding himself unable to deal with the death of his
wife, a woman who coincidentally died the same day as
Crane. The hospital is run by the treacherous Dr.
Armentrout, and here Powers offers the premise that
those whom society shuns—the mentally ill, the physically challenged, the destitute—actually possess supernatural powers that are tied in with the forces of nature.
As Scant Cochran discovers secrets from his own past
and Kootie emerges as the heir-apparent, "Powers
displays an intricate knowledge of viticulture, at least the
equal of his understanding of mythology and modern
culture," declared Tim Sullivan in the *Washington Post
Book World.* The critic lauded the book as "a work of
tatterdemalion brilliance." Writing for *Voice of Youth
Advocates,* John Peacock called *Earthquake Weather* "a
complex and exciting book, merging real places and
people with magic and fantasy in a seamless blend."

Works Cited

Beach, Kevin S., review of *Expiration Date, Voice of Youth Advocates,* August, 1996, p. 171.

Card, Orson Scott, review of *On Stranger Tides, Washington Post Book World,* October 25, 1988, p. 6.

Greenland, Colin, review of *The Anubis Gates, Times Literary Supplement,* July 5, 1987, p. 757.

Hays, Carl, review of *Expiration Date, Booklist,* January 1, 1996, p. 799.

Martin, Sue, review of *The Stress of Her Regard, Los Angeles Times Book Review,* August 27, 1989, p. 12.

Peacock, John, review of *Earthquake Weather, Voice of Youth Advocates, April,* 1998, pp. 58-59.

Sullivan, Tim, review of *Earthquake Weather, Washington Post Book World,* November 30, 1997, p. 6.

For More Information See

PERIODICALS

Kliatt, March, 1997, p. 20.

Library Journal, September 15, 1997, p. 106.

Publishers Weekly, December 18, 1995, p. 44.*

R

RADIN, Ruth Yaffe 1938-

Personal

Born October 8, 1938, in Hartford, CT; daughter of Simon M. and Molly A. Yaffe; married Sheldon H. Radin (a professor), June, 1960; children: one son, two daughters. *Education:* Hartford College for Women, A.A., 1958; Connecticut College for Women (now Connecticut College), B.A., 1960; Southern Connecticut State College, M.S., 1963. *Religion:* Jewish.

Career

Writer. Elementary school teacher in Meriden, CT, 1960-63, and Bethlehem, PA, 1963-66; Congregation Keneseth Israel, Allentown, PA, librarian, beginning 1982. Certified reading specialist, 1980.

Awards, Honors

American Library Association Notable Book and Reading Rainbow selection, both for *A Winter Place;* Books of the Year selection, Child Study Association of America, 1986, for *Tac's Island.*

Writings

FOR CHILDREN

A Winter Place, illustrated by Mattie Lou O'Kelley, Little, Brown, 1982.
Tac's Island, illustrated by Gail Owens, Macmillan, 1986.
Tac's Turn, illustrated by Owens, Macmillan, 1987.
High in the Mountains, illustrated by Ed Young, Macmillan, 1989.
Carver, illustrated by Karl Swanson, Simon and Schuster, 1990.
All Joseph Wanted, illustrated by Deborah Kogan Ray, Macmillan, 1991.
Sky Bridges and Other Poems, New Readers Press, 1993.
Morning Streets, illustrated by Helen B. Santelli, New Readers Press, 1993.

From the Wooded Hill, illustrated by Santelli, New Readers Press, 1993.

Adaptations

Sky Bridges and Other Poems has been adapted for audio cassette, New Readers Press, 1993.

Sidelights

Ruth Yaffe Radin is a librarian, teacher, and author of award-winning picture books such as *A Winter Place* and *High in the Mountains.* Radin's chapter books have also become popular, especially among reluctant readers. These include the popular "Tac" novels, *Tac's Island* and *Tac's Turn,* as well as *Carver,* the moving story of a blind boy's attempts to reintegrate into sighted society, and *All Joseph Wanted,* the story of a young boy whose greatest wish is that his mother be able to read. Radin is noted for handling difficult issues with a light, nondidactic hand, and for writing clear prose and authentic dialogue.

Radin was born in Hartford, Connecticut, and attended college in that state, ultimately earning her master's degree in 1963. Married in 1960, she and her husband make their home in Bethlehem, Pennsylvania, where she has worked as an elementary school teacher, reading specialist, and librarian. Taking the lessons of her educational trade to heart, and also influenced by the stories she read to her own three children, Radin began to write stories and impressionistic descriptions for young people.

Radin's debut book, *A Winter Place,* "speaks of the joys of simply being in the snowy mountains and skating and then coming home," noted Zena Sutherland of the *Bulletin of the Center for Children's Books.* In the story, a family sets out, skates in hand, to find a frozen pond among the frozen hills of farm country. They are searching for " ... a special place high in the hills for skating, not around a rink, but away, on blades that swerve," as Radin described their quest. Reviewing the work in *Booklist,* Ilene Cooper concluded that "lilting language and tranquil pictures combine to make a captivating book." Many reviewers commented on the artwork, by first-time illustrator Mattie Lou O'Kelley, "reminiscent of the best Grandma Moses," according to Daisy Kouzel in *School Library Journal.* A reviewer for *Publishers Weekly* felt that it is "difficult to separate Radin's ballad from O'Kelley's paintings as individual feats," and that the book appears to be created by a single gifted artist, "so tuned-in" is the art to the text.

Radin turned her hand to chapter books with her next work, *Tac's Island.* When ten-year-old Steve goes with his family to spend summer vacation on an island off the Virginia coast, he meets up with one Thomas Andrew Carter, Tac for short, a native Virginian who turns Steve's vacation into an extended adventure. Together the two boys explore the coast and its hidden treasures. Steve and Tac form a lasting bond during this summer, going crabbing together, helping to find a lost two-year-old, and winning free rides at a visiting carnival. "The unpretentious story moves quickly," Denise M. Wilms noted in *Booklist,* "and the boys weather occasional moments of tension in stride." Wilms concluded that the simplicity and "pleasant mood" make *Tac's Island* a good offering for reluctant readers, especially boys who can relate to the characters. A *Children's Book Review Service* contributor echoed these sentiments, concluding that the book should "appeal to reluctant readers and others who enjoy nature and its wonders." *Kirkus Reviews* called *Tac's Island* a "warm story about a short summer friendship which promises to last beyond vacation time," and noted also that Steve and Tac are "likable characters" who "complement each other nicely." Virginia Golodetz, writing in *School Library Journal,* dubbed the book "quiet and gently humorous," and noted especially the "authentic" dialogue and the "sparsely written narrative" that keeps the dialogue flowing.

Radin reprised these characters in a sequel, *Tac's Turn,* in which Tac travels from his familiar Virginia island to visit his new friend Steve at the latter's suburban home in Pennsylvania. Here Tac explores a way of life that is much different than his own. There is some initial tension between the boys as they sort out their fledgling friendship, but bike rides, fossil hunting, and a hot-air balloon adventure cement their friendship once again. "Radin shows insight into how a ten year old would feel spending his first week away from home," Blair Christolon observed in *School Library Journal.* But Tac also brings his common sense to the fore, counseling Steve on how to speak to parents when you're in the wrong. Christolon noted also that the first book in the series, *Tac's Island,* need not be read to appreciate these good friends. *Booklist*'s Wilms concluded that *Tac's Turn* is a "nice pick" for readers, particularly boys who are just breaking away from shorter stories.

Radin returned to the picture-book format in *High in the Mountains.* Ethel L. Heins, writing in *Horn Book,* called this work a "brief poetic text" with "luminescent paintings." Visiting her grandfather high in the Colorado Rockies, a child picks mountain wild flowers, climbs among the boulders, watches deer leap through the forest, and listens to the melody of a stream. Together, the girl and her grandfather camp out that night, following a twisting mountain road to the prize location. Ilene Cooper of *Booklist* offered a favorable assessment of *High in the Mountains,* asserting that "the art and narrative capture the majesty of the Colorado Rockies."

Carver marks a turn in Radin's writing toward more problem-centered stories. In this work, ten-year-old Jon has been blind since an accident eight years earlier. His father died in that same accident, and now Jon is back where he was born, going to school with sighted children for the first time. He finds a new friend, Matt, and through Matt hears about an old and bitter man named Carver. The old man has earned his name because of the lovely wooden birds he carves. It is Jon's ambition to also be able to carve decoys as his father once had. Resistant at first, Carver finally agrees to give the blind boy carving lessons, and eventually boy and man learn from each other; Jon's carving ultimately releases both him and his mother from their prolonged grieving. Constance A. Mellon noted in *School Library Journal* that *Carver* is told simply, in fine prose, and concluded that through Jon's tale, "readers learn gentle lessons about determination, the process of grieving, and the renewing powers of love." *Booklist*'s Deborah Abbott observed that the novel provides a good example of "intergenerational relationships," concluding that Radin offers a gentle message about the "importance of believing in oneself."

In *All Joseph Wanted,* Radin tells the story of an eleven-year-old whose one greatest desire is that his mother be able to read. Joseph is the oldest child of a hardworking dad, and he acutely feels the pressure of helping his illiterate mother cope with daily tasks such as reading simple directions on household products. When his mother tries to get a job, she is stymied because she cannot read the bus schedule. And when she resolves to learn to read, Joseph initially acts as her reluctant tutor. Finally, however, this responsibility is more than the young boy can bear, and his mother agrees to an adult literacy class. Reviewing the novel, Debra S. Gold commented in *School Library Journal* that "Radin portrays a contemporary issue in an honest, yet gentle voice and delineates the tension that evolves between mother and son." Betsy Hearne, writing in *Bulletin of the Center for Children's Books,* called the book "a warm picture of a working class family" and praised the "well-delineated and likable" characters. *Voice of Youth Advocates* contributor Judy Fink maintained: "Without being didactic, this short, well written, and easy-to-read novel, emphasizes the importance of knowing how to read in order to get a job and function in everyday life."

Radin has also written a series of easy poetry readers for primary graders, including *Sky Bridges and Other Poems, Morning Streets,* and *From the Wooded Hill.* Employing simple language and easy rhyming patterns, along with familiar situations, these books entice young readers into the world of verse.

In all of her work, Radin has shown that sincere and even hard-hitting messages need not be sacrificed at the easy-reader level. In her chapter books and picture books, she utilizes straightforward narrative devices and relies heavily upon authentic-sounding dialogue to carry the story. Her characters, including Steve and Tac, Jon and Joseph, are well drawn and memorable, and appeal, as many reviewers have noted, especially to the reluctant readers among young boys.

Works Cited

Abbott, Deborah, review of *Carver, Booklist,* May 15, 1990, p. 1805.

Christolon, Blair, review of *Tac's Turn, School Library Journal,* January, 1988, p. 76.

Cooper, Ilene, review of *A Winter Place, Booklist,* September 15, 1982, p. 118-19.

Cooper, Ilene, review of *High in the Mountains, Booklist,* March 1, 1989, p. 1195.

Fink, Judy, review of *All Joseph Wanted, Voice of Youth Advocates,* December, 1991, pp. 317-18.

Gold, Debra S., review of *All Joseph Wanted, School Library Journal,* January, 1992, p. 116.

Golodetz, Virginia, review of *Tac's Island, School Library Journal,* August, 1986, p. 96.

Hearne, Betsy, review of *All Joseph Wanted, Bulletin of the Center for Children's Books,* November, 1991, p. 73.

Heins, Ethel, review of *High in the Mountains, Horn Book,* September-October, 1989, p. 615.

Kouzel, Daisy, review of *A Winter Place, School Library Journal,* September, 1982, p. 110.

Mellon, Constance A., review of *Carver, School Library Journal,* July, 1990, p. 78.

Radin, Ruth Yaffe, *A Winter Place,* Little, Brown, 1982.

Radin, Ruth Yaffe, *High in the Mountains,* Macmillan, 1989.

Sutherland, Zena, review of *A Winter Place, Bulletin of the Center for Children's Books,* January, 1983, p. 95.

Review of *Tac's Island, Kirkus Reviews,* March 1, 1986, p. 388.

Review of *Tac's Island, Children's Book Review Service,* spring, 1986, p. 132.

Wilms, Denise M., review of *Tac's Island, Booklist,* May 1, 1986, p. 1316.

Wilms, Denise M., review of *Tac's Turn, Booklist,* October 1, 1987, p. 323.

Review of *A Winter Place, Publishers Weekly,* July 9, 1982, p. 49.

For More Information See

PERIODICALS

Kirkus Reviews, October 15, 1991, p. 1348.

New York Times Book Review, February 13, 1983, p. 30.

Publishers Weekly, April 14, 1989, p. 68.

Reading Time, March, 1983, p. 716; October, 1983, p. 62; January, 1990, p. 324; May, 1991, p. 672; May, 1993, p. 692.

School Library Journal, September, 1989, p. 232.

Times Educational Supplement, February 18, 1983, p. 30.*

—*Sketch by J. Sydney Jones*

REYNOLDS, C. Buck 1957-

Personal

Full first name Carolyn; born August 19, 1957, in San Francisco, CA; daughter of Keith E. (a biomedical engineer) and Barbara (a classical piano teacher; maiden name, Ray) Buck; married Michael R. Reynolds (an attorney), August 2, 1980; children: Ryan, Colin. *Education:* University of California, Berkeley, B.A., 1979. *Hobbies and other interests:* Hiking, family activities, painting "cave art" on rocks.

Addresses

Home—1127 Park Hills Rd., Berkeley, CA 94708. *Agent*—Kendra Marcus, 67 Meadow View Rd., Orinda, CA 94563. *Electronic mail*—cbuckart@aol.com.

Career

Buck Art, Berkeley, CA, owner, graphic artist, and illustrator, 1986—. *Member:* Society of Children's Book Writers and Illustrators.

Illustrator

Physiology of the Eye, 2nd edition, Butterworth-Heinemann, 1992.

World Geography and Culture, Globe Fearon, 1994.

Gordy Slack, *I Wish I Could ... Walk with the Dinosaurs* ("I Wish I Could" series), Roberts Rinehart (Niwot, CO), 1997.

Slack, *I Wish I Could ... Buzz with the Bugs,* Roberts Rinehart, 1998.

Work in Progress

Research on ice-age animals and life.

Sidelights

C. Buck Reynolds told *SATA:* "I become very involved in the paintings I create, not only in telling a story but in drawing the viewer into that created world. I strive for accuracy in my art, but also to impart the sense of wonder and beauty I find in nature, from whole worlds to tiny bugs."

* * *

RHUE, Morton
See STRASSER, Todd

ROBINSON, Lynda S(uzanne) 1951-
(Suzanne Robinson)

Personal

Born July 6, 1951, in Amarillo, TX; daughter of George H. Measley and Lois Ann (a school nurse; maiden name, Womack) Heavener; married Wessley I. Robinson (a school administrator), August 10, 1973. *Education:* San Jacinto Junior College, A.A., 1971; Rice University, B.A. (magna cum laude), 1973; University of Texas at Austin, Ph.D., 1984.

Addresses

Home—San Antonio, TX. *Office*—P.O. Box 700321, San Antonio, TX 78270-0321.

Career

Writer. *Member:* Mystery Writers of America, Sisters in Crime, Romance Writers of America, Phi Beta Kappa.

Writings

HISTORICAL ROMANCE NOVELS; UNDER NAME SUZANNE ROBINSON

Heart of the Falcon, Bantam, 1990.
Lady Gallant, Bantam, 1992.
Lady Hellfire, Bantam, 1992.
Lady Defiant, Bantam, 1993.
Lady Valiant, Bantam, 1993.
Lady Dangerous, Bantam, 1994.
Lord of Enchantment, Bantam, 1994.
Lord of the Dragon, Bantam, 1995.
The Engagement, Bantam, 1996.
The Rescue, Bantam, 1998.
The Treasure, Bantam, 1999.

"LORD MEREN" HISTORICAL MYSTERY NOVELS

Murder in the Place of Anubis, Walker, 1994.
Murder at the God's Gate, Walker, 1995.
Murder at the Feast of Rejoicing, Walker, 1996.
Eater of Souls, Walker, 1997.
Drinker of Blood, Mysterious Press, 1998.

Sidelights

Lynda S. Robinson is the author of two lines of historical novels: under the name Suzanne Robinson (Suzanne is the author's middle name) she has written historical romances set in periods ranging from the medieval to the Victorian, and using her first name she has been lauded as the author of historical mysteries set in the days of ancient Egypt. Robinson's interest in history stems from her educational background, which also helped her writing. "I feel that my graduate work in anthropology (with a subdiscipline of archaeology) provided an ideal background for writing," she once commented. "It helped me develop research skills and the ability to understand and recognize the importance of differing cultural values and the paramount importance

Suzanne Robinson
AUTHOR OF *THE ENGAGEMENT*

He was the last man she'd ever expect to come to...

The Rescue

"An author with star quality...Spectacularly talented."
—*Romantic Times*

At the center of Lynda S. Robinson's romance novel, written by the author under the name Suzanne Robinson, is the aristocratic Miss Primrose Dane—on the run after witnessing a murder—and a rogue called Nightshade, the reformed master thief who has been commissioned to find her. (Cover illustration by Alan Ayers.)

of culture and language in shaping individual beliefs and character."

Robinson has enjoyed success with her novels set in old Britain, in which she sometimes blends farce and humor with romance and adventure. In *Lord of Enchantment,* for example, Penelope Fairfax lives alone on an island off the coast of England. She has been banished by her family because of her disturbing powers of precognition. One day, she discovers a wounded man who turns out to be an agent of Queen Elizabeth I. She nurses him back to health; however, since he has lost his memory, both he and Penelope are unaware that he is being pursued by the Queen's enemies. Robinson adds humorous moments with scenes played by Penelope's silly servants. In another romance, *Lord of the Dragon,* set in medieval times, a heroine who has been rejected by her suitor takes revenge on men by disguising herself as a bandit who forces otherwise noble knights to strip naked.

Although the humor in some of these books sometime backfires—a *Publishers Weekly* critic remarked that "too much slapstick [in *Lord of Enchantment*] undercuts what might have been a compelling story"—reviewers have noted with pleasure the historical touches in these books. It is this aspect of Robinson's work that has made her "Lord Meren" series so compelling to many critics and other readers. These mystery books are set in the unlikely age of the reign of Pharaoh Tutankhamen in Egypt. By choosing this setting, Robinson has created for herself the daunting task of not only writing interesting murder mysteries, but also of making her setting realistic and her characters, who live in a culture very alien from ours, believable and sympathetic.

The hero of these mysteries, Lord Meren, is the trusted counselor and devoted subject of the Pharaoh. Along with his intelligent adopted son, Kysen, Meren finds himself investigating unusual murders entangled in court intrigue, family squabbles, and, sometimes, spiritual mysticism. In their debut adventure, *Murder in the Place of Anubis,* Meren and Kysen must learn who killed a despised scribe named Hormin and left his body in a sacred embalming room. Critics found the story to be a promising opener to the series. *Wilson Library Bulletin* contributor Gail Pool especially praised Robinson's historical depictions: "It is difficult to achieve credibility on such foreign soil, but Robinson succeeds . . . . [S]he smoothly works ancient Egyptian mores and beliefs into descriptions, dialogue, and observations. In the intelligent, thoughtful, dignified Meren . . . Robinson creates a fine guide to the culture of old Egypt."

Meren's investigations continue in *Murder at the God's Gate* and *Murder at the Feast of Rejoicing,* the latter of which has been compared to an English country-house mystery. In this case, during a party at Lord Meren's estate, two of his guests are murdered. As he and Kysen try to solve the murders so that the family name does not fall into disrepute, the reader also learns more about Meren and a tragedy in his past from which he has never been able to fully recover. "Lord Meren is sensitively developed," commented *School Library Journal* writer Cynthia Rieben, who added that Robinson leaves out enough about Meren's character to keep him interesting for more books to come. This "fascinating tale of court intrigue and familial squabbling will delight both history and mystery buffs," concluded Margaret Flanagan in *Booklist.*

With *Eater of Souls,* the fourth Lord Meren book, Robinson begins a trilogy within her series. The trilogy involves Meren's investigation into the possibility that Queen Nefertiti, the wife of Tutankhamen's predecessor, did not die of natural causes. In *Eater of Souls,* however, Meren is sidetracked by the murders of people whose bodies are torn apart and whose hearts have apparently been eaten. The rumor is that the victims were killed by Ammut, a goddess who is part lion, part hippo, and part crocodile. Of course, if the killings are indeed from a divine spirit, Meren is powerless to stop them, but the Egyptian detective suspects the murderer is actually a mortal. The problem grows worse when a Hittite prince

dies, making the series of killings both a criminal and diplomatic quandary.

Robinson not only juggles Egyptian history and murder plots in *Eater of Souls,* but also mythology and, as Meren's young daughters get involved in the storyline, teenage concerns that many younger readers can relate to. According to one *Kirkus Reviews* critic, *Eater of Souls* displays the "author's powers of invention and intrigue at their peak." And Tom Pearson, writing in *Voice of Youth Advocates,* declared that "Robinson has an encyclopedic knowledge of Egyptian history and mythology, and a sure touch when it comes to plot and characterization. Lost times and places spring to vivid life at her bidding."

Works Cited

Review of *Eater of Souls, Kirkus Reviews,* April 15, 1997, p. 594.

Flanagan, Margaret, review of *Murder at the Feast of Rejoicing, Booklist,* January 1, 1996, p. 798.

Review of *Lord of Enchantment, Publishers Weekly,* November 14, 1994, p. 64.

Pearson, Tom, review of *Eater of Souls, Voice of Youth Advocates,* April, 1998, p. 50.

Pool, Gail, "Murder in Print," *Wilson Library Bulletin,* May, 1994, pp. 86-87.

Rieben, Cynthia, review of *Murder at the Feast of Rejoicing, School Library Journal,* May, 1996, p. 150.

For More Information See

PERIODICALS

Kirkus Reviews, December 1, 1993, p. 1492; January 1, 1996, p. 28.

Library Journal, February 1, 1994, p. 115.

Publishers Weekly, August 14, 1995, p. 77; April 7, 1997, p. 77; December 22, 1997, p. 57.

School Library Journal, August, 1997, p. 188.

*   *   *

ROBINSON, Suzanne
See ROBINSON, Lynda S(uzanne)

*   *   *

ROSE, Malcolm 1953-

Personal

Born January 31, 1953, in Coventry, England; son of Reg (a machine tool fitter) and Kathleen (a receptionist; maiden name, Robinson) Rose; married Barbara Anne (a teacher), August 2, 1975; children: Colin Mark. *Education:* University of York, B.A., 1974, D.Phil., 1978. *Politics:* "Listing to the left." *Hobbies and other interests:* Science, sports, music, and hill walking.

Malcolm Rose

Addresses

Agent—Juvenilia, Avington, Winchester, Hampshire, England S021 1DB.

Career

University of Liverpool, Liverpool, England, post-doctoral research fellow in department of organic chemistry, 1977-79, biochemistry department, 1979-81, senior experimental officer in department of biochemistry, 1981-83; Sheffield City Polytechnic, Sheffield, England, lecturer in analytical chemistry, 1983-86, senior lecturer, 1986-87; Open University, England, lecturer in chemistry, 1988-96; freelance writer, 1996—. Parent governor of local school. *Member:* Fellow, Royal Society of Chemistry; Scattered Authors' Society.

Awards, Honors

Angus Book Award, 1997, for *Tunnel Vision.*

Writings

Rift, Collins (London), 1985.

The Highest Form of Killing, Andre Deutsch, 1990, published with an additional chapter by Harcourt Brace Jovanovich (San Diego), 1992.
Son of Pete Flude, Andre Deutsch, 1991.
The Obtuse Experiment, Scholastic (London), 1993.
The Smoking Gun, Scholastic (London), 1993, published in the United States as *Formula for Murder,* Scholastic (New York), 1994.
Concrete Evidence, Scholastic (London), 1995.
The Alibi, Scholastic (London), 1996.
Tunnel Vision, Scholastic (London), 1996.
Circle of Nightmares, Scholastic (London), 1997.
Flying Upside Down, Scholastic (London), 1998.
Breathing Fear, Scholastic (London), 1999.

"LAWLESS AND TILLEY" SERIES

The Secrets of the Dead, Scholastic (London), 1997.
Deep Waters, Scholastic (London), 1997.
Magic Eye, Scholastic (London), 1998.
Still Life, Scholastic (London), 1998.
Fire and Water, Scholastic (London), 1998.
Lethal Harvest, Scholastic (London), 1999.
Flying Blind, Scholastic (London), 1999.

Rose's novels *The Alibi, Concrete Evidence,* and *The Smoking Gun* were published as *The Malcolm Rose Collection: Three Degrees of Murder,* Scholastic (London), 1997; also the author of numerous short stories for young adults; Rose's novels have been published in German, Spanish, Catalan, Danish, French, Greek, and Italian.

Work in Progress

Plague, a thriller set in Milton Keynes, England, involving a biological virus.

Sidelights

Malcolm Rose is the prolific author of young-adult suspense novels that often use science to solve the quandaries presented. An instructor in chemistry for many years, Rose's moonlight career as an author of realistic teen fiction proved so successful that he eventually left his teaching post to devote his days to writing on a full-time basis. Rose told *SATA:* "I was born in Coventry, England, in 1953 and began writing stories as a hobby while taking a Ph.D. in chemistry at York University. Writing fiction was my escape from real life. My then girlfriend (now wife) was taking a subsidiary course on children's literature. At one point she read one of my efforts and commented that I ought to try to get it published. I had never thought of writing as anything other than a hobby. Besides, as I thought then, a budding chemist couldn't possibly be any good at it! Anyway, I joined a writers' club to find out how to submit a manuscript and, to cut a long story short, found a publisher in William Collins for my first novel, *Rift.*"

Published in 1985, *Rift* focuses upon Neil, an adolescent in the north of England who has been left home alone for the weekend by his parents—a time-frame during which he unlocks his own supernatural powers. Though Neil has dreamt of physical romance, he also has visions of ghastly events. After his friends hold a seance at his home, Neil attends a theater performance, and the trip home on a bus is waylaid by an industrial accident involving a tanker truck and some deadly acid spillage. The bus driver gets out to investigate, and dies gruesomely. Neil must save the passengers by driving the bus, whose tires have been eaten by the acid, backwards down a hill. Bits and pieces of this trauma have already appeared to him in visions and at the seance. In the midst of this weekend Neil finds romance with a fellow student, and some very bad British-Isles' weather adds to the drama. Jane Woodley, reviewing *Rift* for *School Librarian,* remarked that in this debut work, "[Rose's] inexperience is hardly discernible," and his background in science "provides a technical expertise in the important denouement of the tale." A *Junior Bookshelf* reviewer described Neil's experiences as a "cocktail of horrors," but questioned the suitability of some sexual themes for the book's intended adolescent audience. Finally, a critic for *Growing Point* described the climax of *Rift* as the defining place where "action and temperament come together with unmistakable reality."

Another of Rose's novels with sophisticated themes for young adults, *The Highest Form of Killing* centers on the animal-rights movement and a government cover-up. Once again, Rose's knowledge of chemistry informs the plot, which opens with the discovery of a dead, mutilated dog on the beach. The couple who have found it immediately vanish, but a nearby resident, Mark, saw them being trundled into separate vans. Just before her abduction, the woman managed to phone her brother Derek, a chemistry professor. In turn, Derek enlists Sylvia, a former student of his who is now interning at what turns out to be a top-secret chemical-weapons development facility. Mark, Sylvia's ex-boyfriend and witness to the incident on the beach, joins them to solve the mystery. As *The Highest Form of Killing* progresses, both men compete for Sylvia's affections while all attempt to solve the couple's disappearance and discover why one of Sylvia's co-workers commits suicide with a mysterious vial of a deadly chemical called T42 found near his body.

Catherine M. Dwyer, reviewing the work for *Voice of Youth Advocates,* remarked that though "the premise here is exciting ... readers hoping for a taut suspense novel may be disappointed," which she blamed on too many clever coincidences of plot. In contrast, Lyle Blake Smythers of *School Library Journal* found *The Highest Form of Killing*'s plot well-constructed, while Roger Sutton, in a review for *Bulletin of the Center for Children's Books,* maintained that the author's prose is infused with "a melodramatic quality," but granted that "the story is taut in all the right places [and] the pace is terrific."

The Obtuse Experiment, Rose's next book for teen readers, is set in the near future on board a school cruise for a class outing of juvenile delinquents. A nefarious government minister has conveniently planned for the vessel to run into an iceberg and sink with all inhabitants

to the bottom of the North Sea. A group of aliens, whose mission is to right the wrongs of history before they occur, learn of the ultraconservative political plot and attempt to halt the impending disaster. Rose incorporates serious political themes into the action-adventure tale, which left *School Librarian* reviewer Mike Hayhoe wondering "about the ethical boundaries ... between fiction and propaganda written for adolescent readers." Hayhoe found the group of misfits inadequately characterized, except for a few passages that show off "Rose's more complex talent."

Rose returned to the subject of teens who live on the margins of British society for his 1996 novel *Tunnel Vision.* In this work, Pat, a charismatic youth leader, has covertly laid the foundation for a white-supremacist, apocalyptic cult behind his innocuous "Fellowship" group. Pat's true intent is suspected by Maria, a teen still traumatized by strife in her Central African homeland. Maria becomes friends with Joel, a victim of disfiguring leprosy, who is involved in the Fellowship. Their interracial friendship suddenly puts Joel on shaky ground within the controlling framework of the youth

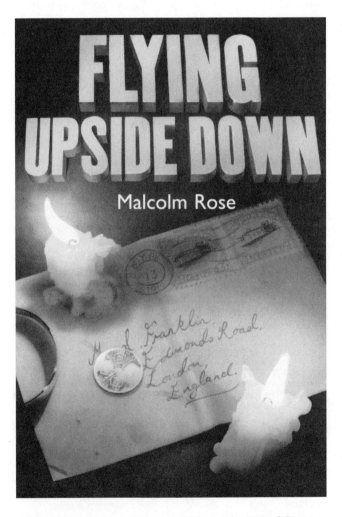

The rising number of teen suicides in the United States motivated Rose to write this young-adult thriller about what happens when two boys who are being bullied at school are threatened in their own homes as well.

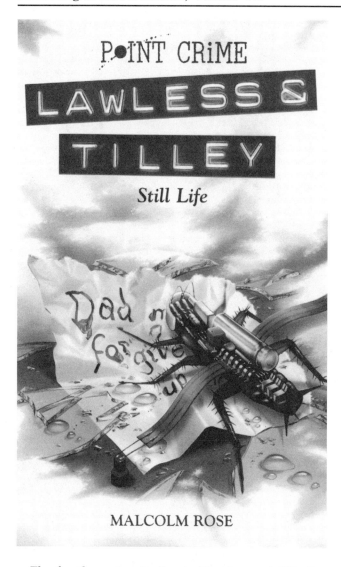

The fourth mystery in Rose's "Lawless and Tilley" series, **Still Life** *presents sleuths Brett and Clare with the daunting challenge of solving the kidnapping of a little girl who has been taken from the woods near her home.*

group. Joel and another Fellowship member are being trained by Pat for a national youth sporting event, and as the plot unfolds the teens uncover a bomb plot to destroy the Sheffield stadium where the event is to be held. Adrian Jackson, reviewing *Tunnel Vision* for *Books for Keeps,* found it "a tense, thought-provoking thriller." Lavishing praise upon both plot and characterization, a critic in *Junior Bookshelf* noted how "the plotting is economical ... and the action can be readily seen to arise out of skillful characterization." Helen Allen, writing in *School Librarian,* found the methods by which the Fellowship lured misfit teens "only too credible and the reader is made aware of how vulnerable people are seduced, sometimes literally, by such organizations."

Malcolm Rose underscores his writing with the investigative and analytical tools he practiced as a lecturer in chemistry. Describing the parallels between chemistry

and writing thrillers, Rose told *SATA:* "Until 1996, I was a lecturer in chemistry at the Open University of the United Kingdom. I carried out research in the fields of chemical aspects of cot death [Sudden Infant Death Syndrome] and the analysis of drugs, and I taught mainly organic chemistry. This job left very little time for writing fiction, which I did mostly after midnight. Perhaps that's why my strongest scenes were set on dark nights! Having put aside my test-tubes and picked up a pen, I am now a full-time writer. In other words, I used to add chemicals together, brew them up a bit and see what happened, but now I mix fictional characters, stir in a bit of conflict and see what happens. Hopefully, either can be explosive! Both are investigations and I have always liked investigating things. I write thrillers and crime stories mainly, highlighting the forensic science that lurks behind police investigations, but my next book is just as likely to be a comedy.

"Many people think it odd and fascinating that a scientist should also be a novelist. In fact, at the Open University there are three scientists who are published novelists. Beside myself, there is a physicist and a biologist, both of whom have been very successful. I do not find it so strange. After all, scientists do write a lot; in particular, they produce textbooks and papers on their research. They also have to be creative and show perseverance to carry out research. Anyone who can stick to a task, is imaginative, and knows how to construct a sentence has the credentials for writing a novel. In addition, my chemical research is aimed at understanding a little better some aspect of human life. A novel also seeks to illuminate some aspect of human life. The aims are similar although the tools are different.

"I now live in Milton Keynes with my wife and teenage son who always read and offer critical comments on my stories before publication. That's a good hint for the next generation of writers. It may be a bit embarrassing at first but reading a story aloud to a small supportive audience is an excellent way of checking its flow and whether the dialogue sounds realistic.

"I get ideas from several places. Newspaper and magazine articles gave me the idea of the smart gun featured in *The Secrets of the Dead.* Also, reports of teenage suicides were the motivation behind my book on bullying, *Flying Upside Down.* When I write, I always listen to music—the louder, the better. A line from a lyric can give me the inspiration for a whole book. This happened with a novel about racism called *Tunnel Vision,* which came from a line in an Asian rap song. Also the ideas for *Son of Pete Flude* and its sequel, *Breathing Fear,* came from songs. Indeed, both books are set in the music industry. My own interest in science fuels many of my stories. Perhaps the most obvious of these is *The Highest Form of Killing* on the topic of chemical and biological warfare. Science often lies behind my crime stories: the baddies using poisons and explosives, the goodies using forensic science. Frequently, I am motivated by outrage. The use of chemistry to kill people in warfare, racist attacks, suicide after bullying, and new weapon development have been perverse inspiration. I am not sufficiently naive that I believe I can solve big problems by writing about them in a novel, but at least I can raise awareness. That is one of my main aims: to make a reader think while he or she is being entertained. And that is why I write for teenagers. Young people have open minds that are receptive to new ideas—probably more so than us boring old adults!"

Works Cited

Allen, Helen, review of *Tunnel Vision, School Librarian,* May, 1996, p. 76.

Dwyer, Catherine M., review of *The Highest Form of Killing, Voice of Youth Advocates,* December, 1992, p. 285.

Hayhoe, Mike, review of *The Obtuse Experiment, School Librarian,* August, 1993, p. 123.

Jackson, Adrian, review of *Tunnel Vision, Books for Keeps,* May, 1996, p. 17.

Review of *Rift, Growing Point,* July, 1985, p. 4471.

Review of *Rift, Junior Bookshelf,* October, 1985, p. 234.

Smythers, Lyle Blake, review of *The Highest Form of Killing, School Library Journal,* October, 1992, p. 146.

Sutton, Roger, review of *The Highest Form of Killing, Bulletin of the Center for Children's Books,* October, 1992, p. 52.

Review of *Tunnel Vision, Junior Bookshelf,* April, 1996, p. 89.

Woodley, Jane, review of *Rift, School Librarian,* December, 1985, p. 359.

For More Information See

PERIODICALS

Books for Keeps, November, 1990, p. 12; July, 1993, p. 28.

School Librarian, November, 1990, p. 160.

Times Educational Supplement, October 11, 1985, p. 26; May 10, 1996, p. 8.

*   *   *

RUSSELL, Ching Yeung 1946-

Personal

Born March 7, 1946, in Guangdong, China; daughter of Ming-Kee (a tailor) and Chui-Bing (Chan) Yeung; married Phillip K. Russell (a social worker), July 4, 1971; children: Jonathan, Jeremy. *Education:* Hong Kong Baptist University, B.A., 1971. *Hobbies and other interests:* Travel, crabbing, reading, walking.

Addresses

Office—P.O. Box 482, Summerville, SC 29484-0482. *Electronic mail*—prussell@dycon.com.

Career

Teacher of seventh-grade Chinese literature and history in Hong Kong; member of public library staff, Summer-

Ching Yeung Russell

ville, SC; writer. *Member:* Society of Children's Book Writers and Illustrators, Authors Guild.

Awards, Honors

Parents' Choice Award, 1994, Charlotte Award, New York State Reading Association, 1996, Charlie May Simon Book Award Master List citation, Arkansas Elementary School Council, 1996, and Nene Award (Hawaii), 1997, all for *First Apple.*

Writings

A Day on a Shrimp Boat, photographs by Phillip K. Russell, Sandlapper Publishing, 1993.

First Apple, illustrated by Christopher Zhong-Yuan Zhang, Boyds Mills Press, 1994.

Water Ghost, illustrated by Zhang, Boyds Mills Press, 1995.

Lichee Tree, illustrated by Zhang, Boyds Mills Press, 1997.

Moon Festival, illustrated by Zhang, Boyds Mills Press, 1997.

Child Bride, illustrated by Jonathan T. Russell, Boyds Mills Press, 1999.

First Apple has been translated into Japanese.

Work in Progress

Six in a Bed and *The Healing,* middle-grade novels; *Ching Ming Festival, Dragon Boat Festival,* and *Someone Stole All My Water,* picture books; *Good-bye Hong Kong,* poetry.

Sidelights

The author of several novels for young readers set in the China of her youth, Ching Yeung Russell has won acclaim for her contribution to multicultural children's literature and portrayals of life in a small, rural Chinese town that retains much of its age-old, family-centered culture. Born in 1946, the author was a small child when Communist leader Mao Tse-tung came to power in 1949. She told *SATA:* "I grew up in a small town in southeastern China, separated from my parents and younger siblings, who had moved to Hong Kong. During that time, I was raised by my uncles and my maternal grandmother. When I was finally reunited with my family at age twelve, my siblings and cousins loved to hear of my adventures in my small town, where I could have the freedom to roam wherever I wanted, something they had never experienced in the bustling, cosmopolitan colony of Hong Kong." At the time of Russell's youth, Hong Kong was still a possession of the British crown, and not part of Communist China. "My small-town adventures fascinated my 'citified' siblings and cousins," Russell continued. "They were even willing to give me their snacks or do my chores if I would tell them of my exploits. I began writing and submitting stories and poems to the Chinese-language newspapers and magazines, many of which were published. My first story, for which I was paid four dollars, was published right after I arrived in Hong Kong. In college, I majored in Chinese literature, never imagining that I would ever need to use English, much less write stories or books in English.

"After I married an American and emigrated to the United States, I decided to learn how to write in English about my adventures growing up in China, so that my husband and children could read what I wrote. I figured that American children would also be fascinated by the escapades of a young girl growing up in a faraway land and in another time. I wrote and submitted manuscripts for more than ten years before Boyds Mills Press offered me a contract."

Russell, who lives in the coastal area of South Carolina, had her first publishing success with *A Day on a Shrimp Boat,* a work that features photographs by her husband, Phillip K. Russell. The next year, Russell finally achieved publication for *First Apple,* which is set in a small, rural Chinese town. In this work, readers are introduced to nine-year-old Ying Yeung, who lives in mainland China with a grandparent, as Russell did as a child. When Ying learns that her grandmother, Ah Pau, has never tasted an apple—such a fruit was a rare and expensive commodity in South China at the time—she resolves to earn the money to buy one for Ah Pau's seventy-first birthday. In the process she has her hard-earned apple stolen, inadvertently commits theft herself,

and makes a new friend. Susan DeRonne, writing for *Booklist,* deemed *First Apple* "a sweet story with a moral," but posited that some of the too-similar names of family members might confuse younger readers. A *Bulletin of the Center for Children's Books* assessment from Susan Dove Lempke echoed that criticism, but found that Russell "conveys the rural Chinese village setting and details of everyday life well," and that Ying is "a likable, energetic young heroine." *First Apple* was also translated for publication in Japan, and won critical acclaim there, as well.

Water Ghost presents Ying with another challenge. She still lives with Ah Pau, and has an occasional conflict with her cousin Kee. But *Water Ghost* centers on the aftermath of the death of one of their classmates, a disabled, orphaned girl who has died in an accidental drowning. The impoverished child had stolen money from a student who was going to pay for a school trip, and Ying was initially accused of the theft. Now she feels tremendous guilt, and when she passes the girl's grandmother, who is selling a dead chicken at the market, she buys the fowl with money she has earned from selling chicken fences at the market that day. Ying's family berates her for wasting the money. Lauren Peterson of *Booklist* called *Water Ghost* a "compelling drama," one whose themes are driven by "ancient Chinese superstitions and the universal need to fit in." *School Library Journal* contributor Carla Kozak found "some awkwardness" in Russell's prose, with its "cadence reminiscent of Chinese," but granted that the distinct style "somehow increases the authenticity" of *Water Ghost.*

Ying's story continues in Russell's next three books, *Lichee Tree, Moon Festival,* and *Child Bride.* In *Lichee Tree,* a fruit tree planted in Ying's honor several years earlier is finally bearing fruit. Ying hopes to sell the lichee fruit at the market and earn enough money to travel to the big city of Canton for a treat. But a wealthy villain wishes to make Ying's cousin Ah So one of his concubines, and when Ah So runs away to escape this fate, the villain takes revenge upon the entire family by seizing their property—including Ying's beloved tree. "More complex than Russell's earlier books, this new title is valuable for its engaging heroine and its unique setting," maintained Margaret A. Chang in *School Library Journal.* Writing for *Bulletin of the Center for Children's Books,* Amy E. Brandt found Russell's tale interesting for its "rich cultural specifics," which include feasts of mudsnails, and declared: "Ying's determination is irrepressible." *Moon Festival* also features Ying and her life in southeastern China, but has no crisis as part of its plot; instead it follows Ying and her friends as they participate in the annual fall festival of the moon. Paper lanterns, celebratory meals, and offerings to a female deity are some of the events that Russell and illustrator Christopher Zhong-Yuan Zhang depict for readers. In *Child Bride,* Ying's paternal grandmother informs Ying that she is to be married immediately, and Ying has no choice in the matter. Feeling helpless, Ying runs away and embarks upon a series of exciting adventures. A *Kirkus Reviews* contributor commented, "the wealth of cultural detail, the curious facts, and vivid descriptions ... will keep readers engaged."

"All of my novels—*First Apple, Water Ghost, Lichee Tree,* and *Child Bride*—have been drawn from my childhood in China," Russell told *SATA.* "The heroine who appears in each of them, Ying Yeung, is me. I plan to write a couple more books and finish my stories in China. Then I will write stories about my life in Hong Kong. I have also written picture books about some Chinese festivals and holidays. Like most successful writers, I have tried to write about what I know best. I plan to translate all of my books into Chinese someday.

"I enjoy learning about other cultures and people's everyday lives in faraway lands. That's why I love to travel. I also like to walk on the beach, and I love to eat all seafood, including conch, squid, and fish with their heads still on. My favorite activities besides traveling are crabbing and shrimping. Living near Charleston, South Carolina allows me to indulge in these passions often."

Works Cited

Brandt, Amy E., review of *Lichee Tree, Bulletin of the Center for Children's Books,* April, 1997, pp. 294-95.

Chang, Margaret A., review of *Lichee Tree, School Library Journal,* June, 1997, pp. 127-28.

Review of *Child Bride, Kirkus Reviews,* February 1, 1999, p. 229.

DeRonne, Susan, review of *First Apple, Booklist,* November 1, 1994, p. 501.

Kozak, Carla, review of *Water Ghost, School Library Journal,* December, 1995, p. 108.

Lempke, Susan Dove, review of *First Apple, Bulletin of the Center for Children's Books,* January, 1995, p. 177.

Peterson, Lauren, review of *Water Ghost, Booklist,* October 15, 1995, p. 405.

For More Information See

PERIODICALS

Booklist, March 15, 1997, p. 1243; September 15, 1997, p. 236.

School Library Journal, September, 1994, p. 222; April, 1999, p. 141.

S

SCAGELL, Robin 1946-

Personal

Name is pronounced "Scad-jell"; born December 14, 1946, in Blackburn, Lancashire, England; son of Alfred Gordon (a television retailer) and Ina Muriel Scagell; married Sally Patricia Peace (a college lecturer), March 26, 1994. *Education:* Watford College, Higher National Certificate in Applied Physics. *Religion:* Atheist. *Hobbies and other interests:* Astronomy, glow worms, photography.

Addresses

Home—1 Milverton Drive, Ickenham, Uxbridge, Middlesex UB10 8PP, England. *Electronic mail*—galaxypix@compuserve.com.

Career

Kodak Research Laboratory, Harrow, England, research assistant, 1965-69; Manchester University, Manchester, England, photographer/astronomer, 1970-71; Marshall Cavendish Publishers, London, England, 1973-92; Galaxy Picture Library, Uxbridge, England, 1992—. *Member:* Society for Popular Astronomy (vice president), British Astronomical Association, Royal Astronomical Society.

Writings

(With Mike Wilson) *Jet Journey,* Marshall Cavendish, 1978.

How to Be an Astronomer, illustrated by David Mallot and Ron Hayward, Silver Burdett (Morristown, NJ), 1981, Macdonald Educational, 1982, revised edition published as *Astronomy for Starters,* George Philip (London), 1989.

City Astronomy, Sky Publishing (Cambridge, MA), 1994, published as *Astronomy from Towns and Suburbs,* George Philip, 1994.

Space Explained: A Beginner's Guide to the Universe, Henry Holt (New York), 1996, published as *Space: An Accessible Guide That Really Explains the Universe,* Marshall (London), 1997.

The New Book of Space, illustrated by Richard Rockwood and Ian Thompson, Copper Beech (Brookfield, CT), 1997.

Stargazing with a Telescope, George Philip, 1999.

Sidelights

Robin Scagell told *SATA:* "A lifelong amateur astronomer, I have been a writer and broadcaster full time since 1992, as well as running Galaxy Picture Library, a photo agency devoted to astronomy and space. Being close to London and available during the day, I often get asked to comment on astronomy and space for the media. I enjoy photographing the sky and even from light-polluted suburban London I can still take photographs that are worth publishing.

"A sideline of mine is glow worms, which I became interested in around 1990. I have been running an ongoing survey of these magical insects since 1991, and often get asked to help conserve colonies of glow worms that are threatened by developments."

For More Information See

PERIODICALS

Booklist, January 15, 1995, p. 883; December 1, 1996, p. 658.

Sky and Telescope, May, 1995, p. 52.

* * *

SEIDEN, Art(hur)

Personal

Born in Brooklyn, NY; son of Frank and Rose Seiden; married Beatrice Rabin (an artist), August 4, 1947; children: Jessica Mae Seiden-Scully. *Education:* Attend-

Art Seiden

ed Pratt Institute and the Art Students League; B.A. (cum laude), Queens College, 1974. *Politics:* Republican.

Addresses

Home and office—Woodmere, NY.

Career

Artist, illustrator. Guest instructor, New York City Community College. *Exhibitions:* National Academy of Design. Seiden's work has also been featured in many American Watercolor Society shows, and is represented in the Kerlan Collection of the University of Minnesota, the Mazza Collection, the Jane Zimmerli Museum of the University of Rutgers, the University of Southern Mississippi, and the University of Connecticut. *Military Service:* U.S. Army, 1942-1945. *Member:* Lotos Club, Society of Illustrators, Artists Fellowship, Art Students League, American Watercolor Society.

Awards, Honors

Best Books for Children, American Institute of Graphic Artists, 1953, for *My ABC Book,* 1956, for *The Story of Noah's Ark,* and 1958, for *Counting Rhymes.*

Writings

AUTHOR AND ILLUSTRATOR

My ABC Book, Grosset & Dunlap, 1953, Putnam, 1983.
The Story of Noah's Ark, Grosset & Dunlap, 1956.
Counting Rhymes, Grosset & Dunlap, 1958.
Little Bunny Learns Colors, Random House, 1982.
Tick-Tock, Putnam, 1982.
Trucks, Platt & Munk (New York), 1983.

ILLUSTRATOR

Alf Evers, *The Little Engine That Laughed,* Grosset & Dunlap, 1950.
Jean Horton Berg, *Three Mice and a Cat,* Wonder Books, 1950.
Jean Horton Berg, *The Noisy Clock Shop,* Wonder Books, 1950.
Snow White and the Seven Dwarfs, Grosset & Dunlap, 1955.
Shannon Garst, *The Picture Story and Biography of Red Cloud,* Follett (Chicago), 1965.
Gladys E. Cook, *Big Book of Cats,* Putnam, 1965.
Lawrence H. Feigenbaum and Kalman Seigel, *This Is a Newspaper,* Follett, 1965.
Joan Potter Elwart, *Animal Babies,* Whitman (Racine, WI), 1966.
Solveig Paulson Russell, *A White Sweater Must Be White,* Grosset & Dunlap, 1967.
Ann McFerran, *The Big and Little Book of ABC's,* C. R. Gibson (Norwalk, CT), 1969.
Phyllis Goldman and Grace Jaffe, *Whatever Happened to Yes?,* Walker (New York), 1970.
John Randolph, *Fishing Basics,* Prentice-Hall (Englewood Cliffs, NJ), 1981.
Janet Chenery, *1 Nose, 10 Toes,* Grosset & Dunlap, 1981.
Lorna Slocombe, *Sailing Basics,* Prentice-Hall, 1982.
Tim Wilhelm and Glenda Wilhelm, *Bicycling Basics,* Prentice-Hall, 1982.
Michael Shows off Baltimore, Outdoor Books (Baltimore, MD), 1982.
Hal Hellman, *Computer Basics,* Prentice-Hall, 1983.
Patricia W. Romero and others, *Tippet Shows off Washington,* Outdoor Books, 1983.
Fred McMane, *Track and Field Basics,* Prentice-Hall, 1983.
Edith T. Kunhardt, *All Kinds of Trucks,* Golden Books, 1984.
Lawrence Stevens, *Computer Programming Basics: An Introduction for Young People,* Prentice-Hall, 1984.
Carl Laron, *Electronics Basics: An Introduction for Young People,* Prentice-Hall, 1984.
Lawrence Stevens, *Computer Graphics Basics,* Prentice-Hall, 1984.
Carl Laron, *Computer Software Basics,* Prentice-Hall, 1985.
Mary Blocksma and Dewey Blocksma, *Easy-to-Make Water Toys That Really Work,* Prentice-Hall, 1985.
Henry F. Halstead, *Boating Basics,* Prentice-Hall, 1985.
Lawrence Stevens, *Laser Basics,* Prentice-Hall, 1985.
Bob Goldberg, *Diving Basics,* Prentice-Hall, 1986.
Mary Blocksma and Dewey Blocksma, *Space-Crafting: Invent Your Own Flying Spaceships,* Prentice-Hall, 1986.

Joanna Randolph Rott and Seli Groves, *How on Earth Do We Recycle Glass?,* Millbrook (Brookfield, CT), 1992.

Helen Jill Fletcher and Seli Groves, *How on Earth Do We Recycle Paper?,* Millbrook, 1992.

Rudy Kouhoupt and Don Marti, Jr., *How on Earth Do We Recycle Metal?,* Millbrook, 1992.

Barry Wilner, *Soccer,* Raintree Steck-Vaughn (Austin, TX), 1994.

Mark Alan Teirstein, *Baseball,* Raintree Steck-Vaughn, 1994.

Dave Raffo, *Football,* Raintree Steck-Vaughn, 1994.

Tom Withers, *Basketball,* Raintree Steck-Vaughn, 1994.

Bert Rosenthal, *Track and Field,* Raintree Steck-Vaughn, 1994.

Lisa Harris, *Hockey,* Raintree Steck-Vaughn, 1994.

John Francis, *Bicycling: How to Play the All-Star Way,* Raintree Steck-Vaughn, 1996.

Thomas J. Nardi, *Karate and Judo,* Raintree Steck-Vaughn, 1996.

Barry Wilner, *Swimming: How to Play the All-Star Way,* Raintree Steck-Vaughn, 1996.

Seymour Brody, *Jewish Heroes and Heroines of America: 150 True Stories of American Jewish Heroism,* Lifetime Books (Hollywood, FL), 1996.

Diane Silcox-Jarrett, *Heroines of the American Revolution: America's Founding Mothers,* Green Angel Press, 1998.

Sidelights

Art Seiden has illustrated numerous books for young people, ranging from the simplest picture books—with little or no accompanying text—for children, to craft and hobby books for young adults. A representative effort in the first category is *Trucks,* a board book collection of a dozen drawings of different kinds of trucks, geared to appeal to preschoolers. The colors used and the amount of detail included are ideal for the comprehension and enjoyment of "toddlers fascinated by large vehicles," according to a critic for *Booklist.* In the category of children's hobby books are two by Mary and Dewey Blocksma, *Easy-to-Make Toys That Really Work* and *Space-Crafting: Invent Your Own Flying Spaceships.* In both instances, the authors were praised for fulfilling the promise of their titles, aided by Seiden's clear drawings illustrating the step-by-step instructions. Seiden's illustrations also enhance the presentation of Diane Silcox-Jarrett's *Heroines of the American Revolution,* a collection of short biographies of women who participated in the war that created the United States of America. Specifically, according to Evelyn Butrico, writing in *School Library Journal,* Seiden's illustrations "set the time and place and enliven the text," making this "an attractive offering" for early elementary social studies units.

Seiden told *SATA:* "I have been illustrating children's books since 1951 and love doing picture books. My aim is to identify with young children; that is why all my illustrations are very easy to understand. I don't like to fill the page with unimportant details that have no relationship to the underlying story.

"This is one thing that many new, young illustrators fail to understand. Parents buy the books but children have to comprehend what they're looking at . . . . New book illustrators [often work] too realistically; many of the artists used to be magazine illustrators and treat each spread in the book as if adults will be reading it."

Works Cited

Butrico, Evelyn, review of *Heroines of the American Revolution, School Library Journal,* August, 1998, p. 155.

Review of *Trucks, Booklist,* November 1, 1983, p. 424.

For More Information See

PERIODICALS

Horn Book, August, 1984, pp. 500-01; September, 1985, pp. 575-76.

School Library Journal, February, 1984, p. 63; March, 1987, p. 153; July, 1992, p. 82.

*   *   *

SEMEL, Nava 1954-

Personal

Born September 15, 1954, in Israel; daughter of Itzhak (a veteran member of Knesset, Israel's parliament) and Margalit (Liquornik) Artzi; married Noam Semel (a theater director), September 2, 1976; children: Iyar, twins Eal-Eal and Nimdor. *Education:* Tel Aviv University, B.A., 1980, M.A., 1988. *Religion:* Jewish.

Nava Semel

Addresses

Home—11a Achimeir St., Ramat Gan 52587, Israel. *Office*—Institute for the Translation of Hebrew Literature, P.O. Box 10051, Ramat Gan 52001, Israel. *Electronic mail*—rawe@infomall.co.il.

Career

Israeli TV, Tel Aviv, production assistant, 1971-72; Galey Zahal (Army Radio), Jaffa, Israel, news producer, 1972-74; "The Culture Show," Israeli TV, Tel Aviv, production assistant, 1975-76; Hed Arzi (record company), Ramat Gan, Israel, record producer, 1976-78; Beth Hatefutsoth (Museum of Jewish Diaspora), Tel Aviv, mobile exhibitions director, 1979-80; *Kolbo* (newspaper), Haifa, Israel, art critic, 1981-88; *Women* magazine, Tel Aviv, columnist, 1989-92; *Studio Art* magazine, Tel Aviv, art critic, 1989-93; Israel *Gallery Guide,* Tel Aviv, art critic, 1994-96; freelance writer, translator of plays, and lecturer on literature, 1996—. Board member, Massuah Institute for Holocaust Studies, and Women's Counseling Center. *Military service:* Israeli Defense Forces (IDF), news producer for IDF Radio, 1972-74. *Member:* PEN International, Israeli Playwrights Association, Israeli Screenwriters Association, Association of Writers and Musicians of Israel, Hebrew Writers Association, Israeli Children's Authors Association.

Awards, Honors

Award from Massuah Institute for Holocaust Studies, 1988, for *A Hat of Glass;* Haifa Award, 1988, and Omanuty La'am (Art for the People) Award, 1990, both for *The Child Behind the Eyes;* National Jewish Book Award, 1991, for *Becoming Gershona;* Israeli Prime Minister Award for Literature, 1996; award for best illustrated book, Israel Museum, 1998, for *Who Stole the Show.* Semel has also received literary grants from the Haifa Culture Foundation, the Wheatland Foundation, the Tel Aviv Foundation, and the America-Israel Culture Foundation.

Writings

FOR CHILDREN; IN ENGLISH TRANSLATION

Gershonah shonah, Am Oved (Tel Aviv), 1985, published in the U.S. as *Becoming Gershona,* translated by Seymour Simckes, Viking, 1990.
Moris Havivel Melamid La-uf, Am Oved, 1990, published in the U.S. as *Flying Lessons,* translated by Hillel Halkin, Simon & Schuster, 1995.

UNTRANSLATED WORKS

Poems of Pregnancy & Birth, Sifriyat po'alim (Tel Aviv), 1982.
Kova zekhukhit: Okovets sipurim shel ha-dor ha-sheni, Sifriyat po'alim, 1985.
Yeled me-aohore ha-enayim, [Tel Aviv], 1988.
Rali masa maotara, Am Oved, 1993.
Ishah al ha-neyar, Am Oved, 1996.
Who Stole the Show, Yediot Achronot (Tel Aviv), 1997.
Liluna, Yediot Achronot, 1998.

Night Poems, Sifriyat po'alim, 1999.

WORKS FOR THE STAGE

An Old Lady (children's play), produced at the Haifa Municipal Theater, 1984.
The Child Behind the Eyes (drama), produced at the Haifa Municipal Theater, 1987.
Qong-Gey the Bell Child (libretto), to be produced at the National Youth Theater.

OTHER

Contributor to *Ha'aretz Book Review* and other Israeli magazines. *Flying Lessons* and *Becoming Gershona* have been translated and published in several European languages; *The Child Behind the Eyes* has been translated and broadcast as a radio play in several languages; other of Semel's works are slated for translation into other languages.

Work in Progress

A Girl in the Dark, "a book about a Holocaust survivor grandmother who tries to reveal her past horrors to her Israeli granddaughter," and *Duty Free,* "a novel about an Israeli man who leaves his country in search of an alternative homeland for the Jewish people."

Sidelights

The author of several books and plays for adults and children, Israeli writer Nava Semel draws heavily upon her experiences growing up in a new nation. Semel was born in Israel in 1954 to Itzhak and Margalit Artzi, both European refugees of World War II and the Holocaust. Her father, active in the Zionist movement that worked toward creating the independent nation of Israel, would eventually be elected a member of the Knesset, the country's parliament; her mother Margalit survived Auschwitz, one of Nazi Germany's concentration camps in Poland.

Semel's family lived in Tel Aviv, then a young city built on the shores of the Mediterranean. Like nearly every other young adult in Israel, Semel spent two years in the army as part of the country's compulsory military service for both men and women. During that time, she produced radio reports for Galey Zahal (Army Radio), then worked as a television production assistant and record producer before earning a degree in art history from Tel Aviv University in 1980. Along the way, she also married a theatrical director, Noam Semel, and gave birth to the first of their three children. Semel began writing art criticism for newspapers and magazines while pursuing her master's degree, and has continued to do so while penning award-winning plays and books for adults and children.

Semel's first published effort, loosely translated as *Poems of Pregnancy & Birth,* was released in 1982. She also wrote a number of short stories that were collected in the 1985 volume *A Hat of Glass* (published only in Hebrew). Many of the stories in *Hat of Glass* deal with themes and issues related to the Holocaust, but as experienced by the children of survivors, including the author herself. By the time her book *Becoming Gershona* became one of the first young-adult novels from Israel to be published in America in English translation, Semel was living in New York City with her family after her husband was posted there as a cultural attaché for Israel.

Semel told *SATA:* "I began 'writing' stories even before I knew how to read and write, by simply telling them to whoever was willing to listen. My childhood, in a small white city on the beach of the Mediterranean called Tel Aviv, was filled with family stories, and not just my own strange family saga. I was constantly surrounded by people who poured into Israel from the four corners of the world, speaking incredible languages and carrying so many personal fates.

"Like my parents, who immigrated from post-Holocaust Europe, people were united by a dream to start a new page in Jewish history in an independent state, though the Hebrew language was a 'sleeping beauty' for 2,000 years.

"I am a typical child of the 1950s, driven by an ambition to achieve a real Israeli identity and become a part of the new generation. Our parents' hopes, sometimes unrealistic ones, were laid on our shoulders.... We were supposed to compensate for the horrors of the past.

"As I grew up and began my writing career, these people and their sad stories became my central literary theme. I finally found the courage to look into the shadow of the Holocaust that haunted not only my own mother, who survived the most horrendous place called Auschwitz, but my whole country."

During World War II, Nazi Germany's systematic attempt to eradicate or deport the entire Jewish population of Europe resulted in the concentration-camp genocide of six million Jews. There had already been a movement underway for a Jewish "homeland," or refuge nation, where any Jewish person could be granted citizenship, but the push for nationhood began in earnest with the emaciated survivors who managed to walk out of the death camps hidden across Eastern Europe at the end of the war. Many of these people made up the adult population of Israel while Semel was a young girl in Tel Aviv. In turn, their children were roughly the same age as Israel itself, a nation founded in 1948.

Becoming Gershona, Semel's first book for young adults, had originally been published in Hebrew in 1985 as *Gershonah shonah.* Five years later it was translated into English by Seymour Simckes and published by Viking. Semel told an American newspaper, the *Jewish Advocate,* that even as late as the 1980s there was no literature that addressed Israel's second generation and their secondhand experiences of the Holocaust. "I was told that writing about it would ruin my career," Semel told Sylvia Rothchild about the publication of *A Hat of Glass.* Her generation had a particular set of hopes and dreams pinned upon it as a result of the war. "We were brought up to break the old stereotype. We were told that we had to build a totally new identity, a new model that had no connections to the Jews of Eastern Europe. We were a blank page, Israelis, born out of nowhere," Semel told the *Jewish Advocate.* Her first young-adult novel explores this matter.

Becoming Gershona tracks one summer in the life of Gershona, an adolescent in 1958 Tel Aviv, as she discovers much about herself and her family. Semel recreates many details that vividly recall life in the new nation in the 1950s, such as food rationing, an absence of trees or grass, and radio broadcasts that intoned names of Holocaust refugees whose families were still searching for them. Yet there is also a mood of great hope and optimism during this time, with new settlers arriving daily. One of them is Gershona's new neighbor, a boy named Nimrod, upon whom she develops a crush. She also struggles with teasing by other children in her neighborhood, who call her "Gershona primadonna." For refuge she scales the stairs to her apartment building's rooftop, where she tends to her beloved pot of radishes.

Gershona's family presents another set of difficulties, however. Her mother, a concentration camp survivor with blue numbers tattooed on her arm, is fiercely overprotective of her daughter. Furthermore, Gershona's grandfather, who has lived in America since the 1920s, inexplicably arrives in Tel Aviv. Gershona learns that 35 years before, he had abandoned his wife and son, who is Gershona's father. Now he is blind, and he and Gershona develop a special bond of friendship. She takes him for walks and describes the sights of the new nation to him.

Elizabeth Gleick, assessing *Becoming Gershona* in the *New York Times Book Review,* gave warm praise to Semel's portrayal of the new nation as well as the Holocaust survivors who created it. Gleick also lauded *Becoming Gershona* as a sympathetic coming-of-age tale. "This story of a young girl's attempts to unravel the unfathomable familial and social knots in her life seems real and immediate—reassuringly so," noted the reviewer. "In the spirit of the young adult genre novels, Gershona finds herself at the end of this book with new knowledge, welcome and unwelcome." Ellen Mandel, writing for *Booklist,* declared *Becoming Gershona* a book for "exceptional readers ... able to appreciate Semel's rich language." *Horn Book* critic Hanna B. Zeiger called the work "a moving portrait of people in a unique time and place in history."

Flying Lessons is the second of Semel's books for young adults to be published in English translation. Centering on another Israeli girl in the 1950s, the novel presents one year in the life of Hadara, who lives with her widowed father, a citrus grower, in a rural Israeli village. Frequently left alone, forlorn Hadara befriends the local shoemaker, Monsieur Maurice Havivel. He is a North-African Jew who tells Hadara that on his home island of Djerba, off the coast of Tunisia, Jews can fly. He also tells her that shoes should never be separated from one another, that they are more attached to one another than are two people in love. He promises to teach Hadara how to fly, and she dreams of becoming a celebrity as the first and only girl in Israel who can do so.

As the growing season progresses, a drought threatens the citrus crop. Arele, a classmate of Hadara's whom she has mistreated because he stutters, is fascinated with the science of citrus agriculture. The woman who owns the only shop in town, a fearsome busybody named Tova, woos Hadara's father. Believing she is indeed ready to fly—despite Monsieur Maurice's cautions—Hadara jumps out of the highest tree in her father's diminishing grove, hoping to reach the clouds and make it rain. Instead she breaks her leg, and Arele must now help her get around. Maurice Havivel, who is haunted by the mountain of children's shoes he once saw, disappears one day. But Hadara realizes that she has instead learned "to fly with both feet on the ground."

Flying Lessons was translated into several European languages. A *Publishers Weekly* commentator called the novel a "deeply moving work" that "weaves dreamlike images and innocent profundity into a coming-of-age-tale of great power." Hazel Rochman of *Booklist* commended Hillel Halkin's translation as "clear and lyrical," noting that "what comes across best is the sense of daily life" in the citrus-growing area of Israel in the 1950s. Liz Rosenberg, reviewing the book for the *Washington Post Book World,* called it "a delicate, sweet, haunting story of the coming-of-age of one ... girl whose hopes, griefs and desires describe a larger world."

Semel continued to *SATA:* "The painful dialogue between parents and their children is a subject I am returning to again and again. How is our present life affected by whatever happened before we were born? Is it possible to open up to each other after such tragedies? Where does the real power of survival come from?

"Writing is the process of digging deep into my soul, like moving up and down in a mysterious elevator. Through my characters and plots I find myself confronting the dark corners of myself—shame, guilt and fears. But once a book is finished, I find out to my amazement that my secret ability to enjoy the precious gifts of life is also being tested. Therefore, I'm grateful for whatever I have and cherish it every day of my life.

"Children are the main protagonists in my books, even in those works which are targeted toward adults. I identify with a child's innocence and wondrous gift to observe reality with truthfulness, frankness, and honesty, which grown-ups unfortunately lose sometimes. Gershona reveals her family secrets and discovers that questions about love, loyalty, and abandonment have more than one answer. Hadara wishes to fly far away from her loneliness and fear of death. Yotam, a boy suffering from Down's Syndrome, still sees the world as a magical place and touches the hearts of his family with his unconditional love."

Yotam is the hero of the monodrama *The Child Behind the Eyes,* first produced at the Haifa Municipal Theater in 1987. Translated into English, it became a radio drama for the British Broadcasting Corporation, and enjoyed successful onstage theater runs in New York City, Nantucket, Massachusetts, and several cities in the U.K. The drama was inspired by a friend of Semel's, a woman who had a son afflicted with a form of mild mental retardation known as Down's Syndrome. The play opens during the middle of the night as Yotam's mother awakens in worry over the events of the coming day, when her son will begin his first day of school. Over the course of the pre-dawn hours, she recalls his birth and the reactions of family and friends to the news of her new baby's disability. She remembers her own mixed emotions to her son as well. Reviewers called *The Child Behind the Eyes* a tear-jerker, but not melodramatic or overly sentimental. It was selected to represent Israel in the 1987 international drama competition, the Prix Italia.

Semel told *SATA:* "In a way, I am also still a child who isn't satisfied with the reality taking place in front of my eyes, seeking other meaning hidden behind it. I always hope to reach a reader who still believes in deep, profound relationship and in the power of the human touch to embrace us, soothe our pain and provide perhaps the only reason for our existence. As long as such a reader exists somewhere, I will keep on writing."

Works Cited

Review of *Flying Lessons, Publishers Weekly,* July 17, 1995, p. 230.

Gleick, Elizabeth, review of *Becoming Gershona, New York Times Book Review,* September 30, 1990, p. 39.

Mandel, Ellen, review of *Becoming Gershona, Booklist,* September 1, 1990, p. 48.

Rochman, Hazel, review of *Flying Lessons, Booklist,* August, 1995, p. 1942.

Rosenberg, Liz review of *Flying Lessons, Washington Post Book World,* March 10, 1996, p. 6.

Rothchild, Sylvia, interview with Semel, *Jewish Advocate,* January 26, 1989, p. 11.

Zeiger, Hanna B., review of *Becoming Gershona, Horn Book,* January-February, 1991, p. 70.

For More Information See

PERIODICALS

Bulletin of the Center for Children's Books, November, 1995, p. 105.

Five Owls, July-August 1990, p. 109.

Horn Book, March-April, 1996, p. 200.

School Library Journal, July, 1990, p. 78; November, 1995, p. 122.

Voice of Youth Advocates, December, 1990, p. 288; December, 1995, p. 310.

SHANNON, David 1959-

Personal

Born October 5, 1959, in Washington, DC; son of Roger (a radiologist) and Martha Shannon; married Heidi (a voice-over artist), 1988; children: Emma. *Education:* Art Center College of Design, B.F.A., 1983.

Career

Author and illustrator of children's books.

Awards, Honors

Best Books, *School Library Journal,* 1998, and "Bulletin Blue Ribbons 1998," *Bulletin of the Center for Children's Books,* 1999, both for *No, David!*

Writings

AUTHOR AND ILLUSTRATOR

How Georgie Radbourn Saved Baseball, Blue Sky/Scholastic, 1994.
The Amazing Christmas Extravaganza, Blue Sky, 1995.
A Bad Case of Stripes, Blue Sky, 1998.
No, David!, Blue Sky, 1998.
David Goes to School, Blue Sky, 1999.

ILLUSTRATOR

Isaac Asimov, *Robbie,* Creative Education, 1989.
Asimov, *Franchise,* Creative Education, 1989.
Asimov, *All the Troubles of the World,* Creative Education, 1989.
Asimov, *Sally,* Creative Education, 1989.
Julius Lester, *How Many Spots Does a Leopard Have? And Other Tales,* Scholastic, 1989.
Rafe Martin, *The Rough-Face Girl,* Putnam, 1992.
Jane Yolen, *Encounter,* Harcourt, 1992.
Rafe Martin, *The Boy Who Lived with the Seals,* Putnam, 1993.
Mark Shannon, *Gawain and the Green Knight,* Putnam, 1994.
Jane Yolen, *The Ballad of the Pirate Queens,* Harcourt, 1995.
Roger Culbertson, *African Folktales,* Running Press, 1995.
Audrey Wood, *The Bunyans,* Blue Sky/Scholastic, 1996.
Jane Yolen, *Sacred Places,* Harcourt, 1996.
Robert D. San Souci, *Nicholas Pipe,* Dial, 1997.

Sidelights

Children's author and illustrator David Shannon worked for a number of years as an editorial illustrator in New York City not long after receiving an undergraduate degree in fine arts. His work appeared in some of the most widely read publications in North America, including the *New York Times* and *Time* magazine. Shannon provided the pictures for works by such noted authors as Isaac Asimov, Jane Yolen, and Robert D. San Souci, and has also written and illustrated several books himself.

David Shannon

Shannon first illustrated several stories by Isaac Asimov that were published in 1989. His next project was Julius Lester's *How Many Spots Does a Leopard Have? And Other Tales,* a collection of Lester's adaptations of traditional African and Jewish folk tales. "The Wonderful Healing Leaves" and "Why the Sun and the Moon Live in the Sky" are two of the dozen stories presented in this compilation. For the tales that are set in Africa, Shannon created images with "rich, warm, earth tones [that] are particularly evocative," maintained *School Library Journal* contributor Kay McPherson. A critic for *Publishers Weekly* termed the book's artwork "striking . . . as full of depth as the stories themselves."

Shannon provided the illustrations for another adaptation, *The Rough-Face Girl,* Rafe Martin's version of an Algonquin folktale. The story features a Cinderella-type title character with scars on her face and arms that are the result of her enforced duties as tender of her family's fire at their home on the shores of Lake Ontario. Every young woman in the Rough-Face Girl's community wishes to become the bride of the Invisible Being, but only the one to whom he is visible can achieve the honor. Her vicious sisters try to prove that they have witnessed his presence, but are exposed as frauds; the Rough-Face Girl, however, has seen the Invisible Being and his accouterments in the natural world around her. In a *School Library Journal* assessment, Susan Scheps called the cover portrait, showing both the title charac-

In his self-illustrated Caldecott Honor Book **No, David!**, *Shannon appeals to the hearts and minds of young children—and the adults who love them—who know first-hand what it's like to be admonished for breaking house rules.*

ter's scars and beauty, "stunning," and found that the inside illustrations "embody the full flavor of the story." A *Publishers Weekly* reviewer praised Shannon's "meticulous research" into Algonquin culture, and commended the "powerful, stylized figures and stirring landscapes." Carolyn Phelan, reviewing *The Rough-Face Girl* for *Booklist,* termed the illustrations "striking and often rich in atmosphere."

Shannon illustrated a second Rafe Martin retelling, *The Boy Who Lived with the Seals.* The work won praise for its presentation of the Chinook legend of a young boy who wanders away from his parents one day, and finds a home with a band of seals in the Pacific Northwest. His parents are saddened, thinking their son gone forever, but one day hear about a boy who lives among the seals, and they steal him away in the dark of night. Shannon's drawings depict the boy's difficult readjustment to human culture and his newfound sense of isolation from the community of his birth. Janice Del Negro, writing for *Booklist,* found *The Boy Who Lived with the Seals* "grippingly illustrated," and praised Shannon for integrating the beauty of Chinook artistic traditions. "His striking acrylic paintings impressively conjure the drama and conflict of the story," added Del Negro. *Horn Book* reviewer Mary M. Burns called Shannon's images

"haunting," and found his pages "reminiscent in their storytelling quality of dramatic murals."

Shannon also provided illustrations for acclaimed children's author Jane Yolen's 1992 book *Encounter,* which depicts the landing of Christopher Columbus on the island of San Salvador, as told through the eyes of a Taino Indian boy. As the story opens, the boy dreams that the coming ships will bring harm to his people, but his Taino elders ignore the boy's warnings. Shannon's drawings show the youth being captured into slavery by Columbus's men, and the ultimate fulfillment of his foreboding dream. This "visionary style," declared a *Publishers Weekly* critic, "is an ideal complement" for Yolen's prose. The commentator added that Shannon's "atmospheric illustrations are of heroic proportions and full of contrast."

Shannon and Yolen teamed up for another book, *The Ballad of the Pirate Queens,* Yolen's lyrical recounting of a true story about the only two women among the dozen outlaws aboard a pirate ship in 1720. When the ship is attacked by a governor's vessel, Anne Bonney and Mary Reade battle the enemy singlehandedly, while the men drink and play cards below deck. All are captured, however, and Bonney and Reade escape the hangman's noose by claiming they are pregnant. A critic for *Publishers Weekly* termed Shannon's illustrations "ironic in their stateliness" with "a sly humor" that helped make the book "offbeat and grimly amusing." Helen Gregory, writing for *School Library Journal,* praised the "depth of [Shannon's] art," which she termed "reminiscent of great classic illustrators working in oil, especially N. C. Wyeth."

Shannon has also collaborated with his brother, drawing the images to accompany Mark Shannon's retelling of the age-old tale of an honorable warrior in *Gawain and the Green Knight.* Based on a Celtic myth, the story presents young, inexperienced Gawain impressing the knights of King Arthur's Round Table by taking up a monstrous intruder's challenge to chop his head off. Gawain succeeds, but the Green Knight simply picks up his own head before departing, reminding Gawain that according to the terms of their agreement, they will meet again in a year's time for another duel. The book follows Gawain's journey to the appointed meeting place and the various challenges he faces along the way, with one variation on the original plot. Hazel Rochman, writing for *Booklist,* asserted that "the glowing, sophisticated paintings ... express the demonic drama of the story."

Continuing the folk-tale theme of his previous artistic endeavors, Shannon penned realistic, full-color drawings for Audrey Wood's *The Bunyans,* a 1996 book that follows an entire family of fictional giants across North America. The Bunyans carve out canyons and construct the Rocky Mountains with their frolic; a famed hot-water geyser in Wyoming has its origins here as Mrs. Bunyan's hot-water faucet. "Better than the text is the BIG artwork," noted Ilene Cooper in *Booklist,* remarking that "this is where most of the humor is." Shannon also illustrated another fable, *Nicholas Pipe,* modernized by renowned reteller Robert D. San Souci. San Souci recounts an old twelfth-century tale about the title creature, a half-man/half-fish, who lives on land but must touch the sea daily to survive. Nicholas falls in love with Margaret, a fisherman's daughter, whose brother was thought to have been killed by merfolk; because of this, her father forbids her to speak to Nicholas. Though the merman saves both father and daughter during a storm, the fisherman turns Nicholas over to the authorities, and although he is carted away far from the sea, love wins out in the end. "Shannon's stunning acrylic paintings are fitting to this powerful story," asserted *School Library Journal* contributor Beth Tegart, while a *Publishers Weekly* critic called *Nicholas Pipe* "a stylish collaboration."

Shannon has also written and illustrated several books himself. The first of these was the children's novel *How Georgie Radbourn Saved Baseball,* the story of the villainous Boss Swaggert, a former major-league baseball star who suffered a slump, was booed off the field, and as a result has made it his life's work to eradicate the sport from the planet. He does this by becoming a rich and powerful media mogul, and even has the President arrested for throwing the first pitch of the season opener. With baseball outlawed, spring ceases to arrive, and the world is one long winter where former ballparks are now prisons for anyone who utters baseball-related slang. Into this world comes Georgie Radbourn, a precocious boy who can only, inexplicably, speak in such terms like "Batter up!" Georgie becomes a cause celebre and makes the evil Swaggert a deal: if he can't hit Georgie's three pitches, the sport will be restored. *Booklist'*s Stephanie Zvirin noted the book's "echoes of an Orwellian future," a "strong, bleak vision Shannon conjures up so well in his dramatic illustrations." A *Kirkus Reviews* critic remarked that at the final showdown, the author-illustrator "gives this contest ... an epic feel—plus a broad streak of comedy."

In *The Amazing Christmas Extravaganza,* another story both written and illustrated by Shannon, Mr. Merriweather suffers the taunts of his neighbor when he puts up just a modest string of lights on his house for the holiday season. Soon he and his nemesis have constructed competing, very elaborate displays that bring a nightly traffic jam of visitors. As a result, the other neighbors turn on the Merriweathers, attacking the Christmas display with common household tools and sporting equipment. "Rarely do pictures have so much narrative in them," noted a *Kirkus Reviews* contributor, who called the sum of the visual parts "startling." Stephanie Zvirin of *Booklist,* noting that *The Amazing Christmas Extravaganza* was aimed at primary graders, remarked that the book has a definite adult appeal in its setup and comedy, while its "brilliant colors, depth, and meticulous details" might lure older children as well. A *School Library Journal* contributor praised Shannon's "deft phrasing and amazing illustrations," and termed *The Amazing Christmas Extravaganza* "a singular tale" likely to "provoke discussion, both with its plot and its remarkable artwork."

Shannon also has penned another story aimed at an even younger audience. The comical *No, David!,* for preschoolers, follows a monstrously devious youngster as he conducts all manner of mischief at his home, including running outside naked. Inside, he draws on walls, plays baseball, puts his fingers up his nose, and breaks things. The title derives from David's mother's incessant admonitions; when his antics push her too far one day, he is punished, but the ending is reassuring. Susan Pine, writing for *School Library Journal,* found that Shannon had created a youngster "whose stick-figure body conveys every nuance of anger, exuberance, and defiance."

Shannon told *SATA:* "I got involved with children's books almost by accident. I was amazed at the quality and variety of children's stories, and more and more found myself drawing things I drew as a boy—baseball players, pirates, knights, and Native Americans. I realized that children's books were what I had been working toward my whole life."

Works Cited

Review of *The Amazing Christmas Extravaganza, Kirkus Reviews,* October 15, 1995, p. 1502.

Review of *The Amazing Christmas Extravaganza, School Library Journal,* October, 1995, pp. 41-42.

Review of *The Ballad of the Pirate Queens, Publishers Weekly,* April 17, 1995, p. 59.

Burns, Mary M., review of *The Boy Who Lived with the Seals, Horn Book,* July-August, 1993, p. 472.

Cooper, Ilene, review of *The Bunyans, Booklist,* September 15, 1996, p. 252.

Del Negro, Janice, review of *The Boy Who Lived with the Seals, Booklist,* March 15, 1993, p. 1321.

Review of *Encounter, Publishers Weekly,* March 9, 1992, p. 57.

Gregory, Helen, review of *The Ballad of the Pirate Queens, School Library Journal,* June, 1995, p. 126.

Review of *How Georgie Radbourn Saved Baseball, Kirkus Reviews,* March 1, 1994, p. 310.

Review of *How Many Spots Does a Leopard Have? And Other Tales, Publishers Weekly,* October 27, 1989, p. 68.

McPherson, Kay, review of *How Many Spots Does a Leopard Have? And Other Tales, School Library Journal,* November, 1989, p. 99.

Review of *Nicholas Pipe, Publishers Weekly,* May 5, 1997, p. 209.

Phelan, Carolyn, review of *The Rough-Face Girl, Booklist,* April 15, 1992, p. 1533.

Pine, Susan, review of *No, David!, School Library Journal,* August, 1998, p. 146.

Rochman, Hazel, review of *Gawain and the Green Knight, Booklist,* June 1, 1994, p. 1832.

Review of *The Rough-Face Girl, Publishers Weekly,* April 13, 1992, p. 57.

Scheps, Susan, review of *The Rough-Face Girl, School Library Journal,* May, 1992, p. 124.

Tegart, Beth, review of *Nicholas Pipe, School Library Journal,* May, 1997, p. 124.

Zvirin, Stephanie, review of *The Amazing Christmas Extravaganza, Booklist,* September 15, 1995, p. 172.

Zvirin, Stephanie, review of *How Georgie Radbourn Saved Baseball, Booklist,* January 15, 1994, p. 939.

For More Information See

PERIODICALS

Booklist, April 15, 1995, p. 1501; September 1, 1998, p. 128.

Horn Book, January-February, 1990, p. 79; July-August, 1992, p. 458.

Publishers Weekly, April 5, 1993, p. 77; February 28, 1994, p. 85; August 29, 1994, p. 79.

School Library Journal, May, 1992, pp. 117-18; April, 1993, p. 112-13; April, 1994, pp. 113-14; October, 1994, p. 138; December, 1996, p. 110.

*   *   *

SLOBODKIN, Florence Gersh 1905-1994

OBITUARY NOTICE—See index for *SATA* sketch: Born January 19, 1905, in New York, NY; died April 29, 1994, in Miami, FL. Children's writer and school secretary. Florence Slobodkin studied at Hunter College and the College of the City of New York. She worked as a secretary for the New York City school system from 1926 to 1964. With her husband, the well-known children's writer and illustrator Louis Slobodkin, she began writing books for the juvenile market. The first of these publications, *Too Many Mittens,* was published by Vanguard Press in 1958, and was followed by *The Cowboy Twins* (1960), *Io Sono, I Am* (1962), *Mr. Papadilly and Willy* (1964), and *Sarah Somebody* (1969). Most were illustrated by her husband. Slobodkin also worked closely with her husband in helping him edit his own children's books.

OBITUARIES AND OTHER SOURCES:

PERIODICALS

New York Times, May 6, 1994, p. B4.
Newsday, May 2, 1994, p. A27.

—Obituary by Robert Reginald

*   *   *

SPAULDING, Norma

Personal

Daughter of Frederick (a laborer) and Clara (Wiggins) Burgess; married Ralph Newman Spaulding; children: Glyn Newman, Merric Newman. *Religion:* Uniting Church in Australia. *Education:* University of Tasmania, B.A. and Diploma of Education; Melbourne College of Divinity, B.Div.

Addresses

Home—1 Malunna Rd., Lindisfarne, Tasmania 7015, Australia. *Electronic mail*—normauca@trump.net.au.

Career

Minister of Uniting Church of Australia, c. 1987—. Also worked as a teacher of languages for ten years. *Member:* Australian Society of Authors, Children's Book Council of Australia, Victorian Writers' Centre.

Writings

The Little Blue Parcel, illustrated by Stephen Michael King, Ashton Scholastic Press (Gosford, New South Wales), 1998.

Contributor to periodicals.

Sidelights

Norma Spaulding told *SATA:* "As a parish minister I am constantly writing: producing sermons and prayers week by week, as well as articles for newsletters and for publication in ministry journals. I also write poetry and have had some published from time to time, but at present my main interest is in writing for children, and especially for the child within. I enjoy music and walking, and I spend as much time as I can with my golden retriever, Esther. I try to bring together my three vocations—teacher, minister, and writer—in a creative, imaginative way which seeks to explore and communicate what it means to be human."

* * *

STOEHR, Shelley

Personal

Born Michelle Stoehr, in Pennsylvania; married Mark Buhler (a photographer); divorced. *Education:* Graduated from Connecticut College (New London, CT).

Addresses

Home—San Francisco, CA.

Career

Writer; modern dance choreographer and teacher; massage therapist. Has performed with a modern dance troupe and as a street entertainer, and has worked as a bartender.

Awards, Honors

Honor book citation, Best First Young Adult Novel, Delacorte Press, 1990, for *Crosses.*

Writings

Crosses, Delacorte, 1991.
Weird on the Outside, Delacorte, 1995.
Wannabe, Delacorte, 1997.
Tomorrow Wendy: A Love Story, Delacorte, 1998.

Sidelights

Shelley Stoehr's novels are about the hard journeys that take some young women deep into themselves. *Wannabe's* Catherine is a good student who daydreams about a writing career, but in her hurry to escape a troubled family life and the social confines of her traditional, working-class Italian neighborhood, she launches herself on an alcohol and cocaine-powered trajectory that lands her dangerously off the mark. Tracey, in *Weird on the Outside,* flees school and the conflicted relationships she has with her divorced parents for a precarious independence as a topless dancer in a New York City strip club. And in *Crosses,* punked-out Nancy and her friend Katie deal with "everything awful" in their lives by compulsively cutting themselves. When they aren't having sex with their more straight-laced boyfriends or chugging vodka secreted out of the house in a shampoo bottle, they are carving crosses into their skin with any sharp object they can find. "When we cut, we're in control—we make our own pain, and we can stop it whenever we want," Nancy explains. "Physical pain relieves mental anguish. For a brief moment, the pain of the cutting is

the only thing in the cutter's mind, and when that stops and the other comes back, it's weaker. Drugs do that too, and sex, but not like cutting. Nothing is like cutting."

Filled as they are with sex, cigarettes, alcohol, drugs, profanity, and domestic violence, Stoehr's first four novels built for her a reputation as a spinner of teen-angst tales whose characters hang from the threads she winds for them out of unhappy means and undesirable ends. Some critics see her work as bold and honest. Others find that its shock value belies a lack of literary depth. Regardless, hers is a contemporary handling of the difficult subject matter out of which some young adult lives are made. Patty Campbell, writing in *Horn Book,* named Stoehr "one of the new young breed of truth-telling young-adult writers."

Born in Pennsylvania, Stoehr grew up on Long Island, New York. She graduated from Connecticut College in New London, where she studied modern dance. She and her husband, a photographer, later moved to New York City, where she was a member of a modern dance troupe, worked as a street performer and a bartender, and took training in massage therapy. She and her husband make their home in San Francisco.

An avid reader (among her young-adult favorites were books by Judy Blume, S. E. Hinton, and Lois Duncan), Stoehr began writing at a young age, and was encouraged by her father, who, she told Campbell, was "a very good editor and critic." Stoehr believes that college students should write books for young adults, since they still have a hold on the emotional reality of teenage life. In fact, she wrote her first novel, *Crosses,* while a college student. After thorough rewriting, and then another reworking of its ending, it was accepted by Delacorte Press, published in 1991, and received a Delacorte honor citation for Best First Young Adult Novel.

Crosses is "not a book to 'like' exactly," according to Teri S. Lesesne, who described it in the *ALAN Review* as an "uncompromising examination of the dark world of adolescents with emotional problems compounded by drug dependencies." In it, two friends, Nancy and Katie, are drawn together by their need to cut designs into their skin when they feel bored or overwhelmed. Their family life is virtually nonexistent: Katie's single mother is promiscuous and mouthy and she mostly overlooks her daughter's misdemeanors, while Nancy's parents are alcoholics who spend their time at home watching television and fighting, sometimes violently. In the story's beginning, Nancy is a good student, but her grades and self-worth suffer as she and Katie get caught in a downward spiral of delinquency. They skip class at every opportunity to get high or drunk, and they sneak out at night to party with their boyfriends or less desirable acquaintances who have access to more drugs.

When the two hit bottom and tragedy strikes, Nancy finds herself in a mental ward faced with some hard decisions about how to take hold of the second chance tenuously held out in her direction by newly sober parents intent on recovery. Graphic and unrelenting, as one drug-using, drunken, hung-over scene is followed by another and then another, *Crosses* is not without its critics. "Nancy's first-person narration is believably angry and self-absorbed, but the book is superficial, lacking any distance or perspective on her problems that would allow them more effect than the thrill of titillation," wrote Roger Sutton in the *Bulletin of the Center for Children's Books.* A *Publishers Weekly* reviewer called it "more a journal than a story."

The main characters in Stoehr's books, each in her own way, explore the appeal and power (usually illusory) of an out-of-bounds secret life, one carried on beyond the knowledge and approval of parents and teachers, or, even further afar, outside of society's expectations of what is appropriate for teenaged women. In Stoehr's second novel, *Weird on the Outside,* Tracey Bascombe is a determined young woman with her sights set on medical school, yet she runs away to New York City, finds housing in a seedy hotel, and becomes a topless dancer—all because she's fed up with her neglectful parents, a biochemist father and a North Carolina manicurist mother who abuses Valium.

Smart and pretty, "Tracey is one of the most interesting female characters in recent YA fiction," according to Campbell, since she is emotionally immature yet also a self-reliant survivor. She learns about sexual power play as she picks up the tricks of her sordid trade, and she taps into the sweaty wisdom of her newfound backstage sisterhood, so that when she winds up in the hospital after being assaulted, she is able to see that she has made the passage into womanhood and is at last ready to go home. *Weird on the Outside* "contains some of the grubbiest scenes of sexual exploitation ever to appear in adolescent literature," according to Campbell, who goes on to say that it is Stoehr's use of demeaning and violent experiences to bring her young character to self-aware-ness "that in the final analysis is most controversial—the idea that a young girl can grow and mature from a stint as a sex worker."

The message earned the novel mixed reviews. "Tracey's descent into booze, cocaine and ever-riskier business counterpoints a murkily developed theme that has something to do with gaining independence or female power; the irony here is never certain," a *Publishers Weekly* reviewer wrote. And though Deborah Stevenson concluded in *Bulletin of the Center for Children's Books* that *Weird on the Outside* is "quite readable, and kids will relish the danger of Tracey's razor's edge existence and thrill to the earthy dialogue," she also described it as "the ultimate made-for-cable rebellion fantasy."

In Stoehr's 1995 novel, *Wannabe,* young Catherine Tavarelli creates a secret life out of a similar need to prove herself. Catherine's story, however, plays itself out close to home and takes its shape as much from family troubles as it does outside forces. Unlike Nancy and Tracey, "Cat" has meaningful family ties. She shows consistent concern for her older brother Mickey with whom she is close, and she feels the influence of a

mother who is always bone-tired and largely ineffective but persistent nonetheless in her efforts to keep the fractious family together. One night when Catherine complains about having to help with the dishes while Mickey gets to do as he pleases, her mother suggests that having her daughter's help is one of her few parental joys: "'Catherine, your brother is pretty much lost to me. If I asked him to help, he might even laugh in my face. So I don't ask. You're a good girl, Catherine. Can't you just let me enjoy it?'"

This simple, brief kitchen scene displays a mother-daughter connection that is rare in Stoehr's novels—most of her parents are drawn as background characters whose influences on their children are minimal or negative—and the scene's irony makes a direct, if unacknowledged, hit to Catherine's conscience, for she is not such a "good girl."

Catherine's parents think she has a job in a late-night cafe, but she really works as a cocktail waitress in a Mafia club, where she wears a wig and red leather boots that get her lots of pinches and ogling, but good tips as well. Catherine is run-down and often ill because she and her friend Erica regularly get drunk and take drugs. She has worries, too: What can she do about Mickey, who has quit college in favor of gophering for drug-dealing mobster wannabes in the neighborhood? How can she save enough money for college and the computer she wants so that she can begin her hoped-for writing career? How can she continue to make good grades and still keep up the nightlife that helps her feel like she fits in somewhere? She starts dating a neighborhood mobster, Joey (in reality an undercover cop), and uses more and more drugs to avoid her problems. Soon Catherine finds herself in dangerous situations in her pursuit of cocaine, with events climaxing in a hold-up scene in which Mickey gets shot in the leg.

Again, the book's reviews were mixed, citing lively characters and provocative, action-oriented scenes, but also a sensational plot, a "too happy and too quick" ending, as reviewer Joel Shoemaker described it in *School Library Journal,* and unsuccessful use of chapters written in Mickey's voice spliced in between those narrated by Catherine. "Cat doesn't plummet as far as the characters in Stoehr's previous books . . . , so her last-minute redemption isn't as absurd as theirs, though it's still tacked on abruptly with no fictional logic for it," Stevenson wrote in *Bulletin of the Center for Children's Books.* A critic in *Kirkus Reviews* added that "the characters aren't likable, even when they are believable, while the lurid world they inhabit is offered in admiring glimpses."

For Stoehr, criticism comes with the writing territory she has chosen, and she seems to take any controversy over her novels' subject matter in stride. "In many ways, I believe, the issues for contemporary young adults are not so different now than they have always been for young people—the main concerns still being sex, drugs, and rock and roll. What's changed more than the issues themselves is how they are dealt with by the media, and the arts, including literature," Stoehr said in a 1995 workshop presentation published in the *ALAN Review.* In it, she defended her fictional portrayals of teenage sex, casual drug use, and profane language by saying that she hadn't "invented any new words" or behaviors, but was simply being honest about teenage life.

"I'm not saying it's impossible to write a young adult novel that speaks to teenagers without using foul language in the work. Many authors don't use foul language and still create beautiful, meaningful young adult novels. It happens not to be the way I write, and more importantly, it's not the way my characters talk," Stoehr added.

She also spoke doubtfully about any potential influence her books might have over young readers. "Don't get me wrong, I'm not pro-drug use. In my books, it's clear that, although there is some casual drug use, wherein my characters don't seem to suffer repercussions, in the end there certainly are some very serious repercussions."

Ultimately, young readers may identify as much with how Stoehr's young characters feel as with what they do. She told Campbell that most young adults experience anger: "They don't fit in anywhere yet. They're not children but they still have to listen to their parents. I certainly thought, as a young adult, that I knew exactly where everything was at, and it wasn't until much later that I realized I didn't know everything."

Such self-discovery doesn't come easily for Cary, the heroine of *Tomorrow Wendy: A Love Story,* Stoehr's novel about a high school girl's sexual identity crisis. Cary is an Audrey Hepburn wannabe who is disconnected from her country-clubbing parents. She has a boyfriend, Danny, but she is more attracted to his twin sister, Wendy. She uses drugs and sex with Danny as distractions from the possibility that she might be gay, relying on the advice of her imaginary friend, Rad, who communicates only through pop music lyrics. The plot is further complicated when Raven, a new girl at school who is openly lesbian, falls for Cary and challenges her denial. Slowly Cary comes to see herself as she really is and begins summoning up the strength for self-acceptance. "Stoehr gives her young narrator a saving sense of irony, and displays a keen appreciation for love's ambiguities and complexities," a critic in *Kirkus Reviews* observed. *School Library Journal* reviewer Miriam Lang Budin, however, wrote that "considering that this book is subtitled 'A Love Story,' there is precious little tenderness." Indeed, *Tomorrow Wendy* features all the sex, drugs, and profane language that Stoehr's readers expect. A *Publishers Weekly* contributor found that in this case, though, the sometimes contrived-sounding but "grittier elements of the story are in clearer service of a theme and message, and when the strands of the plot come together, the impact has force and vigor."

While not necessarily condoning the casual sex and drug use that her characters engage in, Stoehr does believe it's appropriate for young people to read about them. "The most important thing about reading is that they

read, anything," Stoehr said in the *ALAN Review.* "The fact is, reading is good, it's important, and for young adults it doesn't always have to be *The Great Gatsby.*" She added, "We need to worry less about the inevitable sex, drugs, and rock and roll, and more about whether young adults are reading. Once they're reading, and choosing to read because they like it, the other issues become easier to address and conquer."

Works Cited

Budin, Miriam Lang, review of *Tomorrow Wendy, School Library Journal,* March, 1998, p. 224.

Campbell, Patty, "The Sand in the Oyster," *Horn Book,* July-August, 1995, pp. 495-98.

Review of *Crosses, Publishers Weekly,* November 15, 1991, p. 74.

Lesesne, Teri S., "Forget-Me-Nots: Books Worth a Second Look," *ALAN Review,* winter, 1998, pp. 52-54.

Shoemaker, Joel, review of *Wannabe, School Library Journal,* January, 1997, p. 116.

Stevenson, Deborah, review of *Weird on the Outside, Bulletin of the Center for Children's Books,* March, 1995, p. 252.

Stevenson, Deborah, review of *Wannabe, Bulletin of the Center of Children's Books,* March, 1997, p. 258.

Stoehr, Shelley, *Crosses,* Delacorte, 1991.

Stoehr, Shelley, "Controversial Issues in the Lives of Young Adults," *ALAN Review,* winter, 1997, pp. 3-5.

Stoehr, Shelley, *Wannabe,* Delacorte, 1997.

Sutton, Roger, review of *Crosses, Bulletin of the Center for Children's Books,* November, 1991, p. 77.

Review of *Tomorrow Wendy, Kirkus Reviews,* December 1, 1997, p. 1780.

Review of *Tomorrow Wendy, Publishers Weekly,* December 1, 1997, p. 54.

Review of *Wannabe, Kirkus Reviews,* November 1, 1996, p. 1608.

Review of *Weird on the Outside, Publishers Weekly,* December 12, 1994, p. 63.

For More Information See

PERIODICALS

Bulletin of the Center for Children's Books, May, 1998, pp. 340-41.

Voice of Youth Advocates, October, 1991, p. 232; February, 1995, p. 342; April, 1998, p. 50.*

*   *   *

STRASSER, Todd 1950-
(Morton Rhue)

Personal

Born May 5, 1950, in New York, NY; son of Chester S. (a manufacturer of dresses) and Sheila (a copy editor; maiden name, Reisner) Strasser; married Pamela Older (a businesswoman), July 2, 1981; children: two. *Education:* Beloit College, B.A., 1974.

Career

Writer, 1975—. Beloit College, Beloit, WI, worked in public relations, 1973-74; *Times Herald Record* (newspaper), Middletown, NY, reporter, 1974-76; Compton Advertising, New York City, copywriter, 1976-77; *Esquire,* New York City, researcher, 1977-78; Toggle, Inc., (fortune cookie company), New York City, owner, 1978-89. Speaker at teachers' and librarians' conferences, middle schools, and junior and senior high schools. Lectures and conducts writing workshops for pre-teens and teenagers. *Member:* International Reading Association, Writers Guild of America, Authors Guild, Freedom to Read Foundation.

Awards, Honors

Best Books for Young Adults citations, American Library Association (ALA), 1981, for *Friends Till the End: A Novel,* 1982, for *Rock 'n' Roll Nights: A Novel,* 1996, for *How I Changed My Life;* Books for the Teen Age citations, New York Public Library, 1981, for *Angel Dust Blues,* 1982, for *The Wave* and *Friends Till the End: A Novel,* 1983, for *Rock 'n' Roll Nights: A Novel,* 1984, for *Workin' for Peanuts,* 1996, for *How I Changed My Life,* and 1998, for *How I Spent My Last Night on Earth;* Notable Children's Trade Book in the Field of Social Studies, National Council for Social Studies-Children's Book Council, 1982, for *Friends Till the End: A Novel;* CRABbery Award List citation, Acton Public Library, 1983, for *Rock 'n' Roll Nights: A Novel;* Young Reader Medal nomination, California Reading Association, 1983, for *Friends Till the End: A Novel;* Book Award, Federation of Children's Books (Great Britain), 1983, for *The Wave,* and 1984, for *Turn It Up!: A Novel;* Outstanding Book award, Iowa Books for Young Adult Program, 1985, for *Turn It Up!: A Novel;* Colorado Blue Spruce Award nomination, 1987, for *Angel Dust Blues;* Edgar Award nomination, Mystery Writers of America, for *The Accident;* New York State Library Association award, 1995, for outstanding children's literature; International Reading Association-Children's Book Council Children's Choice award, 1996, for "Help! I'm Trapped" series; Notable Book designation, ALA, 1997, for *Hey Dad, Get a Life!*

Writings

FOR YOUNG ADULTS; FICTION

Angel Dust Blues, Coward, McCann, 1979.
Friends Till the End: A Novel, Delacorte, 1981.
Rock 'n' Roll Nights: A Novel, Delacorte, 1982.
Workin' for Peanuts, Delacorte, 1983.
Turn It Up!: A Novel (sequel to *Rock 'n' Roll Nights: A Novel*), Delacorte, 1984.
The Complete Computer Popularity Program, Delacorte, 1984.
A Very Touchy Subject, Delacorte, 1985.
Wildlife (sequel to *Turn It Up!*), Delacorte, 1987.
The Mall from Outer Space, Scholastic, 1987.
The Accident, Delacorte, 1988.
Beyond the Reef, illustrated by Debbie Heller, Delacorte, 1989.

(With Dennis Freeland) *Moving Target,* Fawcett, 1989.
Summer's End, Scholastic, 1993.
Summer's Promise: Lifeguards, Scholastic, 1993.
How I Changed My Life, Simon & Schuster, 1995.
Girl Gives Birth to Own Prom Date, Simon & Schuster, 1996, published as *How I Created My Perfect Prom Date,* Demco Media, 1998.
How I Spent My Last Night on Earth, Simon & Schuster, 1998.

FOR YOUNG ADULTS; "ROCK 'N' ROLL SUMMER" SERIES

Playing for Love, HarperCollins, 1996.
The Boys in the Band, HarperCollins, 1996.

FOR CHILDREN; FICTION

The Diving Bell, illustrated by Debbie Heller, Scholastic, 1992.
Please Don't Be Mine, Julie Valentine, Scholastic, 1995.
Hey Dad, Get a Life!, Holiday House, 1996.
Abe Lincoln for Class President, Scholastic, 1996.
Howl-a-Ween, Scholastic, 1996.
Kidnap Kids, Putnam, 1998.
Close Call, Putnam, 1999.

FOR CHILDREN; "HELP! I'M TRAPPED" SERIES

Help! I'm Trapped in the First Day of School, Scholastic, 1994.
... in My Teacher's Body, Scholastic, 1994.
... in Obedience School, Scholastic, 1995.
... in Santa's Body, Scholastic, 1997.
... in My Sister's Body, Scholastic, 1997.
... in My Gym Teacher's Body, Scholastic, 1997.
... in the President's Body, Scholastic, 1997.
... in Obedience School Again, Scholastic, 1997.
... in the First Day of Summer Camp, Scholastic, 1998.
... in an Alien's Body, Scholastic, 1998.
... in a Movie Star's Body, Scholastic, 1999.
... in the Principal's Body, Scholastic, 1999.
... in My Lunch Lady's Body, Scholastic, 1999.
... in the Camp Counselor's Body, Scholastic, 1999.

FOR CHILDREN; "WORDSWORTH" SERIES

Wordsworth & the Cold Cut Catastrophe, illustrations by Leif Peng, HarperCollins, 1995.
Wordsworth & the Kibble Kidnapping, HarperCollins, 1995.
Wordsworth & the Roast Beef Romance, HarperCollins, 1995.
Wordsworth & the Mail-Order Meatloaf Mess, HarperCollins, 1995.
Wordsworth & the Tasty Treat Trick, HarperCollins, 1995.
The Lip-Smacking Licorice Love Affair, HarperCollins, 1996.

FOR CHILDREN; "CAMP RUN-A-MUCK" SERIES

Greasy Grimy Gopher Guts, Scholastic, Inc., 1997.
Mutilated Monkey Meat, Scholastic, Inc., 1997.
Chopped-Up Birdy's Feet, Scholastic, Inc., 1997.

FOR CHILDREN; "AGAINST THE ODDS" SERIES

Shark Bite, Pocket Books, 1998.
Grizzly Attack, Pocket Books, 1998.
Buzzards' Feast, Pocket Books, 1999.

Todd Strasser

Gator Prey, Pocket Books, 1999.

NOVELIZATIONS

(Under pseudonym Morton Rhue) *The Wave* (based on television drama of the same title by Johnny Dawkins), Delacorte, 1981.

Ferris Bueller's Day Off (based on feature film of the same title by John Hughes), New American Library, 1986.

Cookie (based on feature film of the same title by Nora Ephron), New American Library, 1989.

Home Alone, Scholastic, 1991.

Home Alone 2: Lost in New York, Scholastic, 1992.

Honey, I Blew Up the Kid, Disney Press, 1992.

Disney's "The Villains" Collection, with poems by Mark Rifkin, illustrated by Gil DiCicco, Disney Press, 1993.

The Good Son, Pocket Books, 1993.

Free Willy (based on the screenplay by Keith A. Walker and Corey Blechman; story by Keith A. Walker), Scholastic, 1993.

Beverly Hillbillies, HarperCollins, 1993.

Addams Family Values, Pocket Books, 1993.

Super Mario Bros. (based on the screenplay by Parker Bennett, Terry Runte, and Ed Solomon), Hyperion, 1993.

Hocus Pocus, Disney Press, 1993.

The Three Musketeers (adapted from the novel by Alexandre Dumas), Disney Press, 1993.

Rookie of the Year, Dell, 1993.

Disney's It's Magic: Stories from the Films, illustrated by Philippe Harchy, Disney Press, 1994.

Richie Rich, Scholastic, 1994.

Pagemaster, Scholastic, 1994.

Walt Disney's Peter Pan, illustrated by Jose Cardona and Fred Marvin, Disney Press, 1994.

The Miracle on 34th Street, Scholastic, 1994.

Tall Tale: The Unbelievable Adventures of Pecos Bill, Disney Press, 1994.

Walt Disney's Lady and the Tramp, illustrated by Franc Mateu, Disney Press, 1994.

Ninjas Kick Back, Scholastic, 1994.

Little Panda, Scholastic, 1995.

Man of the House, (based on screenplay by James Orr and Jim Cruickshank; from a story by David Peckinpah and Richard Jeffries), Disney Press, 1995.

(With others) *Free Willy 2: The Adventure,* Scholastic, 1995.

Home Alone 3, Scholastic, 1997.

Anakin (part of "Star Wars Journals" series), Scholastic, 1999.

OTHER

The Family Man (adult novel), St. Martin's Press, 1988.

Over the Limit (teleplay based on *The Accident*), *ABC Afterschool Special,* ABC-TV, 1990.

The Kid's Book of Insults: How to Put down, Dis & Slam Your Best Friends, Troll, 1996.

Kid's Book of Gross Facts & Feats, Watermill Press, 1998.

Help! I'm Trapped in the First Day of School! (screenplay based on Strasser's book), Disney Channel, 1999.

Contributor to periodicals, including *New Yorker, Esquire, New York Times,* and *Village Voice.*

Adaptations

Workin' for Peanuts was broadcast on Home Box Office "Family Showcase," 1985; *Can a Guy Say No?,* based on *A Very Touchy Subject,* was shown as an *ABC Afterschool Special,* 1986, and adapted as an educational video; *Rookie of the Year* was adapted as an audio cassette, 1993; *Next to You,* a feature film with screenplay by Rob Thomas, was based on *Girl Gives*

In this installment in Strasser's "Help! I'm Trapped" series, it is up to Jake Sherman to save the day when his dog, Lance, and best friend, Andy, become trapped in each other's bodies.

Birth to Own Prom Date and released by Twentieth Century-Fox, 1999.

Teacher's guides are available for *Angel Dust Blues* and *The Wave.*

Work in Progress

More "Help! I'm Trapped in . . ." titles; more novels.

Sidelights

A highly regarded author of scores of books for preteens and teenagers, Strasser is "best known for books that are funny but not frivolous and writing that manages to be of high quality while still engaging young readers," according to *New York Times* contributor Kate Stone Lombardi. In works ranging from *Friends Till the End,* the story of a young man stricken with leukemia, to *Wildlife,* a study of the breakup of a successful rock group, Strasser blends humor and romance with timely subjects to address various concerns of teens: drugs, sex, illness, popularity, music. Lacing his work for younger readers with a vein of humor, Strasser has also tantalized even the most reluctant reader to open books with titles like *Hey Dad, Get a Life!, Help! I'm Trapped in My Gym Teacher's Body,* and *Greasy Grimy Gopher Guts.* In addition to his many original works of fiction, Strasser has also written novelizations of many popular motion pictures, including some from the Disney Studios. His understanding of the feelings of children and adolescents has made his works popular with young people.

Strasser was born in New York City, but he grew up on Long Island. While having the same insecurities common to young people, Strasser was blessed with a stable family life, went to a decent summer camp, and credits his sense of humor in the face of trouble to his grandfather, which whom he had a close relationship. Regarding schoolwork, Strasser was an admitted underachiever and, surprisingly, had trouble with reading and spelling. While his efforts in the homework department were often just enough to get by, he would study in depth a subject he found interesting. Some of those favorite subjects included dinosaurs, seashells, and James Bond novels.

During his teen years Strasser held to the "anti-establishment" philosophy that characterized the youth of the 1960s. He grew long hair, listened to heavy metal music, and even attended the Woodstock festival. "Sometimes I think I write YA books because I'm still trying to resolve the conflicts of my own youth," Strasser once noted, recalling the confused messages of the 1960s. "When I say that I hope that each of my books shows an example of a young adult who learns good judgment, I sometimes want to add, 'because I wish I had when I was a teen.'"

After high school Strasser enrolled at New York University. He began to write poetry and some short fiction, but regarded it only as a hobby and did not expect to be published. A few years later he dropped out. During the next two years he hitchhiked around most of Europe and the United States, taking odd jobs whenever money ran low. He performed as a street musician in France and Germany, worked on a ship in Denmark, lived on a commune in Virginia, worked in a health-food store in New York, and was kidnapped briefly by religious fanatics in South Bend, Indiana.

During these wandering years Strasser continued to write, documenting his travels in journals and letters. "Finally it occurred to me that perhaps I should give writing a try as a student and, possibly, some sort of profession," he recalled. Strasser enrolled at Beloit College and began taking courses in literature and writing. The author told Jim Roginski in *Behind the Covers:* "I guess my becoming a writer was really a process of elimination. I tried a variety of things in college. Medicine, law. Nothing worked. My family felt I had to be a business person, or if I was lucky, a doctor or a lawyer. I never really thought I would be a writer."

After graduation Strasser worked temporarily for the public relations department at Beloit, wrote for two years for the *Times Herald-Record,* a Middletown, New York, newspaper, and then became an advertising copywriter for Compton Advertising in New York City as well as a researcher for *Esquire* magazine. "When I sold my first novel I quit my advertising job," Strasser told Roginski. "And then I went the route of the poor struggling novelist. I used to do things like cut my own hair." After *Angel Dust Blues,* Strasser's first novel, was accepted for publication, Strasser used the three-thousand-dollar advance to start a business of his own, a fortune-cookie company called Toggle, Inc. "I ... realized that [the money] wasn't going to last me very long," he told Roginski. "Since I come from a business family, I had some idea of what to do. I just happened to start with fortune cookies."

Strasser found the cookie business more successful than he expected. "It started as a way to come up with a little extra cash while I did my serious writing," he explained to Roy Sorrels in *Writer's Digest.* "In October, 1978, I started with 5,000 cookies hoping to sell them all by Christmas. I sold 100,000!" "To get it going," Strasser continued, "I wore out a pair of shoes hiking from store to store in a seventy-block area of Manhattan. About thirty stores agreed to stock my cookies. They were immediately popular and before long I had sales reps around the city and all over the country." Strasser also found that the business fit well with his writing schedule. As he observed, it gave him the chance to "get up from my typewriter and put my real work aside once in a while. And it's a way to supplement my serious writing. I must admit it's fun. When I look around at other friends who are waiting tables or driving cabs, it makes grinding out fortune cookie messages much more palatable. And I'll never be a starving writer. I can always eat my cookies." Strasser operated his fortune-cookie business until 1989.

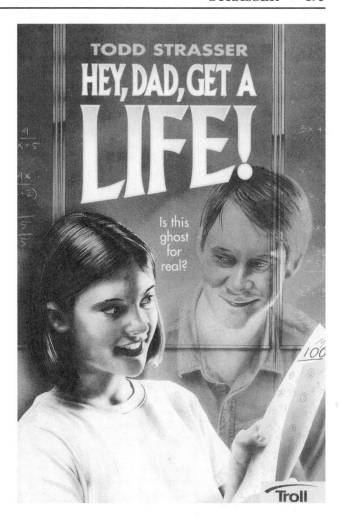

Depicting a family's adjustment to the loss of a loved one, Strasser's novel is a compassionate and nevertheless lighthearted story about two sisters whose deceased father returns as a ghost to watch over them.

Meanwhile, *Angel Dust Blues* appeared in 1979 and won the fortune-cookie manufacturer critical acclaim. The story, about a group of affluent suburban teens who get tangled up with drugs, was based on actual events Strasser had witnessed when he was growing up. Two years later, he published another young-adult novel, again based on his own experiences. *Friends Till the End* focuses on a healthy teen whose friend contracts leukemia and becomes very ill. The story is based on a roommate Strasser had when he first moved to New York City who was also stricken with the disease. Strasser spent many hours visiting his friend at the hospital, not sure if he would live or die.

In 1981, the same year *Friends Till the End* was published, Strasser married Pamela Older, a production manager of *Esquire* magazine, and did a novelization (using the pseudonym Morton Rhue) of the teleplay *The Wave,* the story of how a teacher's experiment with Nazi-like socialization methods failed disastrously. With the critical praise heaped upon his second novel, Strasser was encouraged to make writing for children and young adults his career: he has since gone on to write numerous novels for high-school and middle-grade readers.

Rock 'n' Roll Nights, Strasser's third original novel, was a change of pace from the serious themes of his first two works. The first part of a trilogy, it focuses on "a teenage rock and roll band—something with which I had absolutely no direct experience," he told Nina Piwoz in *Media and Methods.* "However, I grew up in the 1960s when rock and roll was really our 'national anthem.' I relate much better to rock stars than to politicians. I always wanted to be in a rock band, as did just about everybody I knew." "I think the kind of music teens listen to may change, or what they wear may change," Strasser continued, "but dealing with being popular, friends or the opposite sex, or questions of morality and decency ... [I don't think] those things really ever change. I hate to say this, but I think authors tell the same stories—just in today's language and in today's settings."

Strasser would continue the story of the band, called Coming Attractions, in two sequels: *Turn It Up!* and *Wildlife.* In *Wildlife,* published in 1987, band member Gary Specter becomes burned out after Coming Attractions starts touring and begins work on a new album. Meanwhile, personality problems within the band loom larger due to the stress. Lead singer Oscar decides to go it on his own, and another member, Karl, succumbs to drugs and alcohol. *Booklist* contributor Stephanie Zvirin commented that Strasser brings to life "the price fame exacts as well as enough of a sense of the economic burdens and realities of the recording business to intrigue" teen readers. Strasser would revisit the world of teen bands in 1996's *The Boys in the Band,* as a group of four teen musicians, finding that all-girl bands are all the rage, decide that the only way to get in a band over the summer is to audition in drag.

In his more recent works for older teens, Strasser has continued to write hard-hitting, realistic stories about teenagers and their problems. For example, *The Accident,* which Strasser adapted for ABC-TV's *Afterschool Special* under the title "Over the Edge," deals with a drunken-driving incident in which three of four high-school swimming stars are killed. The surviving teen commits himself to understanding what actually happened the night of the accident, in a novel that, in the opinion of *Horn Book* reviewer Margaret A. Bush, "reads well and competently uses the troublesome occurrence of drunk driving and teenage death to provoke thought and discussion on multifaceted issues." *The Complete Computer Popularity Program* deals with questions of the morality of nuclear power; a young boy, whose father is the new security engineer at a local nuclear power plant, must confront the community's hostility, along with his only friend, a "computer nerd."

In addition to illustrating ways to cope with difficult and complex emotions, Strasser has also written several stories that present his young protagonists with physical dangers. *Beyond the Reef* has many of the trappings of a traditional boys' adventure story: at first glance, it seems to be about exploration for sunken treasure in the Florida Keys. However, Strasser focusses not so much on the treasure hunting itself as on one father's obsession with it, which threatens to break up his family. Noting that Strasser's fans would not be disappointed, Susan H. Williamson maintained in her review for *School Library Journal* that the novel's "fascinating plot, coupled with Strasser's vivid writing style and well-drawn characters, will make [*Beyond the Reef*] a popular choice." Also focusing on treasure, *The Diving Bell* finds Strasser in the historical-fiction mode, as he tells the story of Culca, a young girl living in sixteenth-century Mexico. Culca searches for a way to save the lives of young men in her village who are forced by the marauding Spanish *conquistadors* to dive in salvage missions and search the ocean floor for shipwrecked treasure. Calling Culca "a sixteenth-century feminist," *Voice of Youth Advocates* contributor Civia Tuteur claimed of *The Diving Bell:*

A self-described social misfit, high-school senior Bolita Vine sets out to change her image, and in doing so, befriends football captain Kyle Winthrop, with whom she hopes to have a romance. (Cover illustration by Tom Garrett.)

In this title in Strasser's "Against All Odds" series, a plane crash leaves thirteen-year-old Justin lost in the Everglades with an unlikely helpmate—the rebellious teen daughter of his mother's new boyfriend.

"Here is history, adventure, excitement, and a strong heroine all in one setting. What more can a reader ask for!"

Strasser has also produced a large number of light-hearted books for middle-graders. *The Mall from Outer Space* is about aliens who have chosen, for mysterious reasons of their own, to construct shopping centers on Earth. *Hey Dad, Get a Life!* finds twelve-year-old Kelly and younger sister Sasha haunted by their deceased father. Ghostly Dad proves to be a great help around the house—he makes the girls' beds, tidies their room, does their homework, and even helps out on the soccer field. *Booklist* contributor Debbie Carton called the work a "light-hearted and occasionally poignant ghost story" that features "appealing, believable characters and a satisfying plot." Equally laudatory in *Bulletin of the Center for Children's Books,* Deborah Stevenson described *Hey, Dad, Get a Life!* as "touchingly yet surprisingly cheerful," and called it "a compassionate and accessible tale of a family's adjustment to loss."

Several novels reveal Strasser's more quirky, humorous side. *Girl Gives Birth to Own Prom Date* finds ardent environmentalist Nicole taking time off from saving the world to transform her grungy next-door neighbor Chase into the perfect prom date. Praising the novel's "goofy plot twists" and "effervescent dialogue," a *Kirkus Reviews* critic noted that Strasser's "high humor doesn't detract" from his "understated message about noncon-formity and self-acceptance." The author's "Help! I'm Trapped ..." books posit their young protagonists in everything from the unwieldy body of Santa Claus to the summer camp from hell. In *Help! I'm Trapped in Obedience School,* for example, Jake's dog Lance switches bodies with Jake's friend Andy, and while Andy excels at most things doggy—although he never quite acquires a taste for dog food—Jake spends his time in human form chasing squirrels and barking during school. Calling Strasser's tale "briskly paced," *Booklist* contributor Chris Sherman wrote that the "easy, breezy" story would appeal to reluctant readers. *School Library Journal* contributor Cheryl Cufari predicted that readers will relate to the "predicaments in which Strasser's energetic boys find themselves and enjoy this light entertaining read."

"Over the years," Strasser wrote in *Horn Book,* "I had often complained to my wife that I wished that there were some easier way to do research on teenagers, especially in New York where, except for a few weeks each spring and fall, they seem particularly hard to find. Then ... we had our first child, a daughter. Shortly after we brought her home from the hospital, my wife turned to me and said, 'Just think, in thirteen years you won't have to leave the house at all to do your research.' Perhaps that's the best solution: grow your own." His wife turned out to be right; Strasser has received a great deal of inspiration from his children—a son was also born to the author and his wife.

"Whey you live in the suburbs, a lot of your life focuses on the kids," Strasser explained in a *Publishers Weekly* article. "I love writing for kids and teenagers because I feel like they are still impressionable—I can still reach them. I also like to use a lot of humor and teens and kids are more open to that—they get it."

Reflecting on his twenty-year career as an author of books for young people, Strasser told *New York Times* contributor Lombardi: "Now that I have kids, I've become so much more conservative it's incredible. In fact, I think another reason I like writing these books is that you don't have to write about violence, crime and adulterers. I get really emotionally involved in my books, and I don't want to be thinking about those things all day long. In my early books I was more explicit about subjects like sex or drugs. Now I touch on them, but I keep the tone breezy and light. I think you can deal with a serious subject in a humorous way."

Works Cited

Bush, Margaret A., review of *The Accident, Horn Book,* January-February, 1989, p. 82.

Carton, Debbie, review of *Hey Dad, Get a Life!*, *Booklist*, February 15, 1997, p. 1024.

Cufari, Cheryl, review of *Help! I'm Trapped in Obedience School, School Library Journal*, February, 1996, p. 104.

Review of *Girl Gives Birth to Own Prom Date, Kirkus Reviews*, August 1, 1996, p. 1158.

Lombardi, Kate Stone, "For Best-Selling Author, What's in a Name?" *New York Times*, October 12, 1997, Section 14.

Piwoz, Nina, "The Writers Are Writing: I Was a Teenage Boy—An Interview with Todd Strasser," *Media & Methods*, February, 1983.

Roginski, Jim, *Behind the Covers: Interviews with Authors and Illustrators of Books for Children and Young Adults*, Libraries Unlimited, 1985.

Sherman, Chris, review of *Help! I'm Trapped in Obedience School, Booklist*, February 1, 1996, p. 932.

Sorrels, Roy, "The Writing Life: Cookie Funster," *Writer's Digest*, December, 1979.

Stevenson, Deborah, review of *Hey Dad, Get a Life!*, *Bulletin of the Center for Children's Books*, March, 1997, p. 259.

Strasser, Todd, "Changing Hats," *Publishers Weekly*, January 18, 1999, p. 1999.

Strasser, Todd, "Young Adult Books: Stalking the Teen," *Horn Book*, March-April, 1986.

Tuteur, Civia, review of *The Diving Bell, Voice of Youth Advocates*, June, 1992, p. 102.

Williamson, Susan H., review of *Beyond the Reef, School Library Journal*, September, 1989, p. 278.

Zvirin, Stephanie, review of *Wildlife, Booklist*, April 15, 1987, p. 1276.

For More Information See

BOOKS

Children's Literature Review, Volume 11, Gale, 1986, pp. 244-52.

Sixth Book of Junior Authors and Illustrators, edited by Sally Holmes Holtze, H. W. Wilson, 1989, pp. 289-91.

PERIODICALS

Booklist, May 1, 1995, p. 1564; October 1, 1996, p. 344.

Bulletin of the Center for Children's Books, June, 1995, p. 361; February, 1999, p. 219.

Horn Book, January, 1990, p. 90.

Kirkus Reviews, May 15, 1992, p. 676; September 1, 1998, p. 1293.

School Library Journal, May, 1995, p. 123; September, 1996, p. 228; May, 1999, p. 130.

Variety, March 22, 1990, p. 14.

Voice of Youth Advocates, October, 1995, p. 224; April, 1997, pp. 22, 33.

T

TARBESCU, Edith 1939-

Personal

Born October 19, 1939, in Brooklyn, NY; daughter of Benjamin (a furrier) and Esther (a homemaker; maiden name, Malasky) Roseman; married Paul Tarbescu, November 26, 1960 (deceased); married Jacob H. Deutschmann (a stockbroker), May 9, 1982; children: Renata Tarbescu Wilke, Michelle Tarbescu Truly. *Education:* State University of New York, B.A.; also attended Yale University School of Drama. *Politics:* "Democrat/Independent." *Religion:* Jewish. *Hobbies and other interests:* Sailing, hiking, reading, attending concerts and theater, and traveling.

Addresses

Home and office—14 Clark Lane, Essex, CT 06426. *Electronic mail*—edja@mail1.nai.net. *Agent*—Barbara S. Kouts, P.O. Box 558, Bellport, NY 11713.

Career

American Home Products, New York, sales representative, 1982-85; playwright and author of children's books, 1985—. *Member:* Society of Children's Book Writers and Illustrators, Dramatists Guild, National Arts Club.

Awards, Honors

Honorable Mention, Native Peoples Drama Contest, University of Alaska at Anchorage, 1998, for *Molly's Boots.* Notable Children's Trade Book in the Field of Social Studies, National Council for the Social Studies and Children's Book Council, 1999, for *Annushka's Voyage.*

Writings

FOR CHILDREN

Annushka's Voyage, illustrated by Lydia Dabcovich, Clarion, 1998.
Bring Back My Gerbil, Scholastic, 1999.
The Crow (nonfiction), F. Watts, in press.
The Boy Who Stuck Out His Tongue: A Hungarian Folktale (picture book), Barefoot Books (London), in press.

Annushka's Voyage was featured on C-Span's Book-TV, January, 1999.

PLAYS

Wakeville's Trial, produced in Greenwich, CT, 1992.

Edith Tarbescu

Connectus Africanus, produced in New York City, by Yale Drama Alumni Association, 1992.

Mother's Day, produced in Milwaukee, WI, at Milwaukee Repertory Theater, 1993.

Journey Home, performed in a staged reading in New York City, at Westbeth Theatre, 1994.

The Interview (one-act), produced in New York City, by Love Creek Productions, 1996.

Phone Play, produced in Washington, DC, at Source Theatre, 1996.

Molly's Boots, performed in a staged reading at Westbeth Theatre, 1996.

Trio for Two, performed in a staged reading in New York City, at 14th Street Theatre, 1998.

Author of the play *Bal Harbour Rhythm and Blues.*

OTHER

Contributor to magazines and newspapers, including *Connecticut, Hartford Courant, Northeast Magazine, Writer, Christian Science Monitor, New York Times,* and *New York Newsday.*

Work in Progress

Molly's Boots, a screenplay; research for children's books on Navajo and Apache Indians and the native people of Alaska.

Sidelights

Edith Tarbescu told *SATA:* "I grew up wanting to be an actress. I studied acting in New York and worked in summer stock, which I loved. I married young and had children, also when I was young. I realized that an acting career would entail a lot of travel, so I switched to writing.

"I wrote several short stories, and a friend suggested that I turn one of them into a play. I did, and I've been a playwright ever since. After studying playwriting at the Yale Drama School, I had to support my two children, so my writing took a back seat for several years.

"After remarrying in 1982, I started to wear two hats: I wrote books for children and plays for adults. I am now adapting one of my plays into a screenplay, at the urging of a New York agent. I am also researching Alaskan native people for a nonfiction book for children. *The Crow* is about a Native American tribe in Montana. I loved the research!"

Tarbescu's first book for children, *Annushka's Voyage,* is based on her mother's experience as a Jewish immigrant journeying from Russia to America. This fictionalized, first-person account follows Annushka and her sister, Tanya, as they leave their village with two family candlesticks given to them by their grandmother to travel by steamship to New York to be with their father. "The story has charm," enthused a critic for *Kirkus Reviews,* and *School Library Journal* contributor Rosalyn Pierini called *Annushka's Voyage* "a moving tribute to the strength of family ties and the American experience."

Works Cited

Review of *Annushka's Voyage, Kirkus Reviews,* August 15, 1998, p. 1197.

Pierini, Rosalyn, review of *Annushka's Voyage, School Library Journal,* December, 1998, p. 93.

For More Information See

PERIODICALS

Booklist, September 1, 1998, p. 128.
Jewish Book World, winter, 1998, p. 67.

OTHER

Website: http://w3.nai.net/~edja.

*   *   *

TEMPLE, William F(rederick) 1914-1989

Personal

Born March 9, 1914, in Woolwich, London, England; died July 15, 1989; son of William and Doris Temple; married Joan Streeton, 1939; children: one daughter and one son. *Education:* Gordon School, London, 1919-1927; Woolwich Polytechnic, London, 1928-30.

Career

Writer. Stock Exchange, London, head clerk, 1930-50; British Interplanetary Society *Bulletin,* editor. *Military Service:* Served in the Royal Artillery, 1940-46. *Member:* Science Fiction Writers of America.

Writings

FICTION; FOR CHILDREN

Martin Magnus, Planet Rover, Muller (London), 1955.
Martin Magnus on Venus, Muller, 1955.
Martin Magnus on Mars, Muller, 1956.

FICTION; FOR ADULTS

Four-Sided Triangle: A Novel, Long (London), 1949, Fell (New York City), 1951.
The Dangerous Edge, Long, 1951.
The Automated Goliath, Ace (New York City), 1962.
The Three Suns of Amara, Ace, 1962.
Battle on Venus, Ace, 1963.
Shoot at the Moon, Whiting and Wheaton (London), 1966, Simon and Schuster (New York City), 1966.
The Fleshpots of Sansato, Macdonald (London), 1968.

NONFICTION

The True Book about Space-Travel, Muller, 1954, published in the U.S. as *The Prentice-Hall Book about Space Travel,* Prentice-Hall, 1955.

Sidelights

William F. Temple learned his craft amidst the science-fiction writers of pre- and post-World War II England. Inspired by his companionship with writers such as Arthur C. Clarke, John Wyndham, and John Christopher, Temple persevered through an African stint with England's army during World War II to release *Four-Sided Triangle,* a novel toying with love and cloning and the extraordinary dynamics that occur when the two are mixed.

Temple published nine science-fiction books, including the "Martin Magnus" series of books for children. Still, his works never achieved a higher point of acclaim than with his debut novel. His distinctly British prose received an indifferent reception by American critics. As Robert H. Wilcox noted in the *St. James Guide to Science Fiction,* "some readers ... find Temple's work a bit stuffy at times."

Temple himself gave up science-fiction writing after 1968's *The Fleshpots of Sansato.* As he noted in the *St. James Guide to Science Fiction:* "I've read [science fiction] since childhood. At first, uncritically: I didn't notice it was only two-dimensional, i.e., lacked depth, especially in characterization. Then critically: I decided to try to add that third dimension in my writing. Then despairingly: Nobody noticed that I had. Then cynically: Nobody wanted it anyway. They preferred their robots. Then uncaringly: I don't bother to write it anymore."

Works Cited

Wilcox, Robert H., essay on Temple in *St. James Guide to Science Fiction Writers,* St. James Press, 1996, pp. 915-16.

For More Information See

BOOKS

Ashley, Mike, *The Work of William F. Temple: An Annotated Bibliography and Guide,* Bargo Press (San Bernardino, CA), 1994.
Encyclopedia of Science Fiction: An Illustrated A to Z, Granada (London), 1979.*

*   *   *

TIBO, Gilles 1951-

Personal

Born in 1951, in Nicolet, Quebec, Canada; married; children: Simon.

Career

Author and illustrator.

Awards, Honors

Governor General's Award for Illustration (French language category), Canada Council, 1992, for *Simone et la ville de carton;* Governor General's Award for Text (French language category), 1996, for *Noemie—Le Secret de Madame Lumbago.*

Writings

IN ENGLISH TRANSLATION

Busy Critters, illustrated by Sylvain Tremblay, translated by Sheila Fischman, Dominique (Saint-Lambert, Quebec), 1998.

IN ENGLISH TRANSLATION; SELF-ILLUSTRATED

Mr. Clark's Summer Holiday, translated by Sheila Fischman, Doubleday (Toronto, Ontario), 1991 (originally published as *Les Vacances de Monsieur Gaston,* Lemeac, 1987).
Santa Takes a Tumble, Doubleday, 1991 (originally published as *La Degringolade du Pere Noel,* Lemeac, 1987).

Tibo collaborated with Francois Vaillancourt on the design and construction of the illustrations for Mr. Patapoum's First Trip, *the story of two animal friends who experience both unforeseen obstacles and unexpected joys on a journey to find Momo the duck's family.*

The King of Sleep, translated by Sheila Fischman, Double-day, 1991 (originally published as *Le Roi du sommeil,* Doubleday, 1991).

(With Francois Vaillancourt) *Mr. Patapoum's First Trip,* translated by Sara Swartz, Annick, 1993 (originally published as *Le Premier Voyage de monsieur Pata-poum,* Annick, 1993).

"SIMON" SERIES

Simon and the Snowflakes, Tundra Books, 1988 (originally published as *Simon et les flocons de neige,* Livres Toundra, 1988).

Simon and the Wind, Tundra Books, 1989 (originally published as *Simon et le vent d'automne,* Livres Toundra, 1989).

Simon Welcomes Spring, Tundra Books, 1990 (originally published as *Simon fete le printemps,* Livres Toundra, 1990).

Simon in Summer, Tundra Books, 1991 (originally published as *Simon et le soleil d'ete,* Livres Toundra, 1991).

Simon in the Moonlight, Tundra Books, 1993 (originally published as *Simon au clair du lune,* Livres Toundra, 1993).

Simon Finds a Broken Wing, Tundra Books, 1994 (originally published as *Simon et la petit plume cassee,* Livres Toundra, 1994).

Simon Finds a Feather, Tundra Books, 1994 (originally published as *Simon et la plume perdue,* Livres Toundra, 1994).

Simon and His Boxes, Tundra Books, 1996 (originally published as *Simon et la ville de carton,* Livres Toundra, 1992).

Simon Makes Music, Tundra Books, 1996 (originally published as *Simon et la musique,* Livres Toundra, 1996).

Simon Finds a Treasure, Tundra Books, 1996 (originally published as *Simon et la chasse au tresor,* Livres Toundra, 1996).

Simon at the Circus, Tundra Books, 1997 (originally published as *Simon et le petit cirque,* Livres Toundra, 1997).

Simon's Disguise, translated by Sheila Fischman, Tundra Books, 1999 (originally published as *Simon et les deguisements,* Livres Toundra, 1999).

UNTRANSLATED WORKS

Le Dodo des animaux, illustrated by Sylvain Tremblay, Heritage (Saint-Lambert, Quebec), 1996.

L'Incroyable journee, illustrated by Louise-Andree Lali-berte, Quebec Amerique (Montreal, Quebec), 1996.

Noemie—Le secret de Madame Lumbago, illustrated by Louise-Andree Laliberte, Quebec Amerique, 1996.

Les Sept Verites, illustrated by Louise-Andree Laliberte, Quebec Amerique, 1997.

La Cle de l'enigme, illustrated by Louise-Andree Laliberte, Quebec Amerique, 1997.

Les Bobos des animaux, illustrated by Sylvain Tremblay, Dominique, 1997.

Les Cauchemars du petit geant, illustrated by Jean Ber-neche, Quebec Amerique, 1997.

Choupette et son petit papa, illustrated by Stephane Poulin, Heritage, 1997.

L'Hiver du petit geant, illustrated by Jean Berneche, Quebec Amerique, 1997.

Au boulot les animaux!, illustrated by Sylvain Tremblay, Dominique, 1998.

La Fusee du petit geant, illustrated by Jean Berneche, Quebec Amerique, 1998.

Le Chateau de glace, illustrated by Louise-Andree Lali-berte, Quebec Amerique, 1998.

Choupette et maman Lili, illustrated by Stephane Poulin, Dominique, 1998.

Albert aux grand oreilles, illustrated by Louise-Andree Laliberte, Quebec Amerique, 1998.

Alex, le petit joueur de hockey, illustrated by Philippe Germain, Dominique, 1999.

Choupette et tante Loulou, illustrated by Stephane Poulin, Dominique, 1999.

UNTRANSLATED WORKS; SELF-ILLUSTRATED

L'Oeil Voyeur, Les Editions du Cri, 1970.

Monsieur Quidam, l'apres-midi dernier: Un conte a lire tranquillement, Le Tamanoir (Montreal, Quebec), 1976.

La Nuit du grand coucou, Courte Echelle, 1984.

La Nuit Rouge, Quebec Amerique, 1998.

Rouge timide, Soulieres (Saint-Lambert, Quebec), 1998.

Les Voyages du petit geant, Quebec Amerique, 1998.

Les Yeux Noirs, Soulieres, 1999.

Noemie—Le jardin zoologique, Quebec Amerique, 1999.

ILLUSTRATOR

Louis Philippe Cote, *Le Prince sourire et le lys bleu,* Le Tamanoir, 1975.

Grand-pere Cailloux, *Je te laisse une caresse,* Le Tama-noir, 1976.

Grand-pere Cailloux, *Mon petit lutin s'endort,* Le Tama-noir, 1976.

Marie-Francine Hebert, *Abecedaire,* Editions La Court, 1979.

Felix Leclerc, *Le Tour de l'ile,* Editions la courte echelle, 1980.

Malou, *La Fee des lilas,* Graficor, 1983.

Edgar Allan Poe, *Annabel Lee: The Poem,* Tundra Books, 1987.

Marielle Richer, *Au pays de Bombance,* Education Quebec, 1987.

Louis Hemon, *Maria Chapdelaine,* translated by Alan Brown, Tundra Books, 1989.

Bernard Clavel, *A Kenogami: Poemes,* Messidor/La Faron-dole (Paris, France), 1989.

Robert Munsch, *Giant, or Waiting for the Thursday Boat,* Firefly Books, 1989.

Alice Bartels, *The Beast,* Firefly Books, 1990.

Jocelyne Robert, *L'Histoire Merveilleuse de la naissance,* Editions Heritage (Saint-Lambert, Quebec), 1990.

Pierre Filion, *Paper Nights,* Annick (Toronto, Ontario), 1992 (originally published as *Pikolo: Le secret des garde-robes,* Annick, 1992).

Jean-Pierre Guillet, *The Magic Powder,* translated by Sheila Fischman, Quintin (Waterloo, Quebec), 1992 (originally published as *La Poudre Magique,* Quintin, 1992).

Jean-Pierre Guillet, *Castle Chaos,* translated by Frances Morgan, Quintin, 1993.

Jean-Pierre Guillet, *La Fete est a l'eau!,* Quintin, 1993.

Jean-Pierre Guillet, *The Bubble Machine,* translated by Frances Morgan, Quintin, 1994 (originally published as *La Machine a bulles,* Quintin, 1994).

Jacques Flamand, *Lapin Rouge et carotte blanche,* Vermillon (Ottawa, Ontario), 1994.

Pierre Filion, *Pikolo: L'Arbre aux mille tresors,* Firefly, 1994 (originally published as *Pikolo's Night Voyage,* Firefly, 1994).

Sylvie Nicolas, *Billi Mouton,* Editions Heritage, 1996.

Sidelights

French Canadian author and illustrator Gilles Tibo has written and illustrated scores of books for children. Among his most popular are those from the "Simon" series, which feature a young boy of the same name. Internationally recognized for both his writing and artistic talents, Tibo and his works have been embraced by readers and critics from around the world. And, as Hazel Birt, writing for *Canadian Materials,* noted, "His reputation continues to grow with each of his new books." In addition to writing and illustrating books, this self-taught artist has provided drawings for newspapers, magazines, record albums, and movie posters.

Although not Tibo's first work for children, the "Simon" series began in 1988 with the publication of *Simon and the Snowflakes* and has grown to include more than ten volumes, the most recent being *Simon's Disguise,* published in 1999. Over the years, the series has made its way to a number of preschool audiences, including those who speak English, German, Norwegian, and Spanish, not to mention Tibo's native French.

Simon, whom *Canadian Materials* contributor Brenda Partridge described as "a little fellow with a very active imagination," is based on Tibo's own son, Simon. In each book, Simon tries to come up with imaginative ways to change or stop some common force of nature,

A little boy named Simon makes "homes" for animals out of cardboard boxes that he finds in the forest in Gilles Tibo's self-illustrated **Simon and His Boxes.**

like wind or snow or moonbeams. When he realizes he cannot, Simon accepts nature's power and has fun with it instead. For example, in the popular *Simon and the Wind,* Simon yearns to fly with the wind. After imagining many possible ways to do so, Simon realizes that he can't. He does, however, come up with a few things the wind can fly, like a kite. This realization makes him very happy. Or in *Simon in Summer,* Simon searches for ways to make the weather feel like summer all year round. Again, when he realizes he can't, he embraces the coming of autumn instead.

Reviewers had their favorites among the series. *Books in Canada* contributor Welwyn Wilton Katz was disappointed in Tibo's more recent work *Simon Finds a Treasure* for its lack of credibility, but she called *Simon and the Wind* her "favourite picture book of all time." Other reviews were mixed, like this one from a *Quill & Quire* critic who called *Simon Makes Music* "a feast for the eyes," but added that "Simon's story is not quite as satisfying." And Christine Heppermann, writing in *Horn Book Guide,* voiced her disappointment in *Simon Makes Music's* "awkward" rhyme, but felt "the book offers intriguing ideas on the nature of music." Most reviewers, however, complimented Tibo on his beautiful airbrush illustrations. In fact, in 1992 Tibo received a Governor General's Award for his illustrations in *Simon and His Boxes.*

Other popular books by Tibo include *The King of Sleep* and *Mr. Patapoum's First Trip.* Published in 1991, *The King of Sleep* features a monarch named Roger 37 who likes to sleep in stretches of 37 days and whose kingdom exists on a futuristic planet. One day King Roger 37 awakens from a long nap and discovers he is alone—his subjects have left for an interplanetary picnic. Disappointed, the king seeks sleep, but is awakened by a loud sheep. Asleep again after seeing to the sheep, Roger 37 is awakened once more, this time by children from another planet in search of a picnic. King Roger 37, a lover of picnics, gladly plays host. Jane Cobb, writing in *Quill & Quire,* enjoyed the book, calling it "a humourous little fantasy," as did *Canadian Materials* contributor Linda Holeman, who thought Tibo's illustrations were "both fanciful and amusing."

Mr. Patapoum's First Trip, created with Francois Vaillancourt, is the story of an anthropomorphized pig, Mr. Patapoum, who helps a duckling migrate south to meet its family. During their trek through forest, desert, water, and mountains, they meet some friendly animals. Together they overcome a number of obstacles, arriving at their destination safely. For his troubles, Mr. Patapoum receives a hero's welcome and the vacation of his dreams. Gillian Martin Noonan, writing in *Canadian Materials,* described the work as a "delightful story with superb illustrations and a charming ending." Troon Harrison, reviewing the work in *Canadian Children's Literature,* also appreciated the "delightfully illustrated" work, as well as Mr. Patapoum's resourcefulness, imagination, and compassion.

Once labeled "one of Canada's hardest working illustrators" by *Canadian Materials* contributor Hazel Birt, Tibo has since become one of Canada's hardest working children's book writers. Not only does he write and illustrate his own work in addition to illustrating the work of others, he also writes stories for other artists to illustrate. One such work is 1996's *Noemie—Le Secret de Madame Lumbago,* illustrated by Louise-Andree Laliberte. Tibo received a second Governor General's Award for this work—this time for his text. Since then, he has produced more than two dozen books as writer and/or illustrator to the delight of his international audience.

Works Cited

Birt, Hazel, review of *Simon and the Wind, Canadian Materials,* March, 1990, p. 68.

Cobb, Jane, review of *The King of Sleep, Quill & Quire,* October, 1991, p. 36.

Harrison, Troon, review of *Mr. Patapoum's First Trip, Canadian Children's Literature,* summer, 1995, p. 79.

Heppermann, Christine, review of *Simon Makes Music, Horn Book Guide,* July-December, 1995, p. 47.

Holeman, Linda, review of *The King of Sleep, Canadian Materials,* May, 1993, p. 162.

Katz, Welwyn Wilton, review of *Simon Finds a Treasure, Books in Canada,* May, 1997, pp. 33-34.

Noonan, Gillian Martin, review of *Mr. Patapoum's First Trip, Canadian Materials,* October, 1993, p. 189.

Partridge, Brenda, review of *Simon in Summer, Canadian Materials,* September, 1991, p. 233.

Review of *Simon Makes Music, Quill & Quire,* November, 1995, p. 46.

For More Information See

PERIODICALS

Booklist, December 15, 1988, p. 715.

Canadian Children's Literature, Number 60, 1990, p. 138; Number 66, 1992, p. 94.

Canadian Materials, January, 1991, p. 31; November, 1992, p. 309; March, 1994, p. 50.

Quill & Quire, October, 1991, p. 36; October, 1992, pp. 28, 38; October, 1993, p. 40.

School Library Journal, March, 1993, p. 187.*

*   *   *

TYRRELL, Frances 1959-

Personal

Born July 1, 1959, in Kirkland Lake, Ontario, Canada; daughter of Donald H. (an engineer) and Avril J. (a writer; maiden name, Tyler) Tyrrell. Children: Neil Alexander. *Education:* Attended Sheridan College, 1977-78, and University of Western Ontario, 1983-87. *Religion:* Anglican. *Hobbies and other interests:* Gardening, dancing, camping, canoeing.

Frances Tyrrell

Addresses

Agent—Avril Tyrrell, 448 Caesar Ave., Oakville, ON L6J 3Y9, Canada.

Career

Children's book illustrator. *Member:* Canadian Society of Children's Authors, Illustrators, and Performers.

Awards, Honors

Finalist in illustration, Governor General's Literary Award, 1990, for *The Huron Carol,* and 1995, for *Woodland Christmas: Twelve Days of Christmas in the North Woods.*

Writings

AUTHOR AND ILLUSTRATOR

Woodland Christmas: Twelve Days of Christmas in the North Woods, North Winds (Richmond Hill, ON), 1995, Scholastic (New York), 1996.

ILLUSTRATOR

Jean de Brebeuf, *The Huron Carol,* Lester & Orpen Denys (Toronto, ON), 1990, Dutton, 1992.

Marjorie L. C. Pickthall, *The Worker in Sandalwood,* Lester (Toronto, ON), 1991, published in the U.S. as *The Worker in Sandalwood: A Christmas Eve Miracle,* Dutton, 1994.

Joy to the World! (carols), selected by Maureen Forrester, Lester, 1992, Dutton, 1993.

Julie Lawson, *Kate's Castle,* Oxford University Press (Toronto, ON), 1992, Stoddart Kids (Buffalo, NY), 1997.

Alison Baird, *The Dragon's Egg,* Scholastic Canada, 1994.

Woodland Christmas was translated into French and published as *Fete d'Hiver,* Editions Scholastic, 1997.

Work in Progress

Woodland Nutcracker, a picture book, for Key Porter and Ragged Bears (England).

Sidelights

Frances Tyrrell, herself the daughter of a writer, was working as a secretary when the inspiration for her first illustrations came to her. As Tyrrell told *SATA:* "I have been drawing ever since I could hold a pencil, and have never really stopped. There were lovely old books in my life from my early youth—the whole world, it seemed, could be revealed in the beautiful vehicle of the illuminated page. From high school on, I expected to illustrate books myself.

"The ideas for pictures—content and composition— often present themselves to me complete, like a gift dropped into my lap. All I have to do is faithfully reproduce it, in detailed watercolour, which may take up to three or four weeks. The first of *The Huron Carol* images came like that when I was still a secretary, long before the book was even suggested. I stopped typing financial theory for a minute, scribbly-sketched the outline, then returned to tax reform. The resulting painting and three others became greeting cards, which eventually led to the book. I love the history and haunting beauty of *The Huron Carol;* to illustrate it was a joy and privilege."

The author of *The Huron Carol* was Jean de Brebeuf, a French Jesuit missionary to the Huron Nation of the Great Lakes region in the mid-seventeenth century. First translated into English in 1926, *The Huron Carol* is Brebeuf's lyrical version of the biblical saga of the birth of Christ, which Brebeuf wrote down in the Huron language and set in the woodlands in which they lived. He also integrated many elements of indigenous Huron spirituality, such as the Gitchi Manitou deity. Tyrrell's images depict a Huron family expecting their first child. Stranded, they place their newborn in a cradle made of broken bark and keep him warm with rabbit skins. The kings who come bearing gifts are portrayed as representatives of other Native-American nations, and they bring valuable beaver pelts instead of the biblical frankincense and myrrh. Robin Tzannes, a contributor to the *New York Times Book Review,* termed Tyrrell's pictures "rich with the textures of feather, fur and bark . . . . Children and adults will delight in these fine, luminous illustrations."

Tyrrell provided the illustrations for another classic, Marjorie L. C. Pickthall's *The Worker in Sandalwood,* originally published in 1914. This work recounts the mysterious visit of a skilled artisan who helps out a young apprentice woodworker left without food or fire one Christmas Eve, with orders to complete an ornate cabinet by morning. "The illustrations are rich and precise, with fine lines and detail," opined *School*

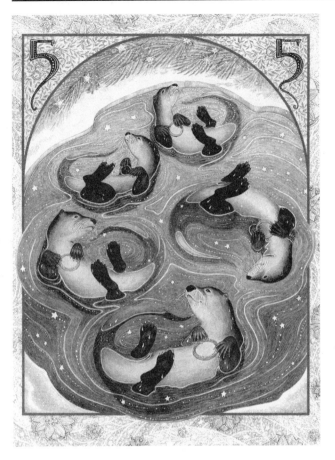

In this fresh presentation of a classic Christmas carol, a young bear presents his true love with gifts from forest and stream. (From Woodland Christmas: Twelve Days of Christmas in the North Woods, *written and illustrated by Tyrrell.)*

Library Journal contributor Jane Marino. A reviewer for the *Montreal Gazette* asserted that "the paintings that grace these pages speak volumes about the artist's skill."

Tyrrell told *SATA* that the inspiration for *Woodland Christmas: Twelve Days of Christmas in the North Woods,* came as she and a friend approached by canoe a remote island in Canada's Georgian Bay. They were surprised to see a black bear walking away from the cabin they had rented, and they joked that perhaps he enjoyed the vacation home in the off-season. Tyrrell

imagined that perhaps Mr. Bear even celebrated Christmas, and that he gave his beloved Miss Bear a series of gifts over twelve days, each gift symbolic of Canada's natural treasures. While the "four calling birds" of the original carol remain, they are presented in watercolor as loons, the bird that also graces Canada's dollar coin; likewise the "five golden rings" are here a quintet of otters swimming in circles, the "ten lords-a-leaping" become lordly moose. The book won praise from reviewers on both sides of the border. "This is a world of magic and fancy," wrote Katherine Matthews in *Canadian Children's Literature,* while Frieda Ling, a reviewer for *Quill & Quire,* asserted that Tyrrell's illustrations "not only portray the animals in all their natural beauty and majesty, but also present the Canadian winter in its stark beauty as well." In an article for *Books in Canada,* Diana Halfpenny declared: "The concept behind the illustrations ... and the pictures themselves, are so charming that young children will pore over them with great delight."

Works Cited

Halfpenny, Diana, review of *Woodland Christmas: Twelve Days of Christmas in the North Woods, Books in Canada,* December, 1996, p. 33.

Ling, Frieda, review of *Woodland Christmas: Twelve Days of Christmas in the North Woods, Quill & Quire,* October, 1995, p. 46.

Marino, Jane, review of *The Worker in Sandalwood: A Christmas Eve Miracle, School Library Journal,* October, 1994, pp. 42-43.

Matthews, Katherine, review of *Woodland Christmas: Twelve Days of Christmas in the North Woods, Canadian Children's Literature,* fall, 1997, pp. 84-85.

Tzannes, Robin, review of *The Huron Carol, New York Times Book Review,* December 6, 1992, p. 91.

Review of *The Worker in Sandalwood, Montreal Gazette,* December 14, 1991, p. J3.

For More Information See

PERIODICALS

Booklist, August, 1994, p. 2052; September 1, 1994, p. 54; September, 1, 1996, p. 138.

Publishers Weekly, September 19, 1994, p. 32.

School Library Journal, October, 1993, p. 44; October, 1996, pp. 41-42.

WARREN, Joshua P(aul) 1976-

Personal

Born October 25, 1976, in Asheville, NC; son of Daniel P. (a land developer) and Peggy D. (a land developer; maiden name, Brigman) Warren. *Education:* Attended University of North Carolina at Asheville, 1995-97.

Addresses

Office—Shadowbox Enterprises, P.O. Box 16801, Asheville, NC 28816.

Joshua P. Warren

Career

Writer, 1991—; book editor in Alexander, NC, 1994-95; Shadowbox Enterprises, Asheville, NC, founder and president, 1995—. Asheville Historical Tour, founder, owner, and president, 1996. Also works as independent filmmaker.

Awards, Honors

Thomas Wolfe Award for Fiction, University of North Carolina, 1996; Aegis Award, 1998; feature film prize, Smoky Mountain/Nantahala Media Arts Festival, 1998, for *Inbred Rednecks.*

Writings

Joshua Warren's Gallery of Mystery and Suspense, World-Comm (Asheville, NC), 1991.

(Compiler and editor) *Speaking of Strange: Residents of Western North Carolina Tell of Their Encounters with the Unexplained,* illustrated by Tim Pedersen, World-Comm, 1994.

Plausible Ghosts: How Could Ghosts Really, Scientifically Exist? This Is How, illustrated by Pedersen and Kristie Ryan, Shadowbox Enterprises (Asheville, NC), 1995.

Haunted Asheville, illustrated by Pedersen, photographs by Mark-Ellis Bennett, Shadowbox Enterprises, 1996.

The Lonely Ameba (for children), illustrated by Pedersen, Overmountain Press (Johnson City, TN), 1998.

(And producer, director, cinematographer, editor, composer, and actor) *Inbred Rednecks* (comedy film), Shadowbox Enterprises, 1998.

Feature writer, *Asheville Citizen-Times,* 1992—. Contributor to magazines.

Work in Progress

The Evil in Asheville, "a supernatural thriller that follows an investigator's research on a haunted castle in North Carolina."

Sidelights

Joshua P. Warren told *SATA:* "I was fortunate enough to have written my first published book at the age of thirteen. Such an early success inspired me to begin shaping my future before most of my peers. It takes a long time to establish yourself as a respectable writer. The sooner one starts, the better.

"My interests are greatly varied. From fiction to nonfiction, children's to adult's, and comedy to drama, I experiment with many genres, forms, and styles of writing. Though the intimacy of a good book is unparalleled, I enjoy the 'storytelling business' in general. This includes motion pictures, songs, and other forms of relating entertaining but substantive tales. I also strive to create works which transcend their medium, allowing the audience to pick up where the work leaves off."

*　　*　　*

WEIHS, Erika 1917-

Personal

Surname pronounced "wise"; born November 4, 1917, in Vienna, Austria; daughter of Arthur S. (a woodworker and businessman) and Vilma G. (a milliner; maiden name, Friedman) Fischl (name later changed to Foster); married Kurt Weihs (an artist, art director, and designer), June 6, 1942; children: Tom (deceased, 1985), John. *Education:* Graduated from Graphische Lehr und Versuchanstalt, Vienna, 1937; attended Leonardo da Vinci Art School, New York City. *Religion:* Pacifist.

Addresses

Home—113 W. 11th St., New York, NY 10011. *Office*—41 Union Sq. W., #1526, New York, NY 10003.

Career

Herbert Dubler, Inc., New York City, designer of greeting cards, 1940-42; freelance painter and illustrator, 1942—. *Exhibitions:* Solo shows at Roko Gallery, New York City, 1950, 1961, 1963, 1967, 1970, 1974, 1976; New York University Contemporary Art Gallery, New York City, 1972; Marist College, Poughkeepsie, NY, 1975; Union of American Hebrew Congregations, New York City, 1982; the Borough President's Gallery, New York City, 1985; Pleiades Gallery, New York City, 1989, 1991, 1993, 1994, 1996, 1998; and the Embassy of Austria, Washington, DC, 1996. Group shows include Whitney Museum of American Art, New York City, 1948, 1949; Carnegie Mellon University, Pittsburgh, PA; Purdue University, West Lafayette, IN; and Ball State University, Muncie, IN. Permanent collections of the artist's works are housed at the Kerlan Collection, University of Minnesota; Museum of the City of New York, the New York Historical Society, the Schomberg Center for Research in Black Culture, the New York City Transit Museum, and Yeshiva University Museum,

Erika Weihs

all in New York City; Slater Memorial Museum, Norwich, CT; Butler Institute of American Art, Youngstown, OH; the Laura Musser Institute, Muscatine, IA; Cape Ann Historical Association, Gloucester, MA; Jane Voorhees Zimmerli Art Museum, Rutgers, NJ; the de Grummond Collection, University of Southern Mississippi, Hattiesburg, MS. *Member:* American Society of Contemporary Artists (chair, exhibition committee, 1996—), National Association of Women Artists (member of oil/acrylic jury, 1983-85; second vice-president, 1987; member of works-on-canvas-jury, 1993-95, and oil jury, 1997-99), Audubon Artists (exhibition coordinator, 1984—), New York Artists Equity.

Awards, Honors

Lillian Cotton Memorial Prize, National Association of Women Artists (NAWA), 1971; citations from Painters and Sculptors Society of New Jersey, 1971, Miniature Art Society of New Jersey, 1980, 1982, American Society of Contemporary Artists (ASCA), 1984, 1992, and Audubon Artists, 1995; Dr. Samuel Gelband Memorial Prize, NAWA, 1978; Sara Whinston Memorial Prize, NAWA, 1980; Charles Horman Memorial Prize, NAWA, 1982; Charles H. Levitt Prize, NAWA, 1983; Charlotte Whinston Memorial Prize, NAWA, 1984, 1995, 1999; Elizabeth Stanton Blake Memorial Prize, NAWA, 1987; National Dr. Maury Leibowitz Award, 1987; Sydney Taylor Picture Book Award, Association of Jewish Libraries, for *Cakes and Miracles: A Purim Tale,* and Philip Reisman Memorial Award, ASCA, both 1992; Aesop Prize, American Folklore Society, 1993, for *Days of Awe: Stories of Rosh Hashanah and Yom*

Kippur; Grumbacher Gold Medal, Audubon Artists, 1995; Children's Books of the Year, Bank Street Child Study Children's Book Committee, 1996, for *Bar Mitzvah: A Jewish Boy's Coming of Age* and *Bat Mitzvah: A Jewish Girl's Coming of Age.*

Illustrator

(And author) *Count the Cats,* Doubleday, 1976.

Jakob Ludwig Karl and Wilhelm Karl Grimm, *Hansel and Gretel,* Simon & Schuster, 1945.

Alice Schneider, *Tales of Many Lands: A Treasury of Fairy Tales, Folk Tales and Legends,* Citadel, 1946.

Johanna Spyri, *Heidi,* Random House, 1946.

Ben Ross Berenberg, *The Snowman Book of Nursery Rhymes,* Capitol, 1948.

Berenberg, *The Big Clock Book,* Capitol, 1949.

Joseph Schrank, *The Cello in the Belly of the Plane,* F. Watts, 1954.

(Co-illustrator with Evelyn Urbanowich) Carol M. Lane, editor, *The Happy Hour Story Book,* Hart, 1955.

Rudyard Kipling, *How the Camel Got His Hump,* Rand McNally, 1955.

Libby M. Klaperman, *Jeremy and the Torah,* Behrman House, 1956.

Marion Belden Cook, *Terry's Ferry,* Dutton, 1957.

Jane K. Lansing, *The Roly-Poly Policeman,* Hart, 1965.

Lansing, *Alphabet Zoo,* Hart, 1965.

Shirley Rousseau Murphy, *The Sand Ponies,* Viking, 1967.

Edith G. Stull, *Good-Bye, Hello,* L. W. Singer, 1967.

Te Ata, compiler, *Indian Tales,* L. W. Singer, 1968.

Michael Baker, *The Mountain and the Summer Stars: An Old Tale Newly Ended,* Harcourt, 1968.

Harry Gersh, *When a Jew Celebrates,* Behrman House, 1971.

Jules Harlow, editor, *Lessons from Our Living Past,* Behrman House, 1972.

Seymour Rossel, *When a Jew Prays,* Behrman House, 1973.

Francine Prose, *Stories from Our Living Past,* Behrman House, 1974.

Seymour Rossel, *When a Jew Seeks Wisdom: The Sayings of the Fathers,* Behrman House, 1975.

Miriam Schlein, *Rosh Hashanah and Yom Kippur,* Behrman House, 1983.

Schlein, *Shavuot,* Behrman House, 1983.

(For adults) Henri Guigonnat, *Daemon in Lithuania,* translated by Barbara Wright, New Directions, 1985.

Lila Perl, *Blue Monday and Friday the Thirteenth,* Clarion Books, 1986.

Miriam Chaikin, *Sound the Shofar: The Story and Meaning of Rosh Hashanah and Yom Kippur,* Clarion, 1986.

Lila Perl, *Mummies, Tombs, and Treasure: Secrets of Ancient Egypt,* Clarion, 1987.

Lila Perl, *Don't Sing Before Breakfast, Don't Sleep in the Moonlight: Everyday Superstitions and How They Began,* Clarion, 1988.

Miriam Gurko, *Theodor Herzl: The Road to Israel,* Jewish Publication Society, 1988.

Lila Perl, *The Great Ancestor Hunt: The Fun of Finding Out Who You Are,* Clarion, 1989.

Miriam Chaikin, *Menorahs, Mezuzas, and Other Jewish Symbols,* Clarion, 1990.

Barbara Diamond Goldin, *Cakes and Miracles: A Purim Tale,* Viking, 1991.

Eric A. Kimmel, *Days of Awe: Stories for Rosh Hashanah and Yom Kippur,* Viking, 1991.

Marguerita Rudolph, adaptor, *How a Shirt Grew in the Field,* by Konstantin Ushinsky, Clarion, 1992.

Carol Carrick, *Two Very Little Sisters,* Clarion, 1993.

Eric A. Kimmel, *Bar Mitzvah: A Jewish Boy's Coming of Age,* Viking, 1995.

Barbara Diamond Goldin, *Bat Mitzvah: A Jewish Girl's Coming of Age,* Viking, 1995.

Norma Simon, *The Story of Passover,* HarperCollins, 1997.

Also illustrator of prayer workbooks published by Behrman House. Contributed illustrations to *The Book of Knowledge: The Children's Encyclopedia,* Grolier Society, 1947, 1958; *Busy Harbors,* Singer/Random House Literature Series, 1969; and magazines.

Sidelights

Since the 1940s, Erika Weihs has worked as a freelance illustrator of children's books. She is also an accomplished painter whose works have been acquired by numerous American museums. Born Erika Fischl in Vienna during World War I, she spent three years in the 1930s at that city's academy of graphic arts. Weihs told *SATA:* "I liked to draw as a young child and had encouragement from my mother and father and teachers throughout my school years. Going on to art school was

Concepts of repentance, prayer, and charity are translated into everyday life in three tales about the Jewish High Holidays, written by Eric A. Kimmel and illustrated by Weihs.

A young Jewish boy who is blind uses his hobby of molding mud from the riverbank to help his mother shape dough into pastries for the villagers during Purim. (From Cakes and Miracles: A Purim Tale, *written by Barbara Diamond Goldin and illustrated by Weihs.)*

a logical follow-up. I was not a student of any one artist. Throughout my student years I was most moved by the work of Kaethe Kollwitz. I also liked Egyptian art . . . . Before entering art school, I flunked mathematics, and Latin I believe . . . all this happened in a different place, at a different time—so very long ago. I left Vienna after Hitler's takeover in the fall of 1938 and landed in New York City via England in the spring of 1940. When I first came to the United States, it was Ben Shahn who most impressed me with his political paintings." During her first years in the city, Weihs designed greeting cards, but quit the job in 1942—the same year she wed fellow artist Kurt Weihs—and became a full-time painter and illustrator.

Weihs's illustrations have graced the pages of many children's books about Jewish history and customs. For *Cakes and Miracles: A Purim Tale,* she created images of a young boy from another time and place to accompany Barbara Diamond Goldin's text. The book won a prestigious award from the Association of Jewish Libraries. Aimed at primary graders, *Cakes and Miracles* is set in Eastern Europe in the late nineteenth century, and centers on Hershel, who is blind. Hershel must help his hard-working mother with chores that keep him from his favorite activity: molding the mud from the riverbank near his home. One day he gets up before his mother and molds some of the dough in their kitchen into the shapes he sees in his imagination. The

dough has been set aside for *hamantashen,* the three-cornered pastries which his mother must sell on the feast of Purim. She bakes the sweets with the dough, and Hershel's unique shapes are a hit with his neighbors. The townspeople flock to buy the pastries, and the local baker wants to give Hershel a job. "The rich, warm illustrations skillfully depict the scenes of village life in this loving story," wrote *Horn Book* reviewer Hanna B. Zeiger. Marcia Posner, reviewing *Cakes and Purim* for *School Library Journal,* declared the book "outstanding" and praised "Weihs's perfectly composed, folk-type illustrations," calling them "rich, yet subtle."

Weihs again brings Jewish culture to life in her illustrations for Norma Simon's classic *The Story of Passover,* first published in the 1960s and reissued in 1997. In this book, Simon recounts the history of the annual Jewish feast that commemorates the Israelites' deliverance from slavery in ancient Egypt. In subdued tones that reflect the reds and browns of the desert and Red Sea area, Weihs's oil paintings "evoke the hardship of the Hebrews as well as the joy of the preparation that modern Jewish families feel each spring," declared a *Publishers Weekly* reviewer.

For Carol Carrick's *Two Very Little Sisters,* Weihs earned praise for helping to evoke the feel of the 1880s with her illustrations. The book recounts the real-life story of two New England women, Lucy and Sarah

Adams, who were just around 4 feet tall as adults. They became part of a circus sideshow for a time, but eventually rejected that lifestyle and began performing on their own, eventually opening a tea room. Martha Rosen, who reviewed *Two Very Little Sisters* for *School Library Journal,* remarked that "the authenticity of detail in architecture, furnishings, and dress gives a vivid sense of time and place." A *Publishers Weekly* critic commented: "Weihs's paintings capture the era splendidly—her flat, primitive style and thinly applied paint convey the feel of an aging canvas."

Weihs has a small studio in Greenwich Village where she paints. The Roko Gallery in New York City began to show her work in 1950, and continued until the mid-1970s. Weihs also has a long affiliation with New York City's Pleiades Gallery. "As a painter I solely work in my studio, from memory, not from life," Weihs told *SATA.* "As an illustrator, I believe the job of an illustrator is not merely to illustrate the text, but to add to it pictorially so as to make the story more interesting and thought-provoking for the child. I like to be in complete control over the visual part of a book. That is, be handed all the pertinent information plus the type-galleys and make a dummy with the type pasted in position and the illustrations sketched. I find this part the most exciting. When I do illustrations in full color, I usually use acrylics or oils. I have done books in pen and ink, Wolff's carbon-pencil, gouache, and scratchboard. I feel that each story requires a different approach and technique, and using a different medium changes one's style. Generally my style is flat, two dimensional. Although I am fascinated with unexpected results I get when I, for instance, do a monoprint, I really prefer a planned approach.

"I need to be moved emotionally, aesthetically, and/or intellectually by art to appreciate it. I am sure everything I ever saw has influenced me. I love nature, the wind in my face, trees, and all growing things. I love the city, and have lived in Greenwich Village since 1947. I am married to an artist, and I have two sons and a grandson, now hopefully in his last year of college."

Works Cited

Posner, Marcia, review of *Cakes and Miracles: A Purim Tale, School Library Journal,* March, 1991, p. 172.
Rosen, Martha, review of *Two Very Little Sisters, School Library Journal,* March, 1994, pp. 213-14.
Review of *The Story of Passover, Publishers Weekly,* January 27, 1997, p. 97.
Review of *Two Very Little Sisters, Publishers Weekly,* August 23, 1993, p. 70.
Zeiger, Hanna B., review of *Cakes and Miracles: A Purim Tale, Horn Book,* July-August, 1991, p. 447.

For More Information See

PERIODICALS

Booklist, February 1, 1997, p. 943.
Horn Book, November-December, 1991, p. 721; March-April, 1993, p. 231; September-October, 1995, p. 620.

Publishers Weekly, January 2, 1995, p. 78.
School Library Journal, January, 1991, p. 99; December, 1992, p. 93; March, 1995, p. 230.

* * *

WILBUR, Frances 1921-

Personal

Born March 8, 1921, in Mankato, MN; daughter of Roswell C. (an educator) and Catharine Corinne (a teacher; maiden name, Creamer) Puckett; married Richard R. Wilford, June, 1945 (divorced, 1968); married William A. Wilbur (a physician), July 14, 1968; children: Margo Wilford Sorenson, Stephen, Katharine Wilford Haines, Geoffrey; stepchildren: Mary Wilbur Wade, May Wilbur Koski. *Education:* Beloit College, B.A., 1942. *Politics:* Republican. *Religion:* Presbyterian.

Addresses

Home—22399 Cupertino Rd., No. 16, Cupertino, CA 95014. *Electronic mail*—hoofbeats4@aol.com.

Career

Writer. Signal Intelligence Service, senior cryptanalyst, 1942-46. Wife of a Foreign Service Officer, stationed at

Frances Wilbur with Giselle, an arctic wolf pup.

the U.S. Embassy in Madrid, Spain, 1947-49, and Italy, 1949-52. Director of a horsemanship camp, 1968-90. Pasadena Red Cross, served as director of Volunteer Office. *Member:* Academy of American Poets, Phi Beta Kappa, Phi Sigma Iota.

Awards, Honors

Milkweed Prize for Children's Literature, Milkweed Editions, 1998, for *The Dog with Golden Eyes;* awards for poetry.

Writings

A *Guide for the Parents of Horse-Crazy Kids,* foreword by Hilda Gurney, Half Halt Press (Middletown, MD), 1990.

A Horse Called Holiday, Scholastic, 1992.

The Dog with Golden Eyes, illustrated by Mark Coyle, Milkweed Editions (Minneapolis, MN), 1998.

Author of "Valley Roots," a history column in *Fence Post,* 1983-92.

Work in Progress

The Horse Next Door, about a Caucasian girl and a Native American girl who become best friends because they own the same breed of horse; *Candle in the Wind,* a mystery for adults, set in Spain in 1947.

Sidelights

Frances Wilbur told *SATA:* "I cannot remember when I did not write. I wrote stories for my school classes. When I was in my thirties, I took an adult education course in creative writing, but at that time I didn't think about writing as a career.

"My parents were educators and great readers. Father constantly gave us books as gifts. When I was eight or nine, he gave me the complete works of Rudyard Kipling in one volume, a real treasure. I read it through many times. If I was reluctant to start a book that he wanted me to read, he would read the first chapter to me out loud. He knew that, when I was hooked, I would finish it by myself. When Father and I did the dishes together, he always recited poetry—Whittier and Long-fellow and Bryant and Emerson. Doing the dishes with him was really fun. I have loved poetry ever since, and I write poetry whenever I am deeply moved. I have won several prizes for my poetry and recently was elected to the Academy of American Poets.

"Father was the principal of our high school, and when I went away to college, he gave me some advice. 'I don't have to tell you to get good grades, because I know you will. But most of all, I want you to have fun.' I took his advice. I went to Beloit College in Wisconsin, graduat-ing in 1942 with teaching credentials for Wisconsin and Illinois, in English, art, French, and chemistry. I was the social chairman and song leader for my sorority, Kappa Delta, the president of Ka Ne, Beloit's creative writing

society, and a member of the Shakespeare Club. I was elected to Phi Sigma Iota for my work in French, and to Phi Beta Kappa. My father died of a massive heart attack a week before I was to return to school for my sophomore year. This tragedy changed my life.

"To eke out my scholarship I took four part-time National Youth Agency (NYA) jobs—working in the Office of the Registrar, reading aloud to a blind girl who planned to teach English at the Illinois State Institute for the Blind (she succeeded), secretary to the head of the speech department, and waiting tables in the self-help dining hall. I also worked at a local stable to pay for my riding lessons. Since I was carrying a heavy scholastic load (eighteen hours), I had to reorganize my schedule, and my grades went up!

"In my senior year at college I received a mysterious letter from the Army War College asking me to enroll in a correspondence course in cryptanalysis (breaking codes and ciphers), that would lead to a job in the Signal Intelligence Service (SIS) in Washington, D.C. I was thrilled, and could hardly wait to get each lesson. I had to prepare the lessons in private and mail them secretly. I would wait until my roommate was asleep, get out of bed, work the next lesson, and get it ready to mail. I graduated in June, 1942, right after Pearl Harbor. The Army War College came through with their job offer. I had ten days at home before I left for Washington. I spent the next four years there and had a blast.

"My college boyfriend asked me to marry him the night before he went overseas. He was gone for three years to England, Africa, and Italy. Ten days after he came home, we were married. He had planned to teach Spanish and worked towards his master's degree from George Washington University while I continued work-ing in the SIS. My husband signed up to take the foreign service exam, passed it, and was appointed a career officer in the diplomatic service. I resigned from the SIS. Our first child was three months old when we received our first assignment, to Madrid, Spain, which was considered a desirable post. We were in Madrid three years and in Italy for four years. I never got homesick, except for the entire United States. I became more appreciative than ever for the privilege of being an American. After we came home, it was two years before I could sing our national anthem all the way through without breaking down.

"My brother encouraged my love of horses, but I really became involved with horses through the Sunday school teacher of our youngest daughter. The teacher's husband operated a small stable not far from our house, and I leased a horse from him. Eventually, I took riding lessons and managed to buy the horse I had been leasing. One summer, I took the kids with me in a borrowed house-trailer and attended the National Equestrian Asso-ciation (NEA) Rating Center in Steamboat Springs, Colorado, so I would be qualified for teaching riding and jumping at accredited colleges.

"I met my second husband, who is a physician from Stanford, through our mutual love of horses and dogs. When we married, between the two of us we had six kids, five dogs, four cars, three horses, and two houses, but we were ONE family. Our children were so much alike many people thought they were true siblings. We bought a ranch in a mountain valley and operated a summer horsemanship camp for twenty years, teaching Combined Training, the Olympic equestrian sport.

"Then I began seriously to write. I needed a book I could put in the hands of the parents of the kids I was teaching, and discovered that I would have to write it myself. So I did. That was *A Guide for the Parents of Horse-Crazy Kids.* It was published by Half Halt Press, a publisher specializing in horse books. My second book was inspired by the first horse I leased. *A Horse Called Holiday* was published by Scholastic and translated into Norwegian, Swedish, and German.

"On our ranch was a very old board-and-batten house, with newspapers from 1894 covering the walls in one of the rooms. I was curious about who built it and when, so I began a search of its history. Along the southern boundary of our property was an extinct gold mine, the mine tailings visible in big piles. I learned that the man who discovered the mine in 1866 had married a fourteen-year-old Indian girl. A number of their descendants lived in or near our valley. This led to a history column, 'Valley Roots' that I wrote for our local newspaper for several years.

"One day I found two Indian arrowheads in the area which I was clearing of rocks so I could ride my horse there. I learned that many Indians had lived in our valley before white men came and settled here, and some had even lived in our old ranch house. I was fascinated by the stories I learned as I became friends with the descendants of those Indians. I began tracing their genealogy, and my husband and I were invited to attend meetings of the local Indian council. I started writing down the history stories, under the title *Pathways into Paiute Country.* Someday I will publish them.

"A girl who was an animator for Hanna Barbera in Hollywood rented a house near our home, a big ranch house we had built. She studied each animal in real life before she drew it, then shipped her work to the city by Federal Express. When she studied wolves for an assignment, she became so devoted to them that she became a licensed breeder of pure-bred wolves. She had ten or twelve of them. The wolves fascinated me as well. My neighbor taught me how to feed them so I could do that for her on the days she couldn't get home in time. I helped her socialize the pups as they grew up. My third book, *The Dog with Golden Eyes,* was inspired by one of her wolves."

The Dog with Golden Eyes is the story of Cassie, a lonely, overweight teenager, and Tokie, the lost dog she secretly adopts. While caring for and researching the animal, which she discovers is an Arctic wolf, Cassie comes out of her shell, loses weight, and learns

responsibility. Offering a favorable assessment of the work in *Booklist,* Susan Dove Lempke asserted: "This is a readable, engaging novel with special appeal for animal lovers."

Works Cited

Lempke, Susan Dove, review of *The Dog with Golden Eyes, Booklist,* September 1, 1998, p. 121.

For More Information See

PERIODICALS

Kirkus Reviews, June 15, 1998, p. 903.
Publishers Weekly, July 27, 1998, p. 78.
School Library Journal, July, 1998, p. 100.

*   *   *

WILLIAMS, Barbara 1925-

Personal

Born January 1, 1925, in Salt Lake City, UT; daughter of Walter (a lawyer) and Emily (Jeremy) Wright; married J. D. Williams (a professor of political science), July 5, 1946; children: Kirk, Gil, Taylor, Kimberly. *Education:* Attended Banff School of Fine Arts, 1945; University of Utah, B.A., 1946, M.A., 1972; Boston University, graduate study, 1949-50. *Politics:* Democrat.

Addresses

Home—1587 E. Ventnor Ave., Salt Lake City, UT 84121.

Career

Writer. *Deseret News,* Salt Lake City, UT, occasional society reporter and columnist, 1944-50; Library of Congress, Washington, DC, secretary, 1946-48, 1951; University of Utah, Salt Lake City, remedial English teacher, 1960-72; *Marriage,* St. Meinrad, IN, children's book reviewer, 1972-76; instructor, creative writing. *Member:* Mortar Board, Phi Beta Kappa, Phi Kappa Phi, Society of Children's Book Writers and Illustrators.

Awards, Honors

First place, Utah Fine Arts Writing Contest, 1965, for *William H. McGuffey: Boy Reading Genius,* 1971, for *The Secret Name,* 1975, for *Desert Hunter,* and 1986, for *Beheaded, Survived;* Children's Book Showcase, 1975, notable book, American Library Association, 1975, and Fifty Books of the Year, American Institute of Graphic Arts, all for *Albert's Toothache;* Children's Choice, International Reading Association-Children's Book Council, 1978, for *Jeremy Isn't Hungry,* 1979, for *Where Are You, Angela von Hauptmann, Now That I Need You?,* and 1981, for *So What If I'm a Sore Loser;* Christopher Award, 1979, for *Chester Chipmunk's Thanksgiving;* Oklahoma Sequoyah Award, 1997, Nebraska Golden Sower Award, Missouri Mark Twain

Barbara Williams

Award, South Dakota Prairie Pasque Award, all 1998, finalist, Nickelodeon Kids' Choice Awards, 1999, all for *Titanic Crossing*.

Writings

PICTURE BOOKS

Gary and the Very Terrible Monster, illustrated by Lois Axeman, Children's Press, 1973.

We Can Jump, illustrated by Mary P. Maloney and Stan Fleming, Children's Press, 1973.

Albert's Toothache, illustrated by Kay Chorao, Dutton, 1974.

Kevin's Grandma, illustrated by Chorao, Dutton, 1975.

Someday, Said Mitchell, illustrated by Chorao, Dutton, 1976.

If He's My Brother, illustrated by Tomie de Paola, Harvey House, 1976.

Never Hit a Porcupine, illustrated by Anne Rockwell, Dutton, 1977.

Chester Chipmunk's Thanksgiving, illustrated by Kay Chorao, Dutton, 1978.

Guess Who's Coming to My Tea Party?, illustrated by Yuri Salzman, Holt, 1978.

Jeremy Isn't Hungry, illustrated by Martha Alexander, Dutton, 1978.

Whatever Happened to Beverly Bigler's Birthday?, illustrated by Emily Arnold McCully, Harcourt, 1978.

Hello, Dandelions!, photographs by the author, Holt, 1979.

A Valentine for Cousin Archie, illustrated by Kay Chorao, Dutton, 1980.

So What If I'm a Sore Loser, illustrated by Linda Strauss Edwards, Harcourt, 1981.

The Horrible, Impossible, Bad Witch Child, illustrated by Carol Nicklaus, Avon, 1982.

Donna Jean's Disaster, illustrated by Margot Apple, Albert Whitman, 1986.

The ABC's of Uniforms and Outfits, illustrated by Sherry Meidell, Winston-Derek, 1991.

FOR MIDDLE-GRADERS

William H. McGuffey: Boy Reading Genius, illustrated by Robert Doremus, Bobbs-Merrill, 1968.

The Secret Name, illustrated by Jennifer Perrott, Harcourt, 1972.

Brigham Young and Me, Clarissa, Doubleday, 1978.

Where Are You, Angela von Hauptmann, Now That I Need You?, Holt, 1979.

Mitzi and the Terrible Tyrannosaurus Rex, illustrated by Emily Arnold McCully, Dutton, 1982.

Tell the Truth, Marly Dee, Dutton, 1982.

Mitzi's Honeymoon with Nana Potts, illustrated by Emily Arnold McCully, Dutton, 1983.

Mitzi and Frederick the Great, illustrated by McCully, Dutton, 1984.

Mitzi and the Elephants, illustrated by McCully, Dutton, 1985.

The Author and Squinty Gritt, illustrated by Betsy James, 1990.

The Crazy Gang Next Door, Crowell, 1990.

Titanic Crossing (fiction), Dial, 1995.

H-E-L-L-L-P! The Crazy Gang Is Back!, HarperCollins, 1995.

NONFICTION FOR CHILDREN

Let's Go to an Indian Cliff Dwelling, illustrated by Robin King, Putnam, 1965.

I Know a Policeman, illustrated by Charles Dougherty, Putnam, 1966.

I Know a Fireman, illustrated by Paula Byrnes, Putnam, 1967.

I Know a Mayor, illustrated by Charles Dougherty, Putnam, 1967.

I Know a Garageman, illustrated by Marvin Besunder, Putnam, 1968.

I Know a Bank Teller, illustrated by Albert Micale, Putnam, 1968.

Boston: Seat of American History, McGraw, 1969.

I Know a Weatherman, illustrated by Russell Hoover, Putnam, 1970.

Desert Hunter: The Spider Wasp, illustrated by Beverly Dobrin Wallace, Harvey House, 1975.

I Know a Salesperson, illustrated by Frank Aloise, Putnam, 1978.

Seven True Elephant Stories, illustrated by Carol Maisto, Hastings House, 1978.

NONFICTION FOR YOUNG ADULTS

Cornzapoppin'!: Popcorn Recipes and Party Ideas for All Occasions, photographs by Royce Bair, Holt, 1976.

(With Susan Arnold) *Pins, Picks, and Popsicle Sticks: A Straight-Line Crafts Book*, illustrated by Arnold, Holt, 1977.

(With Rosemary Williams) *Cookie Craft: No-Bake Designs for Edible Party Favors and Decorations,* Holt, 1977.
Breakthrough: Women in Politics, Walker, 1979.
Breakthrough: Women in Archaeology, Walker, 1981.

OTHER

Eternally Peggy (three-act play), Desert News Press, 1957.
The Ghost of Black Jack (one-act play), Samuel French, 1961.
Just the Two of Us (one-act play), Utah Printing, 1965.
Twelve Steps to Better Exposition (textbook), C. E. Merrill, 1968, 2nd edition, 1978.
The Well-Structured Paragraph (textbook), C. E. Merrill, 1970, 2nd edition, 1978.
(With Carol Grundmann) *Twenty-Six Lively Letters: Making an ABC Quiet Book* (adult), Taplinger, 1977.
Beheaded, Survived (young adult fiction), Watts, 1987.

Sidelights

Barbara Williams is a versatile author of books for all ages, who has penned dozens of volumes over the course of a career spanning more than four decades. She is best known for her stories for primary- and middle-graders that focus on the relationships between children and other family members while exploring issues such as sibling rivalry and family misunderstandings. Her works have been commended for their humorous and authentic presentation of the perspectives of young people who are trying to discover their place in the family. Many of the thoughts and feelings that Williams attempts to capture in her books are based on her personal experiences with her four adopted children or on recollections from her own childhood. *Albert's Toothache,* for instance, one of Williams's best-loved books, has been praised for its exploration of the problems that can arise when parents and children have difficulty communicating. Other highly regarded stories by Williams, including *Chester Chipmunk's Thanksgiving* and *Mitzi and the Terrible Tyrannosaurus Rex,* also portray the tribulations of family life with humor and insight. In addition, Williams has written novels for older readers that vividly depict teenagers in settings as diverse as a modern-day school trip (*Beheaded, Survived*) and the historical sinking of the ship *Titanic* (*Titanic Crossing*).

Williams was born in Salt Lake City, Utah, in 1925, the fifth child of Walter and Emily Wright. Her parents were in their mid-forties by the time she was born, so her childhood was a bit different than most. She never knew her grandparents, and had older sisters who were almost adults themselves. Her other siblings were too old to play with her, and her middle-aged mother was usually too tired to allow friends into their home to play. As a result, Williams grew up with a lot of time to herself, and found that stories were a good form of entertainment. "I was writing stories long before I could write my name," the author noted in the *Sixth Book of Junior Authors and Illustrators.* "As a preschooler I would scribble in a tablet for hours, and then 'read' the stories I'd written to my mother as she ironed my father's shirts and handkerchiefs."

When Williams entered kindergarten, her teacher recognized the young girl's enthusiasm for words and assigned her the task of class reporter. The Salt Lake City newspapers, including the *Salt Lake Tribune,* published a weekly children's section that featured student reports from the classroom. "Thus in kindergarten I not only received my first byline but also met Olive Wooley Burt, who edited the section for the *Tribune* and would later serve as a role model for my life," the author related in her *Something about the Author Autobiography Series* (*SAAS*) essay. Williams continued serving as a classroom reporter for most of her elementary school years, and "was awed every time I was in [Burt's] presence. Not only did she work as a reporter/editor for the *Salt Lake Tribune* and direct a children's radio show for that paper, but she also wrote children's books!"

As she grew older, the young author discovered another reason for indulging her writing talents. "As I look back upon it, I feel sure I must have turned to pencils and typewriters in self-defense," Williams once admitted to *SATA.* "The only non-athlete in the neighborhood (I failed courses in beginning swimming seven times), no captain ever chose me for his team; and I had to find *something* to do while all the other kids were playing football and baseball. As a result, I spent a good part of my childhood living in the realm of my imagination and setting down my ideas on an antique typewriter which I attacked with one finger." She contributed stories and poems to the *Tribune Junior,* a monthly newspaper supplement written by children. After the magazine folded, Olive Burt selected one of her stories and published it in the regular section of the newspaper, thus earning Williams her first paycheck as a writer.

"To be honest, however, writing was only third or fourth in my goals for the future," Williams admitted in *SAAS.* "First, I wanted to be an actress or courtroom lawyer. (The roles seemed pretty interchangeable in my mind.) And second, I wanted to be a mother like my sister Virginia." Williams graduated from high school and entered the University of Utah, hoping to become a lawyer like her self-taught father. She studied English, became involved with drama productions, and wrote for both campus publications and the local paper. As a junior she edited the university's yearbook and later took a special fine-arts course in Canada. By the time she graduated, she had decided against law school and instead hoped to find an interesting job in Washington, DC, where her new husband, J. D. Williams, was soon to start work. "But suddenly Reality set in," the author related in *SAAS.* "Whereas the whole world assumed that J. D., a male, would now begin a career on a professional track, the only question prospective employers ever asked me, a female, was, 'How fast can you type?'"

Frustrated by menial clerical jobs, Williams began taking creative-writing classes while her husband studied for a Ph.D. at Harvard University. She enrolled at Boston University and worked as a graduate assistant while studying for her M.A. degree. Financial problems prevented her from finishing the degree, but she soon occupied herself with raising the first of four adopted children. Writing was never far from the author's mind, however. After the family returned to Utah, Williams organized several friends into a writers' group. At first she focused on plays, indulging her old fondness for drama, and had three of them published. But, in the process of finding things to read to her sons, the young mother had also discovered the children's library. "After a while, I became so smitten with children's books that I lost all interest in playwriting for adults and began writing manuscripts for children's books instead," Williams stated in her autobiographical essay. "I collected dozens and dozens of rejections before it occurred to me that it might be easier to publish nonfiction than fiction."

Williams recalled how much her son Kirk had enjoyed a family trip to Mesa Verde, Colorado, where they explored the ruins of Anasazi cliff dwellings. Query letters resulted in a contract for 1965's *Let's Go to an Indian Cliff Dwelling,* Williams's first published book, which led to several other nonfiction works. Also published in the 1960s was the first of Williams's two composition textbooks, written for remedial students at the University of Utah, where she had resumed graduate studies. When it came time to submit a degree thesis, the author turned in a fiction manuscript. *The Secret Name* was published in 1972, and was inspired by the experiences two of Williams's friends had while fostering a Native-American girl in their family. In Williams's story, eight-year-old Betsy Burnsides has come to live with the Mills family so that she can attend the local school. Naturally, the family experiences a bit of culture shock: some of Betsy's beliefs seem like superstitions to the Mills, and they encounter prejudice from Betsy's classmates and their parents. Nevertheless, with the aid of her nine-year-old "white sister" Laurie, Betsy begins to adjust and becomes a loved member of the family. When a sudden emergency calls Betsy home to the reservation early, Laurie knows she will miss her "sister," but also begins to think about what is best for Betsy.

The Secret Name was well received by critics, particularly because it leaves open the question of whether Betsy would be better off on the reservation, with her own people and heritage, or with the Mills family, who can provide better opportunities for her to learn. "No pat answers are given," a *Booklist* reviewer noted, adding that the two girls' problems "are presented realistically." "Williams writes sympathetically about the children of both cultures," a *Publishers Weekly* critic stated, while *School Library Journal* contributor Cathy Coyle remarked that "interesting information about Navaho art, customs and beliefs is skillfully woven into the story." A *Times Literary Supplement* writer praised the author's characterization and lifelike details, and concluded the reader "is left with many thoughts on which to work, and they are thoughts which do not stop when the story is ended."

Williams soon turned her hand to picture books, penning a series of very popular stories for young readers during the 1970s. Many of these works were inspired by the author's experiences with her own children. *Albert's Toothache,* for instance, came about after Williams's daughter Kim had trouble convincing her mother she had broken a wrist. "She was a hypochondriac, and she just about drove me up the wall telling me about all her aches and pains," the author recalled in *SAAS.* After a nurse saw nothing on an X-ray, Williams thought her daughter was exaggerating once again. When the doctor later informed her that Kim actually had *two* broken wrists, "I felt guilty—horribly guilty—and wrote *Albert's Toothache* as an act of penance." In Williams's story, young turtle Albert is having trouble convincing his family that he is experiencing a terrible toothache—understandable, since no one in Albert's family has ever even had a tooth. After Grandma arrives to visit, however, she solves the mystery by asking the right question: *where* does the tooth ache? "On my left toe," the young turtle replies, where "a gopher bit me when I stepped in his hole."

Critics hailed *Albert's Toothache* for the way it "pokes gentle fun at the communication gap that can exist between young children and the rest of the world," in the words of a *Booklist* reviewer. "This brief tale is as warm as a hug," a *Publishers Weekly* writer likewise commented, praising the conclusion as "surprisingly funny and tender." Zena Sutherland found the dialogue, which makes up most of the story, "very funny indeed," and added in the *Bulletin of the Center for Children's Books* that "there's substance in the way it reflects relationships in human families." Humor that explores the "ridiculous contradictions/confusions" of language makes the book particularly suited to young audiences, Lillian N. Gerhardt observed in *School Library Journal.* The critic concluded that "*Albert's Toothache* is pure gold in support of the refinement of early childhood's levels of humor."

Williams's next picture book, *Kevin's Grandma,* was inspired both by her own longing for the grandparents she never knew as well as by the personality of her second son, Gil. "There has never been a malicious bone in Gil's body," the author explained in *SAAS,* "but from the time he could talk at age two he has been telling whoppers, playing tricks on me, and testing the limits of my sense of humor." In *Kevin's Grandma,* young Kevin competes with his friend's tales of his traditional grandmother by telling him that *his* grandma rides a motorcycle, makes peanut-butter soup, orders them pizza at midnight, climbs mountains, and goes scuba diving. This "story of small-boy braggadocio" is full of "tongue-in-cheek humor," Ethel L. Heins noted in *Horn Book.* "Blithe and bouncy," Sutherland wrote in *Bulletin of the Center for Children's Books, Kevin's Grandma* "has action, humor, variety, tall-tale appeal, and a nice quirk at the ending." A *Publishers Weekly* reviewer similarly enjoyed the humor of the book, concluding: "Just the thing for the doldrums on a dim day is this absurd, sprightly combination of story and pictures."

With *Someday, Said Mitchell,* Williams and Kay Chorao "have hit the bull's eye again," a *Publishers Weekly* writer declared. This story of a little boy who tells his mother of all the ways he will help her when he is big was inspired by the author's son Taylor, who enjoyed assisting his mother with chores even as a small boy. While young Mitchell has big dreams about providing for his mom "someday," she finds little ways for him to be a big help right now. The author and illustrator "zoom in on another warm exchange between preschooler and adult," Betsy Hearne remarked in *Booklist,* adding that "the dialogue is straight from a mother-and-child's day that is going well." *Horn Book* critic Mary M. Burns similarly praised the efforts of both author and illustrator, and called *Someday, Said Mitchell* "a charming mood piece, simply and joyously developed into a litany of love."

Williams produced a dozen picture books during the 1970s, including two more winners featuring animal heroes. *Never Hit a Porcupine* portrays young Fletcher Fox leaving home to make his way in the world. His parents offer him all sorts of advice, from "never tease a bee" to "take your sweater . . . and be home in time for dinner." A *Publishers Weekly* critic wrote that the author "has a real winner in this brisk, endearing story of Fletcher Fox," while *School Library Journal* contributor Cynthia Percak Infantino remarked that "youngsters will enjoy seeing the plucky little reynard 'act his way' through these imagined situations." The Christopher Award-winning *Chester Chipmunk's Thanksgiving* similarly "rivals [Williams's and Chorao's] acclaimed *Kevin's Grandma* and *Albert's Toothache* in charm and meaning," a *Publishers Weekly* commentator declared. In this work, Chester Chipmunk has made a pecan pie for Thanksgiving dinner, but when he asks his neighbors to come share it, they all turn him down because they have other plans. Only Oswald Opossum takes Chester up on his offer, but when the two sit down to dinner they are suddenly joined by the rest of their neighbors, their families, and a spread of extra food. While *School Library Journal* contributor Janet French found that a "querulous air pervades the whole tale, leaving readers with a sense of something short of holiday joy," *Booklist* critic Barbara Elleman stated that "the giving-and-sharing theme sets well in this Thanksgiving story and offers opportunities for discussion."

In her picture book *Jeremy Isn't Hungry,* Williams offers a humorous glimpse of everyday life as older brother Davey tries to keep his baby brother Jeremy occupied while his mother gets dressed. In this "infectiously jolly story," as a *Publishers Weekly* critic described it, every page "is crazy fun and the story as a whole is as suspenseful as a novel." A *Kirkus Reviews* writer praised the "funny, close-to-home dialogue between Davey and Mother," while a *Booklist* reviewer likewise noted that "Davey's problems . . . are hilariously stated in a running conversation between him and his mother." Trouble of a more unusual kind worries the heroine of *Whatever Happened to Beverly Bigler's Birthday?* Beverly Bigler is turning seven, but her family seems to have forgotten her birthday in the wake of her older sister's wedding. "Williams's bubbling story," in which Beverly confuses the wedding cake and gifts for her own but is surprised at the end, "is a nifty

addition to the publisher's Let Me Read line," a *Publishers Weekly* commentator stated. Zena Sutherland of the *Bulletin of the Center for Children's Books* praised the way Williams steadily focuses on Beverly's point of view, concluding that "the story evokes the reader's sympathy even when the light treatment provokes humor."

Although she was enjoying success in picture-book fiction, Williams had not forgotten her roots in nonfiction during these years, producing works on wasps and dandelions for younger readers as well as craft books for older children. In 1979 and 1980 she wrote two well-received books of biography for young adults. *Breakthrough: Women in Politics* and *Breakthrough: Women in Archaeology* both present profiles of women who have achieved success in their respective fields of endeavor. Reviewing *Women in Politics, Voice of Youth Advocates* contributor Patty Tomillo observed: "The profiles offer a clear look at political duties and possible inspiration" for aspiring politicians. "Intelligence and craftsmanship characterize this collection of objective profiles," *School Library Journal* contributor David A. Lindsey maintained, concluding that the book will not only "inform and entertain, it may even encourage some young women to seriously consider a career in politics." *Bulletin of the Center for Children's Books* critic Zena Sutherland called *Women in Archaeology* "a fine example of career orientation, and it's written with vitality in a smooth, informal style." Terming it "interesting and insightful," William O. Autry, Jr. wrote in *Science Books and Films* that *Women in Archaeology* "makes an important contribution to archeological history as well as to the development of career interests in anthropology for women."

In the 1980s, Williams turned to longer stories for middle-graders. Young Mitzi McAllister is featured in a series of works that show her coping with a new family. In *Mitzi and the Terrible Tyrannosaurus Rex,* eight-year-old Mitzi is uneasy about her mother's upcoming marriage, particularly the arrival of two new stepbrothers. Eleven-year-old Frederick is bossy and looks down on Mitzi, while three-year-old Darwin is a little genius who thinks he is a dinosaur. *Booklist* reviewer Barbara Elleman hailed the author's "ear for dialogue and her sensitivity to children's vulnerability," adding that the combination of humor and sympathy creates "an appealing, readable story." Ann A. Flowers favorably compared Mitzi to Beverly Cleary's popular heroine Ramona Quimby, and added in her *Horn Book* review that *Mitzi and the Terrible Tyrannosaurus Rex* is "an amusing, sparkling book about a very real child." Mitzi returns in both *Mitzi's Honeymoon with Nana Potts* and *Mitzi and Frederick the Great.* In the latter book, Mitzi joins her mother on an archaeological dig, only to be disappointed by the rules she has to follow and her stepbrother Frederick's success. "Williams has captured perfectly the frustrations of family life and the enduring affection underneath it," Jane Agnes Furmanak commented in *School Library Journal,* and so Mitzi and Frederick come to a peaceful understanding by the close of the book. The author "sustains remarkably well Mitzi's point of view and feelings," wrote Nancy C. Hammond in *Horn Book,* adding that this novel of family adjustment "may please an audience that finds straightforward family stories less interesting" than adventures.

Williams's 1982 novel *Tell the Truth, Marly Dee* is a similarly "pleasant family story," as Candy Bertelson noted in *School Library Journal.* Set in rural Idaho, the books follows tough sixth-grader Marly Dee Peterson's efforts to be nice to her sworn enemy, classmate Dennis Cunningham. If Marly Dee can succeed, her devout mother has promised to lose the extra weight that is jeopardizing her health. *Booklist* reviewer Ilene Cooper noted that the Idaho setting and Marly's "blue-collar" family "give this first-person story an unusual perspective." Kate M. Flanagan of *Horn Book* found Marly Dee's conflicts with her classmates and particularly Dennis "hilarious," and added that "the author adeptly captures the tenor of preadolescent love." Praising Williams's "skillful" characterization and believable setting, Bertelson concluded that *Tell the Truth, Marly Dee* is "an entertaining, involving story" which is

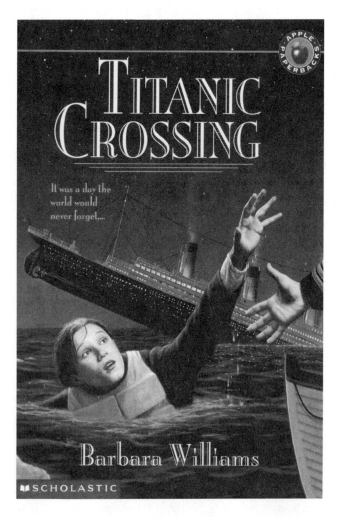

Aboard the ill-fated **Titanic** *on his way home to America in 1912, young Albert Trask is faced with the challenge of saving both his little sister and himself in Williams's well-researched novel based on the historic tragedy.*

"contemporary, yet ... also has an old-fashioned quality."

In 1987 Williams published her first novel for young adults, *Beheaded, Survived.* The title refers to a mnemonic trick for remembering the six wives of King Henry VIII, and the story takes place on a school tour of English historic sites. Fourteen-year-old Jane is shy and feels overshadowed by her confident older sister Courtney; she is also trying to hide her diabetes from the other students so as not to feel like an outsider. Sixteen-year-old Lowell, however, is an outsider by choice, traumatized by his mother's recent death and his father's quick remarriage. When he and Jane are thrown together as "buddies" on the tour, they come to trust each other and a romance ensues. "Williams's romance has a hesitancy based on misunderstandings," a *Publishers Weekly* reviewer observed, "giving it a richness and immediacy that is compelling." In addition, the author's references to literary and historical facts "are authentic," according to a *Kirkus Reviews* critic; "Williams touches on them lightly but makes them interesting." As Zena Sutherland concluded in *Bulletin of the Center for Children's Books:* "Natural dialogue, excellent characterization..., and a smooth development of plot make this an eminently readable story."

Williams turned to actual historical events for the setting of her 1995 novel *Titanic Crossing.* The tragic account of the luxurious ship that sank on its maiden voyage in April 1912 is well known, and provides the backdrop for the story of thirteen-year-old Albert Trask and his family. Albert, his widowed mother Katherine, and his younger sister Ginny have been instructed by Albert's grandmother to return to America. Disapproving of her daughter-in-law's associates in London, Albert's grandmother has sent her son Clay to enforce her instructions. "Tense relationships dominate the first part of the book," a *Kirkus Reviews* critic noted, as Albert tries to act as the "man of the family" and help his mother break free of her in-laws' domination. When the *Titanic* hits an iceberg, however, Albert is given a chance to truly act like a man, as he attempts to find a place for his sister in one of the few lifeboats before the great ship sinks. The wealth of historical details gives the novel an "authentic flavor," according to *Booklist*'s Kay Weisman, making for a "fast-paced adventure that will appeal to history buffs." Roger Sutton of the *Bulletin of the Center for Children's Books* believed that "superfluous foreshadowing" reduced the suspense, but added that "the story does have a grand adventure of an old-fashioned sort." *School Library Journal* contributor Gerry Larson found that this "entertaining blend of fact and fiction" contained "suspense, character development, and pathos amid the dramatic events."

Despite her success with dramatic fiction, humorous books remain the forte of the versatile Williams. In 1990's *The Crazy Gang Next Door,* twelve-year-old Kim Sanders and her mother are watching their neighbor Mrs. Overfield's house when it is invaded by a group of redheaded, wild-eyed children who call themselves the Spikes gang. The gang claim to be Mrs. Overfield's relatives, but their fantastic antics and questionable origin make them a mystery for Kim to solve. "The madcap pace of this zany story never lets up," Connie Tyrrell Burns observed in. *School Library Journal,* calling the book "definitely humorous fare." The Spikes siblings return to bother Kim in the 1995 book *H-E-L-L-L-P! The Crazy Gang Is Back!*. This time the Spikes gang has transferred into Kim's school because Earl Spikes has a crush on Kim—much to her disgust. To try to set up Earl and Kim, the Spikes gang tries to "help" Kim earn a spot on the cheerleading team, wreaking havoc on the school in the process.

While her children once provided inspiration for her writing, "as I grow older ... I find my books are more likely to arise from personal wellsprings rather than from outside influences," Williams revealed in *SAAS.* With her family spread throughout the country, "I'm compelled to search deep within my own recollections of childhood for the sensibilities I record in my juvenile books. Even the protagonist of my two 'Crazy Gang' books, who just happens to share the married name of my daughter (Kimberly Sanders), is not my daughter, Kim, at all, but me, Barbara Wright, as a young student at Bryant Junior High School." Now that her husband has retired, the author added, "there is much we have yet to accomplish—independently—and together. We hope it includes travel, travel, travel, and books, books, books."

Works Cited

Review of *Albert's Toothache, Booklist,* September 15, 1974, p. 103.

Review of *Albert's Toothache, Publishers Weekly,* September 23, 1974, p. 156.

Autry, William O., Jr., review of *Breakthrough: Women in Archaeology, Science Books and Films,* March-April, 1981, p. 216.

Review of *Beheaded, Survived, Kirkus Reviews,* September 15, 1987, p. 1399.

Review of *Beheaded, Survived, Publishers Weekly,* October 9, 1987, p. 90.

Bertelson, Candy, review of *Tell the Truth, Marly Dee, School Library Journal,* November, 1982, p. 92.

Burns, Connie Tyrrell, review of *The Crazy Gang Next Door, School Library Journal,* December, 1990, p. 112.

Burns, Mary M., review of *Someday, Said Mitchell, Horn Book,* June, 1976, p. 283.

Review of *Chester Chipmunk's Thanksgiving, Publishers Weekly,* May 29, 1978, p. 51.

Cooper, Ilene, review of *Tell the Truth, Marly Dee, Booklist,* November 1, 1982, p. 375.

Coyle, Cathy S., review of *The Secret Name, School Library Journal,* October 15, 1972, pp. 3457-58.

Elleman, Barbara, review of *Chester Chipmunk's Thanksgiving, Booklist,* June 15, 1978, p. 1620.

Elleman, review of *Mitzi and the Terrible Tyrannosaurus Rex, Booklist,* June 1, 1982, p. 1316.

Flanagan, Kate M., review of *Tell the Truth, Marly Dee, Horn Book,* October, 1982, p. 519.

Flowers, Ann A., review of *Mitzi and the Terrible Tyrannosaurus Rex, Horn Book,* August, 1982, p. 410.

French, Janet, review of *Chester Chipmunk's Thanksgiving, School Library Journal,* October, 1978, p. 140.

Furmanak, Jane Agnes, review of *Mitzi and Frederick the Great, School Library Journal,* October, 1984, p. 163.

Gerhardt, Lillian N., review of *Albert's Toothache, School Library Journal,* November 15, 1974, p. 3042.

Hammond, Nancy C., review of *Mitzi and Frederick the Great, Horn Book,* June, 1984, p. 335.

Hearne, Betsy, review of *Someday, Said Mitchell, Booklist,* May 1, 1976, p. 1273.

Heins, Ethel L., review of *Kevin's Grandma, Horn Book,* August, 1975, p. 372.

Infantino, Cynthia Percak, review of *Never Hit a Porcupine, School Library Journal,* November, 1977, p. 52.

Review of *Jeremy Isn't Hungry, Booklist,* November 15, 1978, p. 551.

Review of *Jeremy Isn't Hungry, Kirkus Reviews,* October 1, 1978, p. 1069.

Review of *Jeremy Isn't Hungry, Publishers Weekly,* September 18, 1978, p. 167.

Review of *Kevin's Grandma, Publishers Weekly,* March 31, 1975, p. 50.

Larson, Gerry, review of *Titanic Crossing, School Library Journal,* June, 1995, p. 115.

Lindsey, David A., review of *Breakthrough: Women in Politics, School Library Journal,* October, 1980, p. 160.

Review of *Never Hit a Porcupine, Publishers Weekly,* May 9, 1977, p. 92.

Review of *The Secret Name, Booklist,* June 1, 1973, p. 951.

Review of *The Secret Name, Publishers Weekly,* January 22, 1973, p. 71.

Review of *The Secret Name, Times Literary Supplement,* April 6, 1973, p. 382.

Review of *Someday, Said Mitchell, Publishers Weekly,* April 26, 1976, p. 59.

Sutherland, Zena, review of *Albert's Toothache, Bulletin of the Center for Children's Books,* January, 1975, p. 88.

Sutherland, review of *Beheaded, Survived, Bulletin of the Center for Children's Books,* December, 1987, p. 80.

Sutherland, review of *Breakthrough: Women in Archaeology, Bulletin of the Center for Children's Books,* April, 1981, p. 164.

Sutherland, review of *Kevin's Grandma, Bulletin of the Center for Children's Books,* November, 1975, p. 56.

Sutherland, review of *Whatever Happened to Beverly Bigler's Birthday?, Bulletin of the Center for Children's Books,* October, 1979, pp. 39-40.

Sutton, Roger, review of *Titanic Crossing, Bulletin of the Center for Children's Books,* September, 1995, pp. 33-34.

Review of *Titanic Crossing, Kirkus Reviews,* June 15, 1995, p. 865.

Tomillo, Patty, review of *Breakthrough: Women in Politics, Voice of Youth Advocates,* February, 1980, p. 50.

Weisman, Kay, review of *Titanic Crossing, Booklist,* May 15, 1995, p. 1648.

Review of *Whatever Happened to Beverly Bigler's Birthday?, Publishers Weekly,* April 23, 1979, pp. 80, 82.

Williams, Barbara, comments in *Sixth Book of Junior Authors and Illustrators,* edited by Sally Holmes Holtze, Wilson, 1989, pp. 316-18.

Williams, essay in *Something about the Author Autobiography Series,* Volume 16, Gale, 1993, pp. 263-84.

For More Information See

BOOKS

Children's Literature Review, Volume 48, Gale, 1998, pp. 187-208.

PERIODICALS

Booklist, January 1, 1991, p. 939.
School Library Journal, March, 1991, p. 180.
Voice of Youth Advocates, April, 1996, p. 32.

—*Sketch by Diane Telgen*

Cumulative Indexes

Illustrations Index

(In the following index, the number of the *volume* in which an illustrator's work appears is given *before* the colon, and the *page number* on which it appears is given *after* the colon. For example, a drawing by Adams, Adrienne appears in Volume 2 on page 6, another drawing by her appears in Volume 3 on page 80, another drawing in Volume 8 on page 1, and so on and so on....)

YABC

Index references to *YABC* refer to listings appearing in the two-volume *Yesterday's Authors of Books for Children,* also published by The Gale Group. *YABC* covers prominent authors and illustrators who died prior to 1960.

Author Index

The following index gives the number of the volume in which an author's biographical sketch, Autobiography Feature, Brief Entry, or Obituary appears.

This index includes references to all entries in the following series, which are also published by The Gale Group.

YABC—*Yesterday's Authors of Books for Children: Facts and Pictures about Authors and Illustrators of Books for Young People from Early Times to 1960*

CLR—*Children's Literature Review: Excerpts from Reviews, Criticism, and Commentary on Books for Children*

SAAS—*Something about the Author Autobiography Series*